INVESTIGATIVE JOURNALISM

'A surprising book. I'm surprised that it hasn't been done before,
and I'd also be surprised if anyone did it better.'
Roger Cook, *The Cook Report*, Central Television

'a book that no aspiring student of the subject can do without'
Jon Snow, Channel 4 News

Investigative journalism has helped bring down governments, imprison politicians, trigger legislation, reveal miscarriages of justice and shame corporations.
While the results of investigative journalism are widely acknowledged, explanations of it are various.

Investigative Journalism is a critical and reflective introduction to the traditions
and practices of investigative journalism. Beginning with a historical survey,
the authors explain how investigative journalism should be understood within
the framework of the mass media, how it relates to the legal system, the place
of ethics in investigations and the influence of new technologies and the
Internet on journalistic practices.

Combining interviews with journalists, researchers, editors and television
producers, such as Philip Knightley, David Lloyd, John Pilger, Alan
Rusbridger, Nick Clarke, Dorothy Byrne and Roy Greenslade, with an analysis of investigative journalism from the national and local press, radio and
television, such as the *Sunday Times* Insight team, *File on Four*, *Rough Justice*
and *Dispatches*, the authors defend the practice of exposure and investigation
and consider the future of this form of journalism.

Contributors: Hugo de Burgh, Deborah Chambers, Mark D'Arcy, Carole
Fleming, Matthew Kieran, Gill Moore

Editor: Hugo de Burgh is Senior Lecturer in Television Journalism and head
of the Chinese Media Project at Nottingham Trent University. He has worked
as a reporter for Scottish Television and as a television producer for the BBC
and Channel 4 News and Current Affairs.

INVESTIGATIVE JOURNALISM

Context and practice

Edited by Hugo de Burgh

London and New York

First published 2000
by Routledge
11 New Fetter Lane, London EC4P 4EE

Simultaneously published in the USA and Canada
by Routledge
29 West 35th Street, New York, NY 10001

Routledge is an imprint of the Taylor & Francis Group

Typeset in Bembo by Taylor & Francis Books Ltd
Printed and bound in Great Britain by
MPG Books Ltd, Bodmin, Cornwall

British Library Cataloguing in Publication Data
A catalogue record for this book is available from the British Library

Library of Congress Cataloging in Publication Data
Investigative journalism: context and practice/edited by Hugo de Burgh.
Includes bibliographical references and index.
1. Investigative reporting. 2. Journalism. I. Burgh, Hugo de, 1949–

PN4781 .I57 2000
070.4'3 21–dc21   99–043659

ISBN 0–415–19053–3 (hb)
ISBN 0–415–19054–1 (pb)

CONTENTS

CONTENTS

NOTES ON CONTRIBUTORS

The contributors are all members of the Centre for Research into International Communications and Culture at Nottingham Trent University, headed by Professor John Tomlinson.

Hugo de Burgh has worked as a reporter for Scottish Television, a television producer for the BBC and contractor for Channel 4 News and Current Affairs. At Nottingham Trent University he is Senior Lecturer in Television Journalism and heads the Chinese Media Project.

Deborah Chambers is Reader in Sociology of Communication and Culture at Nottingham Trent University. Her research on gender, communication and culture has included the cultural study of the family photograph album, women and suburbanisation.

Mark D'Arcy is a producer with BBC Radio 4. He spent six years working as the BBC's regional local government correspondent in the East Midlands, and two years as the senior political correspondent of the *Leicester Mercury*.

Carole Fleming began her journalism career in provincial newspapers, then moved into radio working in both the BBC and the commercial sector as a reporter and a producer. She is a Senior Lecturer with the Centre for Broadcasting and Journalism at Nottingham Trent University.

Matthew Kieran is a Lecturer in Philosophy at the University of Leeds. He edited *Media Ethics* (1998), is the author of *Media Ethics: A Philosophical Approach* (1997) and co-author of *Regulating for Changing Values: A Report for the Broadcasting Standards Commission* (1997).

Gill Moore is Deputy Head of the Centre for Broadcasting and Journalism at Nottingham Trent University and a Media Law specialist. She is a visiting consultant in media law training for journalists.

ACKNOWLEDGEMENTS

Five of the authors of this book teach student journalists at Nottingham Trent University and the other two, Mark D'Arcy and Matthew Kieran, have been guest lecturers there. We should all like to thank, bearing in mind the difficulties under which academics in other institutions can labour, our Dean, Professor Stephen Chan, and Head of Department, Professor Sandra Harris, for fostering the climate in and providing the facilities with which it is possible for us to both study and teach. We are fortunate in having a Research Unit Head, Professor John Tomlinson, who is both distinguished scholar and generous enabler. Thanks to Julian Ives, Head of the Centre for Broadcasting and Journalism, we have recently moved to a first class broadcasting establishment in which to work and we appreciate all the efforts he has made to achieve that.

We also wish to thank our students for stimulation and for being as enthusiastic about their studies as they are tolerant of our failings; in particular Carole Fleming and Hugo de Burgh would like to thank our first ever class, that of 1998, for their contributions to our development.

The following journalists, student journalists and normal people have contributed to this book in one way or another, and we are grateful to them. Of course, none of them bears any responsibility at all for the failings of the book:

Lindsay Alker, Frances Banks, Martin Bell, John Boileau, Roger Bromley, Dorothy Byrne, Jonathon Calvert, Nick Clarke, Roger Cook, Peter Curtis, Mary Dawson, Clive Edwards, Rob Edwards, Ray Fitzwalter, Jancis Giles, Ed Glinert, Roy Greenslade, Victoria Hawthorne, Steve Haywood, David Heggie, Jeff Hill, Peter Hill, Richard Holloway, Claire Jaggard, Peter Golding, Gary Jones, David Leigh, David Leppard, David Lloyd, Sue MacGregor, Richard McShane, Clodagh Meiklejohn, Sir Anthony Meyer, Jeff Moore, David Northmore, Matthew Parris, John Pilger, Louisa Preston, David Ross, Bob Satchwell, John Sinnott, Jon Snow, Kate Sparks, Tim Tate, Bob Warren, Vivian White and Matt Youdale.

We record conventional, but no less heartfelt for that, thanks to our parents and immediate families for their understanding and encouragement, to the anonymous reviewers for their help and to our publisher Christopher Cudmore for identifying our project as worthwhile and then taking the time and trouble to assist us in realising it.

Hugo de Burgh, Deborah Chambers, Gill Moore,
Carole Fleming, Matthew Kieran and Mark D'Arcy
9 July 1999

Part 1

CONTEXT

1

INTRODUCTION

A higher kind of loyalty?

Hugo de Burgh

It is often said that journalism is the first rough draft of history; by contrast, *investigative* journalism provides the first rough draft of legislation. It does so by drawing attention to failures within society's systems of regulation and to the ways in which those systems can be circumvented by the rich, the powerful and the corrupt. Why does investigative journalism do that? The title of the chapter is taken from the title of a book by a Chinese investigative journalist[1] because it seems to encapsulate what all the British investigative journalists mean when they justify their activities. They are prepared to look beyond what is conventionally acceptable, behind the interpretations of events provided for us by authority and the authoritative, and appeal to our sense of justice, or to the spirit of our laws if not the letter. In this they are no different from the author of *A Higher Kind of Loyalty* who called upon his government's officials to be true to the ideals of what they professed, in that case communism.

The reader will, we hope, find these assertions substantiated in the following pages. A book on investigative journalism is needed because, although everyone knows what investigative journalism is, explanations of it and about it are so various. Some revile the phenomenon and others claim that it saves us; some tell us that it is a fine tradition now being strangled, while others assure us that, because of new technology, its greatest days are coming. It is the subject of debate and is becoming a subject of study.

For whom is this book written?

Although we hope that it will have wide appeal, our work is written with media studies students in mind. For them investigative journalism is one genre of journalism; hence we seek to place it in context, to see how investigative journalism is seen by its practitioners and how it may appear within the wider contexts of public affairs and the study of the media. It is not a 'how to' book. In 1996 David Northmore wrote the first British book on the subject, *Lifting the Lid*; it provides a definition and then proceeds to give invaluable advice to the researcher. In contrast, we are aiming to provide an introduction to the subject for students who see it as a social phenomenon, whether or not they

3

ever practise journalism. While several of the writers of this book teach vocational journalism courses, they believe that student journalists should not merely absorb professional conventions without understanding their limitations; equally they hope that media studies students will ground their analyses in the facts of practice.

This book will also, we believe, be useful to students of disciplines other than media studies for whom some background to investigative journalism is needed. It assumes little prior knowledge about recent investigative journalism that practitioners or those who avidly follow current affairs have. We have attempted to write it in such a manner that students from other Anglophone countries, and from other European countries, will follow and be able to relate the phenomena discussed to their own situations, and this may account for some explanatory remarks which would be otiose for a British audience. The British experience is relevant elsewhere: there are many countries whose media arrangements and ideals are modelled on those of the UK because post-imperial relationships have endured; the BBC has not dissipated its reputation for coverage of integrity and technical quality. In the post-communist world, including China, there is a widespread belief that British broadsheet journalism represents a standard to be emulated. There are many lessons to be learned from comparing UK media experiences with those of other European countries (see, for example, Weymouth and Lamizet 1996).

In the United States, where journalism has been an academic discipline for over seventy years, investigative journalism is well established as a topic of study, and this book will complement some of the American writings and provide a European perspective. It is necessarily an introduction because investigative journalism, although much discussed in Europe, is little researched. We believe that within this book students will find references to virtually any relevant examination of investigative journalism in the UK, and to US material where appropriate. Each chapter is followed not only by a list of references but also by a brief selection of further reading.

Additional aims for this book are that it helps the reader to go deeper into the subject if he or she so wishes, by providing many pointers and references, to stimulate more research, and to encourage new ventures of the kind that have sprung up in the USA and are described in Chapter 4.

How this book is organised

This chapter, after explaining the book, attempts a definition of investigative journalism that can be useful at least for the duration of the read. Through it, and within other chapters too, you will find references to established incidents in the recent life of investigative journalism that illuminate different aspects in different ways. These include the 'Thalidomide', 'William Straw', 'The Connection', 'Goodwin' and 'The Committee' stories.

With Chapter 2 we go to history, with an attempt to show how, gradually, the figure of the investigative journalist emerged from the prototypes that developed. Behind this is the belief that a failure to see journalism as the product of specific historical circumstances which men and women have the power to influence condemns us to accepting the common-sense notion that journalistic freedoms have come to stay because they are a free gift provided with modernity. It is easy for Britons or North Americans to fall into this error, but neither German nor Italian nor Polish journalists would be likely to do so, given the way journalism lost hard-won rights under fascism and communism. There are other lessons to be taken from history of immediate relevance; the destruction of the radical press by mass advertising earlier this century, as analysed by Curran and Seaton (1997) has its echoes and its equivalents today.

Although technology and economics change dramatically, individual responses have an eerie familiarity. Once you have read this book you will be familiar with these names and can decide for yourself whether Pilger is our Cobbett; whether Murdoch, the media prince we love to hate, is the Harmsworth, and Whittam Smith the Renaudot of our era; perhaps England's Paul Foot, in his radical instincts and reasoned research, is the Ida Tarbell of a later century. It may be that cultural context is here at play, more enduring than economic determinists would have us believe.

In Chapter 3 we bring the story up to date and look at recent British investigative journalism. Yet journalism, even investigative journalism, is ephemeral. How can you make interesting revelations of misconduct or the uncovering of crookery that excited people in 1972? By demonstrating that the act of investigation had bearing upon wider social developments that still impinge upon our lives, by evoking historical empathy, by using them as case studies for skills and techniques or by offering them as examples to emulate or avoid. In Silvester's (1994) *Penguin Book of Interviews* there is a selection of enthralling interviews that tell us a good deal about both subject and journalist, usually unintentionally since we look with hindsight, and which perform the exemplary function for the tyro journalist. They are also entertaining. Where in this book cases are described, our intentions are the same.

The task of selecting specimens and of providing some orderly account of investigative journalism is made more difficult by the shortage of preliminary studies. True, journalists write up their cases into books, and they write memoirs; there are books on wide questions of journalism's impact upon society. There are few books like *More Rough Justice* by Peter Hill and his colleagues (1985) that look at genres or journalistic phenomena, and analyses of investigative journalism hardly exist. We call for more studies, but in the meantime Chapter 3 surveys the field.

There are some issues that the student of investigative journalism cannot fail to trip over as he or she looks at the subject. One is the issue of by what right exactly do investigative journalists do what they do, what is this idea of social responsibility that appears to be behind their activity? Another is that of objectivity, discussed energetically in recent years thanks to Martin Bell's challenge. Then there is the question of Watergate and what it stands for. Chapter 4 introduces these discourses.

Journalists tend to see themselves as free agents. The media studies approach is an essential corrective to this and Deborah Chambers demonstrates very clearly in Chapter 5 how debates in journalism can look different when you are in the media studies helicopter, looking down at the global political and economic configurations within which they take place. For example, while Chapter 4 mentions some specific effects of the British 1996 Broadcasting Act claimed by investigative journalists, Chambers looks at the macro effects on the industry of which investigative journalism is a part; if you deploy her perspective, our chapters on law (7) and ethics (8) both look different. For investigative journalism is contained within potent economic and industrial fields with their own rules and exigencies and the political economy approach serves to remind us of this; the great communication empires impose their institutional requirements. She shows us how current commercial pressures are blurring the lines between investigative journalism and other genres. The sociological constraints of professional ideology, social position and employment status are also determining factors; the 'propaganda model' too is a necessary corrective to journalistic hubris.

Freedom of expression is all very well, but for opinion to be well grounded it needs information, verifiable facts and contrasting viewpoints. This is the contribution that investigative journalism can make to the realisation of a public sphere in which all can participate and all have access to the best possible information. In Chapter 6 Deborah Chambers asks whether the ideal of the public sphere is impaired or extended by the phenomenon of globalisation and what may be that phenomenon's implications for investigative journalism.

According to some interpretations, investigative journalism has come to be only for elites; the trend to tabloidisation, also noted in this chapter, means that the consumers of mass market media are denied quality information. This is among the changes to which Chambers draws our attention. She also highlights how the position of women is indicative of some of the broader changes taking place within journalism and points to the questions that are asked about the might of the Anglophone media. Does that might expand or circumscribe horizons? Is our consciousness determined by the economic interests of Anglophone corporations or are we, as some would have us believe, all of one world in which the moral leaders (just coincidentally Anglophone) can crusade cheerfully through other cultures and concerns, content in the knowledge that everyone else is catching up, their copies of Fukuyama in hand?[2] These are the issues addressed by Chapter 6.

American and British journalism share historical and cultural origins and yet display differences that illuminate both. The most significant differences are in the legal and political framework within which journalists operate. The former is discussed by Gill Moore in Chapter 7 in the course of her introduction to English law insofar as it frames investigative journalism. She starts with freedom of expression and considers how this is protected in English law; she evaluates the impact upon the work of investigative journalists of a selection of specific legal provisions and illustrates how the English courts deal with the conflicts that can arise between the various competing rights and interests in matters of reputation, the administration of justice and privacy. She looks at the experiences that lead investigative journalists and their editors to claim that English law inhibits their work and why they call for a legal guarantee to freedom of expression and information. Gill Moore also explains how incorporation of the European Convention on Human Rights is expected to change the environment. She omits one area of law that is often associated with investigative journalists: Official Secrets. It is a very particular field and is dealt with thoroughly in specialist publications.

The law is only one way in which investigative journalism is framed; another influence is professional practice, either through the unwritten rules of routine and common sense, or, more readily identified, through regulation and ethical codes. These are dealt with by Matthew Kieran in Chapter 8. He connects debates about the practices of investigative journalists with general moral principles; draws attention to the piecemeal way in which government, industry and the profession have sought to establish standards of behaviour and to satisfy the critics. He touches upon intentional deception, poor substantiation, the use of the sting, ideas of privacy, sourcing and its problems and the limits of television reconstruction. He shows how regulation and ethics impinge upon investigative journalism and what the specific characteristics of the British situation tell us about investigative journalism in general.

Experienced investigative journalists are very pessimistic about the future of their specialism. The commercial pressures are so great that investigative journalism, generally seen as the most expensive type of journalism but one that does not attract mass consumption, is on the way out unless it can be souped up into comic entertainment such as that of Mike Mansfield or Mark Thomas.[3] People are increasingly pressured for time so that they'll take from the media only what they can use in their own lives; the adversaries are so sophisticated, always steps ahead in information and resources; laws and regulations create limitations; the risks of investigative journalism are too great for the publishers and broadcasters: these are the kinds of comments made repeatedly. Presumably for these reasons – among others – the media managers appear to be disinvesting, with the single exception of the *Express* newspaper, which in 1999 assembled an investigative team. Paradoxically though, it has finally become a subject for university-level study, there appears to be widespread enthusiasm among young people for it and Britain's first Association for Investigative Journalists is being launched.[4]

So where will the investigative journalism of the future be published? Carole Fleming finds an answer in technology. In Chapter 9 she argues that not only will journalists be freed from many of the restraints of the past by having access to much more information independent of the old 'primary definers', thus allowing the investigative journalist to contextualise and compare with relative ease, but journalists will be able to publish and find an audience without some traditional constraints. In a chapter which overviews developments that are changing radically the techniques of and opportunities for investigation as we write, she both gives examples of how the new technology is deployed and provides internet site details to enable the reader to see for him or herself.

The second half of the book, professional practices, introduces the reader to some of the topics that have been investigated in recent years and some of the vehicles deployed. Our bias is towards television because the 1980s and early 1990s saw a great growth in investigative journalism or para-investigative journalism on British television. The subjects chosen by investigative journalists for their attention are without number. We have selected examples which appear to teach general lessons of use to readers anywhere.

We start with radio and a general positioning of investigative journalism within the history of British public service broadcasting. *File on Four* is a powerful exponent of what its editor prefers to call 'evidential journalism' and has made a particular strength of its examination of business issues. We therefore peg a brief survey of business investigations here.

One of the most important fields for inquiry is surely public administration at the local level, where huge amounts of money are expended, all citizens are involved and opportunities for corruption frequent, in no matter what society. For years commentators have lamented the dreadful decline of the regional and local press, the 'silent watchdog'. Suddenly, in 1999 there was a bevy of articles celebrating a renaissance in circulation.[5] Whether this means that there will be a future for investigative journalism at the local level to compare with the USA is doubtful; in Chapter 11 Mark D'Arcy points out how easy it is for the local reporter not to notice the big stories on his doorstep. He also argues persuasively that investigative journalism is very much needed out in the provinces where state power in particular is hardly regulated. The case of Frank Beck and the child abuse scandals provides lessons in journalistic failure, but it also shows what opportunities await the daring reporter and proprietor.

Chapter 12 uses what has abruptly become, with the demise or truncation of several distinguished strands, British television's principal vehicle of investigative journalism. *Dispatches* pioneered the investigative critique of social policy and therefore we concentrate on that angle here, although it has transmitted every possible type of investigative journalism.

In the USA in the 1950s Erle Stanley Gardner, creator of the *Perry Mason* courtroom dramas, first put on television the *Court of Last Resort* which reviewed claims of flawed conviction. Its modern British successor has been BBC's *Rough Justice*, and now *Trial and Error*, made by 'Just Television' for

Channel 4 (C4). The genre has an impressive history of righting wrongs through the application of investigative procedures. We look at that history in Chapter 13, and at one recent programme.

Some years ago Phillip Knightley examined the Gallipoli Myth (he calls it 'the blood icon') which originated from Rupert Murdoch's father, journalist Keith Murdoch, and which represents the Australians of the First World War as 'outstanding troops negligently commanded by British idiots'. The myth has been put to good use by many Australians looking for sticks with which to beat Britain (Knightley 1997: 254–7) and has possibly been an inspiration for Rupert Murdoch's own assaults on aspects of Britain. Knightley's efforts were not welcomed in Australia but his research is a good example of what investigative journalists can do with history; Chapter 14's example is less influential and more ambiguous. It concerns a widely-known case, generally referred to as 'The Cossacks', from the Second World War. It illustrates the relationships between history, politics and journalism and also some of the pitfalls of investigation.

Roger Cook has done more than any other reporter to bring home to large numbers of people what investigative journalism can do and can be. He is criticised for being populist, but he is also immensely popular for it, so he doesn't care. He covers every conceivable subject matter so no one programme is typical; the example chosen for Chapter 15 deals with a rather emotive aspect of environmental degradation in an engaging and exciting way which reveals Cook at his dramatic and ironic best.

Chapter 16 deals with High Politics, the chase of the big beasts by the peoples' tribunes; by way of concrete illustration, we look at the 'Arms to Iraq' scandal and the way in which such a topic is seen as the rightful purview of the investigative journalist. We look at the vehicle for a minister's exposure, the *Sunday Times* Insight, which has the most illustrious pedigree of all the remaining media of investigative journalism.

In the final example we glance at how British investigative journalists examine other countries' sins and the moral and political pitfalls into which they might fall; specifically we look at another piece of television journalism, made possible by the researches of a lone Chinese investigative journalist, Harry Wu, and by the approach of Yorkshire Television's factual units when managed by John Willis and Grant McKee.

What is investigative journalism?

An investigative journalist is a man or woman whose profession it is to discover the truth and to identify lapses from it in whatever media may be available. The act of doing this generally is called investigative journalism and is distinct from apparently similar work done by police, lawyers, auditors and regulatory bodies in that it is not limited as to target, not legally founded and closely connected to publicity. This book will account for this assertion by referring to the way investigative journalism is described in popular culture and professional discourse and by providing concrete examples of how it is realised in society.

In John Grisham's novel and film, *The Pelican Brief*, the character of Gray Grantham is as romantic an idealisation of the journalist as one might hope to meet in popular culture. Not only is he a meticulous desk worker but he is also skilled in the practical arts; his dedication to the public weal is irreproachable, no matter that he is up against powerful and unscrupulous politicians and high officials who will have no compunction in ruining or killing him. As if these gifts were not enough, he is noble to the point of innocence in matters of the heart. This last aspect aside, Gray Grantham, although fictional, is not so very far from the genuine investigative journalists portrayed in two factual books *The Typewriter Guerrillas* (Behrens 1978) and *Raising Hell* (Chepesiuk et al. 1997). The heroic depiction of the journalist, similar to the depiction of heroes of Henty's novels of imperial mission and youthful adventure[6] that were so popular before the Second World War, contrasts with earlier cameos, ranging from the ludicrous Boot in Evelyn Waugh's *Scoop* to the fatuous Hildy in Hecht's *The Front Page* to the repulsive Totges in Heinrich Böll's *The Lost Honour of Katerina Blum*. The idealisation of the reporter is puzzling too because journalists are generally held in the low esteem so appropriately represented by these earlier fictions; yet very large numbers of young people nevertheless want to be journalists, or at least work in the media. Perhaps the low esteem – and, generally, poor wages – is overridden by other considerations such as sense of adventure, being in the thick of 'events' or fame.[7]

It is also, if the anecdotes of teachers of journalism are worth anything, because journalists are conceived of, at their best, as being idealists. The icons of British journalism most often mentioned by students are Martin Bell, Kate Adie, Veronica Guerin, Paul Foot and John Pilger. Of them, the first two are noted for their courage in adversity and unbending principle, while the latter three are also investigators. There are, of course, very many other distinguished investigative journalists, but their names are known more to aficionados of the genre or fellow journalists than to the community at large. Names such as Phillip Knightley, David Leigh, Jonathon Calvert and Michael Gillard are mentioned regularly. What differentiates their work from that of other journalists? What are their motivations? What skills do they deploy? What significance does their work have for the rest of us?

Investigative journalism and dissenting journalism

It is useful at the outset to distinguish dissenting journalism from investigative journalism, although they are often closely connected. It is a long tradition in Anglophone societies to tolerate disagreement with authority and it is a tradition for which writers have fought since at least the seventeenth century. Campaigns on behalf of this or that oppressed party, polemics for a better way of doing things, dissension from the accepted line are usually tolerated, although not easily in wartime, as the BBC's John Simpson discovered when he found himself out of step with the mainstream media during NATO's attack on Yugoslavia in 1999 (Gibson 1999). The wartime examples aside, for important qualifiers as they are, they belong to a category where other factors such as national security, negotiating positions and the safety of personnel may confuse the issue, few would argue today that dissent should be curtailed. Investigation, however, is quite another matter. You may disagree with authority, but you may not necessarily find the evidence of authority's misbehaviour, i.e. investigate.

Dorothy Byrne, editor of C4 *Dispatches*, believes that it is increasingly difficult to surprise audiences with investigative journalism because they increasingly assume corruption to be endemic (Byrne 1999). If she is right, then it is quite possible that the target audience for this book believes that investigative journalism is in principle 'a good thing', even if it also believes that it does not exist. However, there are respectable people around who believe that investigative journalism is 'a bad thing'. It may be that the latter belong to a generation which prefers to believe that authority is usually trustworthy and only occasionally falls into dereliction, whereas the former are convinced that everyone is on the make and that the honest are the exceptions.

One of the most cogent critics of investigative journalism ('the lowest form of newspaper life') believes that it is not a discipline but a cast of mind which is typical of arrogant, privileged and sneering journalists in current affairs who dress up their desire for high ratings and fat salaries in 'nauseating' assertions about 'their responsibilities to society, the nation, the viewers, the truth', assertions in which he sees no justice (Ingham 1991: 355). Bernard Ingham, former Chief Press Secretary to Mrs Thatcher, has diagnosed a number of journalists' diseases, of which the first is pertinent to investigative journalism:

> the conviction that government is inevitably, irrevocably and chronically up to no good, not to be trusted and conspiratorial. This is known as the 'le Carré syndrome' and so sours and contaminates the judgement of otherwise competent journalists as to render them pathetically negative, inaccurate and unreliable. In this context, Watergate has a lot to answer for here – and across the world.
>
> (Ingham 1991: 363)

Ingham believes that the scepticism of investigative journalism is wrong and harmful, but it is not only at the national level at which he worked that politicians and officials question investigative journalists' right to delve. In 1999 Nottingham City Council invested considerable effort in taking C4 *Dispatches* to court to prevent a film being made about children in care; it then began a campaign advocating a change in the law to require that journalists investigate areas of council competence only with council permission and that the police institute checks on them (Lloyd 1999, NCC 1999).

Aside from the *justice* of investigative journalism, or its *right* to exist, some challenge its *competence* to undertake the tasks of scrutinising authority on the basis that where these tasks are necessary there should be legislation to create offices sufficiently skilled and resourced to do that work properly (Kedourie 1988) and this is an interesting critique which deserves to be examined further. Another view of investigative journalism is represented by Charles Moore, editor of the *Daily Telegraph*, who sees it as a distraction from the proper functions of journalism, which are to report and to analyse. He has said, 'there is a higher aspiration than exposing corruption. ... It is to tell people the news, and to interpret it in a way they find interesting, honest and helpful' (Page 1998: 46). However, Moore preceded his remarks by saying, 'I admire much of the work the *Guardian* has done over corruption among some Tory MPs in the late 1980s'.

We might see a contradiction in Moore's views. After all, if the work of the investigative journalist is to be lauded, then surely this is an acknowledgement that it is necessary? It is necessary to those who acknowledge that, sometimes at least, reporting what authority says, or even analysing it, is not enough; because authority may have an agenda that is counter to the general interest; because there are officials and politicians who are swayed by ignorance or self-interest; because there are systems that work to the detriment of people who have no voice. Where there are no institutions capable of performing the functions which investigative journalism has taken on, then to deny the need for investigative journalism is to deny either that these things are possible or that they matter. After all, as the eminent editor of the (London) *Evening Standard*, not normally thought of as an iconoclast, said approvingly that he was advised as a young journalist, 'They lie, they lie, they lie' (Max Hastings on BBC: *Any Questions* 1 May 1999). If they lie, then someone must uncover the truth.

Investigative journalism and the news agenda

News journalism, which has been much written about by academics, has a broadly agreed set of values, often referred to as 'newsworthiness': a typical textbook for trainee journalists states that those events are suitable for news which have proximity, relevance, immediacy, drama and so forth (Boyd 1994). The news journalist makes his or her selection from a range of conventionally accepted sources of information, sources which are in effect the providers of the 'news agenda' and whose regular production of information is diarised; selection from them is made according to these and other criteria of 'newsworthiness'. The multitude of factors that tend to condition his or her acceptance of sources as bona fide and the way in which he or she treats the information has been extensively studied and is reviewed in Shoemaker 1996 and McQuail 1994 among others.

Investigative stories are different in that they may not be on the same agenda. They involve a subject that the journalist has to insist is something we should know about, in effect, by saying 'look at this, isn't it shocking!'; the basis of the insistence is a moral one. In common among the eight cases dealt with in this book is that they cover happenings that journalists believed, or, in the case of Chapter 11 later realised, required attention because they amount to a dereliction of standards. The topics have varying distances from established public moral consciousness; you might say that the subject of cruelty to animals and environmental degradation is well established and that the programme described in Chapter 15 merely satisfies existing moral assumptions. At the other extreme *Dispatches*, in the Chapter 12 example, sought to extend the audience's ideas of what is acceptable, as did Tolstoy's research of war crimes (Chapter 14).

John Pilger considers that the term investigative journalism 'came into common parlance some ten years ago in correlation with the decline of inquiry, curiosity and mission among journalists' (Pilger 1999). This decline he attributes to the domination of media conglomerates by their entertainment interests, changes in employment practises which have made journalists frightened to push, multi-skilling in the newsrooms and the 'corporate solitary confinement' or isolation from the population that has come about thanks to the relocation of news centres and to time pressures. He would like to see the term investigative journalist rejected as a tautology since 'all journalists should be investigative' but does not believe that the conditions at present exist for any but specialists to be so.

Relationship to reporting and analysis

News reporting is descriptive and news reporters are admired when they describe in a manner that is accurate, explanatory, vivid or moving, regardless of medium. Analytical journalism, on the other hand, seeks to take the data available and reconfigure it, helping us to ask questions about the situation or statement or see it in a different way. Clive Edwards, of the BBC's flagship current affairs programme *Panorama*, argues that even though his programme is not always investigative in the sense of resulting from long-term investigation and revelation of the hidden:

> in some sense every week's *Panorama* is telling you about things that you do not know enough about. Even a relatively innocuous subject such as house prices will be treated such as to show you the way they are affecting society and to bring to your attention the problems caused by the situation that most people take for granted. We are trying to get to the bottom of exactly what is happening, the forces behind it.
>
> (Edwards 1999)

Going further than this, investigative journalists also want to know whether the situation presented to us is the reality, as for example in 'Inspecting the Inspectors' (Chapter 12); they further invite us to be aware of something that we are not hearing about at all, as in *File on Four*'s 'Insolvency Practitioners' (Chapter 10) or to care about something that is not being cared about (as in the Chinese prisoners in Chapter 17). At its furthest extent investigative journalism questions the basis of orthodoxy, challenging the account of reality that the powers that be wish us to accept. In Lloyd's words:

> modern information suppliers are very powerful and sophisticated; they create an image of what they want us to believe by taking some aspects of the truth and weaving it into an image that is a denial of the truth. Journalists must not be lulled into believing that this is the truth. We really have got to show that we are up to the task of demonstrating that there are other ways of seeing things, that their premises are wrong.
>
> (Lloyd 1998)

Definitions of significance

Whereas news deals very rapidly with received information, usually accepting what is defined for it by authority (ministries, police, fire service, universities, established spokesmen) as events appropriate for transformation into news, investigative journalism selects its own information and prioritises it in a different way. The distinction is not by any means absolute and neither are news editors as passive nor investigative journalists as active as this simplification suggests. Moreover there are great differences between commercial and public channels, national and regional ones; nevertheless the distinction is broadly true. Taking the events supplied for them, news journalists apply news values in prioritising those events; investigative journalism picks and chooses according to its own definition of significance. What are those definitions?

Investigative journalism comes in so many shapes and sizes that it is not easy to generalise. That stories affect many is the criterion of one journalist; another is content to reveal what has been done to only one victim. There is, though, always a victim and, even if it is collective, always a villain to blame. Usually there is a failure of system, whether that of the administration of justice, or of bureaucratic management, or of the regulatory bodies of this or that sphere. The villains may be so because they stand to make money, as in the business stories sketched in Chapter 10, because they are brutal xenophobes, as in Pilger's revelations of East Timor, or because they are ignorant and deluded as the *Dispatches* series claimed policy-makers and managers to be in an investigation of age discrimination in employment (C4 *Dispatches*: 'An Age Apart' 1993).

All the villains want to stop the story coming out, or at least control its presentation. A common definition of investigative journalism is 'going after what someone wants to hide' although not everything that someone wants to hide is worth going after. Jonathon Calvert, formerly of Insight and the *Observer*, now on the *Express*, says 'I want to expose a bad practice, not a bad person'; the Head of C4 News and Current Affairs, David Lloyd, wants the investigative journalist to ask 'What individual, what institution, does not want this story told, and of what potency are they? The more important the answer, the more engaging the task' (Lloyd 1998). Similarly, Alan Rusbridger, under whose editorship the *Guardian* has been more associated with investigative journalism than any other newspaper in the 1990s, suggests that the quality of target is what defines investigative journalism from mere exposure journalism. He says:

> What's the public interest in a cricketer having a love romp in a hotel room or a rugby player having smoked cannabis twenty years ago? But if elected representatives are arguing a case in Parliament but not revealing that they are being paid to do so, then that strikes at the heart of democracy. That's public interest; this is an easy distinction.
>
> (Rusbridger 1999)

The moral impetus

The urge to get at the truth and to clarify the difference between right and wrong is most clearly evident in the miscarriage of justice stories, where every possible trick has to be used to encourage the audience to see an event as a contradiction of equity and where the audience, if anything, must be presumed to be sceptical of claims of innocence by murderers and thieves. In the revelations of ministerial misconduct over 'Arms to Iraq' (Chapter 16) the context of wars in which extreme suffering was taking place was used to demonstrate the moral dimension to what would otherwise have been minor dishonesties by people in power.

Usually investigative journalists appeal to our existing standards of morality, standards they know that they can rely upon being held by people they know will be shocked by their violation. In this sense they are 'policing the boundaries' between order and deviance, in which case the image of the investigative journalist as intrepidly stepping outside the established order and accusing society is a romantic one; he or she rarely if ever does that. Even in the case of, say, a Serb journalist condemning atrocities by his 'own side' in Kosovo, we must assume that the Serb is appealing to moral standards that he or she believes to be more fundamental to his compatriots than current xenophobia. The *Dispatches* on ageism (C4 1993) can be construed as an attempt to step outside the orthodoxy of the society and appeal, similarly, to a higher moral law. Animal Rights activists might say that they too were trying to extend our moral boundaries. The fact that much investigative journalism ends with legislation or regulation being promised or designed is not therefore an accident.

Methods

The contrast between the news journalist and the investigative journalist is once more instructive. The news journalist takes an event and organises the report of it in a conventional and comprehensible way. If you parse a television news report, the syntax of the process is evident, from the type of shots used to the way in which commentary, interview and effects are employed; documentaries and feature articles also have grammatical structures and investigative journalism is applied to various slightly different models. Just as the novel has widely different variations in form and possible content, so with the journalistic report.

The news journalist's skill lies in his or her ability to recreate the format with new content, content that is accurate and appropriate to the target audience. It is argued by modern observers that news, recontextualised in this manner, falls into culturally-constructed categories. These categories may perform certain social functions but this fact is irrelevant to the journalist when working. What is relevant is that he or she represent events suitably. Starting with Tuchman (1973), researchers have found that journalists, in order to meet deadlines and to manage the vast quantity of input, categorise their raw materials – events – and then apply formula work routines. Tuchman found these categories:

- hard news
- soft news
- spot news
- what a story!

Brundson and Morley (1978: 40) classified story types into four

- the especially remarkable event
- victims
- community at risk
- ritual, tradition and the past.

In 1997 I looked at a regional television news programme and classified it as follows; virtually identical classifications were arrived at independently by two separate classes of students (de Burgh 1998):

- Wow! stories (aka 'Aha! stories' or 'skateboarding ducks')
- heartstrings
- what fun people we are

16

- our kind of folk
- adversity overcome
- fight for rights
- all is well; mankind advances
- wrong-doers cannot escape; the law is our trusty shield.

In 1998 Langer published a study done in very similar circumstances in Australia. He applied the classifications nominated by Brundson and Morley and decided that they were equally appropriate to the objects of his study, with one addition, a classification called 'foolish victims'. Furthermore, Langer looked at the construction of the stories and found that, in addition to the application of basic formulae, particular techniques are used according to the requirements of each category. These techniques belong to the repertoire of meaning-construction and may include the report's framing or cueing within the programme, its positioning, the use of hackneyed representational images, visual techniques from cinematography (framing, composition, lighting, focus, angle, proximity), verbal techniques from acting and so forth. Thus Langer brings together the foci on classification and structuration, or, as he puts it 'narrative construction can bind together certain patterned thematic preoccupations which occur in specific story types' (Langer 1998: 40).

What are recontextualised in these story types are facts. Newsrooms accept facts from established authorities; where there is doubt news reporters will balance two opposing points of view or express the alternative view in the commentary. Evidence is provided by eye-witnesses, corroborated by authority figures, or simply by authority figures alone.

As to investigative journalists, the procedures are similar only insofar as the investigative journalists have to fill a format too, whether it be a radio documentary, a television feature, a certain arrangement of columns in a newspaper or whatever. However, while news journalists are finding their summit meetings, skateboarding ducks, or their stories of hardship overcome and joyous resolution, investigative journalists are going after the truth where it has been obscured, uncovering wrongs and persuading the rest of us to take them seriously, to be affected by their moral reading. This may take any of several forms, some of which are illustrated by the cases dealt with in Chapters 10 to 17:

10 identifying a shameful, even if not illegal, practice as a transgression of moral law
11 revealing abuse of power
12 questioning the factual bases upon which significant assertions are made
13 showing that justice has been corrupted
14 challenging an official account
15 demonstrating how laws can be circumvented
16 exposing the gap between profession and practice
17 disclosing a cover-up.

Ettema and Glasser (1988) have argued that investigative journalists are also telling stories to fit moral types, rather as I have described in news. At the risk of simplifying an extensive argument, I summarise their position in their words:

> The task is accomplished by cueing the audience's response to these characters through the emplotting of events as recognisably moralistic stories and, more specifically, through the skilful use of such story elements as point of view, ironic detail and ritual denial.
>
> (Ettema and Glasser 1988)

To say that investigative journalism fits into cultural categories is not necessarily to diminish it. Even if investigative journalists are less autonomous in identifying wicked things and inspiring moral umbrage than popular culture might have us believe, they may nevertheless be expanding our ideas of what we should think or care about, making us think in a certain way about an event or an issue. Moreover, the claim that they are reaching for 'the truth' is not necessarily rendered absurd by the acknowledgement that there is no truth, in the sense of an absolute hard fact against which to measure their own versions, because what the investigative journalist is after, as with the historian, is a more complete version of the truth.[8] In 1938 Dobrée put it better than I can: 'Most of us have ceased to believe, except provisionally, in truths, and we feel that what is important is not so much truth as the way our minds move towards truths' (cit. in Houghton 1957: 430).

Our minds can move towards a more complete truth by collecting good evidence and by corroborating accounts of people who can either be shown to be disinterested or who speak from different vantage points. Thus, while moral purpose may be a defining characteristic of investigative journalism, so is attention to the evidence used to support that purpose.

In fact, Jonathon Calvert defines investigative journalism by the attention paid to the evidence:

> Some stories you make five calls on, some twenty. When you are making a hundred, that's investigative journalism. The story may land in your lap – it's the substantiation that makes it an investigative story, because when you realise people are lying to you, blocking you, then you have to find different ways of getting hold of the information and it can take a lot longer. Also you have to be very careful when you are making serious allegations against people, then the evidence really matters.
>
> (Calvert 1999)

Alan Rusbridger:

All journalism is investigative to a greater or lesser extent, but investigative journalism – though it is a bit of a tautology – is that because it requires more, it's where the investigative element is more pronounced. In the 1970s Adam Raphael did an investigation of wages paid to blacks in South Africa which required a great deal of time and effort; more recently 'Cash for Questions', 'The Connection' took up so much energy and investment as to deserve the term.

(Rusbridger 1999)

When asked what skills are of most importance to the investigative journalist, those as diverse as Phillip Knightley, Steve Haywood and David Leppard put first the desk skills. By this they mean the thorough knowledge of information sources and types and the rules that govern them, the ability to read documents for significance, and an understanding of statistics. There are good descriptions of the relevance of these skills in Eddy's (1976) and Knightley's (1997) chapters on the thalidomide story. In the cases selected in this book at least eight different families of documents are required research material, and the ability to master them precedes any employment of the interpersonal skills often cited as being essential too; the empathy with others that will get them to talk; the ability to take account of potential impediments to truth such as false memory and question formulation; the gall and wit to doorstep and the ability to efface oneself sufficiently to go undercover if necessary. The most amusing description of those last mentioned skills is probably by the German investigative journalist, Gunther Wallraff (1978).

Investigative journalism versus exposure journalism

There were some questionable uses of the techniques, or the label of, investigative journalism in the 1990s. The use of the sting has become commonplace as a mode of trapping a target into saying something that incriminates him or her, in particular people whose revelations are merely amusing to the spectators rather than useful to society; tabloid newspapers have developed a taste among their readers for this kind of voyeurism, sometimes impugning reputations through research which may be malevolent. Michael Foot, a former Leader of the Labour Party, won an out of court settlement in a libel action against those who accused him of having been a foreign agent, and Richard Gott, a *Guardian* journalist, found himself 'revealed' as a spy before his colleagues and the public.

The most controversial case of confusion between exposure journalism and investigative journalism was that allegedly perpetrated against miners' leader Arthur Scargill in 1990, mentioned in Chapter 15. If the main allegations were baseless, why did Scargill and his colleagues not sue? The answer may lie in the English libel system which makes it all but impossible for any but the very rich, or richly backed, to risk suing for libel; moreover, a libel case is likely to humiliate and embarrass a plaintiff since the defence is often able, in the course of attempting to prove its case, to paint the plaintiff's past or associated activities in the most lurid light possible. Thus unscrupulous media may be able to smear with impunity.

Although investigative journalism is probably associated in the public mind with stings, investigative journalists themselves have to be prodded into remembering that the sting is one of their methods. The sting is the setting of a trap so that the victim demonstrates his or her villainy; it also is convenient in that, since the trap will normally involve taped evidence in which the villain incriminates him or herself by word or deed, the wherewithal to prove the case in a court of law is provided much more effectively than if several people had to be found to swear affidavits, which are, moreover, less compelling evidence. Roger Cook (1999) distinguishes the sting which creates a situation that would otherwise not have arisen – such as persuading a young man to sell the reporter some illegal drug (the William Straw case) – from the sting where the villain is carrying out his or her normal business. The extensive use of this 'method of investigative journalism' at the end of the 1990s to, for example, brand a rugby star as a drug user or identify an MP as the habitué of a massage parlour are hardly on the same level of public interest as, say, the truth about the number of deaths in a war or corruption in the awarding of government contracts.

In June 1994 Jonathon Calvert, then at the *Sunday Times*, went on to the terrace of the House of Commons to pay money to two Members of Parliament, Graham Riddick and David Tredinnick, an event that sparked off several years of exposures known as 'Cash for Questions' or 'Sleaze', discussed in Chapter 3. He regarded it as exposing a practice, not people:

> We had no interest in beating Graham Riddick and David Tredinnick around the head with a stick. What we wanted to show was that there was a culture in Parliament that found accepting money to ask questions of ministers to be acceptable; we didn't think it ought to be so; had we been given longer for that sting we'd have got loads of MPs to take the money, not just those two. We did ten Tories and ten Labour MPs, all chosen completely at random.
>
> (Calvert 1999)

The technique of the sting is used by newspapers less concerned with public interest and more in a titillating exposure. 'It is the public interest element that differentiates the investigation from the exposure' says Rusbridger. Taxed on his newspaper's exposure (without sting) of early 1999 of how one minister (Geoffrey Robinson) lent another (Peter Mandelson) the price of his house he agrees that it was not a major revelation 'but it should have been out in the open'. The difference between investigative journalism and exposure is the public interest element, even if the techniques used sometimes confuse the two.

The other application of the techniques of investigative journalism that has come in for criticism is the excessive employment of television reconstruction, to the extent that the documentary in question is more construction than reconstruction. There have in recent years been so many examples, from the presentation of a Thai child as an underage prostitute who was nothing of the kind; the showing of nefarious meetings which purported to be those between criminals but were those between friends of the producer; the creation of whole sequences demonstrating, in the case of 'The Connection', what the producer would very much have liked to film had it happened. The ethics of this are touched upon in Chapter 8.

Motivations

What are their aims? With clash after clash between journalists and government during the eighteen years of Conservative rule in Britain (1979–1997) it was an understandable assumption that investigative journalism was merely a tactical weapon of the left. The then government was very happy to fuel this prejudice in order to justify its resistance to criticism; however there is no reason to assume that investigative journalism is a prerogative of the left. Scepticism about powerful institutions and privileges has also been an aspect of the attitudes of Conservative Party supporters.

Nevertheless its most prominent practitioners, as with their colleagues in general journalism, have preferred to associate themselves with the left (Weaver 1998: 151). Paul Foot has long been associated with revolutionary socialism but, since we are neither undertaking a psychological profile of Foot nor trying to understand how aspects of English culture manifest themselves through him, this fact can be separated from his work as an investigator of injustices through the *Daily Mirror* column that he wrote for thirteen years. His books alleging injustice include *Who Killed Hanratty?* (1971), *The Helen Smith Story* (1983), *Who Framed Colin Wallace* (1989) and *Murder at the Farm: Who Killed Carl Bridgwater?* (1993); none can have seemed very promising cases at the outset. According to another journalist, Peter Jay, Foot's motivation is moral: 'He has a natural, decent sensitivity to the oppression of the underdogs in society, the less fortunate' (Langdon 1993). Foot himself says he feels 'revulsion at the notion of people being locked up for something they did not do, and the obvious injustice done to them as individuals' (Preston 1999: 3). He goes on:

> It is the responsibility of the individual journalist to find the truth.
> There are things always to be discovered, never believe anything until
> it is officially denied; there is another story which is normally more
> accurate. [It is the job of the investigative journalist] to start the ball

rolling, be inquisitive, ask questions independently of the government and every other power structure inside society. Unless people are there asking questions of those establishments, they become stronger and more reckless.

(Preston 1999: 5)

John Pilger has painted on a larger canvas, making around fifty documentary films as well as writing extensively; his principal theme has been how our governments pursue policies abroad which not only corrupt or wreck other societies but which damage us too and that they do these things for personal glory and to line the pockets of rich men who hide behind them. As he puts it 'the prime role of journalists is to tell people when they are being conned'. His first well known revelation was of the extent of rebellion in the ranks of the US army in Vietnam in the late 1970s, a fact that had not been reported but was having, and would have, an enormous effect upon the prosecution of the war. Later his film *Year Zero* showed what Pol Pot's crazed idealism had done to Cambodia after the slaughtering of millions and the destruction of the cities. He also made an unexpected film on poverty in Japan that gave a very different angle on that country to the take offered by most other journalists who concentrated upon its wealth and power. In the 1990s Pilger returned repeatedly to the sufferings of the East Timor population under Indonesian rule, a rule established by Portuguese and Australian government collusion. In the preface to one of Pilger's books, writer Martha Gelhorn (1992) says:

[Pilger] has taken on the great theme of justice and injustice. The misuse of power against the powerless. The myopic, stupid, cruelty of governments. The bullying and lies that shroud *realpolitik*, a mad game played at the top, which is a curse to real people.

Other established investigative journalists are seen in the same way and have the same view of their aims. They want to affect the way we see events or to make us care about something we have not thought of before; tell us what is and is not acceptable behaviour; champion the weak; accuse the guilty. Phillip Knightley explained why he felt motivated to spent five years of his life on the thalidomide investigation: 'At first journalistic interest ... then, when I had met a victim, moral indignation, outrage ... at the sheer effrontery of men who could put pecuniary interests before their victim's lives' (Knightley 1999).

From a younger generation, Dorothy Byrne, appointed editor of *Dispatches* in 1998 after working on *The Big Story* and *World in Action*, attributes her interest in investigative journalism to the shock she felt when, as a student, she went to West Africa on VSO (Voluntary Service Overseas). She says, 'I knew I couldn't do anything about the suffering, but at least I could tell people who might'. She continues:

There are really important things in the world that people must know about, and if you don't tell them about them then they won't know and they won't be able to do anything about them.

(Byrne 1999)[9]

To summarise, investigative journalists attempt to get at the truth where the truth is obscure because it suits others that it be so; they choose their topics from a sense of right and wrong which we can only call a moral sense, but in the manner of their research they attempt to be dispassionately evidential. They are doing more than disagreeing with how society runs; they are pointing out that it is failing by its own standards. They expose, but they expose in the public interest, which they define. Their efforts, if successful, alert us to failures in the system and lead to politicians, lawyers and policemen taking action even as they fulminate, action that may result in legislation or regulation.

How this situation arose is the subject of the next three chapters.

NOTES

1 See Liu Binyan (1990).
2 Fukuyama has famously argued that liberal democracy is now the only possible form of society. See Fukuyama 1993.
3 It was curious how many of the investigative journalists or editors I interviewed thought fit to mention these two comedians in the context of a discussion about their craft.
4 David Northmore, Tim Fuell, Jancis Giles and Richard Newman, among others, launched Britain's first Association of Investigative Journalists in September 1999. Web site: www.aij-uk.com.
5 For example, see Palmer (1999).
6 Here is a subject of study: are there any similarities between the heroic stories of boys' fiction 1850–1950, of which Henty is the most famous exponent, and this new phenomenon?
7 It suits media managers to confer fame upon their stars, fame that is argued to be coming between the audience and the information, a relationship which should not be corrupted by the personality of the conduit, according to critics. As I write, the main headline of the *Times* is 'My nights under fire in Pristina', promoting the story not only of one of the million desperate refugees but also of the reporter whose pretty face appears next to it (Prentice 1999).
8 This is discussed extensively by Ettema and Glasser (1998: 132). See also two very relevant works, R. J. Evans (1997) and Fernandez-Armesto (1997).
9 However, Byrne is not naive about the motivations of some of those pitching programme ideas to her and claims to take great care to check out the facts she is given lest there has either been deliberate misrepresentation, or journalists are not careful enough or too afraid to tell her when stories do not stand up, or simply do not have the skills. In a casualised industry with no agreed training, investigative journalists may have neither the skill formation nor the hinterland of advice and support provided by the larger current affairs establishments of the past.

BIBLIOGRAPHY

Behrens, J. C. (1978) *Typewriter Guerrillas*. Chicago: Nelson Hall.

Boyd, A. (1994) *Broadcast Journalism, Techniques of Radio and TV News*. Oxford: Focal.

Brundson, C. and Morley, D. (1978) *Everyday Television: 'Nationwide'*. London: British Film Institute.

Byrne, D. (1999) Talk to the students of the MA Investigative Journalism course at Nottingham Trent University, 29 April 1999.

Calvert, J. (1999) Interview with Hugo de Burgh, 28 May 1999.

Central TV (1990) *The Cook Report*: 'Where did the Money Go?' Birmingham: Central TV. Transmitted 5 March 1990, producer Clive Entwhistle, reporter Roger Cook.

Channel 4 (1993) *Dispatches*: 'An Age Apart'. London: Channel 4 TV. Reporter/producer Hugo de Burgh.

Chepesiuk, R., Howell, H. and Lee, E. (1997) *Raising Hell: Straight Talk with Investigative Journalists*. London: McFarland.

Curran, J. and Seaton, J. (1997) *Power without Responsibility: The Press and Broadcasting in Britain*, 5th edn. London: Routledge.

de Burgh, H. (1998) Audience, journalist and text in television news. Paper delivered at the Annual Conference of the International Association for Media and Communications Research, 27 July 1998.

Dorril, S. and Ramsay, R. (1991) *Smear! Wilson and the Secret State*. London: Fourth Estate.

Eddy, P. (1976) *Destination Disaster*. London: Granada.

Edwards, C. (1999) Interview with Hugo de Burgh, 25 June 1999.

Ettema, J. and Glasser, T. (1988) Narrative form and moral force. *Journal of Communication*, Summer 1988: 8–26.

Ettema, J. S. and Glasser T. L. (1998) *Custodians of Conscience: Investigative Journalism and Public Virtue*. New York: Cambridge University Press.

Evans, H. (1997) Prometheus unbound. Iain Walker Memorial Lecture, Green College Oxford, May.

Evans, R. J. (1997) *In Defence of History*. London: Granta.

Faulkner, R. (1998) Tolstoy pamphlet. On the Internet at www.tolstoy.co.uk

Fernandez-Armesto, F. (1997) *Truth: A History*. London: Bantam.

Foot, P. (1973) *Who Killed Hanratty?* St Albans: Panther.

Foot, P. with Ron Smith (1983) *The Helen Smith Story*. Glasgow: Fontana.

Foot, P. (1989) *Who Framed Colin Wallace?* London: Macmillan.

Foot, P. (1993) *Murder at the Farm: Who Killed Carl Bridgewater?* London: Penguin.

Fukuyama. F. (1993) *The End of History and the Last Man*. London: Penguin.

Gelhorn, M. (1992) Introduction. In J. Pilger (1992) *Distant Voices*. London: Vintage.

Gibson, J. (1999) BBC veteran denies bias. On the Internet at http://www.newsun-limited.co.uk/BBC/story/0,2763,43185,00.html

Herman, E. and Chomsky, N. (1995) *Manufacturing Consent*. London: Vintage.

Hill, P., Young, M. and Sargant, T. (1985) *More Rough Justice*. London: Penguin.

Houghton, W. E. (1957) *The Victorian Frame of Mind*. New Haven: Yale University Press.

Ingham, B. (1991) *Kill the Messenger*. London: Harper Collins.

Kedourie, E. and Mango, A. (1988) Talking about the BBC. *Encounter*, 71 Sep/Oct: 60–4.

Knightley, P. (1997) *A Hack's Progress*. London: Jonathan Cape.

Knightley, P. (1999) Interview with Hugo de Burgh, 22 May 1999.

Langdon, J. (1993) High noon at the Holborn oasis. *Guardian*, 29 March 1993.

Langer, J. (1998) *Tabloid Television*. London: Routledge.

Liu, B. (1990) *A Higher Kind of Loyalty*. London: Methuen.

Lloyd, D. (1998) Talk to the students of the MA Investigative Journalism course at Nottingham Trent University, 19 February 1998.

Lloyd, D. (1999) Information passed to Hugo de Burgh, 10 June 1999.

McQuail, D. (1994) *Mass Communication Theory*. London: Sage.

Milne, S. (1995) *The Enemy Within: The Secret War Against the Miners*. London: Pan.

Northmore, D. (1996) *Lifting the Lid: A Guide to Investigative Research*. London: Cassell.

NCC (1999) City wins fight. Press release from Nottingham City Council (NCC), received 8 June 1999. (Further information was requested but not received.)

Page, B. (1998) A defence of 'low' journalism. *British Journalism Review*, 9 (1).

Palmer, M. (1999) Why the locals know best. (London) *Evening Standard*, 5 May 1999.

Pilger, J. (1992) *Distant Voices*. London: Vintage.

Pilger, J. (1999) Interview with Hugo de Burgh, 29 June 1999.

Prentice, Eve-Ann (1999) My nights under fire in Pristina. *Times*, 22 May 1999.

Preston, Louisa (1999) Paul Foot: The role of the journalist in the surveillance of justice. An unpublished essay for Broadcast Practice 3, BA BJ, Nottingham Trent University.

Rusbridger, A. (1999) Interview with Hugo de Burgh, 25 May 1999.

Shoemaker, P. (1996) *Mediating the Message*. London: Longman.

Silvester, C. (1994) *The Penguin Book of Interviews*. London: Penguin.

Tuchman, G. (1973) Making news by doing work: routinizing the unexpected. *American Journal of Sociology*, 79.

Ullmann, J. and Colbert, J. (1991) *The Reporter's Handbook: An Investigator's Guide to Documents and Techniques*, 2nd edn. New York: St Martin's Press.

Wallraff, G. (1978) *The Undesirable Journalist*. London: Pluto.

Weaver, D. H. (ed.) (1998) *The Global Journalist*. New Jersey: Hampton Press.

Weir, D. (1983) *How the Center for Investigative Journalism Gets a Story*. Reading, MA: Addison-Wesley.

Weymouth, A. and Lamizet, B. (eds) (1996) *Markets and Myths: Forces for Change in the European Media*. London: Longman.

FURTHER READING

Ettema, J. S. and Glasser T. L. (1998) *Custodians of Conscience: Investigative Journalism and Public Virtue*. New York: Cambridge University Press.

Evans, H. (1997) Prometheus unbound. Iain Walker Memorial Lecture, Green College Oxford, May.

Northmore, D. (1996) *Lifting the Lid: A Guide to Investigative Research*. London: Cassell.

2

THE EMERGENCE OF INVESTIGATIVE JOURNALISM

Hugo de Burgh

By the mid-nineteenth century the conditions had been created for the appearance of a concept of journalism that has been a model ever since and whose relationship to the polity has been an aspiration and an archetype.

Journalism rapidly developed some professional norms; its own techniques; a variety of genres, of which investigative journalism would be one. Moreover it fed upon the increasing rationalism of intellectual discourse in the period and upon that scientific approach of finding truth from facts which was the Enlightenment's greatest gift; in so doing it advanced the idea of objectivity, or at least impartiality. As with the great popular novelists, investigative journalists married rational observation with moral empathy and made exploitation and abuse an ever more likely topic of analysis, discussion and investigation.

However, when in the early years of the twentieth century, the media became big business, journalism as here defined was threatened. Just as their writings became 'the spaces between the ads' so the moral agenda became merely another commodity, or, like pictures of naked girls, another tool with which to attract a buyer. Public Service Broadcasting (PSB) in the 1960s to 1980s gave investigative journalism a new status, but the decline of PSB has been a severe blow.

Before the nineteenth century

Tales of *Perseus, Horatius* or *Beowulf* and chronicles such as the *Odyssey* or *Leila and Madjnoun* predate writing. With writing there emerged quite rapidly a distinction between stories like these and facts, as the 'Record of Events' was created, a distinction which, in the light of current debates about journalism and reality, may seem to us artificial.

Traditional histories of journalism usually start their tales early, some even as early as 500 BC, because the Egyptians were then producing news reports by writing their hieroglyphics onto papyrus. Around the same time, before the Caesars, the Roman Republic published *Acta Diurnia*, daily events, in the forum. Here is the kind of thing:

Fourth of the Calends of April. The fasces with Livinius the Consul. It thundered; an oak was struck with lightning on that part of Mount Palatine, called Summa Velia, early in the afternoon. A fray happened in a tavern at the lower end of Bankers Street, in which the keeper of the Hog-in-Armour Tavern was dangerously wounded. Tertinius the Aedile fined the butchers for selling meat which had not been inspected by the overseers of the markets.

(cit. in Andrews 1859: 11)

In China, from very early times, government sent out investigators to report on economic and social conditions and on the opinions of the populace. By AD 700 Chinese central government officials had established their own records of events which were sent out to the provincial and county officials. In Europe too, though 700 years later, governments tried to ensure that information on events supported their case both by suppressing alternative views and by publishing their own accounts. King Henry VIII of England (1509–47), in his disputes with Rome and with rebels at home, published his own accounts for wider distribution (Andrews 1859: 23), made possible by the diffusion of paper-making and printing.[1]

One of the earliest reports known in England is that of the Battle of Agincourt in 1415. Its fantastical style was reproduced with the European news pamphlets of the succeeding two centuries, as printers began to publish accounts of current events that were dramatic and also staunchly patriotic and pro-government. Reporting was often vivid, luridly describing, during the time when England was threatened with an invasion from Spain, the 'strange and most cruel whippes which the Spaniards had prepared to whippe and torment English men and women' (cit. in Cranfield 1978) and another detailed the massacres and rapes carried out by Spanish troops in The Netherlands:

James Messier being stricken over his belly, so that his intrailes did issue forth, dyed a few dayes after. The wife of the said Messier was so sore beaten, that she can never be her owne woman again. Peter Riondet, killed as he came out of his bed, although he was seventie yeares olde, his wife is sore hurt, and is hardly likely to recover it

(cit. in Cranfield 1978: 3)

Gradually these kinds of accounts translated themselves into announcements of what was going on in the present rather than what had happened or into records that were intended to influence the present, produced in pamphlet form; in both cases their intentions were political.

The expansion of commerce in the sixteenth and seventeenth centuries created a different demand; the most interested customers of all media were now the traders. In medieval times most trade had been dominated by the state, rural communities were self sufficient, cities tiny, artisans local and traders the appendages of royal and noble households, but this changed over the following centuries and there was a tremendous growth in business. As early as the 1500s the more important trading families of Europe such as the Fuggers and Rothschilds had already had their own private information networks. By the 1600s they were selling their news to other traders and by 1700 *Lloyds List*, a newspaper of business information, was established as a commercial venture. The concept of news as something distinct from chronicle, story or record, therefore, is at least 400 years old.

The career of the Frenchman Theophraste Renaudot (1586–1683) is instructive because it demonstrates both the new entrepreneurship in information and shows an interest in communication distinct from that of the pamphleteers. A fashionable medical practitioner in Paris whose clients included Cardinal Richelieu, he was tasked with inquiring into the health of the urban poor and then to be (in effect) government minister for the poor. He was convinced that one reason for poverty was the inability of people with work to offer to find those who needed it. Towns had grown too large for word of mouth to work, so he set up the *Bureau of Addresses*, a kind of job centre cum notice board cum free advertisement newspaper (Sgard 1976).

It was as a byproduct of his *Bureau of Addresses* that Renaudot found himself collecting news. From collecting information about events, he went on to establish correspondence with knowledgeable people in different parts of the country and he noted what was being said in the pamphlets of the day. The government was concerned about scurrilous pamphlets and decided to licence him to produce a digest of the information that he was obtaining which could be laced with information direct from the government, giving its point of view on events domestic and international (Smith 1979).

The first edition of Renaudot's *Gazzette de France* was published in 1631. This kind of newspaper had existed in Holland and Germany for some time under the name of *corantos*. They had little editorial input, were dependent upon state approval and often subsidies and their circulations were limited to ruling class members and approved recipients. Like his less accomplished equivalent in England, the English printer–publisher Muddiman, he was first and foremost a businessman. They can be described as being of the first generation of information entrepreneur.

While Renaudot was at his most active, England was fighting a civil war. Ideas of equality and human rights canvassed by the Levellers and other radical factions during that war were gaining wide currency, and old authorities were challenged. More than this, the English Civil War provided the opportunity for competing interpretations of events, therefore competing newspapers and therefore polemic and partial propaganda. Conflicting interpretations and competition to get out the news first were very good for news entrepreneurs and by the early 1700s controversy and scathing critique of people in high places were more and more common, with Daniel Defoe and Jonathan Swift epitomising the style.

The English newsletters of the period, or *newesbookes* as they were called, were full of polemic. There was little gathering of news as we would understand it, although the glimmerings of the idea that truth should be sought from facts can be discerned. It was in England that what may be the first theory of the media was adumbrated by John Milton (1608–74) in his *Areopagitica* of 1644; according to Hartley (1992: 150), Milton argued the case that liberty is a condition of national greatness and journalism the means by which that liberty is to be assured. Hartley also makes the point that the idea of the reporter as someone identifying truth, what he calls the 'ideology of the eyewitness' predated the scientism normally associated with the Enlightenment. As the century wore on, there developed that scepticism of the religious mindset and attraction to scientific method, historical investigation and the questioning of all and every institution in ways that had been known to no previous civilisation; this was the basis for the idea of impartial evidence and of the reporter as being the one who gathers such evidence.

There were also economic reasons for the development of the media towards journalism. Printers needed to produce and sell ephemera since books often took a long time to shift and thus tied up their capital in stock. The increase in trade meant that there were well-established means of news distribution via the ports and posting systems that were developing rapidly. There was a growing market. The intellectual and cultural revolution in Europe was both a function of and the stimulus for publishing. Readership was limited to a minority, but by no means as small a minority as in the ancient civilisations. Thanks both to the relative simplicity of the Roman writing and Arabic numeral systems that Europeans now used, to the Protestant Reformation that had encouraged reading in indigenous languages and to other factors promoting literacy, that minority grew and probably grew faster in Northern Europe than anywhere else,[2] except perhaps America. There, Protestant settlers with an intense belief in the value of literacy and a passion for disputation as well as a need to get information from the Europe they had left behind, developed their own periodicals. They created, as in England, an audience, often based upon the coffee house where merchants and officials sat and read and talked; the first modern 'public' which was to be steadily enlarged over the course of the following two centuries and to which journalism became, as in Hartley's characterisation of the *Spectator*, 'an active agent in the *representation* of the imagined public to itself' (Hartley 1992: 153).

Therefore, by the time of William Cobbett (1763–1835) and of the American Revolution (1775–83) there existed not only the newspaper as a conduit of business intelligence but also the idea of the newspaper as a vehicle of political polemic in competition with other propaganda and, inchoate but there, the ideal of truth-seeking. There was a readership, even an embryo public opinion. The Enlightenment had established well the idea of ideas, in other words that there was not one true factual answer to everything based upon religion, but that there were things to be discovered by observation, and upon which opinions might legitimately differ.

The influence of personality may be as important as that of material factors in accounting for the particular direction taken by Anglophone journalism. Why Milton, Defoe, Swift or Cobbett were to reason or act as they did is outside the scope of this survey, but the fact that they did so has influenced journalism. If one of the features of investigative journalism is the fearless uncovering of facts unpalatable to the powerful then Cobbett is a distinguished precursor. Between 1810 and 1812 he spent two years in jail because he had denounced the flogging of militiamen who had protested against unjustified deductions from their pay (Green 1983: 350). In the past information entrepreneurs had gone to prison for offending someone high and mighty or for blasphemy or for getting the official line wrong – but Cobbett went to prison for defending the voiceless. It was an important moment in the development of journalism. How did he arrive at it?

Twenty years earlier, in 1780, Cobbett, the adventurous 17-year-old son of a small farmer signed up as a Redcoat instead of staying around home and labouring. He was sent to North America to fight in the war against the colonists and, while there and doing so well as to be promoted to sergeant major, amused himself with the study of English grammar. That study was to serve as the academic basis for the career of a great early journalist; but it was his own character that supplied the catalyst. Cobbett may have been a conservative in politics, but his journalism was intensely radical and his message was social revolution. He championed the oppressed, the exploited, the marginalised and the cheated.

His first act upon returning to England from America after army service in 1791 was to charge his officers with peculation; he had become outraged by the corruption of the army. However, he had not got his facts correct and the officers invented counter charges so that he had to flee to revolutionary France and then back to America where he spent several years as a passionate pamphleteer condemning the failings of the new democracy and founding periodicals, including *Porcupine's Gazette*. America, too, became too hot for him and he fled back to England where he founded a magazine that launched attacks on corruption and misuse of public funds, unjust laws, low wages and absentee clergy, *Cobbett's Weekly Political Register*, which survived until his death. The quality of his invective found him loyal readers for his investigations and there are good examples in Derry (1968), from which the following is taken. Given the hue and cry created by people in rich countries over population in poor countries over the past thirty years, it is topical as the article from which it is taken exposes Malthusian ideas as theoretical covering for attempts to prevent the poor from breeding because of the cost to the Poor Rates:

> In your book you show that, in certain cases, a crowded population has been attended with great evils, a great deal of unhappiness, misery

and human degradation. You then, without any reason to bear you out, predict, or leave it to be clearly inferred, that the same is likely to take place in England. Your principles are almost all false; and your reason, in almost every instance, is the same ...

It must be clear to every attentive reader of your book on *Population* that it was written for the sole purpose of preparing beforehand a justification for ... deeds of injustice and cruelty.

In 1831 Cobbett was prosecuted for defending striking farm labourers and at the time of his death was being accused of encouraging rioting and rebellion by his championship of rural workers (Green 1983: 164). His career illustrates some important social changes taking place in English society, as well as the connections between ideas, business and politics in France, England and the American states. He was a man who began without any establishment connections; he came from nowhere. It was issues, rather than entrepreneurship, that brought him to journalism. He wrote for a public for whom nobody had written before and in order to communicate with them translated the radical thinkers into simple language that ordinary people could understand when it was read out at inns and street corners. In the past journalists had been more concerned with court and religious politics than with social conditions; Cobbett wrote about matters that affected ordinary people.

Among his achievements are the organisation of an efficient distribution system and the begetting of *Hansard*, the first published account of Parliamentary debates. Most of all, he created a new kind of journalism, providing a model for the radical journalism of the nineteenth century such as that of the *Black Dwarf*. Here is an example:

The people of England have long been in error, it seems, upon the subject of the condition of the *Irish peasantry*; and Lord Castlereagh and Mr Curwen have stepped forward to set them right. It is not true, they say, that Ireland is the most debased and degraded and unhappy country in the world. They are a contented, a *high spirited* and a happy race of mortals ... True it is, that they are almost in a state of nature, as it respects cloathing and habitation: true it is, that their wretched cabins, built of mud, and destitute of cleanliness and convenience, are the very images of the abode of misery and desolation, that the inhabitants of these horrid looking receptacles, which a hottentot would disdain to dwell in, look forth from them in rags and tatters, staring like an unhappy bedlamite looking after some visionary beam of comfort; true it is, that their appearance only excites disgust; yet notwithstanding all this, they are *contented* and *cheerful* and *happy*.

(cit. in Cranfield 1978: 95)

A vigorous, sceptical and irreverent social journalism had appeared, the proclivities of which are demonstrated in the title of one of its most famous mastheads, *The Poor Man's Guardian*.

The nineteenth century

Journalism and the public sphere

In the first years of the nineteenth century newspapers in England could still be bullied by the authorities through taxation, threats of prosecution, offers of help and exclusive information, and the subsidy of government advertising. By 1860 this had changed. Newspapers became relatively independent of politicians. The radical press survived attempts to stifle it. It has often been remarked that the *Times* and a few other papers became the modern equivalents of the Ancient Greek *agora* or places where opinion-formers and decision-makers met to make public opinion. How had this come about?

Different historians give different weight to the various factors at play. Traditional English histories saw the easing of government restrictions on the press as the result of the struggles of progressives (Williams 1957); others have preferred to emphasise the burgeoning power of the new business classes who resisted attempts by the political elite to dominate information (Harris 1996: 106). To Franklin 'undoubtedly the most necessary change was the removal of what opponents dubbed "the taxes on knowledge"', by which he means advertising, newspaper stamp duty and duties on paper all repealed between 1853 and 1861 (Franklin 1997: 78). Technological change made it possible to print and distribute more – and larger – newspapers, and thus satisfy the growing demand. In today's parlance, moreover, the stakeholders in newspapers were many: first, the capital required was large and distributed, such that there were many ready to defend their interest; the revenue from advertisements rendered other sources of funds such as political subvention unnecessary; the readers were influential in guiding the policy of the paper; the inland transport revolution provided a much more extensive market and wide distribution gave to the opinions of the writers an influence that politicians began to fear to contravene.

The pre-eminence of the *Times* was clear; between 1800 and 1860, as Britain's position in the world consolidated a very large class of ascendant internationally-aware, information hungry and influential bourgeois, it became their debating chamber. Thomas Barnes, (editor of the *Times* 1817–41) was their spokesman and informant and he earned new readers by championing causes such as Parliamentary Reform and the victims of the Peterloo Massacre. Rising revenue meant he could spend more on investigation and he and his successors prided themselves on their access to information and their independence from pressure.

A flavour of the situation is conveyed by this well-repeated anecdote. In

1851 the *Times*, edited by John Delane, attacked the French Prime Minister Prince Louis Napoleon. Angry, he demanded that his Ambassador to London either put pressure on the British government to punish the *Times*, or buy a better press through bribery. His Ambassador tried to explain to him that life in England just wasn't like that:

> Someone has told you, Prince, that the hostility of the *Times* and the *Morning Chronicle* was provoked by pecuniary subsidies. Nothing could be more false than such an assertion and, believe me, on such an important subject I would not make a statement without being absolutely certain. ... Although less than in France, political men in England are sufficiently anxious about newspaper criticism to have tried often to buy an organ so widely circulated as the *Times*: but they have always failed ...
>
> (cit. in Cranfield 1978: 160)

That ambassador had correctly noted that, as early as 1851 the *Times* was not amenable to the kind of influence proposed by his Prince.

Whereas in the eighteenth century much of the political conflict had been about personalities, cliques and corruption, now with economic development at home and an empire to exploit abroad, and new classes depending upon both, government policies were of intense interest, both those which touched upon business affairs (foreign treaties, trade policy) or which had a wider constituency (social conditions and taxation). One 1832 paper gave as its aims:

> The abolition of tithes, the repeal of the Corn Laws; a more equitable system of taxation; the abolition of the hereditary peerage; an equitable reduction of the national debt; ... a reform in the expenditure of the crown; and the abolition of all unmerited pensions and sinecures; the doing away with an expensive state religion, and causing society to maintain its own ministers; remodelling the laws, and making the same law for rich and poor; a still more extensive franchise, etc.
>
> (cit. in Cranfield 1978: 134)

Editors welcomed journalists who could identify the issues of the day, analyse them and communicate their relevance to a critical public. These abilities and the new power of the media are illustrated well in the career of a well-known war correspondent.

The idea of the reporter

In 1853 the Crimean War started and William Howard Russell was appointed the *Times* correspondent. As soon as he arrived he reported on the inadequate preparations, insufficient food and lack of shelter for the troops. He did this in two ways, as articles for the paper and as backgrounders for the leaders.

Russell's reports revealed that the British navy was far less efficient than the French; that the French medical services were superior; that the British wounded suffered appallingly; that the officers, through inadequate training, could not cope; that the staff at the headquarters in Britain were negligent and ignorant; that what Raglan and his often brave officers could not do – get changes, get supplies – Russell could. By some accounts (Snoddy 1992) the consequences of such revelatory reporting were that the government fell; a new post, that of Secretary of State for War, was created; conditions for the troops were improved; the *Times* in London got a fund set up to provide medical services; influenced by his journalism Florence Nightingale and others went to the war and built the foundations of a war nursing profession; in time the army commissioning system was reformed thanks to his revelations, a change that would have an important influence on Britain's ability to wage wars. However the extent of Russell's success is disputed in *The First Casualty* (Knightley 1975). For tyro journalists it is nice to know that, as an investigator, he had a presence which today's victims would recognise in Captain Clifford's description:

> a vulgar low Irishman ... but he has the gift of the gab, uses his pen as well as his tongue, sings a good song, drinks anyone's brandy and water, and smokes as many cigars as foolish young officers will let him, and is looked upon by most in camp as a Jolly Good Fellow. He is just the sort to get information, particularly out of the youngsters. And I assure you more than one 'Nob' has thought best to give him a shake of the hand rather than the cold shoulder *en passant*, for [he] is rather an awkward gentleman to be on bad terms with
>
> (cit. in Wilkinson-Latham 1979: 59)

The Crimean War was significant for the development of journalism in that it showed that the profession was earning respect and that the occupation of reporter, as someone who goes out and finds out what is happening, was established. As Stephens (1988) writes, one of the first known to have gone out in search of information rather than merely writing up whatever fell into his lap was Tyas, whose reports of the Peterloo Massacre were influential. Stephens points out the interesting difference between Tyas and his professional successors, in that he did not regard it as part of his duties to meet or interrogate the organisers of the public meeting which was to turn into the Peterloo Massacre of 1819, but simply went as a spectator (Stephens 1988: 243). By the time of Russell, reporters were bearding generals and ministers, to say nothing of more accessible decision-makers, and requiring of them that they clarify their intentions or at least dissemble well.

Sympathy and morality

Before Charles Dickens the novelist came Charles Dickens the journalist who campaigned to ameliorate the condition of the Oliver Twists and Little Nells of his fictional pantheon (Philip 1986: 6). An exhortation typical of Dickens opened a feature article in his own journal, *Household Words*, in 1852:

> Umbrellas to mend, and chairs to mend, and clocks to mend, are called in our streets daily. [But] who shall count up the numbers of thousands of children to mend, in and about those same streets, whose voice of ignorance cries aloud as the voice of wisdom once did, and is as little regarded; who go to pieces for the want of mending, and die unrepaired!
>
> (Dickens, 'Boys to Mend' in *Household Words*, 11 September 1852)

Charles Dickens' literary antecedents lie in the novels of social life that had arisen in eighteenth-century England and in the novel that spoke of ordinary people rather than just the upper classes, more or less a creation of Walter Scott. What he added to the observation and social comprehensiveness of his predecessors was an awareness of the domestic and working conditions in which the poor lived. He shared this with his continental equivalents, Manzoni, Balzac and Zola among them. Emile Zola (1840–1902) was to take a step further; he fused Dickens' awareness and compassion with techniques of observation that we would now call sociological. Like Dostoevsky in Russia, Zola went into the slums and made careful observations of conditions which he then revealed in his writings. The movement born from this was *documentary realism* (Keating 1991). If method defines the investigative journalist then arguably the documentary realists were the first investigative journalists; they also shared an obsession with the condition of the poor,[3] an intense awareness of the miseries caused by the industrial revolution. Old communities had been uprooted, but, much more immediately evident, people had piled into cities in which there was neither the knowledge nor the skill to make their lives bearable by providing decent water, sanitation or food retailing, let alone education, a ready supply of work and protection from exploitation and criminality.

Sharing the tasks of taxonomy and revelation of these phenomena were the early social scientists; the most famous product is probably the seventeen-volume *Life and Labour of the People of London* by Charles Booth, published between 1889 and 1891. Keating reminds us (1991: 305) that, in keeping with the increasing obeisance paid to science and scientific methods, both journalists and scholars claimed objectivity, but there was little that was objective about their *aims*; it was the *method* that was supposed to be scientifically detached. The idea that a distinction can be made between subject selection and method such that commitment or partiality in the former is consonant with impartiality in the latter is an interesting one, with an obvious bearing upon investigative journalism.

The urge to identify and tell of suffering and exploitation cannot be attributed solely to a spirit of inquiry; scientism provided the tools but the motivation came from a combination of that evangelical belief that to do good works is to worship; the optimism that inspired people to believe that a utopia could be built for all (Houghton 1957: 33); the earnestness which infused Victorians to deny themselves pleasures that they might be active in the great struggle to build a better world; a patronising sensibility to the sufferings of the unwashed, born of romanticism, something akin to the sentiments of Dorothea Brooke in *Middlemarch*.

In the latter half of the nineteenth century many writers were both novelists and journalists but around the 1880s there began a gradual bifurcation.[4] H. G. Wells announced that he preferred to be considered a journalist (Parrinder 1972: 297) and his, and others' documentary realist novels were written as adjuncts to journalism. Other kinds of novel, what we might call 'art house' novels, were written by 'artists' and a familiar distinction occurred, bridged in our own day only by American writers such as Tom Wolfe or Gore Vidal.

Objectivity

Between the early years of the century and 1853 the *Times* developed such independence of political influence that it could claim to be reporting objectively and without reference to the interests of the powerful. The date 1853 is significant, because it is then that the Crimean reports of Russell were printed in the *Times*. What had happened to make this possible?

There are four main approaches to the emergence of objectivity: the political, economic, technological and institutional, and they are complementary. Jurgen Habermas holds that impartial or objective information, by contrast with the heavily political and biased news of earlier times, came about with the rise of an informed public opinion in Anglo-America which demanded impartial news. This 'public sphere' consisted of competing groups debating the issues of the day, and these groups wished to be supplied with the same information on which to base their often differing analyses of their interests and the interests of their polities. This public sphere itself was fed and helped to grow, and to grow better informed, by the media which thus enabled a process of political development that culminated in modern democracy (Dahlgren and Sparks 1991).

Schiller (1981) argues that objectivity developed in response to commercial imperatives, i.e. the need to sell to as many people as possible and therefore offend as few as possible; he also emphasises the scientific attitude of empiricism that gradually took hold throughout the nineteenth century and influenced communication as it did intellectual enquiry.

Desmond (1978) largely attributes impartiality to a technical development which had an instant influence upon writing, the telegraph, and a commercial one, the news agency. Before the telegraph, writing was by modern standards long-winded and full of subjective comment and detail. After all, much writing by foreign correspondents was done while waiting several days for a ship. The American Civil War (1862–5) attracted more journalists than any previous war and they were the first to employ the telegraph. Transmission charges were high;[5] every word had to be paid for. Thus the more concise the report, the less it cost to transmit. Correspondents were urged to chop down their material to the minimum of facts and to clarify so that the main points could be identified instantly. When the report was received it could be expanded, and illustrative or subjective material added by the recipient editor.

This new way of reporting very soon led to other changes, in particular the introduction of 'the inverted pyramid'. Copy had to start with the key fact or facts, without preliminaries. Enlargements, filling out, followed sequentially and in the reverse order of importance such that the sub-editor might chop off the lower paragraphs without detriment to the meaning, hence 'the inverted pyramid'. Story-telling, by contrast, leads up to the climax from detail whose relevance is not always clear at the outset. As to the content of that pyramid, they are 'the Five Ws and an H', a codification of essential facts for a story that every news journalism student learns: What happened; Where it happened; When it happened; Who was involved; Why it happened; How it happened. These requirements, forced upon journalists by the telegraph, resulted in much greater accuracy and in better reader comprehension; it became a given of journalism that this kind of objective information, news, was different from more discursive, subjective material.

The next major change was the introduction of news agencies. As Desmond says 'while a reporter might write a report that would be acceptable to his own newspaper, a news agency report on the same subject, going to scores of newspapers, might be wholly unacceptable to some' (Desmond 1978: 217). Agencies had therefore to produce copy that consisted of little more than commonly acceptable facts. Their work provided a check on what newspapers' own correspondents were doing, and a source of comparison. This further accentuated the emphasis upon accuracy and unembroidered fact in news, and the distinction between such news and those parts of newspapers and broadcast schedules where subjectivity was permitted. It also encouraged the idea of the eyewitness as the key to knowledge, which launched the careers of many more special correspondents and inserted the testimonial interview among their tools. Realistic photography, appearing at the same time as the above developments in the 1850s, probably encouraged the belief that there was a reality that journalists could capture. More recent factors in the underpinning of objectivity as a journalistic norm, and the current critique of objectivity, are discussed in the next chapter.

The idea of evidence

The adoption of objectivity as a journalistic norm was simultaneous with the development of the idea that reporters (as we may now call them) used specific techniques particular to their profession – observation of events, enquiry of sources. We can imagine that they were boastful of their accuracy because they saw that not only did this guarantee them a following but also established their status as experts and professionals.

This helped to transform the way journalism was seen – originally seen as mercenary and unreliable polemicists, journalists were being consulted and courted by princes, not only because of their ability to influence opinion but because they were often more knowledgeable than the supposed experts. Such knowledge was also valued by the argumentative Victorian business and intellectual circles whose members increasingly championed the evidential approach, the rational dissecting of outdated institutions and ideas (some of them) and the concept of a public interest (Houghton 1957: chap. 4).

A distinction emerged between those writing the editorials in the office and those gathering news in the field. The report became differentiated from the analysis, as it is today; feature articles appeared, distinct from either, and included what we now call 'human interest'; 'hard' news was distinguished from 'soft' news; literary journalism was introduced; the interview was invented; newspapers campaigned.

The idea of investigation

In 1885 the journalist W. T. Stead sought a girl in the East End of London for sexual purposes, found a 12 year old and bought her. Stead was arrested, tried and imprisoned. However, since his motive had been to stage a publicity stunt and not to take advantage of his purchase his sentence was a short one and he made the whole affair the sting that finally brought success to the campaign to stop child prostitution (Crossland 1996).

William Stead had started life as a 14-year-old clerk in a Newcastle business. He freelanced for the Darlington *Northern Echo* and in 1871, aged 22, he became editor (Griffiths 1992). He was brought up in a Protestant sect devoted to good works and believed that journalism gave him the opportunity to save himself. He was first noticed nationally when he was active in a press crusade in exposing atrocities allegedly carried out by Turks in Bulgaria. He was invited to be assistant editor of the then very influential *Pall Mall Gazette*, of which he became editor in 1883. With that he campaigned for a proactive policy over the Sudan (to save the benighted Sudanese), for the London poor and for modernisation of the navy. Much later he was to campaign for peace and to support the Boers in the Boer War.

The scoop for which Stead is best remembered is 'The Maiden Tribute of Modern Babylon'. The background to the story is that, over a year before

Stead's first article on the subject appeared, tradesmen serving brothels in Brussels had tipped off an English Quaker human rights campaigner, Josephine Butler, about a slave trade in young English girls. Butler managed to find a Belgian police witness but neither British police nor diplomats were interested. The trade was well established, horrifically cruel and well documented by Butler, yet she made no headway in her efforts to raise the age of consent and to get the police to take action.

It was only when W. T. Stead, then editor of the *Pall Mall Gazette*, became involved that the authorities were to take notice. After buying his girl, on 6 July 1885 he published *The Violation of Virgins, The Report of Our Secret Commission* consisting of five pages of detail under such subheadings as 'Strapping girls down' and 'Why the cries of victims are not heard'. It contained a drawn-out account of his own personal investigation.

> The woman of the house was somewhat suspicious, owing to the presence of a stranger, but after some conversation she said she had one fresh girl within reach, whom she would take over at once if they could come to terms. The girl was sent for, and duly appeared. She was told that she was to have a good situation within a few miles of London ... [but] seemed somewhat nervous when she heard so many inquiries and the talk about taking her into the country. The bargain however, was struck. The keeper had to receive £2 down, and another sovereign when the girl was proved a maid.
>
> (*Pall Mall Gazette* 6 July 1885: 5)

The first thing to note about Stead's journalism is that his explicitness was quite novel. We have seen how, two centuries before, newsheets pandered to people's taste for sex and violence, and these kinds of stories continued to be produced but under wraps and in specialist periodicals such as *The Pearl*, which provided stories with such titles as 'Lady Pokingham, or, They all do it' (Cranfield 1978: 212). There had, until Stead, been no place for this kind of stuff in the respectable press, which was full of moral seriousness. Stead changed the style of reporting by conjoining high moral tone with sensational description, the favoured style of many newspapers in Britain today.

Stead got attention not only by prurience, but also by revelation. That this kind of trade existed was almost certainly news to most of his readers. His undercover, investigative style was premonitory. With the help of the specialist, Josephine Butler, Stead carried out detailed preliminary research and undertook a sting, in much the manner favoured by modern investigative journalists. The treatment of the story increased the sensationalism. Stead published it in segments over several weeks, cliff-hangers attracting customer loyalty. His story was talked of everywhere and commented upon by innumerable other papers, circulation rose and touts sold copies at two hundred times the cover price.

Investigative journalism had been invented,[6] just as great changes were about to be demanded of journalism.

Mass media beginnings

As Stead wrote, the conditions for journalism were about to undergo a fundamental development. Although by their own standards their sales figures were impressive, Stead and his admirers failed to notice some of the relevant changes that were taking place in society, or at least failed to capitalise upon their crusading zeal. As with other highbrow editors, Stead had high ideals and great abilities but used them in providing only for a restricted social class – their language still betrayed this, as did the assumptions of culture, knowledge and interests that pervaded the press. Had they been better businessmen they might have noticed that the market was expanding dramatically. They didn't and so, despite all that sensation, they lost out to a different kind of journalist (Williams 1957).

The population explosion that had started in the eighteenth century had continued, with exponential rise in the birth rate and a vastly higher proportion of people living in cities. The money economy was all but universal and retailing outlets had developed everywhere; distribution by road, canal and rail had advanced tremendously. There were better printing presses, cheaper paper and illustrations. Advertising had developed to such an extent that it reduced dependence upon other forms of revenue, reduced the cover price and thus further enlarged the potential market.

As to readership, universal male suffrage and the trades union movement politicised the masses; public education had been introduced and literacy was spreading rapidly; football developed from the 1870s and provided a focus for newspapers, enlarging the market further. By choice and professional formation, few existing journalists were appropriate to take advantage of the opportunities these developments offered. Yet professional journalism and the importance it had gained for newspapers together with the mass market made them commercially successful, and as the media became big business so it attracted people who were first and foremost entrepreneurs rather than journalists. Hence the arrival of the second generation of 'information entrepreneur', epitomised by Alfred Harmsworth (Taylor 1996).

In 1881 a magazine called *Titbits* was born, launched by George Newnes, not a journalist but an entrepreneur. *Titbits* was a collection of short, amusing cuttings from other publications, supplemented with some original gleanings from hosts of stringers; perfectly suited to young people who could read but had no stamina for high culture or wordy elite newspapers. Among its admirers was the 16-year-old Alfred Harmsworth, a keen cyclist who toured the country with other cycling enthusiasts, mainly youngsters who worked as clerks or in shops and who probably read *Titbits* too. Harmsworth became one of the earliest contributors to *Titbits*, and went to work for *Wheel Life*, the cyclists' paper (Williams 1957: 136).

By the age of 21 he was editor of *Bicycling News* and ready to launch his own paper, pretty much a copy of *Titbits*, called *Answers*. Over the next ten years he launched eleven more publications, including *Home Chat* for the housewife, *Chips* and *Pluck* for the errand boy, *Forget-me-not* for factory girls, *Union Jack*, *Halfpenny Marvel* and *Comic Cuts* (Taylor 1996: 19).

In May 1896 Harmsworth's business had a capital of a million pounds and he could attempt to launch into daily newspapers. By that time he had proved, through his commercial success, that he knew what the masses wanted to read. Moreover, he knew how to attract readers through stunts and competitions, selling his publications the same as any other article. When he was offered the failing *Evening News* for a low price he bought it and applied the same principles that had made him successful as a periodical publisher. In time Harmsworth would add many other profitable papers to that one, and become the first modern media mogul.

Several press entrepreneurs were to build their media empires out of the mass market created in the 1870s. Typically they ruled them as despots, but, although as individuals they had strong political views that they sometimes chose to promote, their first consideration was commercial success. Rupert Murdoch is in exactly this mould. When in 1986 *The Sunday Times* was hoaxed over the Hitler's Diaries fraud, the journalists felt ashamed, even humiliated. Rupert Murdoch said: 'Circulation went up and stayed up. We didn't lose money, or anything like that' (cit. in Harris 1996: 567). As far as he was concerned 'we are in the entertainment business' (op. cit.) and other proprietors think the same, for example Lord Matthews of the Express Group 'that's how I look at newspapers ... as money' (cit. in Porter 1984: 153).

With Harmsworth in the 1920s providing for the newly literate classes, ever expanding in numbers, circulation became the most important factor. The broadsheets wanted small select audiences and were increasingly advertising backed as the cost of providing high standard journalism rose; initially advertisers did not influence the content of broadsheets greatly, although in comparison to politics the quantity of feature material grew.

Similar changes took place among the populars, but for different reasons. Advertising was less important – advertisers pay less per capita for advertising to poorer people – but circulation mattered greatly since the populars needed a higher proportion of the cover price and would get what advertising they could only through having large circulations. In order to get them they popularised and sensationalised and simplified. The process of simplifying copy itself, reducing stories to key points, started with the introduction of the telegraph, accelerated with the new populism. Political content was rapidly diminishing in favour of human interest (Curran and Seaton 1997: chap. 5). Intense competition in the period accelerated this trend and brought stunts and the introduction of market research to check that what was being provided was what the masses wanted. As a byproduct of this the radical press died. Political mass market papers could not compete on price, particularly when advertisers were reluctant to advertise in them, or on sensationalism (ibid.).

An exception was the Manchester *Guardian*, supported by a Manchester business and professional community whose members tended to share a religious and liberal political outlook. It was able to remain highbrow and independent in a way that was not open to mass circulation papers. There were others like it, although most were eliminated by the mergers of the 1930s or 1950s.

In summary, the era of the press barons had consequences both positive and negative for British journalism. Many more people read the papers but there was a sharp division between popular and broadsheet journalism in both style and concerns. That the information media could be made into big, profitable businesses was now quite clear, as was the fact that when media are seen first and foremost as businesses, this influences their content. Content is also influenced when advertising is more important than sales. Curran and Seaton argue that business-driven media are different from journalism-driven media (1997). They believe that the press barons limited the range of voices that were heard by ordinary people to those that were acceptable to a few selfish businessmen. Thus the economic depression in the 1930s was not properly analysed and people were allowed to think of it as an Act of God; strikers were calumnied and their ideas marginalised as those of a minority; bogies were created in the public mind – Russia, Jews – and enthusiasms were fostered that were not necessarily healthy, for example empire jingoism (Spurr 1994) and, in the case of the *Daily Mail*, fascism. Curran and Seaton's observations have a particular resonance today, in view of the widespread anguish about journalism's subjection to commercialism and to the power of managers who have no criteria of success but profit.

Commodification

We have seen how the journalism we recognise as such was established by the end of the nineteenth century; Chalaby (1998), building on the ideas of Jurgen Habermas, which are touched upon in Chapter 5, argues that it also came to an end when the media became industrialised.

To Chalaby, in the decades before the mass market, news selection was morally grounded. The press had been polemical, tied to specific parties and points of view; the repeal of the Stamp Acts released the media from these ties and made it possible for a relatively independent and impartial journalism to establish itself. The press no longer needed to kow-tow to narrow sectional interests, whether of the industrial capitalists of Manchester, for example, or the working class, whose press he examines in detail, but sought to serve a much wider constituency. However, as this constituency became much wider, as it became a mass market, it became clear that there were opportunities for profit, and indeed that a greater degree of capitalisation was required to enter such a market.

In the process the media were driven to compete fiercely and this competition pushed them into adapting norms and techniques which greatly changed the nature of the journalism. Journalism, from providing a forum for debate and the wherewithal, unbiased factual information with which to debate, became product to attract audiences, commodities with values according to their power of attraction. The job of the journalist became not to elevate discussion or educate the readers to participation in the *res publica* but to produce such product; unmediated political documents such as the printing of parliamentary debates, disappeared; serious matter was downgraded with the introduction of coverage of a much wider range of activities.

In other words, Chalaby's theory provides an explanation of how journalism adapted as the mass market press became lucrative, attracting entrepreneurs who further commercialised the media businesses and commodified the product. He sees the late nineteenth century as the beginning of a long process of which we see the fruits today in the trivialisation of journalism that is regularly denounced. Postman's aptly named *Amusing Ourselves to Death* (1987) argued that the entertaining, undemanding and ephemeral were distracting us from or just squeezing out important issues.

McManus (1994) gives detailed examples of what he calls 'junk journalism' displacing informative journalism and in chapter 8 provides evidence from case studies of how little effort was made to gather or present background, context or explanation and how reporters are more likely to use emotional or amusing content than the information required to make sense of the story. He explains trivialisation as the result of increasing market-orientated journalism, which he contrasts with normative journalism, and argues that, as with junk food, this 'pap' creates unhealthy desires and dislodges the better quality.

> Even though profit-seeking business has been the enabling foundation of journalism here ever since entrepreneurs succeeded political parties as operators of the press 150 years ago, it has usually been kept in the basement. Now the business of selling news is being invited upstairs, into the temple.
>
> (McManus 1994: 1)

Sparks (1991) identified a widening gap between the informed elite and the entertained masses; others (Golding 1998) argue that all media, including élite media, are becoming more entertainment orientated.

So far so good. Research had long established that various biases were endemic in 'hard' news; a bias in favour of authority, for example, or towards selecting stories that privileged stereotypes. 'Soft' news or those entertaining bits that had gradually supplanted hard were relegated. However, once

43

researchers had grasped the increasing preponderance of soft (also called 'human interest') stories[7] then they began to try to understand them too. As we have seen in Chapter 1, Brundson and Morely (1978), Rutherford Smith (1979), van Poecke (1988) and others all found that events tended to be fitted into existing categories and were made to perform certain functions such as reassure us about authority, or amuse us, or pander to our prejudices; at one extreme was the Charles Stuart case, in which a murder was packaged by reporters neatly to fit conventional stereotypes (young black male, car thieving, white woman, traffic) bearing no relation to reality but every relation to expectation (Berkowitz 1997: 498).

Why is this? News is a genre of journalism; every genre has an identity recognised by producers and consumers, both of whom require obedience to conventions of structure, grammar and vocabulary as well as adherence to the repertoire of themes deemed appropriate to the genre (McQuail 1994). Various studies, including Mazzolini (1987) and Bell (1991) have all come broadly to the conclusion that journalists take events and format them in accordance with the requirements of the genre, themselves rooted in cultural assumptions and commercial requirements.

At its extreme, we might say therefore that journalism so reconstructs the world as to ensure that it fits with its reading of what its audience wants to hear, rather than with reality, and that this has various social implications. Bourdieu has gone much further in his critique, specifically of television journalism, arguing that television journalism, far from enriching the public sphere, is having a number of dangerous effects. Television journalism, he believes, contains and limits ideas and argument; classifies people and forces us to see the world through its classifications (Bourdieu 1998: 22). For institutional, technological, economic and sociological reasons television journalists are able to, and do, impose their own particular constructions and framing upon people and issues: 'the journalistic field is based upon a set of assumptions and beliefs, which reach beyond differences of position and opinion ... the effect is censorship' (Bourdieu 1998: 47).

Chalaby's large scale thesis referred to above appears to be born out by a variety of studies of specific cases of journalism such as Keeble's examination of the way in which the Gulf War was 'created' by the media (Keeble 1998), certain studies of local TV news (de Burgh 1998 and Langer 1998), Cao's comparison of Chinese and British coverage of the Hong Kong handover (Cao 1997) and others. Are these saying that there is no such thing as truth, or that news journalism has nothing to do with truth? No, but that there are tendencies in commodified journalism that make it naive to assume that journalism reflects 'reality'.

Where does investigative journalism fit into this? It may be that investigative journalism, propelled by its moral impulse, is on a quite different plane from the highly-conditioned news journalism that the writers above have sought to interpret, circumscribed by the requirements of format that is itself a requirement of a marketing approach; perhaps investigative journalism is a relic of Chalaby's and Habermas' nineteenth century, with its different values; perhaps, on the other hand, it is just a product (satisfying a desire for pleasurable indignation!), or simply a marketing technique for selling the main product, as with any other media artefact. Suspending judgement, it is now appropriate to look at the investigative journalism of the last thirty years.

NOTES

1   Invented in China in AD 105, paper-making was brought to Europe in the twelfth century. Printing, well established in China in the Tang Dynasty (618–907), was developed in Europe in the 1450s with enormous consequences for the Church, politics and knowledge.
2   For a discussion of the causes of literacy and its influences, see Todd (1987).
3   For more on Zola see Keating 1991: 15–6 and 306.
4   Aspects of these issues are discussed in Dr Lynne Hapgood's unpublished doctoral thesis, 'Circe among the cities'.
5   Desmond (1978) provides fascinating detail on these charges and their influence on the media in history.
6   There were other examples of investigation but more research needs to be done. One that something is known about is the exposure by the *Manchester Guardian* of Kitchener's concentration camps for Boer civilians during the Boer War. See Ayerst 1971.
7   The trend had been identified by Mead in 1926, by Hughes in 1968 and by Barthes in 1977; Fiske and Hartley (1978) noted that they had increased as a proportion of stories. However, the main focus of research remained hard news.

BIBLIOGRAPHY

Andrews, A. (1859) *The History of British Journalism*. London: Richard Bentley.
Ayerst, D. (1971) *The Guardian: Biography of a Newspaper*. London: Collins: 285.
Barthes, R. (1977) Structure of the faits divers. In R. Barthes (1977) *Critical Essays*. Evanston: Northwestern University Press.
Bell, A. (1991) *The Language of News Media*. Oxford: Blackwell.
Berkowitz, D. (1997) *Social Meanings of News: A Text Reader*. Thousand Oaks: Sage.
Bourdieu, P. (1998) *On Television and Journalism*. London: Pluto.
Brundson, C. and Morley, D. (1978) *Everyday Television: 'Nationwide'*. London: British Film Institute.
Cao, Q .(1997) Ideological versus cultural perspectives: the reporting of the handover of Hong Kong in the British printed media. Lecture to the International Political Science Association 17th World Congress, August 1997, Seoul, Korea.
Chalaby, J. (1998) *The Invention of Journalism*. London: Macmillan.
Cranfield, J. (1978) *The Press and Society*. London: Longman.
Crossland, J. Belgium's first child sex scandal. *Sunday Times*, 25 August 1996.
Curran, J. and Seaton, J. (1997) *Power without Responsibility: The Press and Broadcasting in Britain*, 5th edn. London: Routledge.
Dahlgren, P. and Sparks, C. (1991) *Communication and Citizenship: Journalism and the Public Sphere*. London: Routledge.
de Burgh, H. (1998) Audience, journalist and text in television news. Paper delivered at the Annual Conference of the International Association for Media and Communications Research, 27 July 1998.

Derry, J. (ed.) (1968) *Cobbett's England*. London: The Folio Society.

Desmond, R. (1978) *The Information Process: World News Reporting to the Twentieth Century*. Iowa: University of Iowa Press.

Fiske, J. and Hartley, J. (1978) *Reading Television*. London: Methuen.

Franklin, B. (1997) *Newszak and News Media*. London: Edward Arnold.

Fussell, P. (1975) *The Great War and Modern Memory*. New York: Oxford University Press.

Gitlin, T. (1980) *The Whole World Is Watching: The Mass Media in the Making and the Unmaking of the New Left*. Berkeley: University of California Press.

Golding, P. (1977) Media professionalism in the third world: the transfer of an ideology. In J. Curran, M. Gurevitch and J. Woollacott (eds) (1977) *Mass Communication and Society*. London: Edward Arnold.

Golding, P. (1998) The political and the popular: getting the message of tabloidisation. Paper delivered at the Annual Conference of Media, Cultural and Communications Studies, Sheffield. 12 December 1998.

Green, D. (1983) *Great Cobbett*. London: Hodder and Stoughton.

Griffiths, D. (1992) *Encyclopaedia of the British Press*. London: Macmillan: 532.

Hapgood, L. (1990) Circe among cities: images of London and the languages of social concern 1880–1900. Unpublished doctoral thesis. University of Warwick.

Harris, B. (1996) *Politics and the Rise of the Press*. London: Routledge.

Hartley, J. (1992) *The Politics of Pictures: The Creation of the Public in the Age of Popular Media*. London: Routledge.

Houghton, W. (1957) *The Victorian Frame of Mind*. London: Yale University Press.

Hughes, H. (1968) *News and the Human Interest Story*. New York: Greenwood.

Keating, P. (1991) *The Haunted Study*. London: Fontana.

Keeble, R. (1998) *Secret State, Silent Press: the New Militarism, the Gulf and the Modern Image of Warfare*. Luton: John Libbey.

Knightley, P. (1975) *The First Casualty*. London: Hodder and Stoughton.

Langer, P. (1998) *Tabloid Television*. London: Routledge.

McManus, J. H. (1994) *Market-Driven Journalism: Let the Citizen Beware?* London: Sage.

McQuail, D. (1994) *Mass Communication Theory*. London: Sage.

Mazzolini, G. (1987) Media logic and party logic in campaign coverage: the Italian general election of 1983. *European Journal of Communication*, 2 (1): 55–80.

Oliner, S. (1992) *The Altruistic Personality*. New York: Free Press.

Parrinder, P. (1972) *H. G. Wells: The Critical Heritage*. London: RKP.

Philip, N. (1986) *Charles Dickens: A December Vision*. London: Collins.

Porter, H. (1984) *Lies, Damned Lies and Some Exclusives*. London: Chatto and Windus.

Postman, N. (1987) *Amusing Ourselves to Death*. London: Methuen.

Reader, W. J. (1988) *At Duty's Call, a Study in Obsolete Patriotism*. Manchester: Manchester University Press.

Rutherford Smith, R. (1979) Mythic elements of TV news. In D. Berkowitz (1997) *Social Meanings of News: A Text Reader*. Thousand Oaks: Sage.

Schiller, D. (1981) *Objectivity and the News*. Philadelphia: University of Pennsylvania Press.

Sgard, J. (1976) *Dictionnaire des Journalistes 1600–1789*. Grenoble: Presses Universitaires de Grenoble.

Smith, A. (1979) *The Newspaper: An International History*. London: Thames and Hudson.

Snoddy, R. (1992) *The Good, the Bad and the Unacceptable*. London: Faber and Faber.

Sparks, C. (1991) Goodbye, Hildy Johnson: the vanishing 'serious press'. In P. Dahlgren and C. Sparks (1991) *Communication and Citizenship: Journalism and the Public Sphere*. London: Routledge.

Spurr, D. (1994) *The Rhetoric of Empire*. Durham: Duke University Press.

Stearn, R. T. (1992) War correspondents and colonial war. In J. M. Mackenzie (ed.) *Popular Imperialism and the Military*. Manchester: Manchester University Press.

Stephens, M. (1988) *A History of News*. New York:Viking.

Stocking, H. (1989) *How Do Journalists Think?* Bloomington: Indiana University Press.

Taylor, S. (1996) *The Great Outsiders: Northcliffe, Rothermere and the Daily Mail*. London: Weidenfeld and Nicolson.

Todd, E. (1987) *The Causes of Progress*. Oxford: Blackwell.

van Poecke, L. (1988) The myths and rites of newsmaking. *European Journal of Communication*, 1 (14): 23–54.

Walker, M. (1982) *Powers of the Press*. London: Quartet: 116–20.

Wilkinson-Latham, R. (1979) *From Our Special Correspondent*. London: Hodder and Stoughton.

Williams, F. (1957) *Dangerous Estate*. London: Longman.

FURTHER READING

Cranfield, J. (1978) *The Press and Society*. London: Longman.

Curran, J. and Seaton, J. (1997) *Power without Responsibility: The Press and Broadcasting in Britain*, 5th edn. London: Routledge.

Franklin, B. (1997) *Newszak and News Media*. London: Edward Arnold: especially Chapter 4.

Hartley, J. (1992) *The Politics of Pictures: The Creation of the Public in the Age of Popular Media*. London: Routledge.

Smith, A. (1979) *The Newspaper, An International History*. London: Thames and Hudson.

Snoddy, R. (1992) *The Good, the Bad and the Unacceptable*. London: Faber and Faber.

Stephens, M. (1997) *A History of News*. New York: Harcourt Brace.

3

THIRTY YEARS OF BRITISH
INVESTIGATIVE JOURNALISM

Hugo de Burgh

A tradition of investigative journalism

In the 1960s British newspapers faced competition from television and simultaneously, because of the consumer boom, found advertisers demanding more media space. So the newspapers became bigger, and filled the space with big feature and picture reporting. At the same time Doig (1997) has suggested that there was a climate conducive to scepticism and irreverence that made investigative journalism attractive. These factors may account for its eruption.

There had always been 'exposés', understood as real or claimed revelations of something that had been hidden from us but the investigative traditions of reporting that had led, for instance, to exposés of poverty and exploitation in Victorian Britain had fallen into disuse in the serious newspapers. They left that kind of thing to the populars, mainly the Sundays, with their regular 'I made an excuse and left' revelations about prostitution, or 'I name the guilty man' pieces on small-time fraudsters (Leapman 1992: 19). Now similar techniques were to be used for 'socially responsible' journalism in the manner of W. T. Stead.

In 1963 there were two major investigations that have continued to be cited as exemplars: the first was of the triangular relationship between a government minister, Profumo, a Russian secret agent and a call girl. It was extensively researched by *News of the World* investigative journalist Peter Earle, who managed to hide the girl and her associates in a country cottage until he was ready for his story to break (Earle 1963), and also was developed into the first of many Insight books, *Scandal '63*. The second was an exclusive by *Sunday Times* Insight, whose reporter Ron Hall detailed the methods used by a criminal landlord, Rachman, to terrorise tenants (Leapman 1992: 23). By 1969 the *Times* was using bugging devices to gather evidence of Metropolitan Police corruption (Tompkinson 1982). These examples set a trend and by the late 1960s there were many new vehicles for investigative reporting in the national media, aside from the regional and local press that made forays into investigation.[1] Of the three most distinguished, *Sunday Times* Insight is dealt with in some detail later in this book. Two other important and long-lasting vehicles, *Private Eye* and *World in Action*, are not and will therefore be mentioned briefly now.

Private Eye was launched in 1961, then as now funded principally by circulation, and run by a group of well-connected young men whose associations were as varied as arch-Conservative (Auberon Waugh), conservative romantic (Christopher Booker) and left radical (Paul Foot). What they shared was scepticism, lack of deference and satirical wit; brought together they produced a magazine that has been unpredictable, daring and iconoclastic of most shibboleths. As a result it has been despised and hated with fervour; rich men have wasted pots of gold and much energy trying to destroy it, particularly business tycoons and editors. In view of its predominantly satirical approach and the fact that it appears to be read in particular by the moneyed people whom it examines, Richard Keeble has suggested that *Private Eye* is more of a court jester than an investigative medium; however, it has included forensic investigation as part of its repertoire.

Among other achievements, it is claimed that *Private Eye* exposed the shady relationships and manoeuvrings of Prime Minister James Callaghan, corruption in the buildings contracts issued by Wandsworth Council, the Poulson case (see below), the false claims of Dr Christian Barnard, a heart surgeon, sanctions busting by the major UK company British Petroleum in Rhodesia (now Zimbabwe), Irish politician (and later Prime Minister) Charles Haughey's involvement in gun-running for the IRA, the bribing of BBC disc jockeys and many financial and business scandals. In fact it may be in financial circles that *Private Eye*, thanks to the expertise and accuracy of Michael Gillard, has its greatest following (Marnham 1982: 134–7) although its 'Rotten Boroughs' column was in the 1990s believed to be required reading for all local authority decision-makers (see Chapter 11).

Granada Television, a leading company among the holders of UK terrestrial TV franchises known collectively as Independent Television, launched *World in Action* in 1963. When *World in Action* (*WiA*) began it was the first weekly filmed current affairs series on British television:

> For *World in Action*, current affairs meant anything from Government to guilty men, politics to pop. It was a series that was serious in its purpose ... Hewat [the first Editor] operated on the assumption that few viewers would willingly subject themselves to 30 minutes of 'current affairs' unless grabbed by their lapels ... Hewat's achievement was that he created a mass audience for what had till then seemed a preserve of elites.
>
> (Granada 1993)

It was in 1967 that David Plowright set up the 'Investigation Bureau' and *WiA* set out specifically to make investigative programmes. This carried further the Poulson local government corruption scandal of the 1970s, revealed the

mass murders of President Idi Amin of Uganda, sickness among employees of
the UK asbestos industry, the export of UK arms to Argentina while the UK
was at war with that country in the Falkland Islands, corruption in the Irish
beef processing industry, the Pin Down policy by which force could be used
on youths in prison and a notorious miscarriage of justice, the Birmingham
Six, also mentioned in Chapter 13 (Fitzwalter 1998). *World in Action* claims to
have undertaken one of the earliest investigations of the safety of nuclear
power and therefore to have been influential in the decline of that industry; to
have been the first to examine the question of the British Royal Family and
taxation which resulted in 'the Queen agreeing to pay tax as had her ances-
tors' (Granada 1993). It has been widely agreed that *World in Action* has been
an influence upon UK public life and its abolition by Granada Television in
1999 was lamented by many as an indication of diminished commitment to
public service, increasing greed and a diminution of the UK public sphere.

Among the many individual investigations of the period, three have come
to be regarded as classics of the genre: the cases of Poulson, thalidomide and
the DC10 Disaster. All of them are well documented in very competent
books so that no more than a brief summary is needed here.

In 1970 a young English reporter, Ray Fitzwalter, wrote an article in his
local paper, the *Bradford Argus*, on the bankruptcy of architect and public
works contractor Poulson. It was picked up by Paul Foot who then did a 2
page spread on the subject in *Private Eye*. In time this became an enormous
investigation, spawning several broadcast programmes and many articles, and
was instrumental in the establishment of the *Royal Commission into Standards in
Public Life* in 1974. What the journalists achieved was the revelation of
corruption in public administration from the smallest of local authorities right
up to the most senior of national politicians and, in particular in his second
film, Ray Fitzwalter demonstrated every step in the process by which politicians had used, and been used by, Poulson to obtain public contracts by
corrupt means, carry them out incompetently and profit from them greatly
(Granada 1973).

In 1972 the *Sunday Times* started a long campaign to get admission of
liability and thus proper compensation for thalidomide victims. Around 1960
a large drug company, Distillers, had supplied the drug thalidomide to preg-
nant women, which had resulted in 451 babies being born deformed. Despite
considerable publicity, after 10 years still no compensation had been paid and
Distillers was trying to impose a settlement upon claimants representing the
families affected. Harold Evans and colleagues at the *Sunday Times* decided to
investigate the case. As Lord Denning, the judge who refused the request by
Distillers that the *Sunday Times* be forbidden to publish on the case on the
grounds that it was *sub judice*, put it:

> On September 24 1972, the *Sunday Times* published an article headed
> 'Our Thalidomide Children: A cause for national shame'. It drew

attention to the long-drawn out legal proceedings, and said: 'It seems clear that in the new term lawyers acting for Distillers ... will appear with lawyers acting for the children, to seek court approval for a settlement which has been worked out in private over the last few months. Unhappily the settlement is one which is grotesquely out of proportion to the appalling injuries the thalidomide children suffered ... it is little more than 1 per cent of the money made in the last ten years since thalidomide'.

(cit. in Smith 1974: 133)

The investigation mounted by the *Sunday Times* and the campaign based upon it, a campaign which continued for many years, resulted in a better deal for many of the victims of thalidomide than would otherwise have been possible and acceptance by the courts of a public interest argument in the matter of contempt (Evans 1983: chap. 4). Knightley (1997: chap. 10) has however written that the investigation demonstrated failings of British journalism and that, of itself, it achieved little but keeping the issue alive; he believes that it was the campaign among shareholders of Distillers, the company accused, that frightened its board into making the settlement. The issue of what role investigative journalism really played is discussed in Page (1998) and Knightley (op. cit.: chap. 10), which also contains a useful description of the painstaking research necessary for the Insight team to get to grips with the subject. References to the other books on this investigation are to be found in Chapter 10 and other angles on it are considered in Chapters 7 and 8.

Another of the major investigations of the period was also undertaken by the *Sunday Times*, that of the DC-10 air crash of 1974. There is a synopsis in Chapter 10, as well as references.

The profession was impressed by such feats of reportage but established interests and their political representatives were not necessarily impressed in the same way. When journalists looked at the private business interests of UK Prime Minister Harold Wilson's inner circle, the Labour government of the 1970s reacted angrily. A Royal Commission on the Press was set up in 1977 and, among other things, criticised journalists for trying to 'seek discreditable material which can be used to damage the reputation of Labour ministers' (Doig 1997: 196).

In the mid- to late 1970s the UK went through an economic slump; with the print media facing financial problems and upheavals in staffing, newspaper investigations appear to have declined in number. An important vehicle for dissenting journalism gave up that role in the face of populist commercial competition, according to admirers of the *Daily Mirror*, now the *Mirror* (Pilger 1997, Molloy 1997). By the 1980s it appeared that more investigations were being undertaken by television. ITV companies competed to demonstrate dedication to the remits which had been placed upon them by the national regulations covering scheduling and content (Gibbons 1998: 72). The BBC established *File on Four*, the radio investigative series, of which more later (see Chapter 10).

Investigative journalism and Thatcherism 1979–97: years of fear, years of farce

The relationship between British politicians and the media is the subject of other books; however, an overview of British investigative journalism in the period of the Conservative government 1979–97 cannot avoid touching upon it. Roughly speaking, until Mrs Thatcher fell many investigative journalists felt menaced; within three years of John Major's taking her place fifteen ministers had been obliged to resign as there emerged unending risible details of philandering, greed or petty corruption, and fear (at least from the perspective of the journalists) had been replaced by farce.

On the whole the tabloids concentrated upon the smut (there was plenty) while the broadsheets angled on dereliction of public service. The extramarital affairs of insignificant members of the Royal Family (*News of the World* 7 July 1985) were typical of tabloid obsession;[2] in 1986 the Deputy Chairman of the Conservative Party and successful novelist Jeffrey Archer was exposed as having paid £2000 to a prostitute to go abroad; more seriously, in 1988 the *News of the World* revealed that another, notorious call girl, with friends who included many politicians and the editor of the *Sunday Times*, had been issued with a Parliamentary pass. Unjustifiable on any grounds but those of prurience were exposés of the extramarital affair of a football manager, Bobby Robson, and the 3-month long investigation of a then well-known television interviewer, Frank Bough (Bainbridge and Stockdill 1993: 319); the absurd fact that, unbeknown to the then Chancellor of the Exchequer (Norman Lamont), a madam was renting his apartment and details of sundry liaisons of businessmen and soap stars filled up the pages.

More easily justified on the grounds of public interest were the *News of the World* (*NoW*) 1984 exposure of corruption at the government's Property Services Agency, which, as its name suggests, managed the largest real estate portfolio in the kingdom (Macaskill 1984). Other *NoW* investigations resulted in revelations that an IRA bomber was employed in the House of Commons (1987); that some illegal immigrants were paying to get married to local women (who were sometimes married already), stung at the ceremony in 'Operation Gold Ring' (1990), and that a cosmetic surgery clinic which caused disfigurement as well as pain was operating (Bainbridge 1993: 331). Equally, Gary Jones' discovery that the jury had made its guilty decision in a murder case by reference to a Ouija board and an extensive investigation of paedophiles were stories that any medium would be happy to own (Jones 1999). Perhaps the story that was of greatest popular interest was 'Soccer Chiefs and the Vice Girls' (Mahmoud 1998) which described in lurid detail the behaviour, attitudes and crookery of the two bosses of one of the UK's leading soccer clubs, all faithfully recorded by their partner in vice who happened to be the head of *NoW*'s investigations bureau, Mazher Mahmoud. Mahmoud is one of the most colourful characters in modern British journalism, celebrated for his impersonations of Arab Sheikhs in particular.

An important theme of the period was nuclear power, and the casuistry with which its promoters were alleged to have made their case (Foot 1990: 57–63). Notable among the many revelations of duplicity and danger was the Yorkshire Television series and book by James Cutler and Rob Edwards *Britain's Nuclear Nightmare* (1988). It was the first investigation to attend to the high incidence of cancer around nuclear installations, starting a scientific debate that is still ongoing. On the day that it was broadcast, 1 November 1983, Prime Minister Thatcher responded to it in the House of Commons and promised that the claims made by it would be examined urgently. The Black Inquiry was set up and initiated a series of studies which continue today (Edwards 1999) and the (government advisory) Committee on Medical Aspects of Radiation in the Environment resulted. Unfortunately for the intrepid journalists, their efforts were to an extent overshadowed by war, by Ireland and by the unending battles between the media and the government.

As far as the broadsheets were concerned the government's relations with the media started extremely badly with the 1982 Falklands War, when even routine efforts at impartial analysis of the situation were seen as treachery (Meyer 1998). The story of how the government reacted to level-headed analysis has been effectively written up by Harris (1994) and by Adams (1986). Attempts to dig into the mysteries surrounding the Argentine ship, General Belgrano, were furiously resisted and the government brought a case against a civil servant, Clive Ponting, who passed to journalists evidence of ministerial duplicity in this matter towards Parliament (Thornton 1982: 15). The government was frustrated over Ponting, though not in the 1983 case of Sarah Tisdall who had passed information about the arrival in Britain of Cruise Missiles, and this almost certainly stimulated the introduction of a new Official Secrets Act in 1988.[3]

In 1984 John Stalker, a senior police officer sent to investigate alleged criminal behaviour by the Northern Ireland police, was removed from his job; his treatment, and that of Colin Wallace, another apparent victim of government dirty tricks in Northern Ireland, were exhaustively investigated by Paul Foot (Foot 1990: 191; Pincher 1991: 178). There is a long list of programmes dealing with Northern Ireland which were stifled or nobbled in the 1980s (Thornton 1989: 9); *Real Lives* was banned in 1985, and Thames Television censured by the government for questioning its killing of IRA terrorists without trial in its investigation 'Death on the Rock', later exonerated by a public inquiry (Bolton 1990). Of this notorious case Bailey et al. say:

> In 1988, Thames Television broadcast a *This Week* documentary, 'Death on the Rock', investigating the circumstances of the shooting

of three, as it transpired unarmed, members of the IRA in Gibraltar earlier in the year. Government explanations were that the killings were of members of an active service unit of the IRA intent on planting a bomb on the island and that they were shot by members of the SAS acting in self defence. The documentary, however, included evidence from a 'new' witness to the events who asserted that those killed had been shot without warning and with their hands in the air. The documentary rekindled debate about the existence of a 'shoot to kill' policy on the part of the security forces in dealing with terrorists. The documentary was strongly denounced by the Prime Minister, Mrs Thatcher.

(Bailey et al. 1995)

These cases alone indicate the climate of hostility between broadsheet journalists and the government; indeed insults impugning the veracity of journalists in general or the BBC in particular issued almost daily from the mouths of senior politicians. More materially, the government obtained an injunction against the 1987 BBC Radio 4 series *My Country Right or Wrong* on the security services, and had the police raid the offices of BBC Scotland and seize a series of six programmes researched for the BBC by Duncan Campbell, *Secret Society*, going so far as to break into the homes of Campbell and two other journalists. This extraordinary example of government paranoia and the violent behaviour that resulted has become known as the Zircon Affair and has been written up in, among others, Ewing and Gearty 1990.

The late 1980s were also enlivened by the undignified spectacle of Her Majesty's Government trying to ban the memoirs of a former British secret agent (Peter Wright: *Spycatcher*), notwithstanding that the ensuing publicity ensured that the book immediately became available and attractive to large numbers of people who would otherwise have taken not the slightest interest in a rather specialist memoir. The escapade did further demonstrate that the Conservative government continued the policy of its Labour predecessor in trying to make scrutiny of its activities even more difficult by increasing secrecy and censorship. Illustrations of this are too numerous to detail (Ewing and Gearty 1990) but one more must be mentioned. In October 1991 Channel 4 Television (established by the Conservative government in 1982, see Chapter 11) broadcast *Dispatches*: 'The Committee' to the ire of the police who obtained an injunction to hand over all the production documentation under the 1974 Prevention of Terrorism Act in an attempt to discover the sources of allegation that terrorists and police cooperated in Northern Ireland to liquidate other terrorists. The following year C4 was fined £75,000 ($124,000 US) for its refusal to name the sources of the revelations in 'The Committee'.

As much as any ideological commitment to the free market, it may well have been loathing of journalists, and investigative journalists in particular, that

54

was behind the impetus to dismantle the BBC (which did not succeed) and make the broadcast media increasingly commercial (which has to an extent succeeded) (Goodwin 1998: 166; Gibbons 1998). Some of those Conservative politicians most hot for deregulation had been themselves investigated in a 1986 documentary, *Maggie's Militant Tendency*.

The 1990s boom

Nevertheless, contradictory though it may seem, the atmosphere of constant conflict that I have sketched above in fact appears to have stimulated a resurgence of investigative or quasi-investigative journalism, especially on television. An unsystematic trawl of a database for 1995 (*Programme Reports* 1995) suggests that in that year alone on UK terrestrial television there were 300 discrete programmes that could be classified as investigative, this total excluding magazine programmes with investigative elements. As to the media for them, during the 1990s several new current affairs series were born, all of which from time to time did investigative work:

- BBC Inside Story
- BBC Public Eye
- ITV Big Story
- ITV Network First
- C4 Cutting Edge
- ITV First Tuesday
- BBC 40 Minutes
- C4 Street Legal.

The history series BBC *Timewatch* and C4 *Secret History* commenced and C4's *Witness* sometimes undertook historical investigations, for example on the relationship between Sinn Fein, the Irish nationalist political party, and Nazism (C4 1997).

Series or strands claiming to be exclusively investigative that were launched in the 1990s included:

- ITV The Cook Report
- C4 Countryside Undercover
- BBC Taking Liberties
- ITV Beam and Da Silva
- ITV Disguises
- C4 Undercover Britain
- BBC Here and Now
- BBC Rough Justice
- BBC Private Investigations.

Predictions made in 1990 that investigative journalism would not survive increasing commercialisation seemed in 1995 not to have been borne out, indeed it was booming. Investigative journalists suffered some setbacks – *Panorama* withdrew an investigation of corruption by Westminster (local government) Council until after the elections with which it dealt, Central TV cancelled a *Cook Report* on political lobbying (but left the field open to the *Guardian*), possibly under pressure from the lobbyist under investigation, and Paul Jackson, Managing Director of Carlton Television notoriously declared, apropos of the *World in Action* which had increased the awareness that eventually led to the release from prison of the Birmingham bombers, that 'It isn't part of the function of the TV system to get people out of prison. Its function is to make programmes that people want to watch' (Fitzwalter 1999). Nevertheless, investigative journalists also came to grip public attention with a series of investigations into corruption ('sleaze') which involved colourful personalities and well-known institutions.

Sleaze

The 'Cash for Questions' saga kept 'sleaze' in the public eye from 1994 to 1997 and is widely credited with having so damaged the Conservative government as to ensure its defeat in the 1997 General Election. From the point of view of a student of journalism, the main points are these. Soon after the *Sunday Times* had established, in the sting on MPs described in Chapter 1, that Members of Parliament would do favours for money, Mohamed al Fayed, businessman and owner of Harrods, the London store, revealed[4] to the *Guardian* that Members of Parliament with responsibilities related to his interests had been bribed, both by him personally and through a then well-known lobbyist, Ian Greer, to present his case in a variety of ways. It was the fact that, in his view, they had failed to defend his interests while thoroughly enjoying his money that seemed to embitter him. The services for which he had paid included parliamentary questions to ministers and pitches to their colleagues with appropriate ministerial responsibilities. Such representations had been made as if impartially so that those undertaking the lobbying had cheated their colleagues in government as well as Parliament as a whole. In the course of a lengthy investigation of the lobbyist and his stable of hired politicians the journalists uncovered further unsavoury details of many other lobbying activities, in particular of how Greer had attempted to influence government policy in favour of commercial operators wanting to market drugs to youngsters (Leigh and Vulliamy 1997: 126) and in favour of the Serb leader and President of Yugoslavia Slobodan Milosevic at the time that his troops were carrying out atrocities in former Yugoslavia (ibid.: chap. 8).

Much of the investigation was to be confirmed by details obtained only thanks to the libel case attempted, but then abandoned, by Member of Parliament Neil Hamilton. Hamilton was a second rank government minister who, appropriately, had responsibility for those areas of national life in which he had been deeply involved as a covert lobbyist for Ian Greer. The detail of the *Guardian* investigation and of the legal battles that took place are certainly of interest to the student of the media; from a wider perspective what the 'Cash for Questions' saga exposed were the familiar failings of the English legal system discussed in Chapter 7; the inability of the British Parliament to regulate itself with the clarity and transparency of its US counterpart; the tenuousness of UK journalists' freedom to investigate and the failure of politicians to resist Party pressure even when faced with obvious mendacity and even criminality (Leigh and Vulliamy 1997: 244). On the other hand its achievements were important: journalists considered themselves vindicated for their widely-maligned investigations when Hamilton and Greer withdrew their suit, although they did not admit liability, and before long disappeared from public life. The first major revelations of corruption were published by the *Guardian* on 20 October 1994; soon thereafter the government appointed an independent committee, the Nolan Committee on Standards in Public Life, to be set up. This committee has subsequently established new rules for Parliamentary behaviour; its first on-the-ground investigation was to be of Hamilton himself, published by the first Parliamentary Commissioner for Standards, Gordon Downey (Leigh 1999).

The Jonathan Aitken story also turned on the revelation of petty details of expense accounts which, we infer from the effort and energy deployed in hiding them, potentially led to something grander and more shocking, could that something but be pinned down. It was established by meticulous investigation that Aitken, the Minister of State for Defence Procurement,[5] had maintained while a minister a long standing commercial relationship with princes of the Saudi royal family, a relationship which appeared to make him the servant of one of those princes. The sordid details of that servitude are catalogued in Harding et al. 1997. As in the Hamilton case, the target's position was made worse through litigation that both concentrated the minds of the journalists and made it possible for other facts, including in this case some tangential but damaging details about Aitken's personal life, to emerge. In 1999 it was finally established which companies were doing what deals and providing how much in commission to Aitken's associate, who relied upon Aitken's position as minister in the British government responsible for such deals (Pallister et al. 1999).

David Leigh, involved in the investigation from the start, has summarised his view of the story and the achievement: 'Its abiding irony is that – largely because the *Guardian* exposed Aitken's murky trip to the Paris Ritz Hotel – none of the deals came off, and none of the conspirators made a penny' (Leigh 1999). Aitken did, however, go to prison for perjury committed during his attempts to deny his activities.

The extent of the subject matter

From the account above it may appear that UK investigative journalists were obsessed with (1) security matters and (2) sleaze. These were two areas where public authority was touched to the quick, but investigations looked at other areas, broadly classifiable as corporate corruption, public administration, social policy, miscarriages of justice, historical, the environment, high politics and foreign affairs.

Corporate corruption covered such diverse areas as investigations of landlords making fortunes by ripping off the housing benefit system (ITV: *Beam and Da Silva* 18 January 1994) or landlords who harass and illegally evict tenants (C4: *Living in Fear* 25 January 1994). Private security companies were found to be potentially dangerous (ITV: *The Wrong Arm of the Law* 31 October 1994; BBC1: *Out of Order* 21 October 1997). Financial fraud was the subject of several programmes, including C4's documentaries on the Bank of Credit and Commerce International (13 August 1991) and the Barlow Clowes Affair (27 February 1992) and BBC2's on creative accountancy and price-fixing (1 March 1992). The *Observer*, with Michael Gillard as main reporter, tackled corruption in the Inland Revenue (tax authority) (Gillard 1996) and banking scandals at Deutsche Morgan Grenfell (Gillard 1997); Gillard again, but writing in the *Guardian*, looked at how the oil giant British Petroleum assisted the police in Colombia, police with a long record of human rights abuses.

Public administration was examined in a multitude of programmes on education, some more thorough than others, from 'Do Schools Fail Children?' (BBC2 16 November 1993) to 'Inspecting the Inspectors' (C4 1998), discussed in Chapter 11. Serious allegations were made against the police in the matter of crack cocaine (*WiA* 23 November 1992) and we found out how criminals get a new identity (*WiA* 11 March 1996).

Reporters quite regularly posed as the unfortunate or exploitable, starting with a *WiA* on 9 March 1992 in which a reporter posed as one of the homeless and notably in series called *Undercover Britain* (C4) and *Disguises* (ITV).[6]

There are many media dealing with health issues in one form or another. Perhaps the most notable actual investigations in this period dealt with the surprising number of deaths during surgery at a British hospital, whose staff were later charged; shoddy practices among operating theatre assistants (BBC1: *Public Eye* 21 March 1995); there were several programmes on physical abuse of the elderly (C4: *Dispatches* 21 January 1992) or insane (C4: *Cutting Edge* 7 December 1992). Much discussed were investigations into the dangers of contraceptive pills (*WiA*: 'Safe Sex?' 10 July 1995) and cancer clusters near military bases (*WiA*: 'Shadow of the Bomb' 9 September 1996). C4's *Dispatches* claims to have been the first medium to reveal the effect of Creutzfeld Jakob Disease on humans in 1994 (Lloyd 1998).

Revelation that paedophiles had infiltrated charities working with the young in Eastern Europe caused a sensation (*WiA*: 'In the Name of Charity' 3

April 1995); a series of programmes on Indonesia's treatment of its (in effect) colony of East Timor and Australia's complicity in the genocide there was made by John Pilger and screened by Carlton Television (for example on 26 January 1999). A good example of investigative journalists taking up difficult subjects and subjects unpopular to many people is the programme made by *WiA* about the gypsy refugees from Slovakia and Czech Republic (Index 1998). Professional accolades were showered upon two 1995 productions by C4 *Dispatches*: 'The Drilling Fields' by Kay Bishop and Glenn Alison and 'The Torture Trail' by Martin Gregory; it is the folk wisdom of the industry though that such programmes excite only that specialist minority of people unusually interested in foreign affairs which are not salacious. That minority was also interested, if space in the *Guardian* is a guide, in the historical investigations into the treatment of persecuted minorities in the 1930s–50s by Swiss banks and German industries, started by journalist Oskar Scheiben (in the Swiss *Wochenzeitung*). Among many historical investigations undertaken by UK journalists in the 1990s, some touched upon in Chapter 13, one of the most distinguished is surely that by the *Times* reporter Jaspar Becker, who researched the1958–61 famine in China for his book *Hungry Ghosts*.

No survey of investigative journalism can avoid mentioning *Panorama*, Britain's longest running current affairs television programme and the BBC's 'flagship', and yet this programme is probably not widely regarded as principally investigative. It provides reportage, a lot of analysis and some investigation; its decision-makers have always to be careful to remember that politicians will read its programmes as the voice of the BBC. Clive Edwards, deputy editor, describes the programme thus:

> *Panorama* is probably the most famous current affairs programme in the world and is also the BBC's flagship programme. It is under pressure to produce some level of ratings that helps to justify its place on BBC 1, yet at the same time it is also there to be the centrepiece of the BBC's News and Current Affairs operation so that we have to, and want to, do the world's major stories. We will therefore do 'the euro' even though it will not thrill many viewers; we will do it because the programme helps fulfil the BBC's 'mission to explain' serious issues which are going to affect peoples' lives dramatically. You have to work very hard to make some issues entertaining and, no matter how well you do that, they may still get only a small audience. This applied to the Scottish elections, to Rwanda, to the euro.
>
> (Edwards 1999)

Whenever something becomes a major public concern, a 'contentious issue in the public gaze' – mobile phones ('The Mobile Mystery' 24 May 1999; genetically modified foods ('Frankenstein Foods' 17 May 1999), working mothers ('Missing Mum' 3 February 1997) or meningitis ('Every Parent's Nightmare'

22 February 1999) – *Panorama* covers it; but, as Edwards suggests, it also takes on the task of dealing with matters that are not of widespread interest, though by any standard of public importance such as the Scottish elections ('The Battle for Britain' 26 April 1999), biological warfare ('Plague Wars' 13 and 14 July 1998) or Rwanda ('When Good Men Do Nothing' 7 December 1998).

Its investigative journalism of the last ten years has included a revelation of government abuse of the rules on public information ('Getting the Message Across' BBC 1989). Reporter Vivian White examined a public service advertising campaign on television about the re-training of unemployed young people and found that the times that the advertisements had been booked to run were not those that you would use to reach the young unemployed, but ABC1 opinion formers, whose view of the government's approach to youth unemployment, and therefore their votes, might be swayed by such a campaign.

In 'The Great Pensions Gamble' (14 October 1996) the team put a secret camera into a flat and let salesmen from different companies pitch to a member of the *Panorama* team presenting himself as the client (with the same biographical details each time) to see which companies were mis-selling. Early in the life of the 1997 Labour government *Panorama* made a programme about the state of the London Underground system, commonly agreed to need new investment ('Down the Tube' 16 June 1997). The incoming Labour administration had committed itself to the previous government's spending totals but also to modernisation of the Underground. 'Logically, that left only one solution – privatisation' (White 1999). However, the government minister and his associates were against privatisation. After the ministerial interview standard to such an analytical programme, one of the *Panorama* team found a file marked 'Panorama' on the floor of the office in which the interview (with the minister who was hostile to privatisation) had taken place. When the reporter opened it he realised that it contained the minister's briefing notes, which revealed that the government was indeed considering privatisation. Once this useful documentary evidence had been incorporated into the programme and made the desired stink, the programme might well be described as investigative journalism, albeit by chance. Despite the limited interest in foreign affairs, *Panorama* does many foreign stories. One which was rated highly by the critics was Tom Mangold's investigation of the UN weapons inspectors in Iraq and whether they had been penetrated by the CIA ('Secrets, Spies and Videotape' 22 March 1999).

Clive Edwards does not entirely accept the distinction between investigative journalism and the other kinds of journalism *Panorama* may do. He says:

> Every programme we do here has to have some investigative element. There are the long-term, deep investigations such as the programme on the Rosemary Nelson case [21 June 1999], a classic investigation by one of our foremost investigative reporters, John Ware.

He spent months researching it, going through all sorts of referrals because it's legally very difficult. That told you about something you would have had no hope of learning about otherwise. Then there are programmes which are not 100 per cent that kind of deep investigation, but which have an important investigative element. In 'The Mobile Mystery' we revealed that the US industry-funded research body had sufficient research to change its position ... that was unknown and caused a stir at the time. In 'Frankenstein Foods' we showed how the committees that were supposedly safeguarding us had been made up to be packed out with people who would pass anything on the nod. 'To Catch a Cop' [19 October 1998] and 'The Case of India One' [12 January 1998] both exposed corrupt police ... We are always seeking to tell people things that they don't know and what others don't particularly want them to know.

(Edwards 1999)

How long *Panorama* is permitted to fulfil the mission described by Edwards above is much debated, given the pressure upon the BBC to go down market in order to attract ratings from an independent sector become ruthlessly competitive since the Broadcasting Acts of the 1990s. Nevertheless, in 1999 promises were being made by the BBC Governors of more support for current affairs, and *Panorama* was confident that it would continue to investigate.

Given the relatively small proportion of the available viewers that watches current affairs television however, investigative journalism probably meant, for most British people, 'sleaze'. From 1992 the *News of the World* investigated the private lives of minister after minister, six of whom were forced to resign on account of some intimate entanglement. Nevertheless the scope of investigative journalism, as I have tried to demonstrate above, was quite extraordinary. It was a well established feature of British public life in the 1990s. This was possible, as indicated early in the chapter, as a result of developments in the press, consumer demand and broadcasting regulation. Journalists responded in this way to these opportunities on account of their own perceptions of their role in society. These we shall look at next.

NOTES

1   In the late 1960s national media with dedicated investigative personnel included: **press** *Sunday Times* (Insight), *Observer* (Daylight), *Guardian*, *Daily Telegraph* (Close-up), *New Statesman*, *Leveller*, *Private Eye*, *News of the World*, *Daily Mirror*; **television** *World in Action*, *Panorama*, *TV Eye*, *Man Alive*, *The London Programme*.

2   The particular member was Princess Michael of Kent. When I taxed Bob Warren, Executive Editor of *NoW* to justify such an intrusion into privacy (the princess and her lover had been endlessly trailed, deceived and photographed) he replied that since she was 'on the Civil List', i.e. in receipt of public funds, she should behave impeccably or expect to be exposed (Warren 1999).

3   Harold Evans makes a telling point about the difference between the US and UK when he compares the contrasting experiences of Mr Robert MacFarlane in the Iran Contra Scandal and Mr Clive Ponting in the Belgrano affair. In America, MacFarlane, President Reagan's National Security Adviser, was prosecuted for deceiving Congress. In Britain it was the whistle-blower Ponting who revealed the deception of Parliament, not the deceiving Minister of the Crown, who was prosecuted (Evans 1997: 9).

4   Fayed did not reveal everything at once, by any means. The whole exciting story of how the reporters built up their case and fought for it is in Leigh and Vulliamy 1997. Because of what it teaches about journalistic methods, the British polity today and the legal framework for journalism, this book is essential reading for all students of British journalism.

5   Astoundingly, in retrospect, Aitken was promoted to Cabinet rank in 1994 even as information about his behaviour was surfacing.

6   There is no space to discuss the German master of these techniques, Wallraff, here, but his methods and general approach are well described in his book *The Undesirable Journalist*.

BIBLIOGRAPHY

Adams, V. (1986) *The Media and the Falklands Campaign*. London: Macmillan.

Bailey, S. H. and Jones, B. L. (1995) *Civil Liberties: Cases and Materials*. London: Butterworths.

Bainbridge, C. and Stockdill, R. (1993) *The News of the World Story*. London: Harper Collins.

BBC (1989) *Panorama*: 'Getting the Message Across' (reporter: V. White). London: BBC.

Becker, J. (1996) *Hungry Ghosts: China's Secret Famine*. London: John Murray.

Bolton, R. (1990) *Death on the Rock and Other Stories*. London: W. H. Allen.

Brown, G. (1995) *Exposed!* London: Virgin.

de Burgh, H. (1998) Audience, journalist and text in television news. Paper delivered at the Annual Conference of the International Association for Media and Communications Research, Glasgow, July 1998.

Byrne, D. (1999) Talk to the students of the MA Investigative Journalism course at Nottingham Trent University, 29 April 1999.

Carlton TV (1997) *Breaking the Mirror: The Murdoch Effect* (reporter: John Pilger). London: Carlton TV.

Channel 4 TV (1997) *Witness*: 'A Great Hatred'. London: Channel 4 Television.

Channel 4 TV (1998) *Dispatches*: 'Inspecting the Inspectors' (Sarah Spiller). London: Channel 4.

Clarke, D. (1983) *Corruption: Causes, Consequences and Control*. London: Frances Pinter.

Clarke, N. (1998) Spindoctors and the *World at One*. Talk to third year students on the BA Broadcast Journalism course at Nottingham Trent University, 13 November 1997.

Curran, J. (1997) *Power without Responsibility*. London: Routledge.

Cutler, J. and Edwards, R. (1988) *Britain's Nuclear Nightmare*. London: Sphere.

Doig, A. (1997) The decline of investigatory journalism. In M. Bromley and T. O'Malley (eds) *A Journalism Reader*. London: Routledge.

Dynes, M. (1995) *The New British State: The Government Machine in the 1990s*. London: Times Books.

Earle, P. (1963) Enter the blackmail syndicate. *News of the World*, 23 June 1963.

Eddy, P. (1976) *Destination Disaster*. London: Granada.

Edwards, C. (1999) Interview with Hugo de Burgh, 25 June 1999.

Edwards, R. (1999) Information to Hugo de Burgh by telephone 10 June 1999.

Evans, H. (1983) *Good Times, Bad Times*. London: Weidenfeld and Nicolson.

Evans, H. (1997) Prometheus unbound. Iain Walker Memorial Lecture, Green College, Oxford, May.

Ewing, K. D. and Gearty C. A. (1990) *Freedom Under Thatcher: Civil Liberties in Modern Britain*. Oxford: Oxford University Press.

Fennell, P. (1983) Local government corruption in England and Wales. In M. Clarke *Corruption*. London: Frances Pinter.

Fitzwalter, R. (1998) Investigations. Talk to students on the MA Investigative Journalism course at Nottingham Trent University, 26 February 1998.

Fitzwalter, R. (1999) Interview with Hugo de Burgh, 18 March 1999.

Fitzwalter, R. and Taylor, D. (1981) *Web of Corruption: The Story of J. G. L. Poulson and T. Dan Smith*. London: Granada.

Foot, P. (1990) *Words as Weapons*. London: Verso.

Franklin, B. (1997) *Newszak and News Media*. London: Arnold.

Gibbons, T. (1998) *Regulating the Media*. London: Sweet and Maxwell.

Gillard, M. (1996) Revenue paid. *Observer*, 1 December 1996. See also Sadaam's banker. *Observer*, 23 February 1997.

Gillard, M. (1997) DMG – the agony goes on. *Observer*, 19 January 1997.

Gillard, M. and Tomkinson, M. (1980) *Nothing to Declare: The Political Corruptions of John Poulson*. London: John Calder.

Golding, P. (1998) The political and the popular: getting the message of tabloidisation. Paper delivered at the annual conference of the Association of Media, Cultural and Communications Studies, Sheffield, December 1998.

Goodwin, P. (1998) *Television under the Tories*. London: British Film Institute.

Granada Television (1973) *World in Action*: The Rise and Fall of John Poulson (reporter: Ray Fitzwalter). Manchester: Granada.

Granada Television (1974) *World in Action*: Business in Gozo (reporter: Ray Fitzwalter). Manchester: Granada.

Granada Television (1993) *World in Action: 30 Years*. Press Information issued by Granada 7 January 1993. Manchester: Granada Television Ltd.

Harding, L., Leigh, D. and Pallister, D. (1997) *The Liar, The Fall of Jonathan Aitken*. London: Penguin.

Harris, R. (1994) *The Media Trilogy*. London: Faber and Faber.

Index on Censorship (1998) Gypsies: life on the edge. No. 4. London: Writers and Scholars.

Jones, G. (1999) Investigations and the Tabloids. Talk to students on the MA Investigative Journalism course at Nottingham Trent University, 4 March 1999.

Kingdom, J. (1991) *Government and Politics in Britain*. London: Polity.

Knightley, P. (1997) *A Hack's Progress*. London: Jonathan Cape.

Leapman, M. (1992) *Treacherous Estate*. London: Hodder and Stoughton.

Leigh, D. (1999) Aitken, the fixer and the secret multi-million pound arms deals. On the Internet at http://www.icij.org/investigate/leigh.html dated 28 May 1999.

Leigh, D. (1999a) Cash for Questions: A case study in media activism. Talk to members of the Chinese National Media Legislation Working Group held at Nottingham Trent University, 23 February 1999.

Leigh, D. and Vulliamy, E. (1997) *Sleaze: The Corruption of Parliament*. London: Fourth Estate.

Leppard, D. (1997) The Watergate model in UK journalism. Talk to students on the MA Investigative Journalism course at Nottingham Trent University, 27 November 1997.

Lloyd, D. (1998) Talk to the students of the MA Investigative Journalism course at Nottingham Trent University, 19 February 1998.

Macaskill, I. (1984) Scandal in the sun. *News of the World*, 11 November 1984: 10.

Mahmoud, M. (1998) Soccer chiefs and the vice girls. *News of the World*, 15 March 1998: 1.

Marnham, P. (1982) *The Private Eye Story*. London: AndréDeutsch.

Meyer, Sir A. (1998) Talk to the students of the MA Investigative Journalism course at Nottingham Trent University, 10 March 1998.

Molloy, M. (1997) The mirror crack'd. *New Statesman*, 14 February 1997.

National Union of Journalists (1994) *Rules of the National Union of Journalists*. London: NUJ: 50.

Neil, A. (1996) *Full Disclosure*. London: Macmillan.

Nolan, Ld (1995) *First Report of the Committee on Standards in Public Life*, Cmnd 2850-I. London: HMSO.

Page, B. (1998) A defence of 'low' journalism. *British Journalism Review*, 9 (1).

Pallister, D. et al. (1999) Aitken, the fixer ... *Guardian*, 5 March 1999: 1 and 21.

Pilger, J. (1997) Gutted! *Guardian*, 15 February 1997.

Pincher, C. (1991) *The Truth about Dirty Tricks*. London: Sidgwick and Jackson.

Programme Reports (1995) London: The Programme Report Co. (Held at library of Nottingham Trent University.)

Smith, A. (1974) *The British Press since the War*. London: David and Charles.

Thornton, P. (1989) *Decade of Decline: Civil Liberties in the Thatcher Years*. London: NCCL.

Tompkinson, M. (1982) *The Pornbrokers*. London:Virgin.

Wallraff, G. (1977) *The Undesirable Journalist*. London: Pluto.

Warren, R. (1999) Earle and Mahmoud: a comparison of two styles of investigative journalism.Talk to students on the MA Investigative Journalism course at Nottingham Trent University, 11 March 1999.

White, V. (1999) *Panorama*'s place in the Polity. Talk to members of the Chinese National Media Legislation Working Group held at Nottingham Trent University, 11 February 1999.

Williams, F. (1957) *Dangerous Estate*. London: Longman.

FURTHER READING

Harris, R. (1994) *The Media Trilogy*. London: Faber and Faber.

Knightley, Phillip (1997) *A Hack's Progress*. London: Jonathan Cape.

Leapman, M. (1992) *Treacherous Estate*. London: Hodder and Stoughton.

4

SOME ISSUES SURROUNDING INVESTIGATIVE JOURNALISM

Hugo de Burgh

Implicit in all the cases of investigative journalism that we have noted previously, and the basis of the claim to have the right to investigate, is a certain concept of the role of the journalist, a professional discourse of social responsibility. In this chapter we cast a glance at that, at the closely related issue of regulation; at the debate over objectivity and attachment that took place in Britain in the late 1990s and at Watergate, an empowering myth of and a stimulation to investigative journalism. Finally, we note the issue of journalism studies itself.

Professional discourse

Later in this book we look at a series on BBC television called *Rough Justice*, in which reporters re-examine court cases. The series almost invariably leads to a re-opening of the case and a re-trial, because the reporters only research to transmission those cases about which they are very confident of having overwhelming proof that the original court decision was wrong. The successes of this programme, and some others like it, have resulted in some very prominent re-trials, including two re-trials of convicted terrorist bombers who were found innocent thanks to the journalists' investigations.

Between 1992 and 1997 two investigations took place that are generally agreed to have influenced the electorate against the government of John Major, even to have been important instruments of the victory of the Labour party in the 1997 general election. The first was the 'Arms to Iraq' affair, in which the *Sunday Times*' and other journalists not only found that a government minister had been encouraging exports of arms to Iraq against the policy of his own government, but also that one government department was prosecuting the arms salesmen while another was employing them as agents. The second was the 'Cash for Questions' story.

From these and other cases it would seem that British journalists have taken upon themselves the duties of the American journalists who have Watergate as their paradigm. Informing the electorate, expressing public opinion, providing fora for competing views, acting as channels of information between citizens and those in authority and analysing public policy: these are widely agreed tasks. But the most sensational responsibility which journalists have arrogated to themselves is that of checking on authority, by investigation, and challenging it. Prominent journalists resist attempts by government spokesmen to limit their scope; in the words of Nick Clarke, presenter of Radio 4's flagship, *The World at One*, 'Government press officers have no right to tell us what stone we may or may not turn over' (Clarke 1998). Others have a missionary urge 'to search out the weaknesses in the highest levels of government, to expose and to destroy the guilty' (Leppard 1998). In his memoirs the former editor of the *Sunday Times* Andrew Neil has a chapter entitled 'Ruining the Sunday Breakfasts of the Rich and Powerful' (Neil 1996) – an expressive title.

The premise of various journalists is that of a special role for the journalists as scrutineers of all and everyone, the tribunes of the people. In this understanding, their role is analogous to that of the Censorate in ancient imperial Rome and China: censors in both cases were members of the administrative establishment whose job it was to check on the work of the administration, to report deficiencies without fear or favour. In the first *History of British Journalism*, by Andrews in 1859, it was already noted that the media had a policing, or what we now might call a 'deviance defining' role. This at least appears to be how many journalists see themselves; in short, they have a 'social responsibility' theory of the media. From where did the idea originate?

The basis for the belief that journalists have a social responsibility, identified as such by Siebert in the 1950s (Siebert et al. 1963) seems to lie in a number of sometimes contradictory ideas; that the media are the means by which public opinion is formed and influences (in modern society) public policy; that authority requires scrutiny for its own health and for that of the rest of the citizenry, authority meaning not simply government but all those with power and wealth; that the public has the right to a responsive media, and that the public's requirements are made manifest by the market; that the media have a higher responsibility in that they condition that very public, or market to which they are responsive.

Public opinion

From the late nineteenth century onwards public opinion was increasingly important in the calculations of politicians seeking to avoid resistance to legislation or policy. As the numbers and varieties of people who had to be taken account of widened (thanks to public education and extension of the franchise), so the calculations had to be more complex; in recent years it has been no less difficult to know what public opinion is or how it is formed, although both governments and commercial organisations use sophisticated techniques to plumb it and to consult it. Nevertheless, even if the dynamics of public opinion formation are obscure and involve not only the media but culture, economics and psychology, there is general agreement that it influences public policy. Public policy may be conceived by cabals as in the cases of privatisation or devolution, promoted by institutions or marketed by pressure groups, but all these prefer to capture public opinion before they seek to implement policy. In Chapter 16 we discuss the dynamics of this process in a little more detail; for the moment it is sufficient to remark that the ability to provide or refuse access gives journalists power, since they are the conduit by which those who wish to fashion public opinion may reach it.

Realising this power, journalists have not always been content with exercising it as informant and broker; they have chosen to set the agenda. Investigative journalists can be seen as trying to change the agenda by identifying certain events and issues as priorities regardless of what the authorities think. When Prime Minister Major wanted to concentrate upon family values, the *Guardian* and *News of the World* sleaze agendas were very firmly forced upon him. The social responsibility then, is extended from a monitoring function to that of identifying the truth. No wonder people have referred to journalists as a priesthood and that politicians and their spin doctors seek to fill the media slots such that there is no room for agenda-setting by others! (Jones 1999).

Scrutiny

Looked at in this way, investigative journalism can be interpreted as simply a weapon in the battles between two competing powers, media and authority, to set the public agenda. However, to emphasise that alone would be to forget a real need, the need for scrutiny. From the mid-nineteenth century the responsibilities of public administration in the UK grew enormously while the newly-industrialised society became more complex as the population and the infrastructure required for it grew. The ability of existing administrative organs to manage the public domain was limited, and new institutions were established; similarly the limits on the ability of the executive to audit its own activities were to be reached. From the 1830s onwards, in attempts to keep track of public funds and their deployment, central boards of control were set up, as were auditors (Fennell 1983: 16). From these the problems of grafting major increases in responsibility onto the existing system became apparent.

For while British government was limited in its scope and there was no accountability through elections, it was utterly corrupt in the sense we now give to corruption. As in many countries today, it was dominated by cliques which ensured, in the carrying out of public works and other social functions, that any profits or perquisites would accrue to their families, friends and followers. Nor probably was this considered evil unless clearly identifiable harm, such as the journalist Cobbett publicised in his investigation of the virement of militiamen's salaries, could be traced to a particular example of peculation. At the highest level, the Prime Minister was still expected, in the 1850s, to look after his friends with jobs and honours (Blake 1966: 389), although this was to become less and less acceptable as the century progressed.

As the scope of public works grew the incompetence of the contemporary administrative systems to carry them out became obvious. The most famous example is that of the operations of the War Department during the Crimean campaigns, so tellingly condemned by the *Times*, as we discussed in Chapter 2. The late nineteenth century witnessed many reforms, in particular the introduction of a system of entry into public office through a competitive entrance examination. This in turn helped to earn greater respect for the public service such that high expectations of honesty for the public service developed. These were codified not only in the codes of conduct adopted by the various services but in laws.[1]

The development of investigative journalism in Britain in the 1960s and 1970s resulted in a spate of inquiries into maladministration and corruption that shocked Britons, who had come to assume that corruption was something that happened only in foreign parts. It justified journalism by demonstrating that the public service could not be trusted to police itself. Since that time systems of audit and inspection have become much more rigorous, but so has the extent of public administration (Dynes 1995: 335ff) as Mark D'Arcy makes clear in his chapter when he calls for much more investigative journalism to take account of the perils implicit in the growth of government agencies.

The spate of sleaze stories in the 1990s brought home to many the extent of the problem and inspired some appreciation of the need for investigative journalism. Public figures have not been enthusiastic to praise journalists in British public life, so it was a landmark when the Chairman of the Committee for Standards in Public Life wrote:

> a free press using fair techniques of investigative journalism is an indispensable asset to our democracy ... they have a duty to inquire – coupled with a duty to do so responsibly – and in that way contribute to the preservation of standards in public life.
>
> (Lord Nolan 1995)

In sum, there is a belief in social responsibility that fortifies some and assuages the guilt of others; a nineteenth-century concept, its most extreme manifestation has been realised in journalism that challenges both the exercise of authority and authority's attempts to define the issues, doing so in the name of the people and of the self-evident need for scrutiny by the people of those individuals and institutions with power. At its most bold and most impertinent, this journalism is investigative because it applies forensic skills to what we have been told.

However, 'socially responsible' journalism may be being subtly redefined as that which the audience want. When criticised for surrendering to populist taste, some editors defend themselves as being responsive to the audience, the citizenry. This is the report of an interview with the editor of an important regional television news programme in 1997:

> [The editor] believes that the pre-eminent function of the programme is to entertain. He will keep viewers if he can achieve three things: First, interest them sufficiently such that at least one story each night is a talking point at home or in the pub or at work; provide variety such that they do not switch off in the search for something more entertaining; have the chemistry between the presenters concocted in such a way that viewers feel involved by them and attracted to them and their 'story'.
>
> It is the editor who has the most developed conception of his, very different, responsibility to the audience. He does not draw attention to any moral dimension that this approach may have, yet it is implicit in his manner of speaking of it; he believes that his kind of news is democratic, reflects what people want and is appropriate to their needs and that this is not patronising but *right*. This vision is a kind of radicalism – it is absolutely against the old public service ethos and contrasts with the idea of the journalist as serving the peoples' 'interests rather than their desires'.
>
> The editor's vision holds that the task is to 'give people what they want'; help them relax and accept, don't bother them with 'big' things that they 'ought' to know about or which might depress them. There is no false consciousness to be wrestled with in his vision, quite the reverse, it is the elitists who got it wrong.[2]
>
> (de Burgh 1998: 29)

The better Opposition

In some quarters, however, the vision of social responsibility is at quite another extreme. Journalists regard themselves as so much a vital part of the political process that they usurp the tasks of political parties.

> When *Dispatches* started [in 1982] the Opposition was simply not competent at tackling the Thatcher government. That government was initiating a vast range of changes extending into every area of our national life. The orthodox Opposition had no research, no capacity to oppose, no coherence ... little or nothing was being done to interrogate or mediate this revolution. So we started.
>
> (Lloyd 1998)

The editor of the *Guardian* puts it thus:

Journalism today has assumed the role of the Opposition. When you have government with such a huge majority and no effective debate going on within Parliament ... then the role of scrutiny and opposition falls upon the press, especially as the regulatory authorities have been weakened, where many aspects of public life have been privatised so that you do not have the public scrutiny that was (at least in theory) there before. This puts a burden on the press to act as scrutineer over health, local government, water utilities, regulatory agencies, safety agencies and all these areas that are not being investigated.

Moreover, he does not count the cost:

Maybe I'm just a rotten editor, but I never look at each individual day's sales; I never say to myself, if we put the war on page one will we do better ... it would never occur to me to wonder whether Lawrence Dallaglio [a rugby player] would sell more covers than Kosovo, but some newspaper editors do take those kind of decisions ...

(Rusbridger 1999)

In this reading of the social responsibility of journalism, investigative journalists clearly have an important role.

Free market and regulation

It was a widely held assumption of journalists and observers of journalism until recently that the existence of the socially responsible press was due to the free market that enables such commodities to be traded; objective and good quality information is a commodity with a high value in capitalist society. The buyers of newspapers are operating like an electorate; they choose newspapers because of good journalism, thus good journalism is to the commercial advantage of proprietors; advertising, which supports good journalism, is thus the means by which the media are made independent of politicians. In the Cold War era, with the negative example of the media in the Soviet dominated countries, this seemed axiomatic.

Curran (1985) punctured the complacency of this argument with his research which showed that advertising was itself very partial; that as advertising developed it supported newspapers selectively according to the wealth of the readership rather than according to its extent; thus, mass market newspapers had to survive on their cover price whereas elite ones were subsidised by advertising. Radical newspapers, for example, could not compete with those subsidised by advertising, or those that transformed themselves into mass market entertainment rather than organs of serious political discussion. Furthermore, the commercial interests of advertisers, as of proprietors, impact upon content, privileging that which suits the paymasters. This issue is discussed by Chambers in Chapter 5.

According to critics of the argument that capitalism guarantees competing opinions, socially responsible journalism is not at all a function of the free market but of other factors. First and foremost it is a function of professional ethics shared among media managers/proprietors and journalists, ethics that enable them to resist commercial pressures and stand up for what they believe to be in the best interests of society. Those, like Phillip Knightley, who have pointed to the work of *Sunday Times* Insight in the 1970s as the heyday of UK investigative journalism emphasise these factors (Knightley 1999). Second, it is argued that it is government media regulation that makes possible socially responsible journalism; it is having an appropriate system that biases the media towards social responsibility.

In Chapter 1 we looked at some of the criticisms that are made of the quality of modern journalism, and how its alleged irresponsibility is attributed to 'commodification'. Concerns about modern journalism have brought the question of regulation back to the forefront of debate. Before the Thatcher years regulation was seen by many journalists as a tool used by governments to stifle socially responsible (i.e. inquisitive, dissenting) journalism; now it is tending to be seen as a means by which socially responsible journalism may yet be saved. Chalaby (1998) goes so far as to suggest that special regulations during the Second World War improved the quality of the media. However, in the meantime, there is unease at some specific aspects of regulation.

The regulatory framework and television investigative journalism

It has long been argued that the existence of the BBC and the public service obligations placed upon ITV by the 1960s' Acts were responsible for the quantity and quality of current affairs and news in the UK broadcast media. In the mid-1990s investigative journalism appeared to be booming, at least on television. Since that time however, experienced observers of the scene tell us (Greenslade 1999, Fitzwalter 1999) that the number of investigative programmes has reduced. There is no statistical evidence to demonstrate this – as far as I know the data required has not been compiled since 1996 – but some empirical evidence is claimed.

- ITV substitutes for *This Week* have not produced investigative journalism of the same consistent quality;
- *The Big Story, 3-D* and *What's the Story?* have been axed;
- *World in Action* has gone and *Tonight* is not regarded as a substitute;
- *The Cook Report* has, after being threatened with death, been diminished – despite achieving up to 8 million viewers per edition in its last run;
- *Dispatches* has a smaller time-slot. It is also suggested that changes in slot times demonstrate a weakening of commitment by the broadcasters;

- Slot changes for the surviving investigative programmes appear to be delivering smaller audiences.

There are two culprits. First, media managers are accused of being unwilling to invest the time and money required to make good investigative journalism when they can get bigger audiences for less investment. Of course they like sensational investigations, which is why *The Connection*, a programme later found, after exhaustive investigation by the *Guardian*, to be fraudulent, was so welcome, but they will not pay for them, which is why *The Connection* was, in effect, a drama. It is much cheaper to brief actors than to film real villains. The second culprit is the regulatory system put in place by the previous Conservative government.

The 1990 Act, by establishing that the ITV franchises were to be allocated in principle only on financial criteria and that the regulator would impose less stringent requirements on TV companies (and do so by general rules rather than through scheduling), sent out signals that the market was to be the key factor in determining programming scheduling and content rather than the regulators (Goodwin 1998). Some call this 'market forces decide, rather than elites'; others think of it as 'decision-making transferred from the public sphere to somewhere else'.

The practical results are widely agreed to be more populist media, with all channels (including the BBC, mindful of its competition with ITV for share) appealing to a mass audience. In journalism that means fewer foreign stories (with the possible exception of the BBC) and more stories about what until recently were referred to as 'soft' subjects. This much is now common currency and sometimes described as 'dumbing down'. What is perhaps less well aired is the double-bind of regulatory change in the 1990s. On the one hand *less* stringent regulation has broadcasters relieving themselves of the responsibility to put as much resources into serious journalism, of which investigative journalism is only one genre; on the other hand *more* stringent regulation is believed to make it more risky to produce investigative journalism.

The 1996 Act required the Broadcasting Standards Commission (BSC) to establish rules that mean it is now arguably more difficult to make partial, personal view, programmes on controversial matters (Broadcasting Act 1996 55/106–21). The BSC's *Code on Fairness and Privacy*, which resulted from the Act, has, according to Tom Gibbons, 'imposed fairness requirements to provide notice of programme plans and to give rights of reply' (and they) 'impose standards which would be more appropriate to criminal investigations rather than news gathering' (Gibbons 1998). The BSC's *Code* is only part of the framework erected by the Act, although the only one actually required by it.

The Head of News and Current Affairs at C4 says 'the Act [also caused] an updating of the ITC [Independent Television Commission] protocols and made the provision of "due impartiality" more important; the other side has all sorts of purchase on the piece you do and these are formalised in statute'

(Lloyd 1998a). The recent programme he cited in particular was *Continuity IRA*, whose producer, Steve Haywood, agreed with this statement. In support, Haywood referred to the new *Dispatches Rules and Procedures* document, 8 pages long, which he believes to be progeny of the 1996 Act; similar processes have been gone through at the BBC (White 1999). According to Haywood, it is the compliance procedures that make work so difficult. For example, it is almost impossible to be circumspect about your angle when you approach interviewees; before secret filming it is now necessary to have the story completely evidenced. In one case he knew that estate surveyors were performing in a manner that justified their being filmed secretly, but was obliged to first establish that without filming, and only later film it; even then, the lawyers required him to pixillate the faces of the villains caught in the act (Haywood 1999). Sometimes you have to move very fast in order to capture crime on video and it is not possible to go through cumbersome procedures of telephoning back to base for discussion and decision, so that the tight rules effectively ensure you cannot catch the villains. Doorstepping is also made more difficult in the supposed interests of fairness to targets.

Carlton's Head of Legal Affairs, Simon Westrop, has provided similar examples. He has commented that:

> the Broadcasting Standards Commission assumes a capacity to decide on matters of fact which its structure and procedures sometimes do not allow to be carried out effectively or fairly. The BSC frequently demands a degree of evidence from the broadcaster that is simply excessive (far beyond that expected in the civil courts), even in cases where the public interest in properly founded suspicions of wrongdoing can be clearly demonstrated. Perhaps it should be remembered that the regulators of the day acted against the television team who first exposed the corruption of the notorious John Poulson, who was later sent to jail. Perhaps also the BSC should be reminded that the 1998 Human Rights Act incorporates into English law Article 10 on freedom of expression as well as Article 8 on personal privacy.
>
> (Westrop 1999)

By contrast, the current editor of *Dispatches* does not believe that the effects of the Act have been all bad. Dorothy Byrne, formerly of *World in Action* and *The Big Story*, says that standards have risen because of it. 'Our letters are true, our data accurate, our editing fair' and 'we are conscious of the huge power we have when we deal with subjects which affect people enormously, such as cot deaths, measles vaccines, chemicals in the water supply or GM foods'. These improvements have been in great measure enforced by the Act (Byrne 1999).

However, she concurs with Haywood's view in many respects, agreeing that nailing the villains with the tricks of the trade such as set-ups, secret filming and doorstepping are now much more difficult. She is less inclined to find fault with the Act as much as with the procedures of the BSC and ITC, citing as irritating adjudications one in which the complaint of a heroin dealer was taken seriously and another in which the complaint of a slave-owner was upheld (Byrne 1999). She believes that the complaints system has gone too far when 'discussions are held about giving rights of reply to major criminals'. She was angry at being slapped down for invasion of privacy because she filmed crooks selling stolen goods or, in another case, protected species from home. Roger Cook has had much the same experience and was particularly infuriated by the defence of the privacy of a sentenced stalker as well as criticisms that he had given insufficient notice to interviewees who happened to be criminals (Cook 1999).

These limited examples demonstrate something of the frustration of programme makers; they believe that the general orientation of the 1996 Act has made it possible for more barriers to be erected against investigative journalism. The climate of suspicion after the revelations of *The Connection* would not itself have been enough; the Act had provided an instrument well before, an instrument now being used to the full by the BSC. In turn, the trouble this causes is doubtless another reason for not making investigative programmes.

The debate over objectivity

In Chapter 2 we looked at the development of the idea of objectivity and its adoption as a norm by journalists. The manner in which broadcasting was set up in the UK has also been a factor in promoting the concept of objectivity; because of the limit on the number of channels on which radio and television could transmit – and perhaps the high cost of equipment for television broadcasting in the early days – the relatively partisan nature of some newspapers was regarded as inappropriate for broadcasting. Thus there came into being the concept of public service, by which the broadcasters were held to be speaking for the nation and not merely sections of it.

With the internet and digitalisation, the technological basis for objectivity is possibly changing. What has not necessarily changed is the philosophical orientation towards factuality that seeped into the European consciousness from the Enlightenment onwards; although some academics are challenging Enlightenment scientism with relativity and cultural determinism (an interesting discussion of these issues as they relate to history is contained in Evans 1997), journalists appear to retain considerable faith in scientific research, social science empiricism and statistical data.

This faith allows the argument that their impartiality continues to give them a very particular status in society, that journalism is a profession which scrutinises the institutions and the personnel of the polity and provides the facts upon which rational decisions can be made by the electorate as by the decision-makers. Tuchman (1972) has characterised this claim as a 'strategic

74

ritual' deployed by journalists to protect themselves from criticism by offended parties. It is a protective device in that if journalists can claim their job is to report facts rather than opinions they can detach themselves from blame for the (sometimes uncomfortable) facts; the journalist also comes to be judged on his skills of observation rather than his perceived stance. Allan (1997: 315) argues that this professional imperative has been used as 'a weapon with which to resist political interference'. Chalaby finds that it is particular to Anglo–America (Chalaby 1996); nevertheless journalists in many other countries attempt to have this claim accepted at home (Golding 1977).

In recent years journalistic objectivity has been the subject of intense debate. The former BBC war correspondent, Martin Bell, has reported from eighty countries, including eleven wars from Vietnam to El Salvador to Bosnia and is one of the best-known journalists in the Anglophone world. In a series of programmes, a book (Bell 1995) and lectures, he has doubted the cardinal tenet of Anglophone journalism. He has proposed to replace objectivity with 'the journalism of attachment'. In his critique he provides illustrations from his own experience of journalism to support the proposition that 'The mirror does not affect what it reflects; the television image does' (Bell 1997: 11). He shows, for example, how in war time camera crews are used as witnesses to prisoner exchanges, prisoner exchanges that might not take place without the possibility of filming them; how local military commanders will fashion their operations with television coverage in mind. He suggests that war crimes of great scale might not have taken place had there been television cameras. In other words, news does not simply reflect reality, it helps create it. It is also selective.

The guidelines issued by the BBC to its programme makers require that they be impartial and dispassionate (BBC 1996: 14–15), and this is probably a general principle to which most British journalists would adhere. Martin Bell argues that where wrong is being done and where people are suffering, not only is this impossible, but it is inappropriate for a reporter to attempt to be detached, or, as he puts it 'neutered'. He asks rhetorically whether the reporters who uncovered the German atrocities in Europe in 1945 could be expected to be detached; 'if not them, why us?' he asks (Bell 1997: 10).

The war in the former Yugoslavia has had a profound effect upon journalists other than Bell. Some have gone much further than him in their rejection of detachment. While Bell points out that crimes against humanity require accomplices – there is 'not only the hatred that makes it happen, but the *indifference that lets it happen*' (Bell 1997: 15) – Vulliamy says:

> I have to declare a partiality, that I am on the side of the Bosnian Muslim people against a historical and military programme to obliterate them ... I believe that what is happening to the Bosnians cannot be negotiated over or accommodated.
>
> (Vulliamy 1993)

In summary, the journalism of attachment rejects objectivity on the grounds first that it is implausible and secondly that it is immoral.

There has been a reaction to this argument, upholding the possibility of and need for factual reporting. Many journalists have been murdered during the wars in former Yugoslavia; it has been alleged (Hume 1997) that they were mainly murdered by Serbs, because the Serbs assumed that all journalists were against them. They assumed this because the reporting of the war was extremely hostile to their cause, and critics of 'attachment journalism' say that a good journalist should be trusted by all sides, except when evil men have something to hide, because he is the only source of impartially verifiable facts. This situation was achieved in Chechenya, where reporters appear to have managed to gain the respect of both sides. The lesson of these wars for one famous BBC journalist, John Simpson, is encapsulated in what his editor said to him when he was a cub: 'if I wanted to influence the way people thought, I should become a politician; if I wanted to tell them what was going on, I should be a journalist' (Simpson 1997).

According to Simpson, the journalist's job is to get at the facts of situations whether they be political, military or social. Yes, he or she may sympathise with the victims, but the prime task is not to sympathise but to understand. Another writer gives a vivid illustration of how feelings and facts may be confused:

> I vividly remember watching one BBC reporter standing amidst bodies ripped apart by machetes, clearly distressed, throwing his hands up and saying despairingly to camera, 'How can anyone even attempt to explain this – this is beyond explanation, beyond human reasoning'. While all of us can relate to his despair, we must not accept this kind of journalism. A journalist's job is two-fold. It is to give us the facts and it is to seek to explain these facts by attempting to uncover the reasons why events occurred in the way they did.
>
> (Fox 1996)

The argument is: if the journalist is not objective, no one will be; he or she is often the only source of proper information, information upon which rational assessments of the situation can be made. Such information-seeking is a responsibility from which reporters must not shirk. Furthermore, it is argued that emotional detachment is essential. According to Dunkley (1997):

> reporters are starting to believe that they should reflect their emotional involvement in what they report. From there it is only a step, and perhaps not a conscious one, to the selection and manipulation of the facts to favour one side.

Dunkley was appalled by the suggestion of Chief Executive Hall of BBC News that the emotions of those who demonstrated at the death of Princess

Diana in some mystical way represented truth better than facts might do. Hall said: 'by giving voice on our airwaves to ordinary individuals' thoughts and feelings, we [can] get at some kind of truth, which would otherwise elude us, no matter how many facts we assembled' (Hall 1997).

To Dunkley, as to many other observers, detachment is essential if journalists are to exercise their professional functions. Every journalist knows how easy it is to manipulate, either by selection or by mode of questioning. It has never been difficult to traduce audiences with television documentaries, in fact Matthew Parris goes as far as to argue that we delude ourselves if we imagine any factual programming is a record of observation at all.[3] Tom Wolfe's 1998 play about aspects of investigative journalism, *Ambush at Fort Bragg*, has the producer manipulating events thanks to digital technology; only a belief that professional integrity requires detachment could prevent it.

The fiercest critic of the journalism of attachment, Mick Hume, editor of *LM*, believes that its implications are very serious, not only for journalism but for general understanding. Emphasis upon the dramatic and horrific has pushed out the analysis; reporters have, in effect, campaigned for victims. Public policy in Western countries has, he argues, been made on the basis of public opinion that has been manipulated by the emotions and sloppy reporting, in the commercial interest of media owners and shareholders (Hume 1997: 10–11 and 16–17) and at the expense of other groups; reporters have promoted a new image of the journalist as heroic fighter for the oppressed rather than impartial seeker of truth.

However, there has never been a clear distinction; as I discussed in Chapter 1, investigative journalists operate within a framework of moral assumptions just like anyone else, it's just that they make a bigger meal of them. Investigative journalists themselves seem rather ambiguous on the subject. Jessica Mitford puts it prettily:

> I do try to cultivate the *appearance* of objectivity, mainly through the technique of understatement, avoidance where possible of editorial comment, above all letting the undertakers, or the Spock prosecutors, or the prison administrators pillory themselves through their own pronouncements. 'When are you going to get angry?' a friend asked after reading a draft of my article about the Famous Writers. Never, I answered; it is not in my sweet nature to lose my temper, especially in print.
>
> (Mitford 1979: 24)

Paul Foot makes a distinction between objectivity, of which he seems doubtful, and facts, which he respects:

> I'm a little suspicious about impartiality and objectivity, I think facts are facts and you cannot dodge the facts. I'm not an impartial sort of

person, I have very strong views about the way society is run, and how it works, so in that sense I'm not impartial.

(Preston 1999)

John Pilger has often been attacked for his rhetoric, such that one opponent invented the verb 'to pilger', meaning 'to present information in a sensational manner in support of a particular conclusion' (Auberon Waugh). Using rhetoric in support of the cause, opening yourself to the charge of allowing yourself to be so taken in by your campaign that you forget the facts appears to be an occupational hazard of investigative journalism as William Cobbett, who despised impartiality, would have recognised. Yet, notwithstanding Waugh, eloquence and respect for evidence are not necessarily contradictory.

The debate over journalistic objectivity continues; although passionately argued, Martin Bell's journalism of attachment has not, it seems to his colleagues, done away with the need for a belief in truth and objectivity, without which there is little justification for the existence of a profession of journalism. Martin Bell's view doubtless has allies in the academy, where relativity and cultural conditioning are often accepted as the premises of all observation and communication, but so far Anglophone journalists are holding to their beliefs: 'The art of the reporter should, more than anything else, be a celebration of truth. And if that truth offends the dictators, the gunmen, the secret policemen, if it offends lobby groups, vested interests or governments, so be it'. Those words were spoken by BBC reporter Fergal Keane in his 1997 Huw Wheldon lecture, in which he goes on to nominate those things which distinguish the journalist as 'the attachment to the provable', 'intellectual rigour' and 'forensic accuracy'; he goes on to claim that the great journalists understand the world around them because of their 'historical perspective and strategic vision'.

The Watergate myth

I can tell of a generation of British journalists who have Watergate on their brain, and think they could be the next Carl Bernstein, if only they were encouraged to betray every confidence, violate everybody's privacy and read every top secret document

(Brian Walden, cit. in Ingham 1991: 356)

In August 1974 US President Richard Nixon resigned when it was clear that he would be impeached by Congress both for trying to obstruct the official investigation of a burglary, using government resources for party political purposes and dishonestly denying his involvement in other illegal or unacceptable activities. The event that symbolised all the misdemeanours was the burglary at Democratic Party headquarters, based in a Washington office block called The Watergate.

It has often been described how tenacious and courageous reporting of this by the *Washington Post* led to the exposure of the links that proved President Nixon's implication in this and other offences. The full story is told, and the professional techniques and attitudes well demonstrated, in the two reporters' own account, *All the President's Men* (Woodward and Bernstein 1974), and in a film of the same name. The two reporters became icons and have been extensively eulogised; British television has produced regular re-examinations of the case and reflections upon its influence. All journalism in the US since then has been affected, if not dominated, by this feat which is interpreted either as the beginning of a new relationship between journalism and politics or as a demonstration, less of the corruption of US politics than of the efficacy of the system and proof of the important role of journalists in it. At a recent international conference on journalism education,[4] one speaker only half jokingly suggested that the Watergate case and the fall of the President had been concocted in order to demonstrate the superiority of the US system. Less ironically, the editor of *Sunday Times* Insight has described to student journalists how Watergate is his inspiration and his model (Leppard 1998).

The myth can be interrogated on a several grounds. First, it has been argued by Schudson (1992) that the roles of investigative journalism in bringing down the President were secondary relative to those of agencies of government itself; moreover it was other politicians and institutions which 'forced disclosures that kept the Watergate story in the public eye'. Second, Herman and Chomsky (1995) point out that while great attention has been paid to the investigation of a break-in at the headquarters of the powerful Democratic Party, virtually none at all was paid to equally illegal acts at the time by the FBI against targets with less clout. Many other incidences of reprehensible surveillance, provocation and subversion were undertaken in the same period but received little or no attention from Congress or the media; they also note that the bombing of hundreds of thousands of Cambodians by the US Air Force was not investigated with the same relish and draw the conclusion that:

> as long as illegalities and violations of democratic substance are confined to marginal groups or distant victims of US military attack, or result in a diffused cost imposed on the general population, media opposition is muted or absent altogether. This is why Nixon could go so far, lulled into a false sense of security precisely because the watchdog only barked when he began to threaten the privileged.
>
> (Herman and Chomsky 1995: 300)

It cannot, therefore, be argued that Watergate exemplifies the US media at their typical and best as the general watchdog. It may even be that the journalists were partisan, acting on behalf of one powerful group against another.

Moreover, it can be demonstrated that Watergate was neither the beginning of investigative journalism, nor of a new relationship between journalism and politics. Investigative journalism already had a long history in the USA, and a long history of calling politicians to account. By the early 1900s inflation was causing economic discontent, the power of the new rich was a matter for resentment among the urban majorities, huge numbers of immigrants led to machine politics and for all these reasons there was cynicism about the polity and alienation from authority (Desmond 1978: chap. 17). Better printing technology and postal services made market expansion feasible so that there was intensified competition for the new populations of readers.[5] These factors, along with the election of Theodore Roosevelt as President in 1904, may account for the explosion in investigative journalism of the period.

> Collectively their articles pried into practically every political, economic and moral problem of the age. They attacked the evils of city, state and national government, labor unions, big business, Wall Street, life insurance, the press, the medical profession, the food industry, child labor, women's inequality, prostitution and the drug trade. Heavily factual in content, critical in tone, and full of righteous but optimistic indignation, the average muckrake article presented no curative proposals, but simply sought to give the average citizen a scientific description of what was wrong.
>
> (Mowry 1958: 65)

There were at least ten magazines that dealt in this coin and one study estimates a readership of 20 million households out of a population of 90 million (Protess 1991: 39). The most famous is the investigation of the Chicago politicians of Tammany Hall (Stephens 1988: 249), but some of the most impressive in terms of their research dealt with the exploitation of children, such as that by Francis H. Nichols of the children as young as 9 used in wretched conditions in the Pennsylvania coal mines:

> The childish faces are compelled to bend so low over the chutes that prematurely round shoulders and narrow chests are the inevitable result. In front of the chutes is an open space reserved for the 'breakerboss' who watches the boys as intently as he watches the coal. The boss is armed with a stick, with which he occasionally raps on the head and shoulders a boy who betrays lack of zeal.
>
> (Nichols 1902)

One of the best known writers, and one who influenced President Roosevelt, was Upton Sinclair, particularly with his novel about the food processing industry, *The Jungle*. To research it Sinclair both went undercover, another hallmark of the investigative journalist, and trawled for statistical and other factual information.

There were men in the pickle-rooms, for instance, where old Antanas had gotten his death; scarce a one of these had not some spot of horror on his person. Let a man so much as scrape his finger pushing a truck in the pickle rooms, and he might have a sore that would put him out of the world; all the joints in his fingers might be eaten by the acid, one by one. Of the butchers and floorsmen, the beef boners and trimmers, and all those who used knives, you could scarcely find a person who had the use of his thumb; time and time again the base of it had been slashed, till it was a mere lump of flesh ... There were men who worked in the cooking rooms, in the midst of steam and sickening odours, by artificial light; in these rooms the germs of tuberculosis might live for two years, but the supply was renewed every hour.

(Sinclair 1906: 115)

The book became a bestseller but Sinclair did not feel he had achieved what he set out to do. The country became aware of bad practices in the food industries, so much so that Congress passed the Pure Food and Drug Act six months later; but, according to Sinclair himself, the suffering of the workers in the industry went largely ignored (Sinclair 1963: 135).

It has been claimed that investigative journalism resulted in many legislative developments of the period, including the Sherman Anti-Trust Laws, the Pure Food and Drug Act, legislation on Child Labour and pensions for mothers (Protess 1991). Another consequence was the awareness created of the social significance of journalism. No way is this better exemplified by quoting from President Theodore Roosevelt's speech in 1906, when he criticised investigative journalists by likening them to the muckraker in Bunyan's *Pilgrim's Progress*, who is so intent on his job he can see only muck and none of the good things. However he also admitted their importance to society by saying:

there are in the body politic, economic and social, many and grave evils, and there is urgent necessity for the sternest war upon them. There should be relentless exposure of and attack upon every evil man, whether politician or businessman, every evil in practice, whether in politics, in business or in social life.

(cit. in Protess 1991: 6)

Although the great growth in publishing slackened so there were fewer outlets for investigative journalism in the 1920s and 1930s, a tradition had been established. After the Second World War, Ed Murrow (1908–65), a war correspondent, exposed the failure of Senator Joe McCarthy to back up with evidence his claims about communist infiltration in US public life (Bayley 1981: 195, Rosteck 1989). He did it in an early television programme, the

CBS current affairs show *See it now* in 1954. In 1960 he also revealed the exploitation suffered by migratory farm workers in the CBS feature *Harvest of Shame*. Jessica Mitford became famous for her investigations, in particular for her exposé of funeral practices (which became the 1963 book *The American Way of Death*) and penal system (*Kind and Usual Punishment* 1973). I. F. Stone, through the 1950s and 1960s, exposed the flaws in official accounts of the origins of the Korean and Vietnam Wars and the claims of FBI Chief Hoover (Lule 1995).

In November 1969 Seymour Hersh heard about, investigated and reported on the My Lai massacres of 1967. That investigation fuelled the anti-war movement and led to *The Pentagon Papers* which demonstrated the deceptions being carried out by the military leaders upon the electorate during the war. It has conventionally been argued that the climate of suspicion generated by these revelations led indirectly to Watergate.

However, as its protagonists acknowledge, Watergate has become a myth, an icon. The reality is that it was the continuation of a long tradition, that it may have achieved little in comparison with other investigations and also that it can be argued to demonstrate the failings of US journalism. In the minds of many though, its protagonists stand for investigative journalism in the manner perhaps that tales of Wyatt Earp and Davy Crockett in the past stood for the myth of the free frontiersman.

If only you were American

Myth or not, Watergate has ensured that investigative journalism has a high profile in the USA today. Since 1975 the USA has had an organisation of investigative journalists, the Investigative Reporters and Editors (IRE) founded by four well-established journalists and given a fillip by the Arizona Project, in which thirty-eight journalists joined together to research a story that one of their colleagues had been murdered for investigating, eventually ensuring its revelation through simultaneous publication in over twenty media outlets. Today the IRE publishes a journal to keep members up to date with stories and relevant developments in current affairs as well as briefings on, for example, computer-assisted reporting. It provides an index of stories on its website.[6]

The Center for Public Integrity (CPI) explains itself as a 'non-partisan, non-profit investigative research organisation' and makes available studies such as those on the special interests that influence congressional decisions, or possibilities for corruption in State governments. According to Phillip Knightley (1998) it has been responsible for the investigation of the most important investigative stories in the USA over the last few years, including

> the White House providing bed and breakfast for campaign contrib-
> utors, the exposure of the moneyed interests behind the campaign to

defeat Clinton's universal health care plan, and, best of all 'The Buying of the President', a seminal study of the special interests behind the presidential candidates of the 1990s

(Knightley 1998: 40)

These investigations it has handed over to newspapers and television stations 'for little or no cost' and, he believes, this is a trend that may save investigative journalism.

In 1997 the CPI launched The International Consortium of Investigative Journalists (ICIJ). Its members include Englishman David Leigh, the latest twists of whose investigations into the Aitken saga were showcased on the ICIJ's website in 1998, as were the investigations into the looting of the Russian national treasury by Russian mobsters in league with officials. The ICIJ ensures that investigators are up to date on their legal rights and how to realise them, all accessed through the Internet.

Investigative journalists find the Internet bookshop Amazon useful, especially as it gives reviews of relevant books. From California, Facsnet provides information on training and familiarisation courses for investigative journalists, from 'an intensive, one-week Institute on Science to be held at the California Institute of Technology (Caltech)' to a 6-day immersion course in economics. There are many other facilities enjoyed by US journalists that are not yet available to Europeans, many of which can be identified with the help of The Freedom Forum (www.freedomforum.org). Among the multitude of other contact points for investigative journalists, there is also the International Center for Journalism which mainly provides professional development programmes, and the International Journalists' Network which, among other useful assistance, has a fund for investigative journalism.

The research issue

Journalism is studied and written about much more in the USA than in Europe, although, with new courses annually, a first Association for Journalism Education launched in 1998 and three new academic journals launched in 1998–9 in Britain alone, this may be changing. However, not only is there no consensus about what academic subjects journalists should study, there is no coherent idea about how journalism might be studied. So it is not surprising that British and other European academics working on journalism are few and far between and that investigative journalism has hardly been touched on.

Student journalists should know their profession's history and issues and perhaps students of other disciplines should too if, as is often declared, journalism is the mediator of their own work to the rest of the world and of the rest of the world to them. Unfortunately, although we have a few fine texts, many more are needed.

Research could help us understand the role that investigative journalism may have played in British society and politics over the past 150 years and retrieve lost history. It would be interesting to know what subject matter has been most dealt with, and what ignored; there are issues of ethics that require thought; journalism and its relationship to truth needs to be explored. Studies could focus on journalists themselves; Holly Stocking has started to examine journalists' cognitive approaches (1989) and Oliner's studies of altruism (1992) may be a good starting point for studies of motivation. Examining the idealisation of the reporter may tell us a good deal about our society. Individual stories should be analysed from a variety of different angles: how handled, relationships with other institutions in society, public interest, policy making influence, cultural significance, success or failure. My contention that investigative journalism is the first draft of legislation should be held up to scrutiny; is Kedourie's point, referred to in Chapter 1, that investigative journalism usurps the functions of institutions, useful in illuminating the institutional role? What of the idea that investigative journalism galvanises institutions, or responds to popular pressures?

Investigative journalism is not only an Anglophone phenomenon. Courageous reporters expose issues in countries as diverse as Russia, Italy, Turkey and China. Their work deserves study and their efforts recognition. In short, there is great potential in the academic study of journalism and it is to be hoped that universities will recognise this and invest resources in the development of a field which, from the numbers of applicants to courses, continues to inspire.

NOTES

1   The Public Bodies (Corrupt Practices) Act 1889; The Prevention of Corruption Act 1906; The Prevention of Corruption Act 1916.

2   When John Boileau became aware of my interpretation of his work, he asked me to take into account his reaction, a reaction that he wrote to me. Since he expresses it very clearly, I reproduce what appear to me to be his key points: 'I hold these opinions and beliefs only in the context of my job as the editor of a commercial television regional 6.30 news programme … in the context that there is such competition from other channels, and such a variety of other types of news, documentary and current affairs programming, that my job is to decide which part of the target to aim at. … It is absolutely not the case that I despise or would even knowingly disparage other, more intensive, more morally-driven kinds of journalism: but absolutely and clearly that I have decided that such journalism is not appropriate to a pre-watershed, 55 per cent housewife, significantly largely C2, D, E audience at 6.30pm on commercial television'.

3   'The problem with truth on TV is TV itself. Not one rotten apple but the whole damn barrel. Across a whole range of programmes there's a culture of artifice and mendacity. Necessarily. We believe what we see at our peril.' (Parris 1999)

4   International Association for Media and Cultural Studies Research biannual convention, Glasgow 1998.

5   Desmond (1978) Chapter 17 goes into these developments in detail.

6   Full details of the American operations mentioned here, and the sources of quotations, will be found at the following sites:

www.publicintegrity.org/main.html

www.icij.org/home.html

www.icij.org/tools

www.ire.org/history/start.html

www.amazon.com

www.facsnet.org

www.icfj.org

www.ijnet.org

BIBLIOGRAPHY

Allan, S. (1997) News and the public sphere: towards a history of news objectivity. In M. Bromley and T. O'Malley (eds) *A Journalism Reader*. London: Routledge.

Altschull, J. H. (1998) *Agents of Power*. London: Longman.

Andrews, A. (1859) *The History of British Journalism*. London: Richard Bentley.

Bayley, E. (1981) *Joe McCarthy and the Press*. Madison: Wisconsin.

BBC (1996) *Producers' Guidelines*. London: BBC.

Bell, M. (1995) *In Harm's Way*. London: Penguin.

Bell, M. (1997) TV news : how far should we go? *British Journalism Review*, 8 (1).

Bell, M. (1997a) News and Neutrality. Programme 1 of *The Truth is Our Currency*, a series of Radio 4 programmes.

Bell, M. (1998) The journalism of attachment. In M. Kieran (ed.) *Media Ethics*. London: Routledge.

Bell, M. (1998a) Journalists and objectivity. Talk to students and staff at Nottingham Trent University, 27 January 1998.

Berkowitz, D. (1997) *Social Meanings of News: A Text Reader*. Thousand Oaks: Sage.

Bourdieu, P. (1998) *On Television and Journalism*. London: Pluto.

Byrne, D. (1999) Interview with Hugo de Burgh, 22 March 1999.

Chalaby, J. K. (1996) Journalism as an Anglo-American invention: a comparison of the development of French and Anglo-American journalism 1830s–1920s. *European Journal of Communication*, 11 (3): 303–26.

Chalaby, J. (1998) *The Invention of Journalism*. London: Macmillan.

Clarke, D. (1983) *Corruption: Causes, Consequences and Control*. London: Frances Pinter.

Clarke, N. (1998) Spindoctors and the *World at One*. Talk to third year students on the BA Broadcast Journalism course at Nottingham Trent University, 13 November 1997.

Cook, R. (1999) Interview with Hugo de Burgh, 22 March 1999.

Curran, J. and Seaton, J. (1997) *Power without Responsibility: The Press and Broadcasting in Britain*, 5th edn. London: Routledge.

Dahlgren, P. and Sparks, C. (1991) *Communication and Citizenship*. London: Routledge.

de Burgh, H. (1998) Audience, journalist and text in television news. Paper delivered at the Annual Conference of the International Association for Media and Communications Research, 29 July 1998.

Desmond, R. (1978) *The Information Process: World News Reporting to the Twentieth Century*. Iowa: UIP.

Doig, A. (1987) The decline of investigatory journalism. In M. Bromley and T. O'Malley (eds) *A Journalism Reader*. London: Routledge.

Dunkley, C. (1997) Whose news is it anyway? *Financial Times*, 22 September 1997.

Dynes, M. (1995) *The New British State: The Government Machine in the 1990s*. London: Times Books.

Evans, R. J. (1997) *In Defence of History*. London: Granta.

Ewing, K. D. and Gearty, C. A. (1990) *Freedom Under Thatcher: Civil Liberties in Modern Britain*. Oxford: Oxford University Press.

Fennell, P. (1983) Local government corruption in England and Wales. In M. Clarke *Corruption*. London: Frances Pinter.

Fitzwalter, R. (1999) Interview with Hugo de Burgh, 18 March 1999.

Foot, P. (1990) *Words as Weapons*. London: Verso.

Fox, F. (1996) Rwanda: the journalist's role. *The Month*, May 1996.

Franklin, B. (1997) *Newszak and News Media*. London: Arnold.

Gibbons, T. (1998) *Regulating the Media*. London: Sweet and Maxwell.

Golding, P. (1977) Media professionalism in the third world: the transfer of an ideology. In J. Curran, M. Gurevitch and J. Woollacott (eds) *Mass Communication and Society*. London: Edward Arnold.

Golding, P. (1999) The political and the popular: getting the message of tabloidisation. Paper delivered at the annual conference of the Association of Media, Cultural and Communications Studies, Sheffield, December 1998.

Goodwin, P. (1998) *Television under the Tories*. London: British Film Institute.

Greenslade, R. (1999) Interview with Hugo de Burgh, 22 March 1999.

Hall, T. (1997) The people led, we followed. *Times*, 10 September 1997: 22.

Harris, R. (1994) *The Media Trilogy*. London: Faber and Faber.

Haywood, S. (1999) Interview with Hugo de Burgh, 22 March 1999.

Herman, E. and Chomsky, N. (1995) *Manufacturing Consent*. London: Vintage.

Hume, M. (1997) *Whose War is it Anyway? The Dangers of the Journalism of Attachment* London: LM.

Ingham, B. (1991) *Kill the Messenger*. London: Harper Collins.

Jones, N. (1999) *Sultans of Spin*. London: Victor Gollancz.

Keane, F. (1997) The art of the reporter. The RTS Huw Wheldon Lecture 1997. Reprinted in *Television*, the Journal of Royal Television Society.

Kingdom, J. (1991) *Government and Politics in Britain*. London: Polity.

Knightley, P. (1975) *The First Casualty*. London: Pan.

Knightley, P. (1998) *British Journalism Review*, 9 (2).

Knightley, P. (1999) Interview with Hugo de Burgh, 22 May 1999.

Leigh, D. and Vulliamy, E. (1997) *Sleaze: The Corruption of Parliament*. London: Fourth Estate.

Leppard, D. (1997) The Watergate model in UK journalism. Talk to students on the MA Investigative Journalism course at Nottingham Trent University, 27 November 1997.

Lloyd, D. (1998) Talk to the students of the MA Investigative Journalism course at Nottingham Trent University, 19 February 1998.

Lloyd, D. (1998a) Interview with Hugo de Burgh, 9 October 1998.

Lule, J. (1995) I. F. Stone: the practice of reporting. *Journalism and Mass Communication Quarterly*, 72 (3) Autumn 1995: 499–510.

Mitford, J. (1979) *The Making of a Muckraker*. London: Michael Joseph.

Morris, B. (1991) *The Roots of Appeasement: The British Weekly Press and Nazi Germany during the 1930s*. London: Frank Cass.

Mowry, G. (1958) *The Era of Theodore Roosevelt*. New York: Harper.

Neil, A. (1996) *Full Disclosure*. London: Macmillan.

Nichols, F. H. (1902) Children of the coal shadow. *McClure's Magazine*, November 1902.

Nolan, Lord (1995) First Report of the Committee on Standards in Public Life, Cmnd 2850-I. London: HMSO.

Oliner, S. (1992) *The Altruistic Personality*. New York: Free Press.

Parris, M. (1999) Parris on TV. A series for Radio 5 Live (producers: All Out Productions).

Parsons, W. (1995) *Public Policy*. Aldershot: Elgar.

Preston, L. (1999) Paul Foot: the role of the journalist in the surveillance of justice. An unpublished essay for Broadcast Practice 3, BA/BJ course at Nottingham Trent University.

Protess, D. (1991) *The Journalism of Outrage: Investigative Reporting and Agenda Building in America*. New York and London: The Guildford Press.

Randall, D. (1996) *The Universal Journalist*. London: Pluto.

Rosteck, T. (1989) Irony, argument and reportage in Television documentary. *Quarterly Journal of Speech*, 9: 277–98.

Rusbridger, A. (1999) Interview with Hugo de Burgh, 25 May 1999.

Schiller, D. (1996) *Theorizing Communication*. Philadelphia: University of Pennsylvania Press.

Schudson, M. (1989) The sociology of news production. In D. Berkowitz *Social Meanings of News: A Text Reader*. Thousand Oaks: Sage.

Schudson, M. (1992) Watergate: a study in mythology. *Columbia Journalism Review*, May/June 1992.

Shoemaker, P. (1996) *Mediating the Message*. London: Longman.

Siebert, F., Peterson, T. and Schramm, W. (1963) *Four Theories of the Press: The Authoritarian, Libertarian, Social Responsibility and Soviet Communist Concepts of What the Press Should Be and Should Do*. Chicago: Illinois University Press.

Simpson, J. (1997) Save us from reporters who pass judgement. *Sunday Telegraph*, 14 September 1997.

Sinclair, U. (1906) *The Jungle*. London: Laurie.

Sinclair, U. (1963) *Autobiography*. London: W. H. Allen.

Stephens, M. (1988) *History of News*. New York: Viking.

Stocking, H. (1989) *How do Journalists Think?* Bloomington: IUP.

Tuchman, G. (1978) *Making News: A Study in the Construction of Reality*. New York: The Free Press.

Tuchman, G. (1972) Objectivity as a strategic ritual. *American Journal of Sociology*, 77 (4): 660–79.

Vulliamy, E. (1993) This war has changed my life. *British Journalism Review*, 4 (2).

Westrop, D. (1999) Interview with Hugo de Burgh, 22 March 1999. Followed up by e-mail on 24 March 1999.

White, V. (1999) *Panorama's* place in the polity. Talk to members of the Chinese National Media Legislation Working Group held at Nottingham Trent University, 11 February 1999.

Whittle, S. (1999) Interview with Hugo de Burgh, 17 March 1999.

Wolfe, T. (1998) *Ambush at Fort Bragg*. London: BBC Radio 4. (Author/presenter: Tom Wolfe.)

Woodward, R. and Bernstein, C. (1974) *All the President's Men*. London: Quarto.

FURTHER READING

Berkowitz, D. (1997) *Social Meanings of News: A Text Reader*. Thousand Oaks: Sage.

McNair, B. (1998) *The Sociology of Journalism*. London: Arnold.

Protess, D. (1991) *The Journalism of Outrage: Investigative Reporting and Agenda Building in America*. New York and London: The Guildford Press.

5

CRITICAL APPROACHES TO THE MEDIA

The changing context for investigative journalism

Deborah Chambers

Introduction

Investigative journalism has been flourishing in the last three decades of the twentieth century. Recent changes in the media market place are now raising important questions about the future climate in which the profession operates and providing us with clues about the possible changing nature of its practices. By visiting the wider social context in which investigative journalism takes place, in this chapter we identify the economic and cultural constraints being placed on investigative journalism during the early twenty-first century and ask whether they are restricting or reshaping the profession. We begin by inquiring about the values of social responsibility and the public service role of investigative journalism that are upheld in liberal democracies. The mechanisms of democratic accountability embedded in the ideals of press freedom are examined in terms of how effective they are in protecting investigative journalism against partial commercial or state interests. Selected current debates in media theory that relate to investigative journalism are then explored, covering economic and ideological factors which influence the products and practices of journalism. The 'political economy' approach is focused on to assess the impact on journalism of media deregulation, changing patterns of media ownership, and intensified media competition. Classic media research conducted within the 'critical and cultural' approach is then reviewed to explore the ideological factors that influence journalistic reporting. Finally, key changes in media organisations that have led to a casualisation of the journalism profession and the rise in demand for journalistic skills in the form of press officers and public relations staff are visited in relation to these trends.

Press freedom versus state and commercial media interests

Media deregulation has had a major impact on the communication environment in which investigative journalism exists. Having regulated elements of the mass media after the Second World War to safeguard public interests and free speech, Western governments decided to deregulate them during the 1980s to increase competition which it was thought might encourage the development of more diverse and high quality media content. Media regulation had been first prompted by the awareness of the propaganda potential of the mass media. An example frequently quoted in Britain of its powerful influence on people's attitudes and aspirations was Hitler's control over radio broadcasting in Fascist Germany in the lead up to the Second World War. Public service broadcasting in Europe, such as the BBC, was actually strengthened at the expense of commercial media ventures by these media experiences and debates.

During the same period in the United States, the safeguarding of public interest was translated into 'freedom of speech' and inscribed in a written constitution. The US Commission on the Freedom of the Press of 1947 declared emphatically that media ownership and operations are not just to be treated as unlimited businesses but as forms of public stewardship (Blanchard 1977, McQuail 1994). These broad principles of social responsibility were transposed not only into public service broadcasting principles but also into codes of journalistic and broadcasting standards, ethics and conduct across privately-owned media in Britain and the USA to guide journalism between the 'frying pan' and 'fire' of state control and commercial control.

This defence of press and broadcast freedom and codes of professional ethics is an essential form of protection from commercial and state pressures so that the profession can function democratically for the public interest. Journalistic codes deal with criteria such as the provision of reliable, accurate, undistorted and unsensational information yet they differ considerably according to whether they are drawn up by publishers, editors, journalists or regulatory bodies. These interests are often in tension with one another. Publishers and editors emphasise the need for freedom to publish and freedom from vested interests, whereas journalistic codes aim to protect the autonomy of journalists from pressure of publishers and advertisers and call for the confidentiality of sources. Codes of media ethics that apply mainly to journalism cover accuracy, impartiality, respect for privacy, independence, responsibility, respect for law, and moral decency. The codifying of press responsibility is, however, hampered by economic and political constraints. Some of these issues are raised in Chapter 7 on the regulatory and ethical framework of investigative journalism. McQuail states that:

> attempts to codify press responsibility cannot overcome the funda-
> mental differences of perspectives and interests between the various
> participants in the media institution and between the different social
> and political systems in the world. Nor, in practice, has it proved easy
> to reach effective self-regulation.
>
> (1994: 126)

As Hamelink (1999) points out, the right to freedom of expression of opinions, information and ideas with no interference from public or private parties is implied in the provisions in international human rights law on freedom of expression. It is implied in the UK and written as an absolute right of citizens in the First Amendment to the US Constitution. Yet the parties involved have difficulties in translating this right into practice (see Chapter 7 by Gill Moore for a discussion of the legal framework of press freedom). On the one hand, politicians and public bodies argue that press freedom should be forfeited or restrained if it gets abused, threatens good morals or the authority of the state in times of war or other national crises. On the other hand, press freedom can be forfeited if it curtails other rights of citizens. Freedom of speech is an ideal which presupposes that the people speaking are on an equal footing in terms of their knowledge, power and status. In practice, the absolute value of freedom of speech is consistently being overridden by the protection of values that are systematically given a higher priority in Western societies: the reputation, property, privacy and morals of privileged individual citizens and social groups, and of course, the security of the state (Glasser 1986, Curran 1991). As Denis McQuail (1994: 130) states:

> the theory [of press freedom] has been most frequently formulated to protect the owners of media and cannot give equal expression to the arguable rights of editors and journalists within the press, or to audiences, or to other potential beneficiaries, or victims of free expression.

Investigative journalism walks a tightrope through these conflicting demands and priorities. The closer journalists get to those powerful individuals or groups that they spotlight for investigation, the more acute this problem becomes. Protecting investigative reporters' professional principles and practices is vital in a situation where those with power and wealth who typically make up the 'Establishment' are the social category most likely to be under journalistic scrutiny, exemplified by cases such as Woodward and Bernstein's coverage of the 1972 Watergate cover-up in the USA and the *Guardian* exposure of 'Cash for Questions' in Britain between 1994 and 1996.

Both private and state media control pose a threat to freedom of journalistic expression. As Brian McNair (1998: 84) states, 'a liberal democratic political system demands journalistic criticism of elites as a condition of its legitimacy'. Yet in practice, press freedom is being interpreted in a narrow sense in capitalist liberal democracies not as 'freedom of expression' but as freedom to privately own media publishing businesses. This means that property rights are being protected by privileging the freedom to own and publish without state interference. As McQuail (op. cit.) indicates, it is a somewhat bizarre argument to suggest that private ownership of the media guarantees the individual citizen's right to publish. The political economy approach to the media emphasises that the level of private business interests in the media restricts freedom of expression as much as forms of government constraint. In reality, then, there is an underlying contradiction between a negative and a positive concept of press freedom in Western capitalist liberal democracies. The negative sense of press freedom is about an absence of constraint (to publish), and the positive sense is about objectives and benefits in the 'public interest' that transcend those delivered to owners of the press. The problem is that private interests pose as much of a threat to communication democracy as government regulation. Moreover, the libertarian ideal of freedom of speech is too difficult to apply properly to the broadcast media, thus leaving out a vast chunk of the media in Western democracies. As McQuail (1994) points out, the theory of press freedom is of little relevance when applied to cinema, the music industry, the video market, or even to much sport, fiction and entertainment on television, which makes up the bulk of television broadcasting. It also fails to resolve the problems surrounding the role of 'information'. For example, it does not protect the rights of citizens to have equal access to information, to privacy, nor to publication of information unless they happen to own media property. We are also finding difficulties in applying its principles to the Internet and World Wide Web, as Chapter 6 indicates. In practice, then, the principle of freedom of speech tends to protect the owners of the media rather than journalists or the wider public. This poses serious difficulties for the investigative journalism profession as a whole. Although media regulation is now increasingly interpreted by journalists as a defence of socially responsible journalism, proprietors are privileged and protected by rules surrounding ownership while journalistic principles of social responsibility and practices of in-depth research and surveillance are guaranteed little protection.

Media ownership and control

Critics of journalistic performance often overemphasise the extent to which journalists are free agents as Franklin (1997) points out. According to evidence from the research within the political economy approach, journalism's role of servicing democracy by fostering public debate and surveying government power is compromised by growing commercial constraints prompted by media deregulation and privatisation. The political economy theory examines the economic and political dynamics of media ownership and control, and its effects on media practices. This approach is exemplified by the work of authors such as Golding and Murdock (1991), Curran and Seaton (1997), Bagdikian (1988). During the 1980s and 1990s, Western governments encouraged privatisation of the media by relaxing the post-war controls over broadcasting and telecommunications, and restrictions on media ownership were reduced (Murdock 1990). This led to a sharp decline in public control of telecommunications, especially in Western Europe. The deregulation of national media services and lifting of legal limitations of control of capital allowed private media corporations to invest in any country in the world. By investing in nations where labour unions were weak, labour cheap and profits high, multi-national corporations were able to flourish. State deregulation of the media has allowed media moguls such as Rupert Murdoch to extend their media empires. Murdoch now owns Twentieth Century Fox, BskyB, Star TV in Asia, and the publishing company HarperCollins. His newspaper empire embraces the *Australian*, a national newspaper, *New York Post*, and British newspapers, the *Times*, the *Sunday Times*, the *Sun,* and *News of the World.*

The theory of political economy focuses on the relations of the media to the state and the domination of the economy by giant corporations (see, for example, Murdock and Golding 1977, Golding and Murdock 1991, Curran and Seaton 1988 and Ferguson 1990). It emphasises that media organisations are structured by capitalist economies and are necessarily competitive businesses aimed at making profits for shareholders. This means that journalists' products, 'news' and investigative reports, are increasingly treated as commodities and judged by their potential to make profits. In Britain, the rules on media concentration were further relaxed by the Broadcasting Act of 1990 and then 1996 to create a competitive broadcasting market through less strict government regulation. The original intention was to give audiences more control over programme choices while the existing quality of programmes were to remain in place. But higher cost constraints were found to be prohibitive to regional and network programme-making. Commercial competition has been so intense and profit margins so small that earlier public-service commitments and the motivation to produce quality programming have been seriously undermined. Franklin (1997) points out that cheap entertainment programmes such as game shows are now being favoured over quality, in-depth news documentaries in programming schedules. This impacts on the profession of journalism by reducing demand for investigative reporting. The Broadcasting Act of 1996 in the UK was designed to encourage cross-media ownership allowing profit-making enterprise within a media conglomerate to subsidise smaller, newer or ailing non-profit-making enterprises in the larger group. Today's deregulated media are characterised by the combined objectives of making profits from their operations, turning media content into a commodity, and expanding their markets.

The increasing convergence between telecommunications, press and broadcasting, and intensified integration between electronic hardware and software industries have led not only to the concentration of the media in fewer and fewer hands but also to a fast expanding global 'information economy' (see Hamelink 1995, Demac and Sung 1995, Melody 1990 and Paterson 1997). Media organisations are now typically owned by large trans-national corporations who not only have linked controlling financial interests in telecommunications, leisure, and tourism but also in oil, paper, property and the nuclear industry (Bagdikian 1988, Comor 1997). This concentration of media ownership has had a profound impact on the content of the print and broadcast media and on the very nature of investigative journalism. It has led to a reduction in independent media sources, the commodifying of media contents and audiences, and the neglect of minority and poorer sections of the audience. According to the political economy perspective, these factors lead to the marginalisation of opposition views and the reduction of investment in less profitable media activities such as investigative reporting and documentary film-making. Investigative reporting on issues such as nuclear pollution is likely to be severely compromised in circumstances where the media are linked to the nuclear industry through patterns of ownership (Herman 1995). Similarly, reports critical of genetically modified food in 1999 were slow to break world wide, especially in the United States, due to pressures placed on the media by powerful international bio-technology companies. So the main features of concentration of private ownership have been intensified competition, low profit margins, and, according to Franklin (1997) the pressures of censorship by owners have created the context for a trend towards the trivialisation and tabloidisation of information and news.

An approach related to the political economy perspective that examines the place of journalism in capitalist society is the American 'propaganda model' represented by Noam Chomsky and Ed Herman (see Chomsky and Herman 1979, Chomsky 1987). They go further than the political economy approach in their criticisms by arguing that a conspiracy exists among the elites to control the news and information. Rather than there being a pluralist balance between the competing interest of the state and private business to produce a liberal democracy, they claim that the journalistic media serve the joint interests of the state and corporate power of Western societies. The media are subordinated to the interests of a group of political, economic, military and cultural elites, the 'National Security State', which control the flow of information. Herman (1995) has identified five conditions that information must fulfil before it can be transformed into 'information' and 'news' in the United States. These five political economic filters that news has to pass through demonstrate that the US mass media are dominated not by media professionals but by communication gatekeepers made up of a network of powerful profit-making organisations with close links to government and business.

Herman's first filter is the size, concentrated ownership, wealth and profit orientation of the main media firms. Private investors in media businesses tie the media in with controversial multinational companies involved in arms production and nuclear power. This forces the integration of media companies into market strategies and leads them away from responsibility to the democratic process. Media companies are also dependent on government ties for policy support and level of enforcement of anti-monopoly laws.

The second filter is the dominance of advertising as an income source for the mass media. Newspapers obtain around three-quarters of their revenues from advertisers and independent broadcasters obtain almost 100 per cent

(Herman 1995: 84). A media system dependent on advertising drives out media companies that do not subsidise the price of the newspaper through advertising. It ensures that advertisers have a powerful influence on the survival and prosperity of the media industry. Working-class and radical media are unable to attract advertising because they tend to cater for consumers with little purchasing power or who are critical of the market-led system. Advertisers also withdraw their sponsorship of programmes and articles that criticise controversial corporate activities such as environmental pollution, and the financial investment in Third World nation dictatorships and violators of human rights.

The third filter is the dependence of the media on information fed by government and business. In order to save costs, the media concentrate reporters in places where significant news events usually happen, such as The White House, Pentagon, police departments, etc. Journalists' dependence on government sources allows the state to manage and manipulate the media by offering journalists a diet of stories which reinforce a particular ideology and interpretation of events.

The fourth filter is 'flak', consisting of orchestrated attacks on the news media by the government, politicians, big business and powerful interest groups, which is designed to discipline and censor critical media voices.

The fifth filter is 'anti-communism', which continues to be used as a powerful political and ideological control mechanism to shape media discourses.

Although the vocabulary of 'propaganda' smacks of dictator-style media and Cold War/arms race politics, Herman claims that the kinds of dissent topics presented as 'news' are sparing and their existence lends credibility to the dominant ideology and media process. Today, 'Islamaphobia' has been identified as a more recent ideological mechanism of undermining and alienating groups whose views and practices are in conflict with the US security state power block, which has replaced the demonising of left-wing politics and communism that took place within the Cold War era (see for example, Kellner 1992). The repeated association of Muslim culture with terrorism encourages a demonisation of Islamic cultures in the news media. The ethnocentric bias of the Western news media against Muslim cultures was fuelled by the American and British assaults on Iraq in 1991 but has been seriously questioned by journalists during the 1998/99 war. The conspiratorial nature of the propaganda model's analysis is regarded as somewhat extreme by the political economy approach but it contains some insights into the kinds and pressures and challenges faced by investigative journalists in the pursuit of democratic accountability. Governments and big business spend enormous amounts of time and money to erect barriers against in-depth investigations of their activities, as exemplified by those cover-ups, such as Watergate, that do get exposed.

Communication empires and market-driven journalism

An example of the extent to which the dynamics of media ownership operate to control international markets, book publishing, journalistic content, and the reluctance of government legislation against such control is the Patten case. In February 1998, the British broadsheet newspaper, the *Independent*, criticised media tycoon Rupert Murdoch for interfering with the contents of the media. It was alleged that he intervened in his publishing company, Harper Collins, by forcing the company to drop a book being written by Chris Patten, the former governor of Hong Kong. The book, called *East and West*, is about Hong Kong in Asia and in it Patten (1998) criticises the totalitarian regime of the People's Republic of China. Murdoch has commercial interests in China that he wished to protect, so apparently he stepped in to stop the book being published by suspending the duties of the publisher, Stuart Proffitt. Proffitt's departure prompted well known writers – including Doris Lessing, Penelope Fitzgerald, Peter Hennessey and Anthony Storr – to publicly criticise their publisher and threaten to find an alternative publisher. The *Independent* (28 February 1998) accused Murdoch of 'toadying to China's totalitarian regime' in order to extend his television empire into the lucrative Chinese market. One of Chris Patten's complaints was the loss of serialisation opportunities with the newspapers owned by Murdoch, the *Times* and the *Sunday Times*.

Significantly, neither the *Times* nor the *Sunday Times* reported this story on 28 February 1998. Patten responded to Murdoch's action by lodging a writ in the High Court and claimed breach of contract against HarperCollins. In defence, HarperCollins claimed that Murdoch did not try to change Patten's book and did not ask anyone to change it. Murdoch did, however, express dissatisfaction about the decision to publish it. The controversy was fuelled by the publication of a memo sent by HarperCollin's chairman, Eddie Bell, to the head of Murdoch's American publishing arm, Anthea Disney which stated that Rupert Murdoch felt the book had 'negative aspects' (*Independent*, 28 February 1998). The memo also demonstrated Murdoch's concern that the decision to drop the book would threaten John Major's memoirs, which were being written for the same publisher.

The Patten case demonstrates the influence that media owners such as Murdoch have over the contents of the news media and book publishing. Murdoch has been criticised for a number of other interventions in the news media to protect his communications empire. The *Independent* claimed that Murdoch dismissed the editor of the *Sunday Times* (who received a £1 million pay-off) because he was worried that his television broadcasting interests in Asia would be damaged by the newspaper's investigation into 'aid' payments by Britain to Malaysia to obtain building contracts for the Pergau Dam. He withdrew the BBC's World Service channel from his Star TV network in 1994 to appease the regime in the People's Republic of China who were critical of journalist Kate Adie's reports of the Tiananmen Square massacre. Free reporting by the BBC apparently interfered with Murdoch's communication interests in China. Significantly, Murdoch's defence of China has allowed him to obtain a 'special concession' to launch a Mandarin language satellite channel for the Chinese market, called 'Phoenix'. Murdoch cannot risk offending even totalitarian regimes when they constitute the largest global television market (*Independent*, 28 February 1998).

Britain's former Conservative government of the 1980s and 1990s opposed moves to refer Murdoch's newspaper and television acquisitions to the Monopolies Commission. The succeeding Labour government elected in 1997 has also ignored complaints about bad practice such as predatory pricing by the *Times*. The suspicion that Murdoch has influence over government policy has arisen from the British government's reluctance to produce any form of privacy legislation, its caution on European Monetary Union, which Murdoch is known to oppose, and its refusal to deal with predatory newspaper pricing and lack of union recognition by media owners.

A further example of the consequences of the market-driven imperative of information is the emergence of a new consumer-orientated form of investigative journalism. A number of magazine-style consumer advice programmes are now being produced with exposés on a cluster of domestic and lifestyle themes such as holidays, food, home mortgages, and personal finances, exemplified in Britain by BBC1's *Watchdog*. Carefully and sometimes daringly investigated domestic issues and topics are replacing the older style, in-depth current affairs journalism of Granada Television's *World in Action*. The key issues have shifted from international and national political issues to locations and subjects somewhat closer to home by spectacularising domestic, familial and household consumer events, including warring neighbours (for example in *Neighbours at War*, BBC2). It has been suggested that this move indicates a slide from 'hard' to 'soft' journalism, exemplified by the inevitable shift of focus to a sphere that has traditionally been treated as domestic and 'feminine'. But the evidence shows that, from time to time, the 'big guns' of multinational corporations are taken on, confronted and exposed to an audience of millions by hard hitting investigative teams. An example of this is the critical, in-depth analysis of the facts surrounding the multinational giant, Monsanto and the production of genetically modified food reported on BBC Radio 4's *Food Programme* (13 March 1999). It may well be the case that trends towards the commodification of information and news encourage more 'soft news' and 'human interest' stories but this can only be a partial explanation of these developments. When coupled with examples of political exposés such as the 'Cash for Questions' and the *Guardian*'s campaign against corruption of standards in public life, the wider evidence suggests that investigative journalism is yet proving to be effective, flexible and adaptable to some of these key economic and political changes.

Nevertheless, a reduction in newspaper publishing and a rise in magazine publishing has brought about a climate of fierce competition for audiences and readers that places pressure on investigative journalism to change in terms of concept and style. More journalists are now working in entertainment or specialised information provision. The market-driven nature of these changes in journalism is identifiable in the United States where there has been a shift from public affairs reporting on international and national politics to consumer-orientated newspapers (Hallin 1996: 247). Commercial pressure in television journalism has led to the input of market research findings on what audiences 'want to see' in the news in US local-television news (van Zoonen 1998). These changes indicate a significant shift from the public service demo-cratic and professional journalistic imperatives to a new set of journalistic concepts around 'entertainment'.

Van Zoonen cites the example of a new kind of reporter who has emerged in the United States, the 'helicopter journalist' who records sensational action such as car chases, live from the helicopter. Liveness, action and excitement are key entertainment criteria being sought after in the selection of events for the construction of 'information' and 'news'. A further example of market-driven moves towards entertainment style information is the rise of what has been dubbed 'Ken and Barbie journalism'. This involves the male and female duo in local anchor teams who have to be attractive in their appearance and engage in 'happy talk' dialogue as a way of humanising the news. Local television news has had some successes in attracting audiences this way, thereby placing pressure on authoritative national news bulletins such as CBS, NBC and ABC to alter their format as well, much to the annoyance of many journalists (van Zoonen 1998: 40). The erosion of public service ideals and the adoption of these new styles of entertainment journalism, often referred to as 'infotain-ment', are also being experienced in Western European nations such as Britain, The Netherlands and Denmark.

Sources, professional culture and representations

Having looked at the key changes in the political economy of the media that affect investigative journalism, we can turn to the cultural and ideological factors that influence the content of information and news media. Cultural approaches are critical of the political economy perspective on the media. They argue that the structures of media ownership and the supervision and control of journalists' work cannot explain all aspects of information and news production. By examining the contents of the media such as newspapers and television programmes, contributors to critical and cultural studies approaches have claimed that news reporting is largely shaped by cultural and ideological factors. It is useful to trace some of the classic work which has been conducted from the 1970s onwards because it continues to be referred to and debated in media studies, and it helps to pinpoint the key ideological deter-minants that shape the practices and products of journalism. Media studies research outlined below deals indirectly with the particular practices of investigative journalism but the findings provide important clues about the nature of journalistic professionalism, impartiality and the ideological pressures and difficulties faced by all journalists. Investigative journalists' work practices are related to 'news' production in the sense that they share similar kinds of recruitment practices, commercial pressures and organisational constraints in the publication of their reports because they share the same employers, similar professional codes and ethics, and mass communication channels for publishing as other kinds of journalists.

The remarkable consistency of the events, subjects and investigations that become news in western nations is quite striking. Seaton (1995) notes that ease of access to events is generally a stronger determinant of news-making than the significance of the event. News gathering agencies tend to report on events which happen in places that are easy to access, emerge from a reliable and predictable source, exist in a predictable format, and conform to journalists' definitions of news values. For example, specialist reporters find it difficult to expose corruption in the service or profession that they depend on for their sources, such as crime reporting which depends closely on the police for its sources. Seaton confirms media research evidence that '[t]he values which inform the selection of news items usually serve to reinforce conventional opinions and established authority' (Seaton 1995: 265).

A series of British studies on television news bias were conducted by the Glasgow University Media Group in the 1970s and early 1980s. They analysed 22 weeks of British television news coverage of industrial conflicts on all channels. Armed with this extensive videotaped evidence they argued in their first book, *Bad News*, that, far from neutral and impartial, the news is shaped by class biased assumptions. The Glasgow University Media Group (1976a, 1976b, 1982) claimed that news conveys a consistent middle-class ideology because it is biased in three key ways. First, television news misrepresents 'social reality' by deciding the news worthiness of industrial disputes according to criteria other than the facts. News value of events such as strikes is often decided according to criteria such as perceived inconvenience to customers or patients, as in strikes by employees such as nurses, teachers, dustmen or firemen. Second, television news either confirms or fails to question official versions of the economic relations of capitalism. By using a 'restricted code' of news reporting, the dominant ideological consensus is privileged. For instance, industrial disputes, such as the 1975 British Leyland car plant strike, consistently blame the workers rather than balancing reports with evidence about poor management practices and lack of investment in the car plant. The third example of bias is the exclusion of the working class from the media and the creation of a middle class world view and occupational culture by recruiting journalists exclusively from among the middle class. Television media workers are said to have no real understanding of the working class because they are materially and culturally cut off from them. So the dominant middle-class ideology is therefore rarely contradicted by excluding alternative or opposing information.

In 1985 further research was conducted on the British media coverage of war, including the Falklands War, by the Glasgow University Media Group (GUMG). They found that the news reporting of the Falklands War was biased because it was controlled largely by the Ministry of Defence. The journalists' own assessment of public opinion led to the perception that good news should be emphasised and military state and public consensus should be conveyed. The GUMG also found forms of gender bias in war reporting. Women were consistently treated as 'vessels of emotion' by regarding their lives as newsworthy only if they were married to absent servicemen. This emphasised the narrow role for women in society as familial and emotional caretakers of husbands. The status of women in journalism is revisited in more detail in Chapter 6.

The GUMG have been criticised for shortcomings in their approach and interpretation of findings. The shortcomings identified involve problems with the way they interpreted bias, the fact that they ignored institutional factors that influence news production, and the lack of any study of audience receptions of the news (Stevenson 1995). They overemphasised the significance of the social background of journalists at the expense of workplace culture. Other research on media workplace practices came to a different set of conclusions, indicating that the mechanisms of control in media institutions determined by the media industry's links with big business are more fundamental constraints placed on journalists than the professional ones placed on them (Schlesinger 1978, 1990, Kumar 1975). This returns us to the explanations of the political economy approach. Also, in work contexts such as journalism where tasks are event-driven, the valuing of immediacy and speed of news and investigative reporting are often more influential in the construction of the news than the consistency of ideological perspectives (Schlesinger 1990).

The appointment of specialist correspondents in particular fields, such as the 'environmental correspondent' or 'industrial correspondent', is a further factor that can influence the amount of attention devoted to the topic in news construction. Before the 1980s, for example, 'industrial correspondents' and 'labour correspondents' were prominent in newsrooms and so industrial strife was given a high priority. Then, during Thatcher's government in the 1980s, the power of trade unions and organised labour were systematically weakened. Industrial news decreased and the category of industrial or labour correspondent was no longer centrally needed. This further contributed to the marginalising or loss of industrial and labour issues within news agendas (McNair 1998).

Stuart Hall conducted studies of the moral panics that arose around the media reporting of mugging in Britain. He claimed that media texts are not neutral, they are shaped by the belief systems and world views of media-makers and journalists and are therefore 'ideologically' coded. He and colleagues wrote a seminal text in 1978 entitled *Policing the Crisis* about the ways in which the moral panic led by the press about mugging and the erosion of post-war consensus politics were connected to the rise of an authoritarian state in 1970s Britain. The news media over-reacted to the alleged threat of violence by black youth and other 'deviants' who seemed to be threatening the social order. The term 'mugging' was imported to Britain from the United States and used by the dominant culture under the Thatcher government to destabilise consensus politics of social democracy. A spiralling of press reports about mugging was encouraged by more black offenders being sent to court, caused by increased police organisation against deviant members of the black community.

The police were more likely to be approached as sources of information by journalists because black suspects were not considered appropriate definers of reality by virtue of being seen as criminals. So one viewpoint was consistently being reported. The study was significant because it showed the impact that 'primary' and 'secondary' definers of events have on news reporting. Primary definers of events were seen to be structurally dominant groups in society, such as the police and the courts. Secondary definers of events included the media – by journalistically selecting and interpreting information received from these primary definers. Since the police and courts were the only primary definers, their views were given greater ideological weight, which created a high level of cultural closure in the news media's interpretation of the events. This led to a moral panic around mugging. By contrast, in events such as industrial disputes there would normally have been competing primary definers such as trade unions, as well as management.

The 1999 government report into the murder of a black youth, Stephen Lawrence, and its declaration of institutionalised racism in the police force, indicates the currency of such issues and social influences.[1] Lawrence was stabbed to death in South London in 1993 by five white youths who were identified as suspects but not apprehended by the police for approximately three weeks and who have not, to date, been convicted for the crime. A catalogue of incompetencies was cited including the failure of the police to treat Lawrence's condition or the incident as an emergency since they assumed Lawrence had provoked the fight because he was black. Prompted by the lobbying work of Stephen Lawrence's parents, British journalists took the lead in exposing the incompetence, evasiveness and indifference of the Metropolitan Police. The *Daily Mail* even revealed the identities of the five suspects (who could not be prosecuted due to a legal technicality), which prompted a public debate about the ethics of doing so.

Critical of the work of *Bad News* and *Policing the Crisis*, Schlesinger (1990) argues that the strategies of negotiation between journalists and their sources must be looked at as closely as the internal media institutional process in order to understand the complex process of journalistic reporting. He says that media theory should develop a distinction between an internalist and externalist account of the processes of journalism. Whereas the Glasgow group tended to over-emphasise the internal effects of middle class journalistic culture, the *Policing the Crisis* research overstated the police as external definers of events. In his study of Thatcherism, Stuart Hall investigated the ways in which the New Right developed a strategy of 'authoritarian populism' to intensify state control over civil society. He found that Thatcherism was able to weave a whole range of ideological themes into a coherent popular discourse, that is, into a common sense framework of thinking that was conveyed to the mass of society. It was not simply within government that this popular discourse was articulated, but it was precisely through civil society, particularly the privately owned tabloid press, that the agenda of the New Right was communicated to the public.

However, the theme of ideology is somewhat over-emphasised in Hall's studies of the media. He has been criticised for ignoring the ownership and control of the mass media as a key factor of influence on news media. Hall concentrates on the construction of media messages at the expense of an understanding of the political economy of the media, and neglects the increasing integration of distinctive media sectors and the international reach of media conglomerates as a key determinant. Political economists, Golding and Murdock (1979) argue that the ideological variety of the newspaper industry is determined by the distribution of economic resources. The British press is mainly right-wing precisely because of the vast financial outlays needed to enter what are now international markets, and the need for advertising revenue that alternative publications fail to attract. Nevertheless, the critical cultural school raises a number of important issues about the ideological nature of information and news reporting and needs to be combined with the findings of the political economy approach.

The employment of journalists

A further feature of intensified commercial competition emerging from the deregulation of the media is the growing casualisation of the journalism profession, as Franklin (1997) points out. When new print and broadcast technologies were introduced in the 1980s to reduce the costs of news production, management–worker relations were also restructured. Newspaper proprietors and managers were given more powers in their control over printers and journalists and journalists' trade unions were no longer recognised. In place of union negotiated salaries and conditions, individual contracts were offered to journalists which led to sharply differing salaries and conditions of service between employees. Today, journalists no longer have the resources to create a united front against those editorial or management decisions that subordinate journalistic concerns to market and advertising demands.

With developments such as electronic news gathering and digital cameras, journalists have found that their working practices have been extended beyond investigation and writing to include the recording, editing and production of film reports. Franklin (1997: 18) claims that these changes result in the shedding of labour and an erosion in editorial quality of news reports compared to large news-gathering organisations. Increased redundancies have led to a rise in freelance work among journalists as a feature of the growing casualisation of the journalist profession in order to reduce the overhead costs of staff for media businesses. Access to computer technology such as laptop personal computers and the Internet have helped journalists to shift to freelancing (also see Chapter 9 on new technology in investigative journalism). This has led to a significant expansion in freelance journalism. But Franklin is rather gloomy in his forecast about the profession's future, pointing out that:

> Freelances have become conscripts rather than volunteers, with redundancy and lack of job opportunities cited as the major reasons for freelance status. The most able and experienced freelances can write copy for any market, in any house style, to any employer-specified objective, and can deploy the most sophisticated electronic technologies to sustain them.
>
> (p. 19)

This new breed of freelancers work from home and are cut off from the news room and professional culture of journalism with no opportunity to participate in editorial decision-making processes. Franklin suggests that these changes may force further journalistic dependence on editors' demands for particular stories, and allows little time or other resources to engage in in-depth investigative research.

There has been a rise in demand for public relations and journalistic skills by business and government organisations in the form of press offices, press agents and public relations staff in central and local government organisations, political parties and interest groups, voluntary organisations and private corporations (Deacon and Golding 1994, Franklin 1994). Franklin states that a drop in job opportunities in journalism has coincided with this trend. Yet public relations officers have had a significant impact on the editorial content of news media. A key feature of news media in the last couple of decades has been its increased editorial reliance on public relations staff such as press officers at the expense of news journalists, and the proliferation of media material generated by PR. As Franklin states, 'this growing army of journalism-competent public relations specialists and freelances increasingly subordinate such professional values to the requirements of commercial values or political persuasion' (1997: 20). Public relations and press officers are not in the business of investigating in-depth issues in the public interest. They are not impartial, neutral observers but 'hired prize fighters' for sectional interests. Their brief is to persuade rather than inform. The outcome of this trend of buying in journalistic skills for public relations purposes is a privatisation of journalism and may lead to an erosion of the profession's principles of public accountability and public interest.

Conclusion

Investigative journalism has been booming but there is evidence to suggest that the conditions that led to this boom are now changing. Current shifts towards private media ownership by international conglomerates and the intensification of commercial competition and media practices have had a number of profound consequences for the cultural production of 'information' that are gradually impinging on the profession and the news media as a whole. The strong idealism surrounding the profession clearly continues to inspire the expository work outlined elsewhere in this book, but in increasingly new forms of consumer-orientated investigative journalism. Five key consequences of these changes have been identified in this chapter. First, the movement of large private corporations into the public arena has hampered the fourth estate role of journalism as a service to democracy, and undermined the ideal of press freedom by using it to protect the publishing rights of owners of the media. A second effect of deregulation has been the reluctance of governments to control media monopolies. They have been criticised by the political economy approach for being influenced by international media magnates. A third trend is that media deregulation has led to the treatment of information and news as a commodity, leading to a 'tabloidisation' of information and consumer-style investigative journalism through the intensifying competition for audiences and advertisers. A fourth problem is about the difficulties in achieving balanced reporting. A lack of journalistic resources has led to increasing reliance on fewer and mostly primary definers of events and on press officers as sources. A fifth outcome is the increasing dominance of the public relations profession which promotes the privatisation of journalistic skills and ideals. There has also been a distinctive expansion in investigative journalism but Franklin (1997) claims this may be connected to a casualisation of the profession. This remains to be seen. The fate of investigative journalism is tied both to the dynamics of media ownership and control and to the effectiveness of future protection of the profession's role of servicing democracy. When all these factors about the changing environment of journalism are put together, it shows that a fundamental restructuring of state regulatory frameworks is needed so as to safeguard the future of investigative journalism.

NOTE

1   The Stephen Lawrence Public Inquiry Report was an independent judicial inquiry produced by Sir William Macpherson of Cluny, published by the Stationery Office on 24 February 1999.

BIBLIOGRAPHY

Bagdikian, B. (1988) *The Media Monopoly*. Boston: Beacon Press.

Blanchard, M. A. (1977) The Hutchins Commission, the press and the responsibility concept. *Journalism Monographs*, 49.

Carter, C., Branston, G. and Allan, S. (1998) *News, Gender and Power*. London: Routledge.

Chomsky, N. (1987) *Manufacturing Consent*. New York: Pantheon.

Chomsky, N. and Herman, E. (1979) *The Political Economy of Human Rights*, Volumes 1 and 2. Boston: South End Press.

Comor, E. A. (1997) The re-tooling of American hegemony: US foreign communication policy from free flow to free trade. In A. Sreberny-Mohammadi, D. Winseck, J. McKenna and O. Boyd-Barrett (eds) *Media in Global Context, A Reader*. London: Edward Arnold.

Curran, J. (1991) Mass media and democracy: a reappraisal. In J. Curran and M. Gurevitch (eds) *Mass Media and Society*. London: Edward Arnold.

Curran, J. and Gurevitch, M. (eds) (1991) *Mass Media and Society*. London: Edward Arnold.

Curran, J. and Seaton, J. (1997) *Power without Responsibility: The Press and Broadcasting in Britain*, 5th edn. London: Routledge.

Deacon, D. and Golding, P. (1994) *Taxation and Representation: The Media, Political Communication and the Poll Tax*. London: John Libbey.

Demac, D. A. and Sung, L. (1995) New communication technologies and deregulation. In J. Downing, A. Mohammadi and A. Sreberny-Mohammadi (eds) *Questioning the Media: A Critical Introduction*, 2nd edn. London: Sage.

Downing, J., Mohammadi, A., Sreberny-Mohammadi, A. (eds) (1995) *Questioning the Media: A Critical Introduction*, 2nd edn. London: Sage.

Ferguson, M. (1990) Electronic media and redefining time and space. In M. Ferguson (ed.) *Public Communication, the New Imperatives: Future Directions for Media Research*. London: Sage.

Franklin, B. (1997) *Newszak and News Media*. London: Edward Arnold.

Franklin, B. (1994) *Packaging Politics: Political Communications in Britain's Media Democracy*. London: Edward Arnold.

Garnham, N. (1986) The media and the public sphere. In P. Golding and G. Murdock (eds) *Communicating Politics*. Leicester: Leicester University Press: 37–54.

Glasgow University Media Group (1976a) *Bad News*. London: Routledge and Kegan Paul.

Glasgow University Media Group (1976b) *More Bad News*. London: Routledge and Kegan Paul.

Glasgow University Media Group (1982) *Really Bad News*. London: Writers and Readers Publishing Co-operative.

Glasgow University Media Group (1985) *War and Peace News*. Milton Keynes: Open University Press.

Glasser, T. (1986) Press responsibility and First Amendment values. In D. Eliott (ed.), *Responsible Journalism*. London and Newbury Park, CA: Sage.

Golding, P. and Murdock, G. (1979) Ideology and the mass media: the question of determination. In M. Barrett, P. Corrigan, A. Kuhn and J. Wolff (eds) *Ideology and Cultural Production*. London: Croom Helm.

Golding, P. and Murdock, G. (eds) (1986), *Communicating Politics*. Leicester: Leicester University Press: 37–54.

Golding, P. and Murdock, G. (1991) Theories of communication and theories of society. *Communication Research*, 5 (3): 390–56.

Gurevitch, M. (ed) (1982) *Culture, Society and the Media*. London: Methuen.

Hall, S. (1980) Coding and encoding in the television discourse. In S. Hall, D. Hobson, A. Lowe and P. Willis (eds) *Culture, Media Language*. London: Hutchinson: 197–208.

Hall, S. (1982) The rediscovery of 'ideology': return of the repressed in media studies. In M. Gurevitch (ed.) *Culture, Society and the Media*. London: Methuen.

Hall, S. (1988) Thatcherism amongst the theorists: toad in the garden. In C. Nelson and L. Grossberg (eds) *Marxism and the Interpretation of Culture*. London: Macmillan.

Hall, S., Critcher, C., Jefferson, T., Clarke, J., and Roberts, B. (eds) (1978) *Policing the Crisis: Mugging, the State and Law and Order*. London: Macmillan.

Hallin, D. (1996) Commercialism and professionalism in the American news media. In J. Curran and M. Gurevitch (eds) *Mass Media and Society*. London: Edward Arnold.

Hamelink, C. J. (1995) Information imbalance across the globe. In J. Downing, A. Mohammadi and A. Sreberny-Mohammadi (eds) *Questioning the Media: A Critical Introduction*, second edn. London: Sage.

Hamelink, C. (1999) International communication: global market and morality. In A. Mohammadi (ed.) *International Communication and Globalisation*. London: Sage.

Herman, E. (1995) Media in the US political economy. In J. Downing, A. Mohammadi and A. Sreberny-Mohammadi (eds) *Questioning the Media: A Critical Introduction*, 2nd edn. London: Sage.

Hutchins, R. (1947) Commission on the freedom of the press: *A Free and Responsible Press*. Chicago: University of Chicago Press.

Kellner, D. (1992) *The Persian Gulf TV War*. Boulder, CO: Westview Press.

Knightley, P. (1982) The Falklands: how Britannia ruled the news. *Columbia Journalism Review*, September.

Kumar, C. (1975) Holding the middle ground. *Sociology*, 9 (3): 67–88. Reprinted in J. Curran et al. (eds) *Mass Communication and Society*. London: Edward Arnold: 231–48.

McNair, B. (1998) *The Sociology of Journalism*. London: Edward Arnold.

McQuail, D. (1994) *Mass Communication Theory*, 3rd edn. London: Sage.

Melody, W. H. (1990) 'Communications policy in the global information economy', in Ferguson, M. F. (ed) (1990) *Public Communication: The New Imperatives*, London: Sage.

Murdock, G. (1990) Redrawing the map of the communication industries. In M. Ferguson (ed.) *Public Communication*. London: Sage.

Murdock, G. and Golding, P. (1977) Capitalism, communication and class relations. In J. Curran, M. Gurevitch and J. Woollacott (eds) *Mass Communication and Society*. London: Edward Arnold.

Paterson, C. (1997) Global television news services. In A. Sreberny-Mohammadi, D. Winseck, J. McKenna and O. Boyd-Barrett (eds) *Media in Global Context: A Reader*. London: Edward Arnold.

Patten, C. (1998) *East and West*. Basingstoke: Macmillan.

Schlesinger, P. (1978) *Putting Reality Together*. London: Constable.

Schlesinger, P. (1990) Rethinking the sociology of journalism: sources, strategies and the limits of media-centrism. In M. Ferguson (ed.) *Public Communication: The New Imperatives*. London and Newbury Park, CA: Sage.

Seaton, J. (1995) In J. Curran and J. Seaton *Power without Responsibility: The Press and Broadcasting in Britain*. London: Routledge.

Sreberny-Mohammadi, A., Winseck, D., McKenna, J. and Boyd-Barrett, O. (eds) *Media in Global Context, A Reader*. London: Edward Arnold.

Stevenson, N. (1995) *Understanding Media Cultures: Social Theory and Mass Communication*. London: Sage.

van Zoonen, L. (1998) One of the girls? The changing gender of journalism. In C. Carter, G. Branston and S. Allan (eds) *News, Gender and Power*. London: Routledge.

FURTHER READING

Downing, J., Mohammadi, A. and Sreberny-Mohammadi, A. (eds) (1995) *Questioning the Media: A Critical Introduction*, 2nd edn. London: Sage.
Franklin, B. (1997) *Newszak and News Media*. London: Edward Arnold.
McNair, B. (1998) *The Sociology of Journalism*. London: Edward Arnold.
McQuail, D. (1994) *Mass Communication Theory*, 3rd edn. London: Sage.

6

GLOBALISING MEDIA AGENDAS

The production of journalism

Deborah Chambers

Introduction

Because investigative journalism upholds people's right to know about controversial issues and events through media exposure, it is central to debates about the public sphere. The public sphere is a stage, now international in its reach, on which profound economic and ideological struggles are played out about who controls and decides to expose information, who the information speaks on behalf of, and whose voices are excluded and silenced in the process. The ideal of democratic communication expressed in the term 'public sphere' foregrounds the central debates surrounding the nature of balanced public communication among 'equal' citizens. It leads to discussions about the impact of the global reach of media markets on 'quality' forms of information and democratic fora for dialogue.

This chapter begins by looking at the concept of the 'public sphere' developed by Jurgen Habermas (1989), and its implications for investigative journalism. It asks whether there ever was a golden era in which the public interest and democratic ideals of the public sphere existed, whether these ideals and potentials are now being eroded by the globalisation of news media or whether they are being reshaped by new forms of communication. The chapter then looks at some of the key features and relevance of media globalisation to journalism. The deregulation and globalisation of information and news media impacts on the public sphere in a number of ways. Three areas are focused on: the production of Anglo-American and Western information and news by global news agencies, the reporting of international human rights violations, and the status of women in journalism. Chapter 17 takes up the themes of Anglo-American influences and human rights, showing how they are articulated within the specific example of the documentary film *Laogai* (Yorkshire Television 1993) in which a Chinese investigative journalist, Harry Wu, and his wife investigated the human rights violations in China's penal system.

The decline of the public sphere?

Citizenship and membership of the public are manifestations of democracy conventionally measured in Western nations by the right to vote and the right to engage in public debate. Provisions in international human rights law on freedom of expression reflect this by implying that 'people have the right to be informed about matters of public interest' (Hamelink 1999: 106–7). So these provisions indicate that the public sphere needs to be defended as the arena in which this democratic communication of information takes place. By providing a check against excessive power and informing the people about major issues of public interest, investigative journalism performs a vital role in promoting a democratic public sphere (Kellner 1992a).

Habermas studied the ways in which public cultures in social democracies could best conduct rational political debate among differing groups and interests (Habermas 1989, Garnham 1986). He claims that we are now facing a decline in the 'public' and a disenfranchisement of citizens caused by an intensified shift towards privatised consumer-orientated cultures in which information and entertainment become commodities bought and sold for profit. Whether it be through interactive and direct forms such as telephone or the Internet, or through mass and centrally controlled modes of communication such as broadcasting or the press, Habermas's thesis is that the public domain within which we communicate is coming increasingly under the control of private commercial interests. Does the evidence support his claims?

The rights and responsibilities of mass communication can only flourish if unhampered either by the power of the state or the power of commercial enterprise, according to Habermas. He points to a golden era during the rise of a bourgeois 'public sphere' in seventeenth and eighteenth century Europe as an ideal model that has since been lost. This public sphere was located within a civil zone independent of state or commercial control. Members of the aristocracy, intellectuals and bourgeoisie met in coffee houses and salons to engage in open discussions about the arts and politics. Although taking part in debates in this public sphere was exclusive to men of property and high class, Habermas believed that it contained a strong critical potential because this was the first time that the quality of an argument was regarded as more important than the status of the person delivering it (Stevenson 1996). A principle of 'publicity' emerged in which the pursuit of reason and truth outweighed that of private gain, and the notion of a public sphere and the 'public good' came to ensure the exposure of corruption and domination. This principle of publicity coincides with the principles of investigative journalism.

The early newspaper business was said to have been situated within this public sphere during the period of literary journalism up to the nineteenth century. It was not a profit-driven enterprise but part of the leisured interests of the aristocracy, characterised by small handicraft concerns. From the 1870s the public sphere was gradually eroded by the rise of large scale commercial enterprises such as the newspaper industry. The rise of monopoly capitalism began to transform the press into a commercial concern. Literary modes of writing were replaced by the work of specialist journalists who served the private interests of news proprietors. It was being suggested that in contrast to the old print culture of seventeenth and eighteenth century Europe, the products of modern commercial culture such as newspapers, radio television and film were now being consumed in private with little potential for public interaction and debate. The rise of a commercialised and privatised press coincided with a trivialisation and glamorisation of culture and led to the emergence of mass cultural forms. Habermas claims that these changes undermined democratic communication and have brought about a refeudalisation of the public sphere. Today, this sphere of society is being transformed into a commercially manipulated political circus, culminating in public political spectacles such as the American presidential elections (Stevenson 1996). The key claim being made here is that people are nowadays being addressed as 'consumers' rather than as 'citizens'.

In order to point to an example of what a democratic model of public communication could look like, Habermas developed a theory of balanced communication. It was based on an 'ideal speech situation', as an Utopian model, in which people could communicate on an equal basis, free of constraints. The ideal may be impossible to obtain but for Habermas this kind of model is a useful measure of the kinds of communication constraints and imbalances that exist in real life from public protests to investigative journalism. Nick Stevenson (1995) applies Habermas's thesis to the evolution of the British press whereby the commercialisation of newspaper industry led to the two basic types of press, 'quality' and 'tabloid'. The former caters for a small, highly-educated and well-informed audience whose high purchasing power attracts advertisers. The latter attracts a low income group and little advertising power and is therefore dependent on a mass audience circulation. The tabloid press no longer takes on the role of a forum for rational debate. The colonisation of the press by commercial interests is said to have led to the trivialisation of its content and the exclusion of the masses from the crucial debating arenas of our culture. This disenfranchisement of the masses from the centres of political debate means that modern culture now lacks critical forms of dialogue. Along with the erosion of the public sphere, the autonomy of professional communicators such as investigative journalists is also eroded by commercial interests.

This argument is a somewhat nostalgic reinvention of a golden past yet, interestingly, the increased commercialisation of the media has led to renewed defence of public service broadcasting and a re-evaluation of its role in upholding the public sphere in the twenty-first century. Public service broadcasting is seen to occupy a space in civil society that is independent from both state and commercial interests (Scannel et al. 1995). And this is exactly the same role that investigative journalism should be able to play. Both address the public as *citizens* rather than as *consumers* and both offer diverse groups and communities the opportunity – through information communication – to enter into dialogue with one another. In addition to his nostalgia for a by-gone era, we can identify four key drawbacks to Habermas's thesis. First he failed to account for the significant institutional tension between the economy, the state and public service broadcasting as Stevenson (1996) points out. He over-estimated the extent to which the media is responsible for reproducing unequal power relations. The media are not autonomous but reflect existing power relations outside and beyond it. Second, Habermas has been criticised for failing to take account of the active and interpretative ability of audiences, treating them as somewhat passive. Third, the concept of the public sphere excludes women. It tends to legitimate the marginalising and exploitation of women because women have traditionally been excluded from public debate (Landes 1988, Fraser 1992, Ryan 1992, Pateman 1988, Cohen 1996, McLaughlin 1998). These issues are returned to below in the discussion of women and journalism. A fourth criticism is that 'the public' is a constantly shifting concept, being reconstructed all the time. The Internet has been cited as an example of this.

Rather than just another example of the commercialisation of knowledge, as Habermas would have us believe, is online communication via the Internet and World Wide Web a new form of media technology with the potential to reformulate the public sphere? Traditional social contexts of public debate are being reshaped by the emergence of interest-group web sites and the rise of a computer literate public. This new form of communication crosses national boundaries and challenges conventional ideas about the free market of infor-mation. It has proved itself to be an indispensable tool of communication during the 1999 Balkan War between Nato and Serbia. Journalists and civil-ians from Kosovo and Serbia have been able to overcome the censorship of the Serbian state-controlled Tanjug news agency by getting messages out of the war zone through the Internet. The immediacy of this mode of commu-nication is impressive. For example, on 8 May the *Guardian* reported a resident of Nis in Serbia who posted a message on the Internet to say that his father had just returned from shopping and reported the showering of Nato cluster bombs on a crowded market and hospital (which Nato were unable to confirm or refute concerning the collateral damage as they had no personnel on the ground).

The Internet has the potential to constitute a public forum by altering structures of community and political representation (Poster 1997). It is being used to contribute to social and political change by uniting disadvantaged and marginal groups across the world such as the gay community, the disabled and refugees (see Jones 1997). Some argue that the Internet can even become a forum for underground political organisation and critique.[1] Yet there are serious problems about how to evaluate and assess the credibility and merits of the information being produced by the plethora of voices participating in communicating diverse and often contradictory views on the Internet (Grossberg et al. 1998: 381). There has been a vast growth in groups promoting racist material on the net, with around 600 sites available and tens of thousands of hits per month (Bloomfield 1999). This is raising public concern in the wake of racist and homophobic bombing campaigns in London's Brixton, Brick Lane and Soho in April 1999. On the other hand, certain nations – such as Iraq during the period of the 1991 and 1998 Gulf Wars – have been denied access to the Internet and World Wide Web as a result of international trade embargoes that prevent telecommunications businesses from delivering the necessary hardware, software and online facilities to 'enemy' nations. These kinds of actions raise important questions about censorship of information on the net and blocks to the potential for online communication technology to be a tool of peace-making processes. The Internet is essentially a private, commercial project financed by big business and access is limited to those individuals who can afford to pay the fee to access an online computer. Claims for a world 'information revolution' are somewhat misleading given that many parts of the Third World still do not have access to electricity or telephones let alone satellite television or online computers linked to the World Wide Web, as Hamelink (1995) points out.

The Internet exemplifies the trend towards a privatisation of information. But the evidence also suggests that, when accessible, the Internet can be used for or against the public interest. For investigative journalism, it becomes both a crucial tool and a forum for accessing and disseminating information glob-ally (see Chapter 8). But so far, this form of communication cannot guarantee the dominance of truth and reason over private or personal gain in securing Habermas's version of a public sphere. Habermas highlighted the failure of the so-called 'information age' to produce a form of citizenship founded on easy access to reasoned and truthful public debate, and accurate and impartial information. We can agree that the idea of the 'public' is inherently locked into the mass media and that there is a potential for the reinvention of the 'public' through new modes of communication such as the Internet. Yet Habermas did not account properly for the rise of a more international global sphere and the distinctive yet changing nature of local public spheres. The notion of the decline of the 'public' and the rise of privatised information through the Internet raise important questions about the role of investigative journalism and the rise or fall of a public forum in which citizens' 'right to know' can be protected from commercial or state interference.

The globalisation of Western and Anglocentric information and news

The activities of transnational institutions are increasingly ignoring the barriers of the nation state. Discussion about the 'public sphere' and the role of journalism in upholding democratic communication are increasingly taking place in a global context. Sparks (1992) points out that a global public sphere is emerging from which certain elite groups are benefiting, such as the readership of certain quality newspapers. There are also newly emerging local public cultures in Western nations such as Britain in which small groups come together as single-issue protest groups to discuss and publicly protest *global* themes such as animal rights, nuclear disarmament, gay politics and environmental issues, despite being labelled 'single issue'. Many of these groups have produced small-scale and independent press and information networks. Habermas ignored these cultural processes because his writing on the public sphere is grounded in the nation state. To some extent, however, the same kinds of trends are happening on a global scale that Habermas identified in the nation state. During the 1980s and 1990s the deregulation of the media augmented an internationalisation of the flows of media content, expanding the market for television programming, film and news throughout the world.

The term 'globalisation' refers to the intensification of global interconnectedness through a whole range of relations such as international communications and media networks, financial systems, the expansion of transnational corporate activity, and the increasing flow of people including migrants, refugees and tourists across national boundaries (Giddens 1990, Tomlinson 1999). These features of global change provide a strong argument for reassessing the nature of information and news and the practices of investigative journalism at an international level. It is no longer possible to study the national or local news media without referring to these global forces of information circulation (see, for example, Boyd-Barratt 1997 and Sreberny-Mohammadi et al. 1997). There are several contradictory views about the consequences of increasing mass communication between nations and regions. One scenario is that globalisation can lead to international peace and understanding between nations during this post-Cold War period. A second scenario suggests that the rise of transnational media businesses leads to the homogenisation of culture and may erode distinctive national and local cultures across the world through an 'Americanisation' of other cultures, particularly poorer and weaker Third World nations. A third scenario is that global telecommunications systems may lead to a rich cultural diversity and hybridity that is expressive of a local community's complex cultural and economic interconnections with other nations, regions and identities (see, for example, Golding and Harris 1996, Featherstone 1996, Giddens 1990, Tomlinson 1991 and 1999).

The leading news agencies that report and film the news for the press and broadcast media are a good example of organisations that operate in and beyond national boundaries. Powerful agencies such as Reuters (UK) and Associated Press (USA) are international in their reach. In fact, Boyd-Barrett and Rantanen (1998) suggest that they were the first type of global media organisations and multinational corporations to exist. Together with major 'retail' global broadcasters such as CNNI and BBC World Service Television (WSTV), and the Murdoch channels (BSkyB in Europe, Fox in the USA and

Star TV in Asia), these major international news agencies tend to reinforce an Anglo-American tradition of news by narrowing down the diversity of sources in local and national media. By defining the nature of information and news on a global scale they define the very nature of 'local' and 'global' issues and events in Western terms, according to Boyd-Barrett (1997). He claims that international news agencies' origination in the world's ex-imperial capitals and their intimate ties with 'First World' nations are common charac- teristics. They all have wealthy domestic markets to support transnational forays, they sell a similar product – 'spot news' – in a competitive environment, and are dominant partners in relationship with national agencies. The Western- based global news agencies are thereby contributing to the narrow definition and formulation of information and news as events about elite, Western nations and people and their own – albeit internationalised – conflicts and interests. Western interests are taken as the norm in their 'skewed global maps privileging news from Western Europe, the United States and theatres of activity elsewhere which [have] direct relevance to Western concerns' (Boyd- Barrett 1997: 143). The issue is discussed further in Chapter 17 in connection with Yorkshire Television's documentary film, *Laogai*. This kind of evidence suggests that the so-called 'free flow of information' may be predominantly a one-way flow of trade and information from the United States and other Western countries to Third World nations which impacts directly on the quality of information and news production world wide (see, for example, Sreberny-Mohammadi et al. 1997).[2]

Anglo-American information and news products have become important determinants of how global audiences perceive other nations and global issues. Paterson (1997: 148) points out that there is considerable conformity in the images and texts used by broadcasters world wide because so few news *sources* are shared in common world wide. 'Television tells stories best when it can illustrate them with exciting and graphic pictures, but such pictures cost more to provide from Africa than they do from Chicago or London' (ibid.: 152). It is more risky and more expensive to cover world issues, as the discus- sion in the following section about human rights reporting demonstrates. This risk and expense influences the quantity, quality and kind of investigative reporting that gets supported and financed. It influences the overall coverage decisions of the international news agencies and results in the global projec- tion of more events from the USA and the UK than anywhere else in the world. It increases the priority given to news and investigative events and issues in the USA, the UK and other Western nations. The shift from tradi- tional investigative reporting to consumer-style investigative journalism has been justified by appeals to notions of 'efficiency' and has also led to an emphasis on the cheaper production of 'pre-packaged' news events (Carter et al. 1998: 4). Videos of the same news stories from the same sources are placed in almost the same slot in newscasts all over the world on the same evening according to Malik's (1992) evidence. This confirms that international television news coverage is increasingly becoming homogenised (cit. in Paterson 1997). The world wide conformity of news coverage is taking place at the same time as the proliferation of news services that are ideologically identical, Anglocentric and share the same information sources.

Investigative journalism and human rights

International communication about human rights issues relies heavily on public exposure by investigative reporting. The democratic model of Western investigative journalism has had, through its reports, far-reaching liberating effects on regimes that violate human rights. The global news agencies' reports of events such as the Tiananmen Square massacre in 1993 in China are the kinds of examples we can point to. Yet human rights reporting demands a form of investigative journalism that is dangerous and costly, and is not adequately supported by the information media world wide (Hamelink, 1999: 112). Although the trend towards global digital information technologies allows unprecedented access to information, it is a market-driven industry in which the commercialisation of information 'implies that price and not public interest is the decisive factor'.

Hamelink (1996) suggests that investigative journalism is gradually being transformed into 'safe' journalism by the transformation of information into a commodity. By this he means that reporting on human rights violations is becoming very expensive to support effectively because it operates in, and is resourced by a market-driven context where competition for profits is paramount. Journalists have been killed and injured in a number of dangerous situations across the globe resulting in a dramatic rise in their insurance premiums. With up to thirty bodyguards being used by the large American broadcast networks to protect their staff in dangerous circumstances, most broadcasters will not send their journalists to perceived international 'trouble spots'. The very form of cover needed for war correspondents' 'forays' inevitably makes objective and accurate reporting very difficult. This was shown in the Falklands Crisis of 1982 and the Gulf War of 1991 where journalists were obliged to travel on the British and Allied Navy bulk carriers and continuously received their protection from the side of the Allied Forces in reporting the events (see, for example, Knightley 1982 and Kellner 1992b). Journalists were compromised in their attempts to report impartially about the actions of the British or Allied forces. Human rights violations caused by the Allied forces during the 1991 Gulf War were not reported in the Anglo-American media (Kellner 1992b).

When liberationist forces as well as oppressive regimes violate human rights, as in the case of the South African ANC during the apartheid struggles of the 1980s, opinions are divided about which side to accuse of violations. White South African journalists were under great pressure not to report human rights violations. In the 1990s Middle East war between Israel and the

Islamic group Hizbollah, the latter were typically labelled as the terrorists by the deployment of specific vocabulary as, for instance, the 'pro-Iranian Hizbollah' in descriptions about the tribe in news reports (Trendle 1996). Being financially supported and armed by the USA, Israel tended to be treated by Western, particularly American, journalistic reports as the 'good guys'. Israel invaded and imposed a 9-mile deep 'security zone' in Lebanon in 1982 which journalists have referred to as the 'so-called security zone' and sometimes the 'Israeli occupied zone'. Claiming that this stretch of Lebanese land is Israel's security zone implied that Israel's security is more important than Lebanon's experience of invasion (Trendle 1996). The Lebanese civilians are the populations who have suffered most in terms of casualties. For example, in 1996 Israel launched a prolonged bombing attack of southern Lebanon, in the so-called 'Grapes of Wrath' operation, which led to the death of around 200 Lebanese civilians. The Western press have tended to rely on reports from the Israeli militia which are rarely balanced by details of casualties suffered by the Lebanese or Hizbollah. Both sides of the war have been violating human rights, but one side, the stronger military power – is implicitly supported by Western journalists while the Lebanese civilians' suffering has largely been ignored.

These are examples of the kinds of dangers and constraints that journalists have to face and work under in their attempts to produce balanced reports about human rights violations both in war and peace time. There are several factors involved in the construction of Western-centric, often Anglocentric, standpoints and the decline in media reporting of human rights violations. Two key factors have been identified here. First, journalists are often forced to rely on protection from the military personnel of one side of the dispute, thereby encouraging accounts from that government's viewpoint. Second, the difficulty of access to non-Western sources and protagonists is compounded by an over-dependence on official sources and sources from nations which are Anglo-American or Western friendly.

The commercialisation of information deters the media from providing sufficient resources to finance the quality investigative reports needed for public debate about international human rights. Apart from the Non-Government Organisations (NGOs), such as Amnesty International, there are few avenues beyond the mass media in Western societies for publicising human rights violations. In fact, NGOs themselves rely on the media for the effectiveness of their campaigns. As Hamelink (1996) states, violations take place precisely because people do not protest about it. So long as human rights issues do not get publicly debated through the mass media it is likely that international forms of human rights protection will remain weak. Well-informed public debate is essential to a globalising world order and investigative journalism should be allowed to play a central role in creating it. But governments do not appear to be ready to organise world debate and neither does big business.

Women and journalism

The lack of research information on the role and status of women in investigative journalism within media and communication studies makes it difficult to address the topic, but research conducted in several countries during the 1980s about women across print and broadcasting journalism provides indications about their standing within the profession as a whole. The findings have consistently revealed that newspaper and television journalism is dominated by men in the sense that women are over-represented in the 'low grade' positions while they are under-represented at the executive producer level (Skidmore 1998, Dougary 1994, van Zoonen 1994 and 1998). There is even evidence that women with equivalent experience and qualifications as their male colleagues are paid less for doing the same work. Van Zoonen (1998) shows that these kinds of inequalities result from recruitment practices that tend to favour men, coupled with discriminatory attitudes among some decision-makers. She also reported contributing factors, shared by many other professions, of the burden of childcare placed on women but not on male colleagues who had children as well as sexist behaviour towards women within the professional culture.

Public communication can only contribute effectively to a democratic public sphere if women are able to participate on equal terms with men yet, as McLaughlin (1998) and others have pointed out, Habermas's model of the public sphere excludes access for women. Ideas of 'publicity' and the 'public sphere' are profoundly problematic to women in societies where an ideology of 'separate spheres' has sustained powerful myths of segregated gendered space. The suggestion is that 'men's issues' tend to be equated with the 'public sphere' and deemed as serious and newsworthy events whereas 'women's issues' are often associated with the 'private' or 'domestic sphere' and given a lower status and priority (Davidoff and Hall 1994). McLaughlin recommends that we integrate Habermas's concerns about democratic participation in communication with the findings of critical studies on women and communication.

Interestingly, the history of past famous investigative journalists uncovers the crucial role that women in journalism have played in political struggles to place women's rights and needs on the agenda within the public sphere. At the end of the nineteenth century, a small number of middle-class women were gradually benefiting from the kind of educational resources enjoyed by middle-class men, providing them with the opportunity to develop careers in a context that, looking back, we can identify and claim as investigative journalism. Women journalists and authors such as Annie Besant, Vera Brittain, Katherine Glasier, Edith Nesbitt, Maud Pember Reeves, Margaret Haig Thomas and Beatrice Webb rose to prominence by promoting women's issues, often amid hostile responses from male colleagues. Many women investigative journalists of this period were socialists and active members of the

117

Fabian Society and women's organisations such as the Women's Trade Union League, and the Women's Social and Political Union.

Annie Besant investigated and publicised the effects of population growth on the poor within her campaigns for birth control and women's rights between the 1870s and 1900s. Newspapers such as the *Times* labelled Besant's booklet on *The Laws of Population* (1884), which advocated birth control to reduce overcrowding and poverty among working class families, as 'filthy, lewd and obscene' (see, for example, Manvell 1976, Saville 1970 and Taylor 1992). Besant launched her own newspaper, *Link*, and publicised a number of women's issues including the dangerous working conditions and phosphorous fumes that women factory labourers had to put up with at the Bryant and May match factory in London. Maud Pember Reeves was a journalist who also placed women's issues on the public map by forming the Fabian Women's group in 1908 and campaigning for equal rights for women and state support for motherhood. She wrote a report on a 4-year study of the daily lives of working-class families in Lambeth, conducted by the Fabian's Women's Group, called *Family Life on a Pound* (Pember Reeves 1912). Another prominent woman in the profession is Beatrice Webb who wrote a number of Fabian Society pamphlets, some with her husband, Sidney Webb, on topics such as socialism, the Labour movement, and equal wages for women from the 1890s onwards. Beatrice and Sidney Webb started up the *New Statesman* in 1913 to promote socialist reform. Vera Brittain is also well known for her work as an investigative journalist and author. She contributed centrally to publicising women's rights by writing for a feminist journal called *Time and Tide* during the 1920s and investigating the role and position of women in employment and in marriage. As her views became more radical she moved from the Liberal to the Labour Party. Brittain became a pacifist during the Second World War and as a fierce opponent of nuclear weapons she actively participated in the formation of the Campaign for Nuclear Disarmament (CND) in 1957. Not only does the history of the first waves of women in investigative journalism need to be systematically recovered but they also need to be connected to an initiative of researching the position of women in the profession today as an important part of the centring of women's lives and practices within local and global communication networks.

Looking at today's investigative journalistic environment in Britain, David Lloyd (1998), founder of Channel 4's *Dispatches* and his successor as commissioning editor, Dorothy Byrnes (1999), claim it to be one of the first investigative mediums to undertake investigative reports on what were originally considered to be 'women's subjects' and even referred to dismissively in the trade as 'daytime TV'. Single parenthood, child cruelty, safety at work, ageism and the treatment of the elderly were among the subjects investigated by the programme, which they believe have contributed to the opening up of opportunities for women to express their voice within investigative journalism and counterbalance typically masculine topics that have characterised the profession such as arms dealing, spies, and the Mafia. Before moving to *Dispatches*, Dorothy Byrnes worked for several years with Granada's *World in Action* first as a researcher and then as a producer in the 1980s. Although she was not the first woman to work on the programme, she did experience being the only woman on the team at the time. In recalling her memory of it, Byrnes remarked that 'even ten years ago, it was so male dominated it was just extraordinary. At meetings it felt like going into the gents' toilet'. [3] When she became producer on *World in Action*, Byrnes was the second woman in its history who had been working as a researcher on the programmes who was then promoted to producer. Although it was a path well trodden by men, she explains that if women aimed to be producers they usually had to leave and look to regional programmes to employ them as producers. The first programme Byrnes produced for *World in Action* was on rape in marriage, which actually contributed to a change in the law in Britain so as to be defined as a crime. She was initially told that this subject was suitable only for morning television. Similarly, a programme she produced on women frightened to go out at night was not considered to be 'a story' by an experienced producer. Byrnes (1999) points out that women's subjects are now not only seen as valid subjects of investigation but as the saviour of current affairs in today's climate.

Notwithstanding the difficulties that women face in the profession, a number of contemporary structural changes point to the possibility of a future rise in the number of women journalists. Figures on employment patterns compiled by UNESCO indicate a rise in the number of female journalism students, notably in Europe and the USA (Gallagher 1995). But we need to be cautious in our optimism about possible future improvements as many female students experience barriers in graduating from journalism training to employment in print and television media – as shown by Gallagher's data on female employees in the European media. There may have been a rise in women employees in the last fifteen years but van Zoonen points out that it has not been particularly impressive. Women seem to drop out of journalism in their early 30s to have children because the profession makes it difficult for women to combine parenthood and career. Research evidence shows that men's lives and experiences tend to be privileged in the organisational structures and work cultures of journalism. Sexism operates in the newsroom through routines and conventions such as training within a system of rewards and punishment. For example, news that focuses on women, such as the women's department, 'society news' and so on, has often been emphasised as 'trite' and of low status by being offered as punishment assignments (see for example, van Zoonen 1994, Melin-Higgins and Djerf Pierre 1998). Female graduates still tend to move into public relations and information management jobs rather than journalism. When they do take on jobs in journalism, they are more likely to move into what are conventionally considered to be low status areas of journalism such as magazine publishing and the entertainment side of news television. The long term drop in the number of newspapers and rise in magazines is a pattern that is likely to determine a shift in employment to the latter. The dominance of magazines will further encourage the move towards more consumer-style investigative reporting and more journalists working in the entertainment fields of travel and sport. Sparks (1991) notes that the magazine sector is more open to women than press and television, suggesting that the shift from newspaper to magazine publishing will be linked to the feminisation of the profession.

Women's status and their inclusion as news sources still tends to be determined by their relationship to men – as wives, mothers, victims of crimes and disasters (Holland 1987). Questions have been raised about whether women journalists produce a different, more 'feminine' kind of news. But some researchers are sceptical of the idea that there is such a thing as a 'woman's perspective' that can produce a blurring of 'hard' and 'soft' news (van Zoonen 1991, 1994). In fact, van Zoonen predicts that the rise of market-driven journalism, with its emphasis on entertainment, 'human interest' stories, audience desires and emotional involvement will be the key factors that open up the profession to women. Yet the shift towards 'soft' news, consumer-style investigative reporting, 'info-tainment' and a sexualisation of tabloid style news are not the kinds of transformations that serve the public interest in the way that conventional investigative journalism does. These newer forms of journalism are neither examples of the 'femininising' of information and news nor good journalism but, rather, part of the trend in the shift to market-orientated 'consumer journalism' which gives priority to this so-called 'soft news'. The treatment of successful investigative reporters such as Veronica Guerin, one of Ireland's leading crime reporters who was murdered in 1996, illustrates some of the prejudices surrounding the role of women at the 'hard' end of underworld crime reporting. Her tragic death led to the kinds of criticisms that are far less likely to be levelled against male colleagues. Attacked on three occasions before her murder, and having received death threats targeted at her husband and threats of sexual assault targeted at her son, Veronica Guerin was posthumously criticised in the media for placing her career above her family (see O'Reilly 1998). [4] Many issues are raised by Guerin's death including the spectacularising of crime news, and the lack of protection for crime journalists. Yet as a woman investigative journalist, she was condemned as simply *too* successful in her knowledge of Dublin's underworld: she was perceived as 'ruthless' in the pursuit of her job – a charge not levelled against male war correspondents.

Conclusion

Quality investigative journalism has proved to be an essential tool of democratic communication, connecting social groups and actions across distances during periods of crisis and rapid political change in the last two decades of the twentieth century. Examples include historical events such as the collapse of the Soviet-style politics in Eastern-bloc nations, protests for political reform in The People's Republic of China, Thailand, Kenya and also the indigenous land rights of First Peoples, world trade and environmental issues (see, for example, the debates in Mohammadi 1999). The early women investigative reporters who have been involved in placing women's rights on the public agenda have shown the importance of campaigning and investigative reporting to creating public awareness of oppressed groups in society. Yet the market-driven imperatives of a global media do not necessarily guarantee the production or protection of the conditions needed to sustain this kind of journalism into the future. The economic, organisational and ideological constraints placed on investigative journalism by global news agencies often lead to the promotion of Anglocentric news standpoints. The concurrent shift of journalism in Anglophone Western nations towards the production of more so-called 'info-tainment' and human interest stories places individual journal-ists under great pressure to conform. In a climate of demand for more 'consumer-style' investigative reporting, the profession has a difficult role to play in its attempts to provide equality of opportunity to women at all levels within the profession, and to place human rights and women's issues centrally on the agenda at the level of information and representation.

Investigative journalism's critical principles of serving the public interest through committed expository reporting need to be strengthened within the political project of creating a more democratic and communicative culture. It seems that democratisation of communication through equal access to all, including women and other groups who have been traditionally silenced or marginalised, can only be ensured through the formal protection of the infor-mation media from both the state and commercial interests. Habermas's notion of the public sphere contains many problems but by exploring them critically we can at least imaginatively reconsider ways in which the media can be democratically reconstructed towards such protection. Thus, as we have seen, some scholars hold out hope for the democratising potential of both public service broadcasting and the Internet which may help us to rethink and reshape the public sphere.

Nevertheless, we need to remain cautious in our assessment of the new kind of publicity emerging in the global era. Public service broadcasting is being rapidly undermined by deregulation and the market-driven direction of information media while new and exciting 'online communities' are often excluding the very same people who are traditionally and currently excluded from the conventional media forum of public debate. Internet use is finan-cially prohibitive to the majority of the population in Third World nations as well as the poor of the West and some of the most sexist and racist material goes out on the Internet on a regular basis, shielded by anonymity. Studies of the role of investigative journalism in the twenty-first century need to be part of a radical reassessment of the media's role in upholding principles of democratic communication, the 'public interest' and universal access to global communication so as to guarantee the inclusion of social groups who are marginalised by a market-driven information media.

NOTES

1   In a collection of essays about histories and cultures of the Internet edited by Shields (1996) the implications of the Internet for both commercialised leisure and political organisation are examined.
2   For a discussion of the impact of globalisation and deregulation policy on communication technologies in developing-world countries such as Iran, see Mohammadi (1999).
3   I am grateful to Hugo de Burgh for drawing my attention to the talks delivered by David Lloyd (1998) and by Dorothy Byrnes (1999) to the students of the MA Investigative Journalism course at Nottingham Trent University.
4   I wish to thank Hawthorne (1999) for drawing my attention to these issues.

BIBLIOGRAPHY

Baehr, H. and Dyer, G. (eds) (1987) *Boxed In: Women and Television*. London: Pandora.

Bagdikian, B. (1988) *The Media Monopoly*. Boston: Beacon Press.

Benhabib, S. (ed.) *Democracy and Difference: Contesting the Boundaries of the Political*. Princeton, New Jersey: Princeton University Press.

Besant, A. (1884) *The Laws of Population*. London: Annie Besant.

Bloomfield, R. (1999) Fascists at large. *Time Out* (London), 5 May 1999.

Boyd-Barrett, O. (1997) Global news wholesalers as agents of globalisation. In A. Sreberny-Mohammadi, D. Winseck, J. McKenna and B. Boyd-Barrett (eds) *Media in Global Context*. London: Edward Arnold.

Boyd-Barrett, O. and Rantanen, T. (1998) The globalization of news. In O. Boyd-Barrett and T. Rantanen (eds) *The Globalisation of News*. London: Sage.

Boyd-Barrett, O. and Rantanen, T. (eds) (1998) *The Globalisation of News*. London: Sage.

Byerly, C. M. (1995) News, consciousness, and social participation: the role of women's feature service in world news. In A. Valdivia (ed.) *Feminism, Multiculturalism and the Media*. London: Sage.

Byrnes, D. (1999) Talk to the students of the MA Investigative Journalism course at the Centre for Broadcasting and Journalism, Nottingham Trent University, 29 April 1999.

Calhoun, C. (ed.) (1992) *Habermas and the Public Sphere*. Cambridge, MA: MIT Press.

Carter, C., Branston, G. and Allan, S. (eds) (1998) *News, Gender and Power*. London: Routledge.

Cohen, J. (1996) Democracy, difference and the right to privacy. In S. Benhabib (ed.) *Democracy and Difference: Contesting the Boundaries of the Political*. Princeton, New Jersey: Princeton University Press.

Comor, E. A. (1997) The re-tooling of American hegemony: US foreign communication policy from free flow to free trade. In A. Sreberny-Mohammadi, D. Winseck, J. McKenna and O. Boyd-Barrett (eds) *Media in Global Context, A Reader*. London: Edward Arnold.

Dahlgren, P. and Sparks, C. (eds) (1991) *Communication and Citizenship*. London: Routledge.

Davidoff, L. and Hall, C. (1994) *Family Fortunes: Men and Women of the English Middle Class 1780–1850*. London: Routledge.

Demac, D. A. and Sung, L. (1995) New communication technologies and deregulation. In J. Downing, A. Mohammadi and A. Sreberny-Mohammadi (eds) *Questioning the Media: A Critical Introduction*, 2nd edn. London: Sage.

Dougary, G. (1994) *The Executive Tart and Other Myths*. London: Virago.

Downing, J., Mohammadi, A., Sreberny-Mohammadi, A. (eds) (1995) *Questioning the Media: A Critical Introduction*, 2nd edn. London: Sage.

Featherstone, M. (ed.) (1996) *Global Culture: Nationalism, Globalisation and Modernity*. London: Sage.

Ferguson, M. (ed.) (1986) *New Communication Technologies and the Public Interest*. London: Sage.

Ferguson, M. (ed.) (1990) *Public Communication: The New Imperatives*. London and Newbury Park, CA: Sage.

Franklin, B. (1997) *Newszak and News Media*. London: Edward Arnold.

Fraser, N. (1992) Rethinking the public sphere: a contribution to the critique of actually existing democracy. In C. Calhoun (ed.) *Habermas and the Public Sphere*. Cambridge, MA: MIT Press.

Gallagher, M. (1995) *An Unfinished Story: Gender Patterns in Media Employment*. Paris: UNESCO Reports on Mass Comunication, 110.

Garnham, N. (1986) The media and the public sphere. In P. Golding and G. Murdock (eds) *Communicating Politics*. Leicester: Leicester University Press: 37–54.

Giddens, A. (1990) *The Consequences of Modernity*. Stanford: Stanford University Press.

Golding, P. and Harris, P. (eds) (1996) *Beyond Cultural Imperialism: Globalisation, Communication and the New International Order*. London: Sage.

Golding, P. and Murdock, G. (1979) Ideology and the mass media: the question of determination. In M. Barrett, P. Corrigan, A. Kuhn and J. Wolff (eds) *Ideology and Cultural Production*. London: Croom Helm.

Gray, A. (1992) *Video Playtime: The Gendering of Leisure Technology*. London: Routledge.

Grossberg, L., Wartella, E. and Whitney, D. C. (1998) *Mediamaking: Mass Media in a Popular Culture*. London: Sage.

Habermas, J. (1989) *The Structural Transformation of the Public Sphere*. Cambridge: Polity Press.

Hamelink, C. J. (1995) Information imbalance across the globe. In J. Downing, A. Mohammadi and A. Sreberny-Mohammadi (eds) *Questioning the Media: A Critical Introduction*, 2nd edn. London: Sage.

Hamelink, C. J. (1996) Communications and Human Rights. Lecture delivered at the Centre for Research in Communication and Culture (CRICC), Department of English and Media Studies, Nottingham Trent University, May 1996.

Hamelink, C. (1999) International communication: global market and morality. In A. Mohammadi (ed.), *International Communication and Globalisation*. London: Sage.

Hawthorne, V. (1999) *Veronica Guerin 1959–1996*. Unpublished student dissertation, BA Broadcast Journalism course at Nottingham Trent University.

Hobson, D. (1982) *Crossroads: The Drama of a Soap Opera*. London: Methuen.

Holland, P. (1987) When a woman reads the news. In H. Baehr and G. Dyer (eds) *Boxed In: Women and Television*. London: Pandora.

Jones, S. G. (ed.) (1997) *Virtual Culture: Identity and Communication in Cybersociety*. London: Sage.

Kellner, D. (1992a) Television, the crisis of democracy and the Persian Gulf war. In M. Raby and R. Dagenois (eds) *Media, Crisis and Democracy*. London: Sage.

Kellner, D. (1992b) *The Persian Gulf TV War*. Boulder, CO: Westview Press.

Knightley, P. (1982) The Falklands: how Britannia ruled the news. *Columbia Journalism Review*, September.

Landes, J. (1988) *Women and the Public Sphere in the Age of the French Revolution*. Ithaca, New York: Cornell University Press.

Lloyd, D. (1998) Talk to students of the MA Investigative Journalism course at Nottingham Trent University, 19 February 1998.

Malik, R. (1992) The global news agenda. *Intermedia* 20 (1).

Manvell, R. (1976) *Trial of Annie Besant*. London: Elek.

McLaughlin, L. (1998) Gender, privacy and publicity in 'media event space'. In Carter, C., Branston, G. and Allan, S. (eds) *News, Gender and Power*. London: Routledge.

McLuhan, M. (1964) *Understanding Media*. London: Routledge and Kegan Paul.

McQuail, D. (1994) *Mass Communication Theory*, 3rd edn. London: Sage.

Melin-Higgins, M. and Djerf Pierre, M. (1998) Networking in newsrooms: journalism and gender cultures. Paper presented at the International Association of Media and Communication Research Conference, Glasgow University, Scotland, July.

Melody, W. H. (1990) Communications policy in the global information economy. In M. F. Ferguson (ed.) *Public Communication: The New Imperatives*. London and Newbury Park, CA: Sage.

Mohammadi, A. (1999) Communication and the globalisation process in the developing world. In A. Mohammadi (ed.), *International Communication and Globalisation*. London: Sage.

Mohammadi, A. (ed.) (1999) *International Communication and Globalisation*. London: Sage.

Mohanty, T.C. (1991) Introduction: cartographies of struggle: Third World women and the politics of feminism. In T. C. Mohanty, A. Russo and L. Torres (eds) *Third World Women and the Politics of Feminism*. Bloomington: Indiana University Press: 1–47.

Mohanty, T. C., Russo, A. and Torres, L. (eds) (1991) *Third World Women and the Politics of Feminism*. Bloomington: Indiana University Press.

Morley, D. (1980) *The 'Nationwide' Audience*. London: British Film Institute.

Morley, D. (1986) *Family Television: Cultural Power and Domestic Leisure*. London: Comedia.

Murdock, G. and Golding, P. (1977) Capitalism, communication and class relations. In J. Curran, M. Gurevitch and J. Woollacott (eds) *Mass Communication and Society*. London: Edward Arnold.

Nelson, C. and Grossberg, L. (eds) (1988) *Marxism and the Interpretation of Culture*. London: Macmillan.

O'Reilly, E. (1998) *Veronica Guerin: The Life and Death of a Crime Reporter*. London: Vintage.

Pateman, C. (1988) *The Sexual Contract*. Cambridge: Polity Press.

Paterson, C. (1997) Global television news services. In A. Sreberny-Mohammadi, D. Winseck, J. McKenna and O. Boyd-Barrett (eds) *Media in Global Context: A Reader*. London: Edward Arnold.

Pember Reeves, M. (1912) *Family Life on a Pound*. London: Fabian Society.

Pendakur, M. and Kapur, J. (1996) Think globally, programme locally: privatisation of Indian national television. In M. Baile and D. Winseck (eds) *Democratising Communication? Comparative Perspectives on Information and Power*. Cresskill, New Jersey: Hampton Press.

Poster, M. (1997) Cyberdemocracy: Internet and the public sphere. In D. Holmes (ed.) *Virtual Politics: Identity and Community in Cyberspace*. London: Sage.

Press Complaints Commission (1994) Code of conduct. In *Press Complaints Commission Report*, 23, January/February: 36–9.

Rakow, L. and Kranich, K. (1991) Women as a sign in television news. *Journal of Communication*, 41 (1): 8–23.

124

Ryan, M. (1992) Gender and public access: women's politics in nineteenth century America. In C. Calhoun (ed.) *Habermas and the Public Sphere*. Cambridge, MA: MIT Press.

Saville, J. (1970) *Annie Besant: Selected Pamphlets*. London: Kelley.

Scannel, P. (1995) Public service broadcasting and modern public life. In T. O'Sullivan and Y. Jewes (eds) *The Media Reader*. London: Edward Arnold.

Scannel, P., Schlesinger, O. and Sparks, C. (eds) (1992) *Culture and Power: A Media, Culture and Society Reader*. London: Sage.

Shields, R. (ed.) (1996) *Cultures of Internet: Virtual Spaces, Real Histories, Living Bodies*. London: Sage.

Skidmore, P. (1998) Gender and the agenda: news reporting of child sexual abuse. In C. Carter, G. Branston and S. Allan (eds) *News, Gender and Power*. London: Routledge.

Sparks, C. (1991) Goodbye Hildy Johnson: the vanishing serious press. In P. Dahlgren and C. Sparks (eds) *Communication and Citizenship*. London: Routledge.

Sparks, C. (1992) The popular press and political democracy. In P. Scannel, O. Schlesinger and C. Sparks (eds) *Culture and Power: A Media, Culture and Society Reader*. London: Sage.

Sreberny-Mohammadi, A., Winseck, D., McKenna, J. and Boyd-Barrett, O. (eds) (1997) *Media in Global Context, A Reader*. London: Edward Arnold.

Stevenson, N. (1995) *Understanding Media Cultures: Social Theory and Mass Communication*. London: Sage.

Taylor, A. (1992) *Annie Besant*. Oxford: Oxford University Press.

Tomlinson, J. (1991) *Cultural Imperialism*. London: Pinter.

Tomlinson, J. (1999) *Globalisation and Culture*. London: Polity.

Traber, M. and Nordenstreng, K. (1993) *Few Voices, Many Worlds*. London: World Association for Christian Communication.

Trendle, G. (1996) Hizbollah, Israel, and peace in the Middle East. Lecture delivered at the Centre for Research in Communication and Culture (CRICC), Department of English and Media Studies, Nottingham Trent University, May 1996.

UNESCO (1980) *Many Voices, One World: Towards a New, More Just and More Efficient World Information and Communication Order* (McBride Report). The International Commission for the Study of Communication Problems. Paris: UNESCO/London: Kogan Page.

van Zoonen, L. (1991) A tyranny of intimacy? Women, femininity and television news. In P. Dahlgren and C. Sparks (eds) *Communication and Citizenship*. London: Routledge.

van Zoonen, L. (1994) *Feminist Media Studies*. London: Sage.

van Zoonen, L. (1998) One of the girls? The changing gender of journalism. In C. Carter, G. Branston and S. Allan (eds) *News, Gender and Power*. London: Routledge.

FURTHER READING

Boyd-Barrett, O. and Rantanen, T. (eds) (1998) *The Globalisation of News*. London: Sage.

Carter, C., Branston, G. and Allan, S. (eds) (1998) *News, Gender and Power*. London: Routledge.

Sreberny-Mohammadi, A., Winseck, D., McKenna, J. and Boyd-Barrett, O. (eds) (1997) *Media in Global Context, A Reader*. London: Edward Arnold.

Stevenson, N. (1995) *Understanding Media Cultures: Social Theory and Mass Communication*. London: Sage.

7

THE ENGLISH LEGAL FRAMEWORK FOR INVESTIGATIVE JOURNALISM[1]

Gill Moore

Freedom of expression and freedom of information are two fundamental mutually supportive principles that underpin the work of all journalists. The ability to gather and disseminate information is constrained and influenced by a wide variety of factors, including commercial, legal, ethical and political considerations. A myriad of statutory provisions, subject to constant change, amendment and development exists in English law and creates a minefield for press and broadcasting journalists alike. These legal rules are supplemented by a number of regulatory codes, which seek to govern issues relating to broadcasting standards and to confront concerns relating to media ownership.[2] The media itself provides codes of journalistic ethics and practice that provide day-to-day guidance for journalists and attempt to reflect society's view of the public interest, a notoriously nebulous concept. These various constraints provide a complex framework for the activities of investigative journalists. The very nature of their work will often bring them into conflict with individual, commercial and official interests alike. This chapter identifies a number of selected areas of conflict and considers how the English law seeks to draw the balance between the various interests involved and its subsequent impact upon the activities of the investigative journalist. It is beyond the scope of this chapter to provide a comprehensive discussion of the legal provisions in existence in English law. The text is not intended to be a 'how to' guide for budding investigative journalists, instead, the aim is to provide a selective study of a number of key areas, providing the opportunity for a more critical analysis and discussion to take place.[3] The omission of topics, such as the legal restraints relating to official secrets, is not to diminish their importance, and the reader is invited to explore such areas through texts identified in the further reading list. Finally, the reader is reminded that the law cannot be seen in isolation. Investigative journalists, for example, will often have a story 'lawyered' or 'legalled' before its publication. At this stage the legal adviser is often compelled to trust that the journalist concerned has adhered to certain basic ethical standards, and even then, the story may be pulled for commercial reasons.

Introduction

Investigative journalists argue that they perform an important function in society, uncovering corruption, injustice, wrong-doings and generally highlighting issues of public concern.[4] If they are to undertake the role of watchdog then they must do so in a responsible manner, maintaining the highest professional and ethical standards whilst working within the letter and spirit of the law.

For many editors and journalists the law appears to present a formidable set of hurdles and barriers restraining the work that they seek to undertake in the public interest. For others, the legal provisions appear ineffective as a means of controlling intrusive media coverage and may actually serve to encourage sensationalism and trivialisation.[5] When covering a story, investigative journalists face moral and ethical dilemmas which may bring them into conflict with the law. Most areas of dispute, though they may turn on differing facts, centre upon the tension between the investigative journalists' right to freedom of expression and competing rights associated with a variety of other interests. This chapter focuses upon a number of selected key areas of conflict and considers how a number of English legal provisions impact upon the work of investigative journalists.[6] An analysis of the legal constraints is undertaken within the context of the wider debate associated with freedom of expression.

The opening section of the chapter examines the significance of freedom of expression to the work of investigative journalists and considers how that interest is protected in English law. Subsequent sections reflect upon a number of significant areas of conflict – in particular, disputes between investigative journalists' free speech interests and those based upon the interests of reputation, privacy, and the administration of justice. The relevant legal provisions in these three broad areas will be outlined and evaluated to establish whether they directly or indirectly inhibit the work of investigative journalists.

Freedom of expression, English law and the investigative journalist

Freedom to communicate enables public and private debate on numerous important issues that affect all our lives in a variety of ways. Investigative journalists have on many occasions called upon this argument in support of their actions in uncovering wrong-doings.[7] There are a number of philosophical rationales submitted in support of the protection of this core right. In a Western liberal pluralistic model of society, commonly used arguments are based upon the belief that freedom of expression enables citizens to seek the path to *truth* (Mill 1859), to *democracy* (Meiklejohn 1965) and to *self-fulfilment*.[8] Although it is generally acknowledged that freedom of expression is a core right it will inevitably conflict at times with other competing interests.

Investigative journalists may believe that it is in the public interest to publish a story, but in communicating such information disputes can arise concerning the 'harm to others' (Mill 1859) that may be inflicted. This harm may be based upon, for example, the harm done to a personal or commercial reputation, infringing the right of an individual to a fair trial or damaging the security of the nation state itself.[9]

If freedom of expression is acknowledged to be such an important human right and of particular relevance to investigative journalists, how well is that right protected in English law?

The rights of citizens in most Western democracies are enshrined in a Bill of Rights or a written constitution. This formal statement, asserting the importance of a number of fundamental rights, provides a framework for judicial decision making in dispute resolution. In many countries, such as Canada and Sweden, freedom of speech is guaranteed through constitutional provision, which protects and guarantees key individual rights.[10] The relevant judiciary may have to deal with the issue of resolving conflicts between these interests, but rights such as free speech are enshrined in a written document and are thus given equal (if not greater) status in any dispute.

In the United States Constitution the First Amendment states 'Congress shall make no law ... abridging the freedom of speech, or the press'. Enshrined within the framework of a written constitution, this provides a clear indication of the importance of free speech and a free press without mentioning any restrictive conditions or special requirements. In practice, the First Amendment operates as a concept that is subject to scrutiny by the American judiciary and limited by the 'clear and present danger' test.[11] The American approach, however, preserves a recognition of the core importance of free speech.

The United Kingdom does not have a written document that details fundamental rights in this way.[12] In English law a great many interests have the effect of squeezing out the standing of free speech. Common law and statutory provisions provide a variety of means to restrain freedom of expression and the work of investigative journalists. Limitations have been developed by a Parliament that historically had no obligation to consider free speech issues when enacting provisions. In addition many decisions that effectively restrict speech may not even be subject to judicial control. The various provisions have evolved in a piecemeal fashion; the courts appearing happier to apply and expand legitimate limitations particularly where there is no similar legislative enactment protecting free speech.

In 1998 the European Convention on Human Rights was incorporated into English law, although it does not come into force until October 2000. The Convention guarantees a number of basic rights and freedoms, including freedom of expression.[13] Until this major step takes effect there is no clearly defined concept of freedom of expression in English law; it exists only as a residual right. However, the Human Rights Act, which facilitates this fundamental change, retains Parliamentary sovereignty. As a result, if an English statute is unclear the judges will be called upon to interpret it in line with the convention. If a statute is clear in its meaning, however, the judges will be required to apply it even if it appears to breach the convention.[14] Consequently, fundamental rights and freedoms that are afforded constitutional status in countries like the United States will still not be safeguarded by the courts and Parliament of the UK.

Incorporation of the European Convention on Human Rights will grant a means of providing a quasi-constitutional basis for the protection of free speech in English law. Prior to its incorporation, journalists have relied upon the Convention in an attempt to uphold their right to free speech and support their work in exposing wrong-doings and investigating matters of public concern. A number of successful cases have been brought before the European Court of Human Rights at Strasbourg, indicating that human rights are not adequately protected under English domestic law.[15] From October 2000 journalists will be able to claim that their right to freedom of expression has been infringed by relying directly upon the Human Rights Act. It remains to be seen how far the courts will uphold freedom of expression when this interest conflicts with existing domestic statutory provisions.

Summary

The history of the state regulation of speech in English law has resulted in a case by case reaction that has failed to consider or give effect to the long term benefits of free speech, and that has had a tendency to exaggerate the 'harm to others' principle. Following the incorporation of the European Convention on Human Rights into English law, the judiciary will be provided with an opportunity to enhance the status of free speech in the United Kingdom. This may have important implications for the work of investigative journalists, who will no doubt call upon the Convention to challenge the numerous legal provisions that continue (rightly or wrongly) to inhibit their activities.

Investigative journalists, English law and reputations

Of all the legal constraints that impinge upon the work of investigative journalists, the law of defamation is one of the most intrusive.[16] On the one hand it provides the opportunity for individuals and organisations to suppress publications on matters of public importance, to stifle debate essential to the democratic process, to gag the media in its potential role as the public's watchdog and to threaten the closure of media outlets. On the other, it is suggested that legal provisions relating to the protection of the individual's reputation encourage a higher level of professionalism from working journalists. Certainly the fear of expensive litigation acts as a spur to journalists and editors to maintain accuracy in their reporting.

It is commendable that the law should be seen to encourage quality reporting. However, when combined with circulation and competition pressures placed on media organisations, those same legal provisions produce a framework that influences and dictates editorial decision-making in a way that in reality has little to do with ensuring high levels of accuracy or the protection of reputations (Vick and Macpherson 1997). It is ironic that court cases involving defamation actions provide the media with a legitimate opportunity to revisit every lurid detail of a story, whether or not allegations made are true.[17]

The law of defamation exists to protect the reputation of the individual from unjustified attack. The provisions relating to libel and slander in English law have evolved over many years.[18] The main principles are at present based in statutory enactments and much highly entertaining case law. The difficulty in maintaining an appropriate balance between freedom of expression and the protection of an individual's personal or professional reputation is reflected in the complexity of the legal rules. Changing perceptions in society regarding the meaning of reputation further complicate the issue.[19] Technological developments and the ever-faster systems of global communications have also exacerbated the problem.

In English law, defamation is seen as 'the publication of an untrue statement, which reflects upon a person's reputation and tends to lower him in the estimation of right-thinking members of society generally or tends to make them shun or avoid him'.[20] Exactly what can amount to a defamatory statement can vary dramatically. Examples range from allegations that a company deliberately concealed the side-effects of a drug,[21] untrue claims that a major retailer knowingly exploited overseas child labour[22] to 'offensive and distressing' false allegations that a pop singer appeared on stage wearing no knickers.[23]

The law of defamation in the United Kingdom represents a game of Russian roulette for investigative journalists. A number of key considerations must be taken into account at every stage of the publishing and broadcasting process. These include:

1   Is the allegation true?
2   Can the investigative journalist prove the allegations?
3   Is the subject of the story likely to sue?

Is the allegation true?

As an issue of journalistic ethics all investigative journalists should only publish that which is true.[24] Few would argue with the basic premise that if media organisations take the decision to run with a story that is not based on the truth or is carelessly researched, then they should be brought to account. Through the use of skilful, accurate and balanced writing investigative journalists should be able to avoid expensive litigation. In addition, larger media outlets may have the luxury of in-house legal advice, sympathetic to the working practices of journalists. The defences of fair comment, justification and privilege seek to draw an appropriate balance between the right to reputation and freedom of speech. The defence of justification (truth) has been particularly important in defeating claims for provisional orders of the court which can be used to censor publications whose wrongfulness has not yet been established.

The main difficulty for investigative journalists is not simply whether the allegation that is made is true, but whether it is possible to prove this in a court of law.

Can the investigative journalist prove the allegation?

An individual wishing to bring a libel action has to show the following; first that the words used bear a defamatory meaning; second that those words refer to the plaintiff; and third that they have been published to a third party. There is no requirement to show an intention to defame, and if the statement is in a permanent form there is no need to prove any actual harm.[25] Most significantly, the plaintiff does not have to prove that the statement is false. Indeed there is a presumption of falsity, and it lies with the investigative journalist to prove that the allegations made are true. For many investigative journalists and media organisations this evidential burden is too great. The fear is that the particularly onerous burden of proof in defamation cases has a dampening or 'chilling effect' on free speech and can be exploited by wealthy, unscrupulous individuals. Alan Rusbridger (1997) argues that editors 'would be foolish to risk their papers on too robust journalism whilst the law operates as it does'.

The investigative journalist must not only be in a position to prove the truth of the allegation as intended, but also any possible libellous meaning inferred. Following a *World in Action* investigation, 'St Michael: Has the Halo Slipped?', broadcast in 1996, the national retailer Marks & Spencer brought a libel action against the programme makers Granada Television, claiming that the programme contained false accusations that seriously damaged their much valued reputation. Granada argued before the court that the programme carried a meaning different from the one suggested by Marks & Spencer. In an unprecedented move the judge in the case asked the jury in advance of the trial what meaning the *World in Action* programme conveyed to its viewers. When the jury decided in favour of Marks & Spencer's interpretation, Granada agreed to pay £50,000 damages, plus Marks & Spencer's costs of £650,000, as it was unable to prove those meanings. The decision may present problems for investigative journalists in the future, as this legal development has the potential to deny them the opportunity of a full trial to which, in free speech terms, they are arguably entitled. Ian McBride, Managing Editor, Factual Programmes, for Granada Television commented:

> We can confidently endorse and encourage the standard of our inves-
> tigative journalism. But to have to ponder and second guess our fate
> in a short-cut route through the libel roulette puts another burden

and potential hazard in the way of inquiring, challenging journalism and the communication of important if uncomfortable, truths to the public.

(*Guardian*, 14 March 1998)

The requirement to prove the truth of all factual assertions made will inevitably result in a degree of self-censorship by the media. Investigative journalists may well believe the truth of their allegations but face many hurdles in proving them in a court of law. The information they require to satisfy a court of law will often rest with the plaintiff. Witnesses may be difficult to track down. The journalist may have promised confidentiality to a particular source. A witness may not seem particularly credible in the eyes of an unpredictable jury and the cost of bringing a water-tight defence can be prohibitively high. These factors may combine to force a media organisation to make an out of court settlement with the plaintiff, which by implication suggests that the subject matter of the allegation is squeaky clean and that standards in journalism have slipped ever lower. Of greater concern is the impact on editorial decision-making. An editor may alter an article to avoid litigation and as a result issues of public concern may not be aired. Editors may be deterred from publishing a story at all, or may simply strangle an investigation at birth. Whilst defamation provisions are, of course, relevant to all journalists, the concern is that media corporate culture may see little or no point in supporting investigative journalism, opting instead for compliant, bland reporting.

This so-called 'chilling effect' has long been recognised in the United States.[26] In the landmark case of *New York Times v Sullivan*, the Commissioner of Public Affairs for the city of Montgomery, Alabama sued the *New York Times* for libel.[27] Many of the allegations proved to be factually incorrect, but the US Supreme Court reversed a jury damage award and found in favour of the newspaper. The court established the principle that to prevail in a defamation action, it is for the *plaintiff* (a public official in this case) to prove the falsity of any factual claims made against them. Additionally the plaintiff must demonstrate that the defendant published a false or defamatory statement with the knowledge that the statement was false, or with a reckless disregard of its truth or falsity.

The decision recognises that while an individual whose reputation has been tarnished should be able to seek redress through the law, that right is subject to the First Amendment protection of freedom of expression. The case established the so-called 'actual malice' standard and acknowledged the importance of open robust criticism of public officials. In subsequent cases the US courts extended the principle to include not just public officials but also public figures.

The American approach illustrates the importance of the constitutional status of freedom of expression when drawing a balance between conflicting interests. Libel litigation does of course still exist in the United States. In a number of interviews with US editors Weaver and Bennett (1993: 9) discovered that although they are 'concerned about the threat of defamation actions, and the possibility of adverse judgements ... they are far less concerned than their British counterparts'. It appears that the *New York Times* case has not brought about a rise in reckless reporting. American journalists are able to operate secure in the knowledge that their judicial system recognises freedom of speech based arguments in defence of their publications. The suggestion is that this has refocused attention upon the importance of high ethical standards of accuracy and integrity within journalism.[28]

The 'chilling effect' is recognised to a limited extent in English law. Barendt (1993) explains that the defences of absolute and qualified privilege, which allow journalists to report on matters in Parliament and before the courts, are based on the notion that free speech on matters of public importance outweighs the need to protect a reputation. It is difficult to see why this principle cannot be extended in some form to provide a general public figure and public interest defence that would allow responsible journalists to conduct investigations and compile reports more freely. The Faulks Committee considered creating a new head of qualified privilege, but concluded that there was insufficient evidence to confirm that the media were in fact deterred from reporting events by the UK's libel laws.[29] The issue was further debated by the Neill Committee, but it was feared that such a defence 'would mean, in effect, that newspapers could publish more or less what they liked, provided they were honest, if their subject happened to be within the definition of a "public figure". We think this would lead to a great injustice'.[30] A public figure defence was rejected during debates over the Defamation Bill with the then Conservative government endorsing the conclusions of the Neill Committee.[31] It was suggested that any development of such a defence should be left to the judiciary who were best placed to balance free speech against other interests.

An opportunity for the judiciary to develop a public interest defence was provided in the landmark case of *Derbyshire County Council v Times Newspapers Limited*.[32] Finding for the newspaper Lord Keith stated in his judgement, 'It is of the highest public importance that a democratically elected body, or indeed any governmental body, should be open to uninhibited criticism'. As a result the principle was established in English common law that local authorities are unable to bring an action for damages for defamation as it is deemed contrary to the public interest for the organs of government, whether central or local, to have that right. The decision is important as there is a clear recognition of the importance of free speech, particularly at its 'core'. Whilst Barendt notes that the 'decision has potentially enormous implications for the development of this controversial area of law' (1993: 450) he points out that it is hard to justify any distinction drawn from the case between an attack on a public office and one on a public official. It follows that if a local authority is unable to sue in defamation because it would inhibit free speech, then the same logic must be applied to public officials and similarly by analogy to public figures and corporations. While the English courts do not appear willing to embrace a Sullivan type defence which includes the wider concept of public figures, it is hard to justify the rejection of a public official defence. Such an approach would provide greater protection for 'core' political speech, vital to the dissemination of information in a healthy democracy.[33]

Attempts made to extend the common law principle of qualified privilege in *Albert Reynolds v Times Newspapers Limited*, appear to confirm the doctrine that the media may have a stronger claim to a public interest based defence in certain specified circumstances.[34] Although the ruling is welcome, the decision imposes a heavy evidential burden on the party seeking to rely upon it. It remains to be seen whether the case represents the 'English Sullivan'.[35]

The lack of enthusiasm displayed by both the legislature to enact a public figure defence, and the judiciary to extend qualified privilege in English law represents a missed opportunity. There are many cases that illustrate how politicians and other public figures have attempted to make use of English libel laws to restrain the media and legitimate public debate on matters of public concern. In a notorious case, former Conservative cabinet minister Jonathan Aitken used the English libel laws in a cynical attempt to protect his political career. Following allegations made in the national newspaper the *Guardian* and the television programme *World in Action* that he had breached ministerial guidelines and was financially dependent on the Saudi Arabian royal family, Aitken asserted:

> If it has fallen to my destiny to start a fight to cut out the cancer of bent and twisted journalism in our country with the simple sword of truth and the trusty shield of British fair play, so be it, I am ready for the fight.
> (Press conference, 10 April 1994)

Aitken commenced a libel action, but in a dramatic turn of events new evidence was uncovered part-way through the trial which indicated that he had lied to the court. Aitken abandoned his case, instigating a swift and cutting response from both the *Guardian*, 'Jonathan Aitken has impaled himself on the simple sword of truth' (20 June 1997) and Granada Television, 'Jonathan Aitken's chosen weapon was a dagger of deceit, not the sword of truth' (20 June 1997). The story centred upon sleaze and corruption, and the subsequent legal action serves as a reminder of the value of quality investigative journalism, and how those in positions of power have the potential to abuse the law of defamation to serve their own interests. Condemnation of the disgraced minister was unanimous. The *Press Gazette* observed, 'That unity should be used to harass and pressure the new Government to show it can make fundamental reforms and cut out the real "cancer", the libel lottery which eats away at investigative journalism' (*Press Gazette* 27 June 1997).

Although media organisations have on occasions successfully justified their investigations and resulting exposés, it should be noted that this has often only been possible following expensive and extensive research undertaken by both journalists and lawyers, trawling for documents to be used in their defence in a court of law.[36] Whilst large media organisations may be in a position to undertake such activities and pay high-powered lawyers, the same cannot be said for editors of small publications and production companies.

Is the subject of the story likely to sue?

A key question that editors and journalists ask themselves when investigating, constructing and writing a report is how litigious the subject of their story is. The press mogul Robert Maxwell serves as a cautionary reminder of an individual who did not shy away from legal action. It was common knowledge that Maxwell would sue unless a publication was 100 per cent true. Fearful of expensive litigation, journalists did not publish details relating to his financial misconduct until after his death.[37] Similarly, editors are quick to comment that stories concerning the police are altered or suppressed because they are perceived as being highly litigious (Barendt et al. 1997).

The law of defamation is in the main a civil action.[38] This means that the individual who claims that their reputation has been damaged by a publication has the choice whether or not to sue. The fear of high costs, lack of legal aid and the unpredictable nature of a jury trial may well dissuade a potential litigant from commencing legal action. The introduction of 'no win, no fee' schemes in defamation cases may, however, mean that more individuals will be in a position to consider legal action.[39] The prospect of a large compensation award may further serve to dispel any apprehensions. The level of damages in a libel action is determined by the jury and can vary considerably. Robertson and Nichol suggest (1992: 102) that 'the alarming escalation of damages in recent cases is best explained as the response of ordinary people to falling standards in the popular press.' Despite reforms, which allow the judge to offer guidance to the jury on the level of damages[40] and also enable parties to appeal against excessive awards,[41] they continue to be capricious and extravagant.[42]

Journalists and editors are also influenced by the factors identified above. Costs may cripple a plaintiff; they can also be very damaging to all branches of the media, especially when combined with a massive award in damages.

The Internet, defamation and investigative journalists

The advance of the global communications network raises a number of regulatory and legal questions.[43] The World Wide Web, Internet and e-mail systems provide new fora for forthright and open debate,[44] creating a libertarian culture that is resistant to institutional control. It is suggested that the

Internet 'interprets censorship as a form of damage and seeks to find ways round it' (Lloyd 1997: 9).

While cyberspace does not respect national boundaries, creating jurisdictional and enforcement difficulties, nonetheless, it is misleading to suggest that it is beyond regulation. Investigative journalists may, as a result of the new 'virtual society' (Gould 1996), have enhanced tools with which to undertake their activities,[45] but they remain subject to the defamation provisions outlined above. While a number of gaps exist in the legislation, if the author of the libellous material can be identified then he, she or the online media organisation concerned can be sued.[46] While the maverick or independently operative investigative journalist may, by retaining anonymity and through the use of 'mirroring'[47] be able to disclose matters on the Internet and avoid legal liability for any inaccuracies, this is not an option available for online media organisations. Certainly such outlets will be seeking to obtain commercial benefits attached to being clearly identified as the publishers of an exclusive exposé. As a result the requirement to ensure accuracy and the ability to prove the truth of the allegations made remains paramount. The growth of 'forum shopping' allows those aggrieved by the instantaneous and potentially highly damaging spread of defamatory statements across the globe to commence their legal action in the country of their choice. It comes as no surprise to learn that Britain, with its highly repressive libel laws, will often be found at the top of such a shopping list.

Summary

It is acknowledged that an individual must have the right to protect their reputation from false and damaging allegations and that investigative journalists bear a responsibility to maintain high ethical standards of accuracy and professionalism. Many journalists believe, however, that the libel provisions that exist in English law fail to give sufficient weight to the importance of freedom of expression, and that this impacts upon editorial decision-making, encouraging trivialisation and threatening serious journalism.

The investigative journalist, English law and the administration of justice

The law of contempt serves as a further constraint upon the work of investigative journalists. Contempt operates both to protect the rights of an individual to a fair trial and the administration of justice generally. The US constitution acknowledges that 'Everyone has the right to a speedy trial, by an *impartial* jury' (emphasis added) and the courts have to draw a balance between this interest and the freedom of the press as enshrined in the First Amendment. This core interest is similarly protected under the European Convention on Human Rights. Article 6(1) states, 'In determination of his civil rights and obligations, or of any criminal charges against him, everyone is entitled to a fair and public hearing within a reasonable time by an independent and *impartial* tribunal' (emphasis added). While Article 10 enshrines the right to freedom of expression, it does so subject to the restrictions prescribed by law and necessary in a democratic society in the interests of 'maintaining the authority and impartiality of the judiciary.' Article 6, therefore, provides a legitimate justification for a restriction on free speech under Article 10(2).

The challenge for any legal system is to draw an appropriate balance between the interest of protecting the legal process and the principle of freedom of expression. Any conflict normally falls to the judiciary to resolve.

Generally the arguments put forward to justify the infringement of freedom of expression in this way are based upon the following key points:

1   the right to a fair trial;
2   protecting the proper administration of justice;
3   protecting the authority of the judiciary; and
4   the issue of anonymity.

The right to a fair trial

All democratic constitutions make it clear that individual citizens have an inalienable right to a fair trial. The media frenzy that surrounds certain news events can give rise to misleading, inaccurate, exaggerated and relentless coverage, raising serious questions concerning the issue of prejudicial publicity. In the US, the trials of ex-footballer and one time actor, O. J. Simpson and of English au pair Louise Woodward act as a cautionary reminder of the power of the circulation driven media and its potential to influence the outcome of legal proceedings.[48]

Pre-trial publicity and actual trial coverage may prejudice the decision-making process of a jury in determining liability or guilt. In English law, however, it is impossible to assess the true impact of media coverage upon jury deliberations. Section 8 of the Contempt of Court Act 1981 makes it an offence to 'obtain, disclose or solicit any particulars of statements made, opinions expressed, arguments advanced and votes cast by members of a jury in the course of their deliberations in any legal proceedings'.[49] The section, introduced to ensure that jurors are free from any pressure to justify their decision, has the additional effect of stifling academic research into this area and arguably may also inhibit the activities of investigative journalists working to uncover miscarriages of justice. The Report of the Royal Commission on Criminal Justice (1996) recommended that Section 8 should be repealed. Although there is a lack of empirical research to prove the link between media coverage and tainted trials, there have been a growing number of appeals by defendants in criminal cases in England. These appeals are based on the grounds that the defendant was unable to receive a fair trial as a result of prejudicial press reporting.[50] The general belief that trial by media is undesirable provides strong justification for the vigorous contempt provisions in England.[51]

Protecting the proper administration of justice

There is a strong public interest argument in protecting the due process of the law. This principle reflects the interest of the parties to a legal action (see above), but goes further by suggesting that any inappropriate interference will undermine public confidence in the system itself. This can be illustrated by the disturbing increase in the number of criminal cases that have been stayed in England because judges decided that media coverage would make a fair trial impossible.[52] In October 1995 the trial of Mr Geoffrey Knights was abandoned following submissions that he could not receive a fair trial as a result of newspaper reports surrounding his arrest in connection with the wounding of a cab driver. The same year the trial of Mr Tony Hassan and Mr Anthony Caldori was also abandoned after their lawyers argued that the national tabloid newspaper, the *News of the World*, had published an article in September 1994 which was prejudicial. It is crucial that individuals have the right to a fair trial, but it is equally important for individuals to be brought before the courts and for justice to be given the opportunity to be done.

Protecting the authority of the judiciary

As an aspect of maintaining the administration of justice, the law of contempt is also justified by the contention that it reinforces and protects the authority of the judiciary. Legal provisions enable the judge to ensure that trials proceed without inappropriate interruptions and that orders of the court are respected and complied with.

The issue of anonymity

A number of legal provisions exist, which together with the Contempt of Court Act 1981, operate to keep certain aspects of legal proceedings secret in an effort to protect privacy and confidentiality interests. Examples include protecting the anonymity of the complainant in rape cases, the justification of which is provided by the belief that anonymity will encourage other victims to come forward.[53] Similar safeguards are available to protect witnesses from intimidation and to preserve the confidentiality of trade and official secrets. Numerous statutory provisions also exist to protect children in both civil and criminal proceedings. Provisions contained within the Youth and Criminal Evidence Act 1999 may have serious implications for the work of investigative journalists.[54]

The arguments against restrictions

Although it is acknowledged that freedom of expression interests may have to be compromised to a certain degree, the arguments against such restrictions are compelling and suggest that such constraints should only be countenanced in clear and pressing circumstances. The fundamental principle operating in support of this contention is that justice should be seen to be done.[55] Robust examination of the legal process ensures the accountability of the judiciary and discourages the insidious growth of 'secret courts' (Barendt 1993). Media coverage of trials may also have an educational value, providing the public with an invaluable insight into the workings of the courts and the legal system. Publicity surrounding cases may serve to discourage perjury and encourage individuals to come forward with information vital to the course of justice. There are numerous examples of investigative journalism that can be cited in support of the importance of an open system of justice, and minimal media restrictions. The media coverage surrounding the thalidomide scandal serves as a classic illustration (see page 140).

Investigative journalists need to be aware of the law of contempt as it impacts upon their activities in a variety of ways. For example, stories that uncover illegal activities may well result in arrests and court appearances. Alternatively the subject of an investigation may already be subject to proceedings or restriction orders from the court. In such cases the law will determine how the story can be covered, if it can be covered at all.

The conflict between the right to a fair trial and the investigative jour-nalist's right to freedom of expression is not an easy one to resolve. Media excesses do result in gross contempts, and the challenge is to establish a system that draws an appropriate balance between the needs of freedom of expression and the administration of justice. Does English law achieve the right balance?

The English position: a case study[56]

Until 1981, the English provisions relating to contempt were to be found within the common law. Over many years the judiciary had developed a set of principles that established a strict liability offence. The media were at risk of being in contempt if they published during the *sub judice* period. At common law this was a vague term which included an indeterminate time span applying both before and after civil and criminal proceedings. During this period of time the journalist who intentionally published material that created a real risk that the proceedings in question might be prejudiced ran the risk of prosecution.

Decisions in contempt cases brought before 1981 provide 'an important insight into judicial attitudes to the protection of freedom of expression' (Boyle 1982: 592). There was growing concern that the application of the law was resulting in the suppression of open public debate on matters of public importance and that the broadness of the test adopted by the courts was out of all proportion to the actual risk to the administration of justice. The Phillimore Committee considered reform of the law in 1974. Matters, however, came to a head when the national newspaper, the *Sunday Times* was brought before the courts over its campaign against Distillers, the manufacturers of the drug thalidomide.

The parents of the thalidomide children had been seeking compensation for some time from the manufacturers of the drug, which, it was believed, had caused their terrible deformities. The pre-trial proceedings had gone on for some considerable time and the *Sunday Times* began a campaign on behalf of the victims to highlight their plight. Distillers argued that such coverage prejudiced their right to a fair hearing before the courts. The Attorney General commenced contempt proceedings against the newspaper and although the case was appealed to the House of Lords, the court imposed an injunction banning further publication on the story. While it was recognised that there was a conflict of public interests, the House of Lords felt that 'trial by the press' would undermine public confidence in the administration of justice. Harold Evans, editor of the newspaper at the time, commented 'our case and their judgements met each other only as the express on the up-line meets an express on the down, flashing past each other in a blur' (Evans 1994: 80).

The *Sunday Times* took their case to the European Court of Human Rights, arguing that the injunction banning publication breached Article 10 of the European Convention on Human Rights.[57] In a decision hailed as a victory for press freedom, the European Court confirmed that although it was legitimate for a state to enact legal provisions to protect the authority of the judiciary, these were only sustainable in as far as they were 'necessary in a democratic society'. By a majority decision of 11 to 9, the court declared that the free speech interests in discussing an important public issue outweighed the interests of justice in this particular case.

The thalidomide story is often cited as a classic example of investigative journalism. It also serves to provide a useful reminder of how the English law of contempt as it stood at the time constrained the work of those campaigning to remedy an injustice. The resulting legal action was symbolic on a number of levels, none more so than the recognition that English law failed to provide an appropriate balance between the interests of justice and freedom of expression.

As a direct response to the ruling of the European court, the UK government enacted the Contempt of Court Act 1981. The changes introduced a number of liberalising measures. The time limits on the application of the statutory contempt provisions were more clearly defined, and the test for liability appeared to move towards a greater recognition of free speech interests.

In addition and of particular relevance to the work of investigative journalists is that a public interest defence was introduced by Section 5 of the Act.[58]

This defence, which was introduced specifically to respond to the criticisms made by the European Court of Human Rights in the thalidomide case, may not apply to publications that focus on the detail of a case before the courts. Indeed it is arguable that had the defence been available to the *Sunday Times* it would not have protected them from an injunction banning their coverage of the scandal.[59]

Although the legislation is an improvement on the pre-1981 position, it is submitted that the provisions contain a number of weaknesses that continue to impact in a detrimental way upon the work of investigative journalists and also fail to prevent media excess. Inconsistent signals from the judiciary as to what will amount to serious or substantial prejudice have resulted in difficulties for editors in judging how to cover a particular story.[60] In July 1997, News Group Newspapers was fined £50,000 for publishing an article in the *News of the World* which, it was suggested, brought about the abandonment of a criminal trial. It is common practice for journalists involved in investigations that uncover criminal activities to inform the police of their findings shortly before publication. In this way, the journalist is able to run the story in the knowledge that the subjects of the investigation will not have the opportunity to escape justice or destroy valuable evidence. The subject of the investigation will generally be 'helping the police with their inquiries' and although the case may be *active*, there is an obvious benefit to society in taking a flexible approach to the issue of prejudicial media coverage in such circumstances. In the *News of the World* case, journalist Mazher Mahmood had been carrying out an investigation into an alleged counterfeit currency scam. Mahmood informed the police of his findings and on 10 September 1994 the police made a number of arrests in connection with the alleged conspiracy. The *News of the World* ran an article under the banner headline, 'We Smashed £100m Fake Cash Ring.' The story gave details relating to the criminal backgrounds of two individuals who were subsequently charged. Although the trial did not start for a further ten months, the media coverage was deemed to have been prejudicial and News Group Newspapers was found guilty of contempt. The decision leaves investigative journalists in an impossible situation. Len Gould, editor of the *People* commented, 'In our opinion this is a dangerous judgement which places obstacles in the path of investigative journalism and fails to serve the public interest. Some old fashioned common sense is required' (*The People*, 20 July 1997).

Rather confusingly the 1981 Act did not remove the possibility of a journalist being convicted for common law contempt.[61] Although the prosecution must show an intention to prejudice the case, the fact that neither the defences nor the active period as defined under the Contempt of Court Act 1981 will apply can only reintroduce an element of uncertainty for journalists.

The Internet, contempt and investigative journalists

The current English legal provisions operating to protect the administration of justice face new challenges with the growing importance and the irresistible impact of the Internet. While the English courts may impose legal restrictions upon all journalists it is increasingly apparent that such orders cannot keep the lid on the 'ever expanding, unmanageable morass of inter-tangled material' (Edwards and Wealde 1997b: 20) that is the World Wide Web. In 1997 investigative journalist Dawn Alford ran a story in the *Daily Mirror* alleging that a senior cabinet minister's son had been involved in drug dealing. Although the article did not name the minister or the youth concerned, media outlets were keen to reveal their identities.[62] In a dubious legal decision, however, an injunction was granted under Section 2(2) of the Contempt of Court Act 1981, preventing the English media from identifying the 17-year-old youth and thereby retaining anonymity for his father as well. In addition, Alford was arrested for possession of cannabis obtained as a result of her undercover activities. The case raises a number of concerns relating to ethical and privacy considerations. In addition it highlights the dilemma facing the investigative journalist who, in seeking to obtain evidence to support the allegations made, may find themselves subject to prosecution! In terms of the law of contempt, the case illustrates how legal provisions can be invoked too readily at the expense of freedom of expression and information. But such measures are becoming increasingly ineffective with the easily accessed and very often anonymous nature of information placed on the Internet, for while the English newspaper buying public were in the dark, the Internet identified to all those with access to it that the minister concerned was Jack Straw.

The law of contempt and confidential sources

Of additional concern and particular importance to the work of investigative journalists is the limited protection offered under Section 10 of the Contempt of Court Act to journalists who wish to maintain the confidentiality of their sources. As every journalist knows, sources are the lifeblood of a good story.[63] On many occasions such sources are willing to be named; indeed it may be vital to produce the individual as a witness to defend a defamation action. There are, however, circumstances when a source will only come forward and provide information on the understanding that their identity will not be disclosed. It is in such circumstances that investigative journalists may find they are in conflict with the law. Such a conflict occurred following the broadcast of a television programme entitled 'The Committee', which formed part of a series of programmes known as *Dispatches* made by Box Productions for Channel 4. The programme alleged that there was widespread and systematic collusion between members of the RUC and loyalist terrorists that had resulted in at least twenty sectarian murders in Northern Ireland over the previous two years. Much of the information for the programme was provided by source 'A', who played a role on the explicit understanding that Box Productions and Channel 4 would protect his identity. Under powers contained within the Prevention of Terrorism Act 1989, the police successfully applied for orders requiring Channel 4 to disclose information that would invariably lead to the identification of the source. Following a refusal to comply with this request, Channel 4 and Box Productions were found guilty of contempt.[64]

Section 10 of the Contempt of Court Act 1981 appears to confer a qualified privilege upon investigative journalists and others, allowing them to refuse to disclose the identity of a source of information. The section is subject to a number of exceptions, allowing the court to insist upon disclosure when it is 'necessary in the interests of justice or national security or for the prevention of disorder or crime'. While the section recognises the public interest in protecting sources and the importance of confidentiality to freedom of expression, it enables the court to consider the particular facts before them and balance the competing interests. However, case law would suggest that with a few exceptions the approach adopted by the House of Lords has failed to give sufficient weight to the interests of free speech, rendering the statutory protection illusory.

In 1996, the European Court of Human Rights ruled that a court order requiring journalist Bill Goodwin to reveal a source breached Article 10 of the European Convention on Human Rights.[65] The case was hailed as a victory for investigative journalism. Goodwin's counsel, Geoffrey Robertson QC commented in the *Daily Telegraph* (28 April 1996) that the Contempt of Court Act 1981 would have to be amended to provide greater protection for journalists and bring English law into line with the European Convention. To date the law remains unchanged and, despite the Goodwin ruling, a number of subsequent decisions indicate that the law is less than clear on the issue of upholding a journalist's right to protect a source.[66] The Public Interest Disclosure Act 1998 may serve to ameliorate some of the difficulties associated with whistle-blowing and protecting sources, although the emphasis in the act appears to be upon employment protection and compensation rather than freedom of expression and information. The act prevents whistle-blowers from being treated unfairly, but requires that disclosure only be made to one of a limited group of individuals, which can include the employer, but does not include journalists.[67] Disclosure may only be made to 'unspecified persons' if the matter is of an exceptionally serious nature and the individual has acted in good faith, for no personal gain and having previously raised their concerns with their employer, legal adviser or in accordance with the whistle-blowing procedure. Whilst an improvement, the provisions still beg several questions.

It remains to be seen whether incorporation of the European Convention on Human Rights into English law will help to resolve the issues surrounding journalistic confidentiality. What is clear is that any legal requirement to disclose the identity of a source acts as a severe blow to investigative journalism, undermining its ability to expose corruption and wrong-doings.[68]

Summary

The law of contempt and a variety of statutory provisions exist in English law to protect the public interest in the administration of justice. While this is acknowledged by most Western democracies to be an important principle, it is also recognised that such restrictions will impact upon the interests of freedom of expression and should therefore only apply in 'legitimate' circumstances.

The English provisions provide only vague guidance for working journalists. The judiciary are left to determine cases on an individual basis. Inconsistent decisions of the courts, the disparity in approach taken by the Attorney General in commencing contempt actions, and the Internet technology revolution have encouraged journalists to test the boundaries of what is and is not legal in English contempt law. This uncertainty cannot be good for the administration of justice or for investigative journalism.

The investigative journalist, English law and privacy

The work of the investigative journalist raises inevitable conflicts between freedom of speech and the protection of privacy. The very nature of investigative journalism involves potentially intrusive activities. Once again, the law is required to draw a balance between these conflicting interests. In many countries, such as Germany, the United States, France and Canada, a right to privacy is recognised as part of their domestic law.[69] In addition a number of jurisdictions provide constitutional protection for the privacy of their citizens. In the US, for example, a more general constitutional protection is also available.[70] Article 8 of the European Convention on Human Rights guarantees that 'Everyone has the right to respect for his private and family life, his home and his correspondence'. The incorporation of the convention into English law will provide the judiciary with the opportunity to develop a consistent approach to the protection of privacy interests. There is, however, no specific statutory protection for privacy in English law, although a variety of statutory, common law and equitable rules exist which may offer incidental limited protection against invasions of privacy.[71] In addition, a number of regulatory codes exist which allow individuals to seek some redress for inappropriate invasions of their private lives.[72] The situation is further exacerbated by the rapid and expanding use of the Internet, raising concerns relating to security, confidentiality and ownership of private and personal information.

A number of attempts have been made to introduce some form of statutory protection for privacy.[73] All have failed to become law. In addition a variety of reports have been produced which considered proposals for reform in this area.[74] Demands for change have often followed notorious media intrusions. The public hostility to intrusive media coverage of the private lives of public figures was exemplified by the public's reaction following the death of Diana, the Princess of Wales in 1997.[75] Many journalists believe that the legal restraints that already exist in the UK provide sufficient protection of privacy. Investigative journalists fear that if a privacy law were to be introduced then their ability to expose wrong-doings would be inhibited even further. In contrast, there are many who believe that without such a provision it is impossible to curb media excesses. Once again, the challenge is to provide an appropriate level of protection against unwarranted invasions of privacy, while enabling the media to investigate and publish stories that raise issues of public interest.

How is privacy protected in English law?

The investigative journalist's ability to access, gather and publish information in the UK is subject to a great many statutory and common law restrictions. Individuals with a legitimate desire to protect their private lives also deploy these provisions, with varying degrees of success. The English courts have been willing to extend established forms of action to provide a remedy in some, though not all cases.[76] In the hands of less scrupulous individuals and organisations, these same provisions have been used as a means of restraining the work of investigative journalists.

With the help and advice of the legal profession, investigative journalists have developed methods of avoiding many of the legal pitfalls placed in their way. It is not possible to detail all the various provisions that create this patchwork of protection for privacy and the resulting potential minefield for journalists, but a number have been selected by way of illustration.

The laws of trespass and nuisance provide some relief for property owners who believe their privacy is being invaded.[77] As a result, the snooping journalist can be required to leave private premises. However, this does little to deter the tenacious journalist, for there are always alternative ways to 'get the story'. The use of long-distance cameras, aerial photography and a wide variety of surveillance devices cannot be restrained by the law of trespass.[78] Similarly many investigative journalists who wish to interview an individual will undertake this in a public place, or by means of a scam whereby the target is invited to alternative premises.[79] In this way the law of trespass is simply side-stepped.

In recent years the law of copyright has been used to protect privacy interests and has been invoked in an attempt to curtail unwanted media revelations. The subject of an investigation by the media can call upon the law of copyright to prevent the publication of, for example, private photographs and diaries. Although this may cause some inconvenience for investigative

145

journalists, the difficulty can be resolved by invoking the defence of fair dealing, or by taking their own film footage and photographs of the target in public and/or private locations (subject to the law of trespass). Having no ownership in the item, the target cannot then use the law of copyright to protect their privacy or prevent publication.

Of greater concern, however, is that the law of copyright can be used to identify journalists' sources. Stories drawn to the attention of the media by moles and whistle-blowers require as much verification as possible before the outlet concerned will publish.[80] Corroboration of allegations of corruption and wrong-doings may be contained within confidential reports and private (and public) correspondence. The law of copyright can be invoked to prevent the publication of such documents and also to insist upon their return. Fair dealing and public interest defences are available to defend such breaches of copyright.[81] However, the requirement to return leaked documents may serve to identify sources to whom journalists have promised confidentiality.[82]

A further illustration is provided by data protection legislation, which provides some protection for privacy interests and is of particular relevance to the growing debate surrounding concerns relating to privacy and computer technology. The legislation acknowledges the difficult balance to be drawn between individual privacy and media freedom in relation to the collection of information. The individual has the right to ensure that personal data has been collected fairly, is only held for a lawful purpose, is accurate and that there is no unauthorised disclosure of the information held. The provisions create a number of difficulties for investigative journalists. They may be denied access to information essential to the investigation of a story, whilst the subject of their inquiries may have the legal right to access information held on file by the journalist. An unfettered right to access journalists' records in this way could be abused by the rich and the powerful and effectively curtail responsible investigative journalism. Targets would be able to establish exactly what was known about their activities, they would have the opportunity to discover the identity of sources and challenge any information held which was not obtained 'lawfully' (this might include secret filming and recording). The Data Protection Act 1998 provides an exemption from the requirements of the legislation for 'special purposes', which includes journalism. It remains to be seen how this exemption is applied in practice.

The law of breach of confidence provides a final example of how established principles in English law have been refined to safeguard privacy interests. Originally developed as a means of protecting commercial secrets, in recent years it has been extended to protect secret information belonging to both individuals and organisations. Fenwick and Phillipson (1996) argue that the flexibility of the doctrine of confidence in English law provides a potential means of protecting individual privacy. In *Francome v MGN Ltd* it was used in legal argument to prevent the publication of material obtained by a journalist who had taped a number of the plaintiff's private telephone conversations.[83]

Inevitably the doctrine raises particular concerns for investigative journalists. The law of confidentiality has the potential to restrain publications about the workings of central and local government.[84] The doctrine may also serve to discourage whistle-blowers from coming forward with information worthy of investigation by journalists,[85] although the Public Interest Disclosure Act 1998 makes confidentiality clauses void in certain circumstances.[86] Despite these major concerns, it should be noted that a public interest defence supporting publication is available, if it can be shown that this outweighs the public interest in preserving a confidence and preventing disclosure.[87] Once again, it falls to the judiciary to determine an appropriate balance between these conflicting interests.

If the piecemeal development of the protection of privacy in English law is unacceptable to both 'victim' and journalist, would a privacy law resolve the issue? Attempts to define the scope of such legislation have met with inevitable problems. It is particularly difficult to provide a clear distinction between that which is public and that which is private. These spheres of interest are not mutually exclusive (Paton-Simpson: 1998) and it is often where the two meet that the investigative journalist's work begins.

It is assumed that any privacy law, were it to be introduced, would include a public interest defence. Although an extensive defence would provide some relief for journalists, it relies upon the judiciary to balance any competing interests. In addition, the very nature of investigative journalism involves a preliminary period of research, which by implication involves intrusion, some of which may cross over into the 'private' sphere. A public interest defence may not provide protection for such activities as it could be difficult for journalists to satisfy this test in the early stages of their inquiries. This would seriously inhibit investigative journalism.

In both Germany and Canada the courts have developed principles for balancing privacy against free speech interests. Craig and Nolte (1998) argue that the Canadian and German approach provides a structured and coherent system for the resolution of such conflicts. The judiciaries in these two countries have developed a multi-factored approach, which is used in individual cases to balance the competing rights. The courts take into account such factors as the status of the individual claiming privacy; the location; the nature of the information and its relevance to public debate; what motivates the publication and whether the story could have been covered in some other way to limit any invasion of privacy.

Incorporation of the European Convention on Human Rights will provide the English judiciary with an opportunity to develop a similar approach to the protection of privacy in English law whilst recognising the importance of free speech (Article 8 is to be balanced by Article 10). Many journalists fear that if a distinct Privacy Act were to be introduced this would distort the balancing process, as the courts would respect such a provision as the clear will of Parliament. Such a statute, when combined with the English libel laws and data protection provisions would have to be balanced with some sort of freedom of information legislation. On 24 May 1999 the UK government published a long awaited draft freedom of information bill. The proposals are, however, widely criticised as being overly restrictive, and in any event it is anticipated that they will take several years to become law.

Summary

British journalists are accused of intrusive, prurient and unnecessary invasions of private lives almost daily. Article 8 of the European Convention on Human Rights, and a variety of statutory, common law, equitable rules and ethical codes of conduct provide some redress for the victims of such media excesses. However, the same provisions enable others to restrain the work of investigative journalists under the pretext of protecting privacy interests, and as a consequence suppress the exposure of wrong-doings. The introduction of a privacy law might provide an opportunity to curb the unacceptable face of journalism, but would have to be balanced effectively against the important concepts of freedom of information and expression.

Conclusion

This chapter has sought to focus attention on the extent to which English law affects the work of the investigative journalist. From the premise that both ideologically and practically the concept of freedom of speech is fundamental to the work of investigative journalists, a number of key legal constraints have been examined. Whilst the three main areas selected for consideration raise particular points of interest, they reflect the same key debates: most of the legal provisions that exist in English law and impact upon the work of investigative journalists can be justified in principle, but it is how they are formulated, applied and developed by a Parliament and judiciary which is not under a constitutional duty to consider free speech issues that lies at the heart of the debate. The balance that is drawn between the various interests and the fundamental principle of free speech determines the boundaries of investigative journalism. The chapter has provided an analysis of how the balance is drawn in English law in the areas of reputation, privacy and the administration of justice, but such an analysis could be applied equally well in a number of other contentious areas. For example, it may apply in considering the legal provisions relating to the activities of local and central government, commercial organisations, and the very strictly regulated area of official secrets.[88]

While the law struggles to resolve the difficulties inherent in the transnational and all pervasive nature of the Internet, some investigative journalists may enjoy a period of relatively unfettered freedom of expression.[89] That opportunity and facility should be embraced enthusiastically but with the highest professional and ethical standards, and in the certain knowledge that as access to the Internet increases, governments will be attempting to find the legal means to exercise control over the new global information networks.

The targets of investigative journalists' activities believe that the media abuse the public interest justification argument, push the limits of the law and disregard regulatory and ethical codes of conduct simply for commercial gain. Investigative journalists argue, however, that at present they labour within a framework of legal and regulatory restraint that encroaches upon their work both directly and indirectly. While there is no easy solution to the conflict that can inevitably arise between rights, journalists in the United Kingdom believe that many of the provisions that exist can be used by the powerful and privileged to suppress stories of public importance, and undermine their role as public watchdog.

NOTES

1 The term 'English legal system' extends to both England and Wales. Scotland, Northern Ireland, the Isle of Man and the Channel Islands have separate systems.
2 For further reading on the issue of regulating the media see Gibbons 1998.
3 For an excellent 'how to' book see Greenwood and Welsh 1999.
4 See for example Mullin 1986 and Foot 1993. See also Chapter 13.
5 See in particular the section on privacy, and Chapter 8.
6 In a work of this nature it is not possible to include an analysis of all the legal provisions that impinge upon the work of investigative journalists. A further reading list is provided at the end of the chapter.
7 See *The Sunday Times v UK* 2 E.H.R.R. 245.
8 Representational democracy may not, however, provide the best access to freedom of expression. See Bagdikian 1989 or Held 1987.
9 The issues surrounding official secrecy and investigative journalism are not covered in any detail in this text. Please refer to the further reading list for recommended texts.
10 See, for example, the Canadian Charter of Rights and Freedoms (s.2), the Spanish Constitution, Art. 20, the Swedish Constitution, Chap. 2, Art. 1(1).
11 For further discussion see, Kingsford–Smith and Oliver (eds.) 1990, particularly Lewis, 'Journalists and the First Amendment' p. 1–15.
12 See the Magna Carta (1215) and the Bill of Rights (1688), though these do not contain references to major rights and freedoms.
13 The basic rights enshrined in the convention include: the right to life; freedom from torture or inhuman or degrading treatment, slavery, arbitrary arrest and detention; the right to a fair trial; the right to privacy, family life; freedom of expression, religion and association; the right to marry and found a family; the right to education; freedom from discrimination.
14 Note the judges do have the power to declare the provision 'incompatible' with the convention. This can signal a Parliamentary fast track amendment procedure.
15 See *Sunday Times v UK* (1980) 2 E.H.R.R. 245.
16 This chapter focuses on the English law of defamation as a civil wrong. Libel is also a criminal offence which takes two main forms: (1) defamatory libel, and (2) blasphemous, seditious, and obscene libel. For further discussion of these topics the reader is referred to the further reading list. The reader is also invited to

consider the growth in malicious falsehood claims to protect a reputation. See *Kaye v Robertson* (1991) F.S.R. 62. See also the section on privacy.

17 A fair and accurate report of judicial proceedings in a court within the United Kingdom, published contemporaneously, is protected by absolute privilege.

18 For textbooks on defamation law please see the further reading list.

19 See for example a set of three cases, involving the entertainer Liberace, the pop singer Jason Donovan and the ex-MP David Ashby. Each of these cases considered whether it is defamatory to refer to someone as a homosexual. It is interesting to note that the two more recent cases do not make it clear whether a jury would take the view that calling someone a homosexual is defamatory. Both cases suggested that such statements were nonetheless defamatory as they implied that the subjects of the accusations were *lying* about their sexuality.

20 See for example *Sim v Stretch* (1936) 52 T.L.R. 669.

21 The BBC was ordered to pay Upjohn, a pharmaceutical company, damages following allegations made in a *Panorama* programme, 'The Halcion Nightmare', broadcast in 1991. An employee of Upjohn, Dr Royston Drucker, was awarded £75,000; he was said to have been defamed 'in an emphatic and vivid form by an explicit statement in a popular television broadcast'.

22 On 7 January 1996 the *News of the World* claimed that Marks and Spencer knowingly exploited child labour. George Carman QC for Marks and Spencer stated that this 'struck at the heart of Marks and Spencer's reputation for conducting business in a totally honest manner.'

23 Dolores O'Riordan, a singer with the band The Cranberries received a public apology and a donation to the charity Warchild in April 1996 from the national newspaper the *Sport*.

24 See Chapter 8 and the discussion surrounding *The Connection*, an award winning documentary by Carlton Television, which became the subject of an investigation by the *Guardian* who exposed the programme as largely a fake.

25 This includes a defamatory statement in writing, or broadcast on radio or television.

26 See also Germany, India and The Netherlands, which recognise a public interest defence to a defamation action.

27 376. US 254 (1964).

28 For further discussion see Chapter 8.

29 Cmnd 5099, 1975 paras. 211–15.

30 The Neill Committee on Practice and Procedure in Defamation.

31 See Media Lawyer 3 (1996) 25–7.

32 (1993) 1 All ER 1011.

33 See also *Goldsmith and Another v Bhoyrul and Others* 1997 4 All E.R. 268, and Chapter 10.

34 (1998) 3 WLR 862. See also Loveland 1998.

35 The *Reynolds* criteria were applied by the Court of Appeal in *Saif al Islam Gaddafi v Telegraph Group Ltd* (1999) Tolley's Communications Law Vol 4, 2 p.75. The case was also interesting as it considered the issue of protecting journalists' sources. See also Hamer (6 November 1998) *Press Gazette*.

36 See the defamation actions brought against the national newspaper the *Guardian* by former Member of Parliament Neil Hamilton and Jonathan Aitken. See also Leigh and Vulliamy 1997.

37 Note, the defence of qualified privilege is available to individuals, including journalists, who pass on evidence of a criminal offence to the police, though this does not cover any related publication.

38 Although very few cases are brought, libel does also exist as a criminal offence. See Sir James Goldsmith's action against *Private Eye* in 1975 which is discussed in Ingrams 1979. See also Spencer 1977.

39 The first defamation action using a conditional fee agreement involved Luisa Morelli and Vincent Coyle, who successfully sued *The Sunday Times* (PA News, 21 December 1998).

40 See *John v MGN Ltd* (1996) 2 All E.R. 35.

41 See *Rantzen v MGN Ltd* (1993) 4 All E.R. 975 and *Tolstoy v UK* (1995) 20 E.H.R.R. 442.

42 See Johnson and Dyer '"Scapegoat" doctor wins libel damages of £625000' the *Guardian*, 24 February 1996.

43 For example intellectual property, competition, security and privacy issues.

44 See, for example the technique known as 'flaming', where essentially abusive messages are posted on bulletin boards.

45 See Chapter 9.

46 See *Rindos v Hardwick* (1994) in which a newsgroup was ordered to pay compensation for defamatory material displayed on the Internet. Unreported, Supreme Court of Western Australia, 31 March 1994. See comment in Edwards and Wealde 1997a. See also, *Western Provident Association v Norwich Union Health-Care and Norwich Union Life Insurance, Times* 18 July 1997. Note, Internet Service Providers may also face liability, although section 1 of the Defamation Act 1996 may provide a defence if it can be shown that they took all reasonable care in relation to the publication.

47 'Mirroring' is the copying of a web site onto multiple servers, probably in different countries, where different laws may apply. If one copy of the web site is shut down – whether for legal or technical reasons – the content will still be available at another web site address.

48 The 'fair trial/free press' conflict in the US is outlined in Overbeck 1996.

49 See *Attorney-General v Associated Newspapers Ltd. And Others* (1994) 1 All E.R. 556.

50 See *R v Taylor and Taylor* (1994) 98 Cr. App. Rep. 361.

51 Additional statutory provisions exist which place a number of restrictions upon media reports of legal proceedings. For example, there are strict rules regarding media coverage of committal hearings under section 8 of the Magistrates' Courts Act. For further discussion see Greenwood and Welsh 1999.

52 See Clare Dyer, 'Media coverage stops trials', *Guardian*, 27 October 1995.

53 For further discussion see the considerations of the Advisory Group on the Law of Rape, Cmnd 6352 (1975).

54 See Media Lawyer, no. 19 and 20.

55 See *Ambard v Attorney-General for Trinidad and Tobago* (1936) A.C. 322.

56 See also Chapter 16.

57 *Sunday Times v UK* (1980) 2 E.H.R.R. 245.

58 Section 5 states that, 'A publication made as or as part of a discussion in good faith of public affairs or other matters of general public interest is not to be treated as contempt of court under the strict liability rule, if the risk of impediment or prejudice is merely incidental to the discussion.' See the application of the section in *Attorney General v English* (1982) 2 All E.R. 903.

59 See *Attorney-General v TVS Television Ltd, Times*, 7 July 1989.

60 Compare *Attorney-General v MGN Ltd* (1997) 1 All E.R. 456 and *Attorney-General v Piers Morgan and News Group Newspapers*.

61 See section 6c, Contempt of Court Act 1981 and *Attorney General v Newspaper Publishing plc* (1988) 2 All E.R. 906. Compare with *Attorney General v Sport Newspapers Ltd.* (1991) 1 W.L.R. 1194.

62 The minister's son was entitled to the protection of the law of contempt, which prevented prejudicial media reporting once the case became active. However, the provisions contained within the Children and Young Persons Act 1933 preventing the media from identifying the young person only take effect in relation to court *proceedings*. Please note these legal provisions are the subject of review and amendment under the Youth and Criminal Evidence Act 1999.

63 See Chapter 8.

64 *DPP v Channel 4 Television Co Ltd and Another* (1993) 2 All E.R. 517.

65 *Goodwin v UK* (1996) 22 E.H.R.R. 123.

66 See *Camelot Group plc v Centaur Communications Ltd* (1998) 1 All E.R. 251.

67 See section 43C–F. The Public Interest Disclosure Act 1998 inserts new sections into the Employment Rights Act 1996.

68 See Allan 1991.

69 The Privacy Act 1974 (US). The Canadian Protection of Privacy Act 1974. The French Civil Code, Article 1382. The German Civil Code, 823(1).

70 See *NAACP v Alabama* 357 US 449 (1958), *Sweezy v New Hampshire* 354 US 234 (1957), *Massiah v United States* 377 US 201 (1964).

71 See *Kaye v Robertson* (1991) F.S.R. 62.

72 See The Broadcasting Standards Commission, The Press Complaints Commission, The Independent Television Commission and the Radio Authority. See also Chapter 8.

73 See for example: Lord Mancroft in 1961, Alex Lyon in 1967, Brian Walden in 1969, Sir William Cash in 1987, John Browne in 1988 and Lord Stoddart in 1989.

74 See: 1970 The Justice Report, *Privacy and the Law*; 1972 The Younger Committee, *Report of the Committee on Privacy* Cmnd 5012; 1981 Law Commission *Breach of Confidence* No 110, Cmnd 8388; 1990 The Calcutt Committee, *Report of the Committee on Privacy and Related Matters* Cm 1102; 1993 Sir David Calcutt, *Review of press regulation* Cm 2135; 1993 Lord Chancellors' Department, *Infringement of Privacy*, Consultation Paper; 1993 National Heritage Select Committee, *Privacy and Media Intrusion*.

75 See also *Kaye v Robertson* (1991) F.S.R. 62 and the action taken by Diana, Princess of Wales in 1994 against Mirror Group Newspapers to prevent the further publication of pictures taken secretly of her working out in a private gym.

76 Privacy interests have been protected in various ways by, the law of trespass, nuisance, defamation, malicious falsehood, breach of confidence, harassment, copyright, data protection, contempt, reporting restrictions, interception of communications and contract.

77 Although in *Kaye v Robertson* (1991) F.S.R. 62 the argument that flashlight photography amounted to trespass to the person was rejected by the court.

78 *Bernstein v Skyways* (1978) 1 QB 479.

79 See Chapter 15.

80 See previous comments on the Public Interest Disclosure Act 1998.

81 See *Lion Laboratories v Evans and Express Newspapers* (1984) 2 All ER 417.

82 See *Secretary of State for Defence v Guardian Newspapers* (1985) AC 339.

83 The private tapping of telephones is also an offence under the Interception of Communications Act 1985 s 1. Secret recordings are also controlled by regulatory codes, see Chapter 8.

84 See *Attorney-General v Jonathan Cape* (1976) QB 752, *Attorney-General v Guardian Newspapers Ltd* (1987) 3 All ER 316 and *Attorney-General v Guardian Newspapers Ltd* (1990) 1 AC 109.

85 See *BSC v Granada Television* (1981) 1 All E.R. 417 and *Lion Laboratories Ltd. v Evans* (1984) 2 All E.R. 417.

86 The Public Interest Disclosure Act 1998, section 43 J(1).
87 See *X v Y and Others* (1988) 2 All E.R. 648.
88 See the further reading list.
89 As previously stated in the section on defamation, the Internet is subject to legal regulation, but raises a number of challenges. See Lloyd 1997.

BIBLIOGRAPHY

Allan, T. (1991) Disclosure of journalists' sources, civil disobedience and the rule of law. *C.L.J.*, 131.

Bagdikian, B. (1989) The lords of the global village. *The Nation*.

Barendt, E. (1993) Libel and freedom of speech in English law. *P.L.* 449.

Barendt, E., Lustgarten, L., Norrie, K. and Stephenson, H. (1997) *Libel and the Media: The Chilling Effect*. Oxford: Oxford University Press.

Boyle, A. (1982) Freedom of expression as a public interest in English law. *P.L.* 574.

Craig, J. and Nolte, N. (1998) Privacy and free speech in Germany and Canada: lessons for an English privacy tort. *2 E.H.R.L.R.* 162.

Edwards, L. and Wealde, C. (1997a) *Law and the Internet: Regulating Cyberspace*. Oxford: Hart.

Edwards, L. and Wealde, C. (1997b) Regulating cyberspace: is there a role for law? *Computers and Law*, 19.

Evans, H. (1994) *Good Times Bad Times*. London: Phoenix.

Fenwick, H. and Philipson, G. (1996) Confidence and privacy: a re-examination. *C.L.J.*, 55 (3): 447.

Foot, P. (1993) *Murder at the Farm – Who Killed Carl Bridgwater?* London: Penguin Books.

Gibbons, T. (1998) *Regulating the Media*. London: Sweet and Maxwell.

Gould, M. (1996) Rules for the virtual society. *10 Int Review of Law, Computers and Technology*, 199.

Greenwood, W. and Welsh, T. (1999) *McNae's Essential Law for Journalists*. London: Butterworths.

Held, D. (1987) *Models of Democracy*. California: University of California.

Ingrams, R. (1979) *Goldenballs*. London: André Deutsch.

Kingsford-Smith, D. and Oliver, D. (eds) (1990) *Economical with the Truth: The Law and the Media in a Democratic Society*. Oxford: ESC Publishing Ltd.

Leigh, D. and Vulliamy, E. (1997) *Sleaze: The Corruption of Parliament*. London: Fourth Estate.

Lloyd, I. (1997) *Information Technology Law*. London: Butterworths.

Loveland, I. (1998) The constitutionalisation of political libels in English common law? *P.L.* 633.

MacDonald, B. and Petheram, M. (1998) *Media Ethics*. London: Mansell Publishing Ltd.

Meiklejohn, A. (1965) *Political Freedom: The Constitutional Powers of the People*. Oxford: Oxford University Press.

Mill, J. (1974[1859]) *On Liberty*. Harmondsworth: Penguin Classics.

Mullin, C. (1986) *Error of Judgement: The Truth about the Birmingham Bombings*. London: Chatto and Windus.

Overbeck, W. (1996) *Major Principles of Media Law*. New York: Harcourt Brace College Publishing.

Paton-Simpson, E. (1998) Private circles and public squares: invasion of privacy by the publication of 'private facts'. *3 M.L.R.* 318.

Robertson, G. and Nichol, A. (1992) *Media Law*. London: Penguin.

Rusbridger, A. (1997) The James Cameron Lecture, 22 May 1997. Copies available from James Cameron Lecture, Delta House, Imber Court Business Park, Orchard Lane, East Mosley, Surrey.

Spencer, J. (1977) *Criminal Libel – Skeleton in the Cupboard. Crim. L.R.* 383.

Vick, D. and Macpherson, L. An opportunity lost: the united kingdom's failed reform of defamation law. On the Internet at http://www.law.indiana. edu/ fclj/ v49/no3/ vick. html

Wacks, R. (1995) *Privacy and Press Freedom*. London: Blackstone.

Weaver, R. and Bennett, G. (1993) New York Times Co v Sullivan: the 'Actual Malice' standard and editorial decision-making. *Media LandPrac*14 (1): 2.

FURTHER READING

Media law

Baker, R. (1995) *Media Law: A User's Guide for Film and Programme Makers*. London: Blueprint.

Carey, P. (1996) *Media Law*. London: Sweet and Maxwell.

Creech, K. (1996) *Electronic Media Law and Regulation*. Oxford: Focal Press.

Crone, T. (1991) *Media and the Law*. London: Butterworth.

Greenwood, W. and Welsh, T. (1999) *McNae's Essential Law for Journalists*. London: Butterworth.

Robertson, G. (1992) *Freedom, The Individual and the Law*. London: Penguin.

Robertson, G. and Nichol, A. (1992) *Media Law*. London: Penguin.

Freedom of expression and information

Barendt, E. (1985) *Freedom of Speech*. Oxford: Clarendon.

Birkinshaw, P. (1988) *Freedom of Information: the Law, the Practice and the Ideal*. London: Weidenfeld and Nicolson.

Birkinshaw, P. (1990) *Government and Information: The Law Relating to Access, Disclosure and Regulation*. London: Butterworth.

Dworkin, R. (1971) *The Philosophy of Law*. Oxford: Oxford University Press.

Dworkin, R. (1978) *Taking Rights Seriously*. London: Gerald Duckworth and Co Ltd.

Dworkin, R. (1992) *A Matter of Principle*. Oxford: Clarendon.

Fenwick, H. (1998) *Civil Liberties*. London: Cavendish.

Thomas, R. (1991) *Espionage and Secrecy: the Official Secrets Acts 1911–1989 of the United Kingdom*. London: Routledge.

Defamation

(See also Media law list)

Carter-Ruck, P. and Starte, H. (1997) *Carter-Ruck on Libel and Slander*. London: Butterworth.

Duncan, C. and Neill, B. (1995) *Defamation*. London: Butterworth.

Milmo, P. and Rogers, W. (1998) *Gatley on Libel and Slander*. London: Sweet and Maxwell.

Contempt

Lowe, N. (1996) *Borrie and Lowe's Law of Contempt*. London: Butterworth.
Lowe, N. and Sufrin, B. (1996) *The Law of Contempt*. London: Butterworth.

Broadcasting/Regulation

Burton, H. (1997) Digital broadcasting in the United Kingdom. *CTLR*, 3 (1): 33.

Privacy

Wacks, R. (1993) *Personal Information: Privacy and the Law*. Oxford: Clarendon Press.

Copyright

Edenborough, M. (1995) *Intellectual Property Law*. London: Cavendish.
Flint, M. (1997) *A User's guide to Copyright*. London: Butterworth.
Philips, J. (1994) *Intellectual Property Law Handbook*. London: Butterworth.

Internet law

Wealde, C. and Edwards, L. (eds) (1997) *Law and the Internet: Regulating Cyberspace*. Oxford: Hart.

Useful web sites

All new Acts of Parliament since 1996: www.hmso.gov.uk/acts.htm
The Campaign for Freedom of Information: www.cfoi.org.uk/
Collection of the most important human rights treaties worldwide: www.umn.edu/humanrts/
Data protection: www.homeoffice.gov.uk/datapr.htm
Dictionary of legal terminology: www.wwlia.org/diction.htm
The European Court of Justice search facility for full text of recent judgements: www.Europa.eu.int/jurisp/cgi-bin/form.pl?lang=en
Government press releases: www.coi.gov.uk/coi/coihome.html
The Home Office: www.homeoffice.gov.uk/index.htm
Homepages for UK government organisations: www.open.gov.uk/
The Lord Chancellor's department: www.open.gov.uk/lcd/lcdhome.htm
Official texts from the EU: www2.echo.lu/eudocshome.html
Server run by the European Commission offering a wide range of information: www.Europa.eu.int

8

THE REGULATORY AND ETHICAL FRAMEWORK FOR INVESTIGATIVE JOURNALISM

Matthew Kieran

Good investigative journalism

Professional and ethical constraints

Journalism can usefully be characterised, in part, as an unofficial Fourth Estate which has the function of pursuing and covering stories that concern the political, legal or social interests of the public as citizens. It relies on the Lockean notion of an implicit contract (Kieran 1997: 21–63). The basic Lockean thought is that citizens must be made aware of the nature, workings and characters of those in government so they are in a position to exercise their will as citizens and judge those to whom power is entrusted on their behalf. The news media have certain privileges to act on our behalf in keeping watch over those who affect our lives. The purpose is to ensure just and fair government, due process in law, its application and enforcement, revealing corrupt and scandalous practices and informing us about events that affect the social fabric of our society. But it is important, further, to distinguish investigative journalism from standard news reporting. Standard news reporting is essentially reactive – it involves looking for stories of the day that have a public or human interest element to them, chasing up the institutions or people involved to check facts, motivation, intention, allegations and conveying to the public the nature and significance of the event involved. Investigative journalism is, by contrast, a more drawn out, murkier and sometimes much more tedious process. For although the general ends involved are the same as those of standard news reporting investigative journalism is necessarily concerned with matters such as corruption and illegality which it is difficult to discover, prove and thereby reveal to the public. The distinction is not a straight-forward hard and fast one but rather a matter of degree. Nonetheless, it has to be borne in mind when considering the regulatory and ethical considerations that are pertinent to investigative journalism.

Now the essential aims of investigative journalism give rise to various professional constraints which, as journalists, they are ethically required to adhere to. Given that investigative journalism aims at uncovering and revealing the truth about a matter of public concern, investigative journalists are required to stick to truth-adhering methods. Indeed, as is pointed out in Chapter 11, this may even require familiarity with the basic methods of the social sciences and the basic skills of critical reasoning in order to ascertain whether claims made have a reasonable scientific basis, are generalisable or the methodology unsound. Thus the quest for truth is tightly linked to procedural matters such as checking the authenticity and trustworthiness of one's sources, following up claims made to see if they bear out in fact, constitute plausible if unproved speculation or downright lies, attempting to discover if there are any motivations at work other than those presented and so on. Obviously such procedures are not sufficient to ensure that the truth of a matter will be discovered. But they are the only way of ensuring that an investigation is likely to get at the truth of the matter (Kieran 1998: 23–36). Carelessness about such procedures is thus professionally culpable and, in this respect, constitutes a moral failure to live up to the responsibilities of one's job.

An obvious example of a failure in this regard concerns *The Sunday Times*'s 'exclusive' story of 19 February 1995 that Michael Foot, former leader of the Labour Party, had worked for the Soviet KGB. Yet on inspection it transpired that, at best, the *Sunday Times* had mischaracterised their one and only source's claims. All that had happened was that Michael Foot had, at one time, met various Soviet emissaries. Given that this was true of many if not most left-wing politicians at the height of the cold war this hardly constituted news, let alone the assertion that Foot had gone on to work for them. Hence the *Sunday Times* was, in the face of legal action, forced to retract the 'story' (albeit in a small section on page 2 of the paper) and pay substantial undisclosed damages.

A more problematic case concerns the Channel 4 commissioned documentary *Daddy's Girl*. The film maker Edmund Coulthard followed, amongst others, Victoria Greetham and her putative father Marcus Greetham around for months filming for the programme – and they certainly provided compelling material. But 24 hours before transmission the documentary was pulled from transmission because it turned out that Marcus Greetham was not Victoria's father at all but 29-year-old Stuart Smith, Victoria's boyfriend. Although highly plausible, the film-makers had failed to check if a Marcus Greetham existed, whether he really worked where or owned what he claimed.

Although carelessness about professional responsibilities is culpable, it is as nothing when compared to the case of someone intentionally abrogating them. In 1998 Carlton Communications was forced to admit that a television documentary they had commissioned, broadcast and which had won many awards, *The Connection*, was guilty of at least sixteen instances of outright deception. The original allegations were made by the *Guardian* in May 1998, this was followed by a 6-month Carlton internal independent inquiry, headed by Michael Beloff QC. The *Guardian* of Saturday 5 December 1998, carried extensive coverage of the report and its findings. It was found that the audience of up to 4 million who watched the programme on ITV was thoroughly misled. The two central theses of the documentary concerning the 'revelation' of a new heroin route from Colombia through to Britain were found to be entirely unproven. The deceptions included misleading the audience as to the location of an interview with the putative No. 3 in the Cali drugs cartel – it actually took place in the producer's hotel bedroom as opposed to the mysterious location the camera crew were represented as having been escorted to under blindfold. Even more astonishingly the three central characters of the 'documentary', including the No. 3 from the drugs cartel and the drugs smuggler, were found to be actors paid for their parts by the producer rather than who they were represented as being. Indeed Marc de Beaufort, the producer, was found to have paid for the drug smuggler's trip into Britain. Moreover, what was represented as one continuous smuggling trip turned out to have been two entirely separate trips (the first time the 'smuggler' had been turned away at customs). The documentary had been run on many international channels and in the US *60 Minutes*, the high profile CBS documentary series, ran a programme explaining to its audience of millions how it had come to run segments from *The Connection*.

Such intentional deception, motivated by the producer's desire to make a sensationalist documentary programme to make a reputation for himself, is deeply immoral given the ends of investigative journalism. Far from seeking the truth, truth promoting methods were sacrificed at the altar of expedience for the sake of personal gain. There is nothing wrong with producing life-like dramas. But to present a dramatic fiction as fact is not, whatever else it may be, good investigative journalism.

However, one might think that at various points investigative journalists, to be effective as such, will have to be immoral. True moral goodness, it is often thought, requires refusing to contemplate immoral actions whatever the consequences. Yet very often successfully investigating hidden scandals or corruption requires journalists to misrepresent themselves, deceive, lie, intrude into privacy and in extreme cases even break the law, all actions we normally presume are wrong. If investigative journalists were required to be morally good they would be unable to penetrate the murky world they need to investigate and thus would be unable to do their job. It is something like this thought that underlies the presumption of many journalists that at a certain point ethical considerations are excluded from the sphere of investigative journalism – getting one's hands dirty is something that comes with the territory.

But this is to confuse moral innocence with moral goodness. To be sure a moral innocent, who by definition is unaware of the evils of the world, would have no truck with performing actions that are less than morally ideal. But this can only be possible in a world where one does not have to face evil and immorality. In such a world investigative journalism would not need to exist. But in our less than ideal world we are often required to sacrifice moral ideals in order to uphold that which is right – and this is itself a moral obligation.

The point of regulation

It does not, however, follow that the ends of investigative journalism thereby justify any means used to fulfil them or that anything or everything is licensed by such considerations. Rather, what does follow is that certain actions we normally think of as immoral can be, under certain strict conditions, morally justified. Consider an analogy. Generally we hold killing to be a deep moral evil. Yet under certain conditions, those of self-defence for example, it may be morally justified. But this is only so where one's life is threatened and the threat cannot reasonably be neutralised by actions short of killing. So the means used must be proportionate to the threat involved and no more. Similarly with investigative journalism. Such matters as deceit or intrusion into privacy may be justified – but only where they are absolutely required to establish proof of serious corruption, deceit or immorality that significantly harms others. Moreover, journalistic actions that abrogate the relevant moral considerations are very often not illegal in any way. As outlined in Chapter 6, some of the legal requirements on British journalists are fairly strict, especially when compared to the legal constraints on US journalist. Nonetheless, there are ethical considerations that arise independently of legal prohibitions and are more properly considered and treated as regulatory matters.

This explains a major part of the rationale for regulation – to ensure that journalists adhere to the moral obligations incumbent upon them and to clarify when and where they are morally justified in acting in ways we would under normal circumstances regard as immoral. Enforcement is required given the commercial, political and psychological pressures involved in investigative journalism. As we saw in the case of *The Connection*, the pressures are such that someone lacking moral integrity may easily be drawn into abrogating some of the most fundamental requirements of good journalism. Moreover the culture of investigative journalism could itself be subject to moral slippage in the increasing acceptance of dubious practices over time – such as presenting dramatic reconstructions as the representation of the actual events themselves – and regulation helps to put a brake on such slippage.

There are, though, various problems with regulation as it exists in Britain. There are several different bodies with different powers of enforcement and legal status which regulate investigative journalists working in different parts of the industry – such as the Press Complaints Commission, the ITC, the Broadcasting Standards Commission not to mention the codes of practice issued by each ITV company, the BBC and Channel 4. This renders regulation over investigative journalism a somewhat confusing matter since different codes and regulations are held to apply to investigative journalists depending on whether they are working for the BBC, an ITV company or for a newspaper. More significantly the relation between regulation and the ethical requirements investigative journalists are motivated to take seriously diverges due to the different powers of enforcement the different respective bodies have. The Press Complaints Commission is a self-regulatory body whose board is mainly constituted by editors from the major dailies. Its powers of enforcement are incredibly weak – at most amounting to the power of expulsion. Hence, despite lip service, it often seems that it is used as a rhetorical device designed to minimise possible government legislation. Conversely the ITC, which regulates independent broadcasting in Britain, has extensive powers, including the ability to fine companies severely as happened to Carlton in *The Connection* case, and even withdraw a company's franchise and thus effectively put them out of business. Hence the ITC code is taken much more seriously because its powers of enforcement are relatively strong. Such things make a difference to the extent to which an investigative journalist is motivated to take regulation seriously. Nonetheless, such powers are not sufficient to guarantee adherence to good journalistic norms.

Deceit in investigation

Obviously without trust investigative journalists cannot fulfil their function as the Fourth Estate. Yet, on the other hand, they cannot nor should they be too trusting and must often use deceitful means to achieve their goals. Hence journalists may have to break the very bonds of trust on which they depend. Honesty, openness and truth-telling are not in need of justification. But deception or lying clearly is. So we need to understand when and where deception may be justified in investigative journalism.

Deceit, public interest and proof

Consider the case, as discussed in Chapters 2 and 14, of the *Sunday Times* investigative Insight team in investigating the 'Cash for Questions' scandal. In 1994 there had been rumours going around that various lobbying firms had been exercising undue influence on MPs to ask questions on their behalf in the House of Commons. The rumours suggested that various incentives and financial remuneration had been offered to facilitate this process and lobby groups had been making inflated claims about their power and influence. Yet there was little hard core evidence to back any of these rumours up. So the Insight team decided to set up a sting operation. Acting as *agents provocateurs*, they set up a fictitious company nominally dealing in arms and blanket approached a sizeable group of MPs from all parties. Only two MPs responded and met up with one of the journalists, who pretended to be the chairman of the company. The journalist then explained he wanted a question to be asked in the House of Commons since he needed information that may affect a putative arms contract of his company. Conservative MPs Graham Riddick and David Tredennick both initially agreed to ask the suggested question in the House for a fee of £1,000. The *Sunday Times* then ran the story as an exposure of corrupt practices in the House of Commons. This seems to be an obvious case where lying and deceit is justified in the name of the public interest. It is a deeply serious matter if MPs elected on the basis of representing the interests of their constituents, and the public at large, are asking questions on the basis of shadowy financial inducements.

Yet it is not as straight-forward a matter as things superficially appear. For it is far from obvious whether the investigation revealed endemic corruption or the isolated shady behaviour of two MPs. Imagine a lecturer has heard vague rumours of students trying to cheat on her course. At the start of the next class, she lets her students know she has their exam paper before her. Then, at the end of the lecture, she deliberately leaves it there to see if any students will cheat by looking at it. Having rigged up a camera she sees that one or two students out of a large class do so. What does this show? Only that when presented with a rather tempting way of cheating, and believing they would be unlikely to be caught, a small number of people may put self-interest before moral obligations and cheat. But this is merely a reflection of the way human nature is – as Aristotle recognised we are often tempted by and sometimes succumb to acting against what we know to be right and good (Aristotle 1976: 226–57). The teacher's little sting operation does not establish that either of the two students or anyone else had been cheating prior to the set up.

Such considerations suggest that those involved in cases like those of the *Sunday Times* 'Cash for Questions' scandal are guilty of hypocrisy. For they are lying and deceiving people in order to expose them as liars and deceivers – without being able to prove that independently of the deceit the journalists perpetrated that either of the two MPs, or indeed any other, had been guilty of such corruption. This is important because given the increasing commercial and sensationalist pressures, journalistic culture must resist sliding down a slippery slope from acceptable instances of deception to those that end up manufacturing states of affairs for which there is no real independent evidence. Such moral slippage would be self-defeating – increasingly the public would come to distrust investigative journalists claiming to 'reveal' events by deception. Hence investigative journalism would be rendered impotent.

This is not to deny that there are grounds for investigating here. That there were rumours of MPs taking bribes to ask questions did constitute *prima facie* evidence that there may have been something corrupt going on, though only of a rather weak kind. But the methods used to investigate the possible problem could not have hoped to substantiate the rumours. For the sting itself was incapable of verifying or falsifying either any link to whether the prior activities supposedly being investigated had actually been taking place or, even assuming they had, whether the people involved were one and the same. Thus the means of investigation employed in this case, based on deceit, were unjustified.

161

Contrast this with the *Guardian*'s investigation of the same year into the then British government minister Jonathan Aitken, later imprisoned for perjuring himself in a libel case he pursued against the paper. It seemed they had good reason to believe that Aitken had received various 'gifts' and stayed at the Ritz Hotel in Paris on various occasions without having declared this to Parliament. Given the potential of bribery or unwarranted influence involving a government minister there is a strong public interest in pursuing the matter. However, verifying the accusations meant not only that the *Guardian* had to prove Aitken stayed at the Ritz, but who actually paid the bill. If they had approached the hotel saying they were investigating the possibly deceitful and improper conduct of a British minister they would hardly get the relevant details. So on House of Commons note paper they faxed the hotel asking to be sent a copy of the relevant bill, which they duly received. Deception is again involved, but here it constitutes the only way of revealing potentially corrupt practice and, crucially, actually constitutes a means of proving what is suspected. Not only must deceit be justified in terms of the public interest but it must constitute a means by which corruption can potentially be revealed and proven.

Privacy

Invasion of privacy is another area where we need to think very carefully about when, where and under what conditions investigative journalists may be justified in abrogating the ethical constraints we normally hold. In the first instance we should bear in mind a distinction that often fails to be made between secrecy and privacy. Secrecy involves the intentional and deliberate concealment of actions, events or information (Bok 1984: 10–14, 249–64). But not everything that is kept secret is private nor are private matters necessarily deliberately concealed. For example, the kind of local state corruption or child abuse scandals Mark D'Arcy is concerned with in Chapter 11 are often kept secret and hushed up by those involved for obvious reasons – but it could not be claimed that they are by their nature private matters. Conversely, the nature of someone's sexuality is a highly personal and private affair – and yet it is something about which many people are not secretive.

The value of privacy

Before examining the criteria determining whether an investigative journalist's invasion of privacy is justified or not, we must first consider why privacy is important (Kieran 1997: 74–86). We tend to assume privacy is a fundamental requirement of a humane or civilised society. Of course, just because something is valuable it does not follow that we have a right to it. Friendship is an important human good but it does not follow that I have a right to have friends and therefore others have a duty to befriend me. However we consider privacy to be a right for several reasons. First, as classical liberalism holds, because of the importance of autonomy. Although the defences of liberalism offered by philosophers such as Locke, Kant and Mill are vastly different, nonetheless they agree on at least one central claim: namely that we should be free to think and act as we choose, given it does not significantly harm others, and this includes the freedom to make moral mistakes. The point of the state is to provide a framework that ensures our freedom from the interference of others. Such considerations underwrite the assumption that one of the deep evils of totalitarian states is the denial of individual privacy in the name of the collective good. Hence, as Parent (1992: 92–109) has argued, the presumption is that privacy is a right since it affords a bulwark against the state or social groups acquiring power over us to our disadvantage. If privacy were not recognised as a right then we would be unprotected from threats of manipulation and coercion regarding our thoughts and behaviour. For example our sex lives should be protected as a matter of right, as long as we do not harm others, so we are free to pursue our desires as we choose shielded from social pressures of prurience, blame and condemnation. Second, certain crucial kinds of human relationships, such as friendship and love, require privacy to flourish within. Last, privacy is also important since without it we would be unable or less likely to pursue certain activities that enable our individual self-development. It is important to realise that privacy does not merely concern information – our privacy can be intruded upon by someone rummaging through our house or bank account details without their being able to glean any private information about us at all. Privacy concerns certain areas of our lives over which we exercise autonomous control and which it is not the business or right of others to concern themselves with unless we so choose. So the right to privacy is based on a recognition of ourselves as free rational agents for whom it is psychologically crucial that certain areas of our lives are considered private and protected as such in order to be able to fulfil certain fundamental human needs, desires, goals and for our relationships to flourish.

Developing privacy rights

It is for these reasons that regulatory bodies are particularly keen on ensuring the protection of people's privacy even beyond the legal protections of privacy. Interestingly the previous version of the Press Complaints Commission's code of practice stated:

> Intrusions and enquiries into an individual's private life without his or her consent including the use of long-lens photography to take pictures of people on private property without their consent are not generally acceptable and publication can only be justified when in the public interest.

Note: Private property is defined as any private residence, together with its garden and outbuildings, but excluding any adjacent fields or parkland. In addition, hotel bedrooms (but not other areas in a hotel) and those parts of a hospital or nursing home where patients are treated or accommodated.

Yet there is something deeply problematic about mapping the notion of privacy directly onto an extension of the notion of private property rights as distinct from public places. For private affairs, activities or relations are often conducted in public or quasi-public places but it does not follow that eavesdropping, recording or photographing them cannot constitute an intrusion into privacy. In recognition of this the code of practice was altered, with effect from January 1998, to:

i   Everyone is entitled to respect for his or her private and family life, home, health and correspondence. A publication will be expected to justify intrusions into any individual's private life without consent

ii The use of long lens photography to take pictures of people in private places without their consent is unacceptable

Note: Private places are public or private property where there is a reasonable expectation of privacy.

It is the qualifying note at the end which is crucial, adducing the test of reasonable expectations as to what may be considered private even when in the public sphere.

However, the right to privacy can be overridden where information or activities an individual may choose to keep private should be placed within the public sphere. So, as Belsey puts it:

where some information about an individual that he or she would prefer to keep private *should* be in the public domain, then putting it there is not overriding that individual's right to privacy because no such right ever existed concerning this aspect of a person's life ... all invasions of privacy are unjustifiable.

(Belsey and Chadwick 1992: 77)

The boundaries between the private and public areas of people's lives may be drawn in different places according to the nature of the institutions or the status of the figures journalists are dealing with. Indeed, there is strong evidence that such distinctions converge closely with the public's general attitudes towards journalistic privacy intrusions (Kieran et al. 1997: 82–93 and 122–34). Very roughly:

1   Public figures who occupy positions of power and influence in society. Politicians are an obvious case, though this category may include civil servants, professionals, business people and criminals by virtue of the fact that they either exercise power on our behalf, have public or professional responsibilities or have broken the law.

     It is crucial to recognise that only information that potentially relates to the breaking of the relevant responsibilities or duties is relevant to the public interest here.

2   Public figures created or sustained by publicity, the obvious case being people who come under the term celebrities. One might take the line that given such people's careers depend upon publicity they have, tacitly, entered into a Faustian pact. This gives the media legitimate entrée into covering their private lives – whether they consent or not (Belsey and Chadwick 1992: 72–92). But judgements here need to be rather fine grained. Obviously an actor such as Nigel Hawthorne became a public figure by virtue of his talent and dramatic success. So, in an important way, his career was somewhat sustained and furthered by the associated publicity. But since he never proffered for public consumption information about his sexuality, for example, digging into and revealing aspects of his sex life cannot be justified. Whereas the same does not hold true for one, such as Pamela Anderson, whose celebrity status has been promoted by revealing and cultivating a public appetite for just such information.

3   People who become public figures not through their own choice but involuntarily due to the nature of events – what might be termed innocent victims or bystanders. For example, someone caught up in a tragedy or news events. Here, unless strictly relevant to how and why they got caught up in the story, private information about such individuals is strictly irrelevant and such individuals have very strong privacy rights indeed.

Furthermore, it is important to recognise that those whose privacy is intruded into, in order to substantiate investigative claims, have at least a right to reply. First, because it may turn out that the evidence uncovered may have an alternative explanation. Second, even where this does not appear to be the case, those accused should have a chance to answer the allegations being made against them as a matter of principle. Last, because the public themselves should be placed in the best position possible to make up their own minds – and without the opportunity having clearly been given, even if not responded to by the accused, the possibility that someone has been unfairly characterised in the journalistic report is one the audience may take seriously.

Cheque book journalism

One interesting contemporary contrast between standard practices in investigative journalism in Britain and the US concerns the use of cheque book journalism. In the US it is shunned as a pernicious and corrupting practice whereas in Britain it is, at least in certain circles, common practice.

Criminal cases and regulatory evolution

In Britain the practice is certainly not illegal as such nor does cheque book journalism *per se* abrogate any of the relevant regulatory codes – rather it only constitutes a violation in very particular circumstances. The Press Complaints Commission's code of practice, effective since 1998, states:

i   Payment or offers of payment for stories or information must not be made directly or through agents to witnesses or potential witnesses in current criminal proceedings except where the material concerned ought to be published in the public interest and there is an over-riding need to make or promise to make a payment for this to be done. Journalists must take every possible step to ensure that no financial dealings have influence on the evidence that those witnesses may give.

    (An editor authorising such a payment must be prepared to demonstrate that there is a legitimate public interest at stake involving matters that the public has a right to know. The payment or, where accepted, the offer of payment to any witness who is actually cited to give evidence should be disclosed to the prosecution and the defence and the witness should be advised of this.)

ii   Payment or offers of payment for stories or information, must not be made directly or through agents to convicted or confessed criminals or to their associates – who may include family, friends and colleagues – except where the material concerned ought to be published in the public interest and payment is necessary for this to be done.

Notice that even here the regulation does not absolutely prohibit payment since it may be justified on grounds of public interest where the payment is necessary – presumably where without the financial incentive there would be no information.

The reason for picking out criminal related matters for special circumspection in relation to cheque book journalism should be fairly clear. Imagine a criminal case comes up in which there is a huge amount of public interest. Witnesses in the trial are approached by journalists proffering offers of large sums for the rights to their exclusive story after the trial – as long as their story proves to be of sufficient interest.

The media coverage of the murder trial of sports and media personality O. J. Simpson and the wildly divergent US and UK media coverage of the trial of the English au pair Louise Woodward served to highlight the potential dangers involved in the media coverage of trials generally. Indeed, in Britain cases such as the trial of Michelle Taylor, who had her murder conviction quashed in 1993 because the Court of Appeal judged news coverage of the original trial had been prejudicial, are less infrequent than one might like to think. But add to the dangers of prejudicial coverage the practice of cheque book journalism and the potential for undermining the judicial process is severely heightened.

The temptation for witnesses to talk up their testimony in court in order to ensure snaring the money for their exclusive, especially where large amounts are involved, would no doubt be great to some people. Moreover, even someone who consciously strives to set aside such considerations whilst giving their testimony may still be unconsciously influenced to emphasise certain aspects of their testimony, such as presenting speculation as fact or generally over-dramatising their role in events. For there is reasonably good psychological evidence to suggest that people sometimes unconsciously act to maximise their self-interest even at the expense of their self-conscious goals. Thus cheque book journalism in relation to criminal proceedings has the potential to corrupt the judicial process and undermine the justice that such proceedings are set out to enforce. This is a deeply serious matter and any such potential influence must be kept out at all costs – for it would be a heinous matter were such influences to causally effect in any way the nature of a verdict or sentence passed. True procedural justice requires critical detachment from contaminating influences to the largest extent possible.

In fact, such considerations arose in relation to the investigation and murder trial of Fred and Rosemary West. The *Daily Mirror* and *Sunday Mirror*, amongst other papers, had given or proffered money to actual or potential witnesses in 1994 and 1995. Before this case no complaints had previously been brought to the Press Complaints Commission regarding newspapers' involvement in criminal proceedings. In the light of the evidence provided by the Chief Constable of Gloucestershire Constabulary, the Commission revised its code in November 1996. The new clause places a burden of justification on the editor to prove that payment is in the public interest and, moreover, must be disclosed to the parties involved in the trial. Although in their 1996 Complaints and Adjudications ruling the Commission felt it could not then make a ruling retrospectively based on this clause, and thus felt it could not consider the actual complaint made, nonetheless this case rightly led to the strengthening of press self-regulation in this regard.

Legitimate cheque book journalism

It might be thought that if cheque book journalism is pernicious in this way then it should be prohibited entirely. For surely the same considerations apply to both criminal and non-criminal matters. Indeed, Harris has argued that it would be reasonable for codes of practice to condemn cheque book journalism as a practice quite generally on this basis (Belsey and Chadwick 1992:

74). People may similarly be tempted to talk up affairs they have had with public figures, to invent details or present speculation about a public figure as fact in order to ensure that their story merits the payment of a nice fat fee. The public figure may then suffer gross mischaracterisation, which puts them in a bad light and public opinion may turn against them on the basis of these misrepresentations. Although there is no potential cost in terms of judicial verdicts or sentences being influenced, nonetheless the cost to someone's public reputation may be great and constitute a significant harm.

Indeed, from a distance it might be taken as a mark of the less than salubrious culture of British journalism that such a practice is regarded as morally permissible. The potential for distorted, misleading and gratuitously sensational revelations being made seems to be greatly enhanced where money enters into the motivational equation. Financial reward may tempt individuals into exaggerating or presenting speculative gossip as fact in order to ensure they get the proffered cheque or, indeed, hoax journalists entirely.

However, such considerations entail only that great caution is required in making use of this practice rather than showing there is something corrupt about it as a matter of principle. Consider, for example, the fact that many people write biographies and memoirs for which they receive financial remuneration from their publishers. We do not consider that making a profit outlining the biographical stories or events in other people's lives is inherently morally wrong. Moreover, in the case of investigative journalism, it may be the only way that someone can be induced into revealing potentially vital information required to substantiate allegations. Often people are afraid for their own reputations, jobs or safety, and though far from being sufficient to get them to open up, financial reward can provide an incentive that may help the individual to overcome or come to terms with such fears.

There is something rather distasteful about individuals being paid for information which we perhaps should expect people to disclose anyway. Of course there is a distinction to be drawn between financial costs incurred in order to protect sources and actual financial reward for disclosing information. Yet in the latter case, typically those who are being rewarded seem singularly undeserving of any financial reward at all. For often they are themselves villains or accomplices in the scandal involved or, perhaps, are betraying loyalties they should be upholding merely for the sake of material gain. Nonetheless, that the practice may often be distasteful in this way does not, of itself, show the practice to be morally bankrupt. Rather, though less than ideal, where this is the only way of getting the relevant information it may be morally justified despite certain morally undesirable side-effects.

It might be useful to consider two rather contrasting cases in this light. Darius Guppy, a society figure convicted of fraud, was paid for an interview he gave to *Hello!* magazine whilst still serving part of his prison sentence. Given that *Hello!* is a glossy, uncritical, society and celebrity gossip magazine, it is hardly surprising that there was nothing of public interest, as distinct from what certain sections of the public may be interested in, and the Press Complaints Commission thus upheld complaints on such grounds holding that the articles 'merely served to glorify the crimes that Guppy had committed' (PCC August–September 1993). By contrast, complaints about the *Times* 1998 serialisation of Gitta Sereny's book about the 1960s child murderer Mary Bell were judged rather differently. The Commission found there was indeed a compelling public justification – issues addressed included the nature of the criminal justice system and whether it damages children, how being brought up in circumstances of depravity and being abused may have related to Bell's own crime, and the first thorough account of how child criminals are dealt with by the penal system (PCC July 1998).

Sources and confidentiality

It is a common feature of journalistic codes of practice that they specify journalists have a moral obligation to protect confidential sources of information. Hence the British National Union of Journalists code of conduct states 'a journalist shall protect confidential sources of information' and, similarly, the American Society of Newspaper Editors statement of principles holds that 'pledges of confidentiality to news sources must be honoured at all costs, and therefore should not be given lightly. Unless there is clear and pressing need to maintain confidences, sources of information should be identified.' Of course, the emphasis rightly remains upon identifying sources wherever possible. But under certain conditions this is impossible and, where the information is in the public interest, honouring confidentiality is a deeply serious matter. The reasons for this are fairly substantial ones. Investigative journalism, by its very nature, is often heavily reliant on sources who wish their identity to remain anonymous or to be protected in some way. Without promises of confidentiality or anonymity which the source can trust in, investigative journalists would often be unable to get crucial information about scandals or substantiating corruption. Thus once such commitments are made they are heavily binding. If it were common practice for such commitments to be made and then broken, sources would not trust journalists and reveal information to them. The consequences of loss of anonymity could result in harming their career prospects, the loss of their job or even, in more extreme cases, result in physical retaliation and life threatening situations.

The dangers of anonymity and confidentiality

But there are many dangers associated with the common use of anonymous sources and the reporting of confidential information. First, the use and attribution of confidential information to anonymous sources can often belie or even encourage slack, careless journalism. It is often far easier, when in search of a good story, to report unattributed quotes, allegations or information than painstakingly and carefully checking whether the claims made can be substantiated. Hence the possibility of misrepresentation of states of affairs may be allowed to go unchecked.

Second, the sources themselves may be confiding information because they have a particular agenda to push. For example, both in the UK and the USA political journalists have increasingly been subjected to what has come to be known as the art of spin doctoring. A significant element here concerns the use, or perhaps abuse, of anonymous sources. Journalists looking to investigate a possible story are fed leaks of reports anonymously or given juicy quotes by politicians or press officers as long as they remain unattributed. The real purpose in so doing is often not so much a matter of revealing the truth of the matter to a journalist as furthering the personal or political agenda of the parties involved. The pay-off involved is that the journalist will get such information, which may help his or her career, as long as the sources are not divulged. The ease with which falsehoods, unsubstantiated allegations and misrepresentations can be made is greatly heightened since there is no potential cost to the unidentified source. Such considerations apply not just to the political arena, though they may have particular force here, but generally. The worry is that investigative journalists, in respecting sources' requests for confidentiality, are wide open to being manipulated and abused by their source in the interests of political, business or other wider agendas.

Responsible granting of anonymity

One possible response is to condemn outright the entire practice of using anonymous sources in this fashion. For example, Tony Benn MP in a 1996 BBC *Panorama* programme on political spin doctors, condemned outright the use of anonymous sources by political journalists. The underlying thought is that such a practice is not just corrupt in many cases but turns out to be wholly unnecessary. On the one hand someone may be seeking to use anonymity as a cloak for making scurrilous, unfounded allegations in order to undermine, unjustifiably, colleagues, opponents or business competitors. In which case giving such allegations the oxygen of publicity, without identifying the source and thus precluding the possibility of redress, is corrosive, harmful and wrong. On the other hand, it may be that the allegations made are, in part or wholly, ones which can be substantiated. If this is the case then, the line of thought goes, all well and good and no-one need protect their identity. For then the allegations can be shown by investigation to be substantiated and the source need not fear for themselves because they are protected by law from being sacked, intimidated or harmed. The cloak of confidentiality can only foster harmful deceit.

Yet such a line of thought shows a desperately naive understanding of the ways of the world. That the law prohibits the kind of retribution a source may rightfully fear does not ensure that it will not be taken. It is of little consolation to someone who suffers intimidation at work, beatings or whose life is threatened that this is illegal. Moreover, a source and the investigating journalist may not even be in a position to know if the allegations being made, in all honesty and good faith, can be clearly substantiated by independent evidence as yet. Without the promise of confidentiality, and trust on the part of the source that this commitment will be fulfilled, many a scandal would be unlikely to be revealed. When one considers that sometimes whistle-blowing often involves revelations about corruption in the very forces supposed to enforce legality one can recognise why sources may not be prepared to trust in the legal protection that may be afforded were their identity to be revealed.

It is true that certain exceptional individuals are often prepared to take enormous risks to their livelihood and even life in order to reveal injustice. But many people are not nor could they be expected to be such moral saints. Many people of ordinary good character can only be persuaded to blow the whistle on illegal or immoral practices given assurances of confidentiality and anonymity – if not for their own sake then for the sake of their family and loved ones.

There does remain a perpetual problem with confidential sources revealing secret or confidential information – and this concerns proof. At least in the early stages of investigation a journalist may have little or nothing to go on except the information coming from their anonymous source. The evidence that is then accumulated, independently of the source's information, may be consistent with what the source has revealed but be insufficient on its own to substantiate the claims made. Thus verification is a difficult often nigh impossible task. But one minimal, weaker test here is important – corroboration. For where this is the case it is the duty of the investigative journalist to seek out corroborating testimony from other sources. The more the stories converge the stronger reason there is to think that, *prima facie* at least, there is a case to answer.

Having suggested that confidentiality and anonymity of sources are morally justifiable and integral to good investigative journalism, we might nonetheless hold that the practice of making such commitment is perhaps too widespread and easily granted. Where the allegations made are hardly of the first import in terms of public interest but, for example, involve attributions of a scurrilous character, granting confidentiality is gratuitous and only serves the interests of sensationalism and the political or financial motivations of those making the allegations. Sadly this is a far from uncommon state of affairs.

In relation to confidentiality it is also important to bear in mind the dangers to investigative journalists themselves. In investigating criminal cases journalists may find themselves threatened by incriminated parties if they don't reveal where they got their information from. Such are the dangers of the job and the obligation not to break the confidence is absolute – assuming the source has not themselves deceived the journalist and they will be harmed if the journalist breaks a promise. A more difficult scenario is where a journalist may find that the legal courts demand that his or her source be revealed on pain of contempt of court and thus imprisonment. As can be seen from Chapter 6 there is currently a state of uncertainty regarding the status of legal requirements made by court order requiring journalists to reveal their sources and the tensions with the European Convention. But leaving such uncertainty to one side journalists, as we all do, have a moral duty to obey the law whatever it may be. Nonetheless, the duty is a defeasible one – it may be overridden where countervailing moral considerations outweigh the obligation to honour the law. Where a law is fundamentally corrupt or deeply unjust then our obligation to obey it may be rescinded. In the case of investigative journalism it may be that the legal requirement made upon the journalist, to reveal his or her source's identity, is of such a nature – where this is the case the journalist has a moral duty to defy the law.

Reconstructions

Finally, investigative journalism has duties to the audience not just in terms of methods of investigation but also in terms of presentation. The issue arises with particular force in the case of television documentaries and the role of dramatic reconstructions therein. The point of investigative programmes and documentaries is to convey to the audience not just allegations about a particular person or event but to make clear exactly what the nature of the events was, how they occurred, why they happened, in what sequence and, most important of all, what evidential and rational basis the programme has for making the claims made. In essence the aim is to present a case to the audience making it clear what reasons there are for the audience to concur with the conclusions of the programme whilst also flagging reasons that remain for doubting them.

The use of mocked-up sequences and dramatic reconstructions in documentaries is common practice. Often people wish to remain anonymous and won't trust being filmed in shadow or having their voice synthesised, so someone is brought in to act out the part and utter the anonymous source's words for them. A sequence of events may be quite hard to describe, the relevant detail may be cumbersome or tricky, and it may be much easier to convey the right kind of impression of what happened by dramatisation – not to mention making the documentary more telegenic. Or it may be that the actual filmed or tape recorded evidence is scratchy, fits badly together and is hard to discern. These are common enough reasons taken to justify reconstructions in contemporary investigative programmes. At least in large part the rationale is simple and not all that different from other journalistic practices. For example, it is common enough for journalists to rewrite or make up quotes from interviewees because they seem to express more clearly the actual thought the interviewee was trying to communicate. As long as this is checked with the interviewee, to rule out misunderstandings on the part of the journalist, there seems to be nothing wrong – the actual sentence quoted was not one literally uttered as such by the interviewee but it articulates more clearly what exactly the interviewee was trying to get across. The rationale underlying reconstructions, in part at least, would seem to be the same. Moreover, given that reconstructions must be labelled as such on screen there would seem to be little room for confusion.

But the major worries here concern the acceptable limits of dramatising, reconstructing or constructing events in the service of a 'higher truth'. For there are fine distinctions that need to be drawn between dramatising events we know to have happened, dramatising events we have good reason to believe happened, dramatising events merely as they might have happened and dramatically representing events as if they happened when, in fact, they did not.

The Connection documentary, discussed at the beginning of this chapter, falls into the last category. In essence it presented fiction as fact to the audience and as such constitutes a heinous abrogation of the most basic of journalistic commitments. Although this is only the most extreme of cases the dangers attendant here are more pervasive than might be presumed. Apart from anything else the financial and commercial pressures involved in making such programmes are great and the temptation to sensationalise or vivify the nature of a documentary can be quite strong. One obvious way of doing so is by gratuitously using dramatic reconstructions to make the programme more telegenic. The way in which such dramatisations are used can, despite the rest of the programme's content, give a misleading impression that the grounds for believing what the programme claims are stronger than they in fact are. Hence a programme may dramatise what elsewhere has been presented as a possible sequence of events and, through so doing, give the misleading impression that this is what is 'known' to have happened. In such cases dramatisation is used to create interest for its own sake in the programme rather than aiming at a rational and balanced understanding of what the audience has most reason to believe. One might be tempted, as Matthew Parris suggested in considering such matters, to hold that television is necessarily a deceptive medium. To quote Parris:

> Life isn't good television. To make good television it's essential to contrive and manipulate moving images. The only danger is that viewers might actually believe it. So why don't we just let go? Why don't we drop the pretence of worthiness, the unequal struggle to see this as a trustworthy medium and admit that television – all television – is entertaining nonsense?
>
> (Parris 1999)

But it would be an over-reaction to condemn reconstructions outright or to conflate the conventional artifice of programme making with deception. Since, for the reasons given, reconstructions can have an extremely useful, informative and non-misleading role to play. Rather it would be more adequate to recognise that they are perfectly legitimate under certain conditions. Namely if, and only if,

- the journalistic team can substantiate the dramatisation independently in a manner which shows they have sufficient grounds to claim that they either know this was or probably was the case;
- these independent grounds are made perfectly clear in the programme and the validity of the reconstruction is shown to rest on these grounds;
- the reconstruction is labelled on screen as such to the audience and it is made clear whether the dramatisation is being presented in terms of what is known to be the case, believed to be probable or merely a representation of what might plausibly or possibly have happened.

Where these conditions are met the audience are not deceived and thus in the best position possible to make up their own minds as to whether the evidence presented to them is sufficient to warrant the nature of the dramatisation or whether it is unsubstantiated speculation.

Such constraints are crucial precisely because it is so tempting to use reconstructions in a misleading fashion, especially given the highly competitive nature of the commercial market nowadays. Without ingraining such constraints within the culture of investigative journalism, and the external reinforcement of effective and meaningful regulation to back it up, it is likely that reconstructions will increasingly be used to spice up documentaries which seem to be going nowhere, have failed to establish very much or are not considered telegenic enough. If a documentary is not important, interesting or worthy enough without the use of gratuitous reconstructions then it should not be broadcast at all.

Conclusion

The examination of some of the most pressing ethical and regulatory issues concerning investigative journalism shows that we can legitimately demand investigative journalists to respect basic moral considerations. However it is crucial both that individual journalists and the culture of investigative journalism at large appreciate exactly what those considerations are and how they apply. For without a conscious appreciation of what considerations justify what kinds of action, where and why, it will be all too easy and tempting to assimilate immoral practices given the attendant pressures on journalists. Where such criteria are not respected the danger of investigative journalism coming apart from its aims and responsibilities looms large. Indeed, as the respected Howard Kurtz has warned in relation to journalism in the US, we must constantly resist the pressures that would make investigative journalism 'part of the vast entertainment culture which seeks to amuse and titillate and shies away from the risks of old-style muck-raking as media corporations have grown wary of abusing influence or offending the public' (Kurtz 1994: 5).

Good investigative journalists will seek the truth, adhere to truth respecting standard methods, such as fact checking and corroborating sources, intrude into privacy only under the constraints outlined above and seek to convey to their audience an open, verifiable, reason based understanding of the scandal or events uncovered. These obligations arise straight-forwardly from what it is to be an investigative journalist in conjunction with the relevant moral and regulatory considerations that may be involved. The role of regulation consists in, at the very least, providing an external motivational force against commercial, political or vested interests for ensuring that this remains the aim of investigative journalism and, at its very best, in reinforcing the dispositions already inherent in journalistic practice to make sure it stays that way.

BIBLIOGRAPHY

Aristotle (1976) *Nichomachean Ethics* (trans. J. A. K. Thomson). Harmondsworth: Penguin.

Belsey, A. (1992) Privacy, publicity and politics. In A. Belsey and R. Chadwick (eds) *Ethical Issues in Journalism and the Media*. London: Routledge.

Bok, S. (1984) *Secrets: On the Ethics of Concealment and Revelation*. Oxford: Oxford University Press.

Harris, N. (1992) Codes of conduct for journalists. In A. Belsey and R. Chadwick (eds) *Ethical Issues in Journalism and the Media*. London: Routledge.

Kieran, M. (1997) *Media Ethics: A Philosophical Approach*. Westport, Conn.: Praeger.

Kieran, M. (ed.) (1998) *Media Ethics*. London: Routledge.

Kieran, M. (1998) Objectivity, impartiality and good journalism. In M. Kieran (ed.) *Media Ethics*. London: Routledge.

Kieran, M., Morrison, D., and Svennevig, M. (1997) *Regulating for Changing Values: A Report for the Broadcasting Standards Commission*. London: Broadcasting Standards Commission.

Kurtz, H. (1994) *Media Circus*. New York: Random House.

Locke, J. (1955) *A Letter Concerning Toleration*. New York: The Library of Liberal Arts.

Locke, J. (1963) *Two Treatises of Government*. New York: Cambridge University Press.

Mill, J. S. (1982) *On Liberty*. Harmondsworth: Penguin.

Parent, W. A. (1992) Privacy, morality and the law. In E. D. Cohen (ed.) *Philosophical Issues in Journalism*. New York: Oxford University Press.

Parris, M. (1999) *Parris on TV*. London: BBC. (All Out Production for Five Live, Producer David Prosser)

Press Complaints Commission (1993) Huins v *Hello!* In *PCC Report, August–September 1993*. London: Press Complaints Commission.

Press Complaints Commission (1996) *Daily Mirror, Sunday Mirror, Daily Express and News of the World*, Complaint by Chief Constable of Gloucestershire Constabulary. In *PCC Complaints and Adjudications 1996*. London: Press Complaints Commission.

Press Complaints Commission (1998) Complaints against the press concerning payments for stories from convicted criminals. In *PCC Adjudication, July 1998*. London: Press Complaints Commission.

Reiss, H. (ed.) (1970) *Kant's Political Writings*. Cambridge: Cambridge University Press.

Schoeman, F. D. (ed.) (1984) *Philosophical Dimensions of Privacy*. New York: Cambridge University Press.

FURTHER READING

Calcutt, D. (1993) *Review of Press Self-Regulation*. Cmnd. 2135. London: HMSO.

Christians, C. G., Fackler, M. and Rotzoll, K. B. (1995) *Media Ethics: Cases and Moral Reasoning*. White Plains, New York: Longman.

Fallows, J. (1996) *Breaking the News*. New York: Pantheon.

Klaidman, S. and Beauchamp, T. L. (1987) *The Virtuous Journalist*. New York: Oxford University Press.

Snoddy, R. (1992) *The Good, the Bad and the Unacceptable*. London: Faber and Faber.

9

JOURNALISM AND
NEW TECHNOLOGY

Carole Fleming

Introduction

The root of every investigation is information, and the job of every investigative reporter is to find information, evaluate and analyse it, and communicate it in a way that informs and interests a wide range of people. The problem is finding the right kind of information from the myriad of sources and distribution media – the traditional print form, broadcasting, the Internet and electronic data services. Moreover it has to be recognised that information is not neutral: it is ideological. That is to say, as Stuart Hall argues, that because meaning is not given but produced, different kinds of meaning can be attached to the same events. The way that certain information is recurrently 'read' or signified is an ideological force, and the dominant means of social signification in the modern world is the mass media (Hall 1982). Journalists obtain their information from sources that want their interpretation of events to be the accepted one, which is not to say that it is false, but that it is presented in a context that gives credibility and legitimacy to their interpretation, while marginalising or delegitimising alternative constructions. This explains the rise of *spin-doctors* whose job is to peddle information to journalists in a selective manner that emphasises the angle they want and downplays others.

As Philip Meyer points out: 'In a world where the amount of information is doubling every five years, it takes a specialist to understand, let alone communicate, very much of it' (Meyer 1991). This suggests that the role of journalists is to interpret information and present it in an understandable form. But to view journalists as existing in a vacuum, outside or above the society they live in, is unrealistic. Journalists tend to fall into three categories: those whose wages are paid by large media organisations; those whose wages are paid by small independent outlets, including minority interest publications; and freelance journalists who sell their products to the previous two kinds of outlets. This means all journalists work under certain constraints. Some of these are brought about by the working practices of journalists, for example the need to be 'first with the facts' that forces them to work to tight deadlines. These preclude in–depth research or analysis and perpetuate the conventions for selecting, researching, interpreting and presenting facts, as Curran and Seaton observe (1995: chap. 5).

Added to this are the economic and political constraints (outlined in Chapter 5) under which journalists work. The majority of journalists work for organisations whose main objective is to make profit. Even where the journalist is freelance, that is, not bound to a particular outlet, in order to sell their stories they must conform to the *style* – the particular signification – of that organisation, which means giving preference to one particular interpretation of information over others. Generally that interpretation is one that supports the existing structures of society under which media organisations make profits. This is further reinforced by the concentration of media ownership by large transnational corporations with a diversity of economic interests,[1] who encourage the practice of targeting an audience to enhance advertising revenue. As Nicholas Garnham points out, cultural theorists like Hall claim 'there is a systematic tendency of the media to reproduce the ideological field of society in such a way as to reproduce also its structure of domination' (Garnham 1979), while for political economists like Dallas Smythe, 'the crucial function of the mass media is not to sell packages of ideology to consumers, but audiences to advertisers'(Smythe 1981). In either event, information is manipulated to benefit the organisations who pass it on to audiences, which means, as Peter Golding and Graham Murdock point out, 'the audience's position as a commodity serves to reduce the overall diversity of programming and ensure that it confirms established mores and assumptions more often than it challenges them' (Golding and Murdock 1996).

In this chapter I will argue that the technology now available has the potential, if not to reverse this situation, at least to go some way to redressing it. This will be achieved not through the much hailed 'information revolution', but by a change in the conventions of journalism and the modes of publishing brought about by technological advances. By using computers to aid them in accessing and analysing information, journalists will be better equipped to access alternative interpretations of events and information, which would allow audiences the opportunity to arrive at their own interpretation, rather than a manipulated one. It may even put a different meaning on Bernard Cohen's observation that the press 'may not be successful much of the time in telling people what to think, but it is stunningly successful in telling readers *what to think about*' (McCombs and Shaw 1997). Perhaps more importantly, computers will also provide them with a way to publish their findings to a reasonably large audience free from the political constraints of traditional publishing. While many electronic publications are already owned and controlled by established conventional news outlets like the *Electronic Telegraph* and BBC Online in the United Kingdom, and the *New York Times* and *MSNBC* in the USA, Matt Drudge has shown that stories deemed too politically sensitive for large organisations to publish, like the Clinton–Lewinsky sex scandal can be effectively published by an individual. The Monica Lewinsky scandal broke in January 1998, and although journalists working for traditional publications had information about tapes she had made admitting a sexual relationship with President Clinton, they hesitated to publish it until after it appeared on the Drudge Report website (www.drudgereport.com).

Of course it has to be recognised that any changes in the conventions of journalism, such as which topics should be discussed and which interpretation privileged will not transform the profession overnight. The future of conventional news publishing is assured well into the future, and traditional broadcasters and publishers are already staking their claim in the new forum of the World Wide Web. But as Bill Gates so famously said: 'the Internet is this big, big thing' (San Jose, 7 May 1996) and I will argue it has the *potential* to return journalists to the pamphleteering days of early journalists like Thomas Paine, whose self published works *Common Sense* and *The American Crisis* helped in the American War of Independence by providing information and opinion that went directly against the establishment.[2]

That said, the Internet is not a panacea for all problems in accessing information. Despite its rapid growth in the 1990s, vast tracts of the world, especially in the developing south, still have no connection to a telephone, let alone a computer and modem, and as Victor Keegan of the *Guardian* points out, 96 per cent of Internet sites are located in the rich twenty-seven nation OECD area.[3]

Nonetheless, the technological advances being made through computers and digitalisation open areas that were previously restricted, if not closed, to investigative journalists. Traditionally journalists start an investigation on the basis of a rumour or a noted incongruity. From there they track down people involved in the issue either as victims, perpetrators or experts on the subject, and facts stored in a variety of published material until a complete picture is produced. All this takes a lot of time in locating people, actually managing to talk to them either face to face or by telephone or fax, verifying the information given by people, finding the relevant documents and accessing them. With the aid of technology the time it takes to find people and information is considerably reduced, the range of accessible information is increased – not least because often it can be accessed from one place – and data can be analysed more efficiently.

Computer assisted journalism

In the following sections I shall outline the modes of technology now available to journalists and their implications for the professional practices and their products. Essentially there are four main tools available to journalists with a computer, a modem and the appropriate software: the Internet, which covers e-mail, the World Wide Web, FTP, newsgroups and listservs; commercial information services; spreadsheets; and databases. The following section explains each of these tools, and illustrates their uses.

The most important word in the phrase 'computer assisted journalism' is 'assisted'. The computer is there to aid journalists, not to replace them or dominate their working practices. As Neil Reisner, a computer assisted reporting specialist at the Miami Herald told a media conference in 1997:[4] 'Computer-assisted reporting does not, in itself, make better stories. It does let us ask better questions so we can write better stories'.

The Internet

As most people know, the Internet is simply a network of computers that can communicate with each other. It started as four networked computers at the Advanced Research Projects Agency Net (ARPANET) at the University of California in 1969, and had grown to over 16 million connected computers, or hosts, in 1997.[5] The problem was that until the 1990s when the World Wide Web took off, gaining access to computers on the Internet and the information they stored required specialist knowledge. What the web did was to make access 'user friendly' through the use of software called a web browser.

The World Wide Web

The World Wide Web is the best known aspect of the Internet. In 1993 it had 130,000 pages[6] and 5 years later it carried over 30 million. The most common criticism of the web is that because anyone can, and does, set up a web site it is difficult to 'separate the gems from the junk'. Web sites essentially come from five main sources:

1   academic institutions
2   governments
3   non-profit making organisations and associations
4   commercial companies
5   individuals.

Of these, all but the last can be of use to journalists, to obtain independent expert opinion (academic institutions), to obtain official facts (government sites), to get information from alternative but credible sources like Greenpeace or Oxfam (organisations and associations), and as an easy reference or archive store (companies). Although not all sites run by individuals are valueless, it is generally held that the majority are the equivalent of junk mail, the exceptions being those posted by professional journalists that often contain 'hot lists' of sites with useful and/or unusual information. An example of such a site is FACSNET (www.facsnet.org), which describes itself as a journalists' Internet resource service, 'operated by journalists for journalists'.

As well as sites with information in them, there are sites to help navigate through the millions of pages available on the Web. These are directories or search engines that work in different ways. Some like Yahoo and UK Plus are compiled by human beings who check the content of the sites listed on their directories. Others, like Alta Vista and Infoseek are compiled by robots (computer programs) and have no human involvement. They operate by sending a software agent out onto the web to trawl for new sites and catalogue them. Then there are subject specific search sites, which use a combination of humans and robots to catalogue sites dedicated to specific topics, such as Findlaw (www.findlaw.com).

Once familiar with the World Wide Web, journalists can use it to check facts and figures quickly, to get background information about stories they are working on, to contact experts, to compare the views of various interest groups. All this, of course, could be done without the use of a computer, but it would take much longer and rely upon the journalist already having relevant contacts to use as a starting point. More importantly, the use of the World Wide Web gives a journalist access to information and people regardless of their geographical location.

Useful sites for journalists

The list of useful sites for journalists is potentially endless, and often a matter of personal preference. Most Internet experts, like Randy Reddick, author of *The Online Journalist*, advise individuals to get to know two or three search engines thoroughly and learn their capabilities. Search engines generally have a news index that links to most online news organisations. It is also relatively easy to link to most government sites through the search engine index. Less obviously, there are also some more specialised sites that journalists can tap into, some of which are listed below.

www.networksolutions.com/cgi-bin/whois/whois   This site is useful to find out who runs a particular web site. The site queries the database of registered domains and gives the names, address and telephone numbers of those behind the site, which can help in evaluating any information from a particular site. As in the real world it is vital for a journalist to check any source, rather than accept information at face value, so this is an invaluable site. Often just knowing where the site originates from is enough. For example, the address for the administrator of the site for Radio Free Europe/Radio Liberty is in Washington DC.

www.geocities.com/CapitolHill/Lobby/4179/index.html   This site is run by British investigative journalist Danny Rosenbaum, and describes itself as an investigative journalism resource. It has a range of useful contact numbers for journalists, as well as the Tony Blair Dossier, which is a vast unofficial collection of information about the British Prime Minister.

www.usus.org   USUS is 'the usually useful Internet Guide for journalists' – and it is. As well as a description of the history and development of the Internet, and an introduction to various techniques for research, it has very useful links to sites of value to journalists.

www.facsnet.org   This is a site created 'by journalists for journalists' to give them help tracing sources online, advice on Internet resources, and briefings on top issues. It also has several online tutorials on how best to use your computer to help with stories.

www.cais.net/makulow/vlj.html   This site was created by a full-time Internet guru in Washington DC. As well as being of general interest it links to the WWW Virtual library which is an extensive catalogue of sites of use to journalists dealing with every conceivable topic.

www.mailbase.ac.uk   This is an electronic discussion list for the UK higher education community. Some lists are moderated or closed, but you can browse the archives for ideas, search for people and subjects, and track down UK academics or research. Very useful for finding experts who can often give access to 'victims'.

www.amazon.com   This is the site of Amazon books, the largest online book-store in the world. From here it is possible to track down recent publications, which is another good way of contacting experts in any given field. Once the author and publisher is known it is then possible to track them down using something like Infoseek (www.infoseek.com). By entering the name of the publisher it is possible to get details including a telephone number, and often a web site and e-mail address.

www.foreignwire.com/index.html   This site is produced by professional journalists and offers news and analysis of international affairs. It has a mailing list and a good archive that is valuable for background information.

www.nato.int   This is the NATO web site and has mostly text documents. It is useful because NATO does a lot of grass roots research in a wide range of countries, including Britain and the USA, and these documents are available here.

www.who.ch   This is the World Health Organisation site. It has a lot of statistics about disease trends and drugs in various countries. It can also help to find experts at universities, government agencies and think-tanks around the world.

www.undcp.org/index.html This is the site for the United Nations International Drug Control Programme. It contains mainly overview statistics.

www.ifs.univie.ac.at/~uncjin/stats.html This is part of the United Nations Crime and Justice Information Network. This site is for the World Crime Survey and has criminal statistics for lots of countries.

There is so much information available on the Internet that it can be daunting, but many journalists feel it is an area that can increasingly aid their work. As the group of journalists behind USUS note on their web site:

> for research the Internet will become nearly indispensable and as important as the telephone is at present. The Internet will be a fundamental tool to search for a story, for information, for experts or insiders. Note the word 'search' instead of 'surf'. The difference is to find needed information and contacts in contrast to finding them by accident. The secret is to learn how to exploit the Internet's massive network of information tools
>
> (www.usus.org)

E-mail

Electronic mail, or e-mail, cuts out the need for a journalist to be in a particular location to either research or file a story. It provides a way for messages to be sent from one computer to another anywhere on the network, and was one of the earliest applications for computer networks. There are many different programs available to send and receive e-mail but the essentials are the same: a file, or message, is sent from one named computer user to another named computer user. Since 1992 when Multipurpose Internet Messaging Extensions became available these files need not just be text, but can also be spreadsheets, audio or video.

As more and more people go online, e-mail is becoming increasingly useful for accessing sources. Its main advantage is that it is quick, with access worldwide at the press of a button. Another is that it is convenient. The person being contacted does not have to be available when the message is sent: it just sits there until they check their mail, then they are able to reply with a few simple key strokes that cut out the need for stamps, envelopes or looking up telephone numbers and ending up with an answer phone. This aspect is particularly useful when contacts are overseas: messages can be sent and replied to without worrying about time zone problems.

Moreover, e-mail is the basis for Newsgroups and Listservs (explained in the next section) which allow access to interest groups that might not be among the contacts of a particular journalist. Through them a journalist can access a wide range of people not previously known or met.

Despite the fact that e-mail is the most sophisticated tool on the Internet, having been used for over thirty years, it still has some problems. The first is finding the address of the person you want to communicate with, and although there are a number of e-mail directories available on the Internet, it is still often difficult and time consuming to track people down in this way. The best method is still to telephone the individual or their organisation and ask for the address, although increasingly it is possible to find an e-mail address by tracking down the web site of organisations and individuals using one of the Internet search engines.

Another problem is that, despite a reply coming from the e-mail address of your contact, you have no way of knowing for sure that it was written by them and not a subordinate or assistant, so sending e-mail to someone you do not know can be dangerous. Reddick says:

> Once you have established a relationship with a source ... you will find person to person email can be an invaluable tool. After a long telephone interview or face-to-face session, you may find that your notes are unclear in certain crucial places. E-mail is an effective tool to ask your source to clarify information.
>
> (Reddick and King 1995: 91)

E-mail also has problems connected with privacy and security. Although it appears to be a private method of communicating, there is no way of knowing who has access to the e-mail address you sent the message to, and therefore who is able to read it. As well as secretaries and assistants being able to access them, e-mail messages can be reviewed by the administrators of the computer systems through which messages are sent. Many companies monitor their employees' e-mail, and in America the FBI monitors the e-mail of people they are investigating. Perhaps the best known example of this was in the mid-1980s when Oliver North stored e-mail messages on disk relating to the Iran-Contra arms for hostages incident. Despite having deleted the messages from the hard disk of his office computer, investigators were able to retrieve them to use against him. For these reasons e-mail should be avoided when dealing with any sensitive issues. As Bill Thompson, an online journalist who played an important role in creating websites for the *Guardian* and the *Observer* newspapers says:

> There are many ways in which access to e-mail can help a working journalist, just as a fax machine, telephone or company car can make life easier. However each is a tool which must be used properly. Relying on any one method to the exclusion of all others, or ignoring the different characteristics of the communications medium chosen, can lead to problems.[7]

Newsgroups and listservs

Newsgroups and listservs are a useful way for journalists to contact people in an unofficial capacity, to get what journalists call 'a human angle' on their stories. Essentially they are methods of one person communicating with many electronically. Listservs work via e-mail: once registered with a listserv group or 'list', every message sent to the discussion group is sent to every other person in the group. Newsgroups, or Usenet groups as they are also known, do not send mail to individuals, but instead to a central 'bulletin board'. On joining a newsgroup, access is given to the central server where messages can be read, replied to or posted.

The advantage newsgroups have over lists is that they allow individuals to dip into and out of the 'discussion', and prevent individual e-mail systems being clogged by dozens of messages from members of the discussion group. Lists have the advantage that they tend to be frequented by the same type of people – for example lists for journalists or those specialising in a particular field – so users tend to get to know each other, and the quality of the responses can be more easily verified. Obviously being able to contact specific groups of people easily is a great aid to journalists, especially if it is a story that has international implications. For example, one of my students working on an investigation into the rising number of secondary school exclusions in England and Wales, wanted to compare the situation in other countries. He found a list that dealt with the topic, and posted a request for information. Within a week he had received responses not only from people in England and Wales, but from Australia, Italy and Canada which gave his piece an international dimension that, at best, would have taken weeks to achieve non-electronically.

However, it is impossible for journalists to know the level of expertise of people making comments in discussion groups, so a certain amount of caution has to be used. Once identified as being useful, reporters need to check the credentials of their online sources in the same way as they would check someone they met casually who appeared to have interesting information.

Newsgroups can also be used in an indirect way to give a journalist a broader outlook on the story they are working on. By tuning in to the discussion of a particular topic, aspects of the topic that might be overlooked or deemed unimportant by some are often discovered. Interestingly, the Pentagon routinely monitors newsgroups to gauge the political mood of the country and get the opinion of users.[8]

Useful newsgroups and lists

To join a list one usually sends a message to the listserv's e-mail address and 'subscribes' to the named list. Once a member of a list, you receive every piece of mail sent to that list, and in turn every message you send to the list is sent to every other member. This can mean receiving dozens of messages every day, so use with caution.

NICAR-L discusses investigative reporting at listserv @lists.missouri.edu
NEWSLIB discusses researching stories at listserv @ripken.oit.unc.edu»
FOI-L discusses freedom of information issues at listserv @listserv.syr.edu

There is also a directory of newsgroups at www.dejanews.com that allows you to search, read and post information.

FTP

FTP Stands for File Transfer Protocol, and essentially it is a language that allows computers to send and receive files from other computers that may be distant and using a different operating system. This is one of the least user-friendly aspects of the Internet, and requires a reasonable degree of computer literacy to operate it, and FTP client software on your computer. Typically FTP is used to obtain specific files from research institutes or libraries. The main problem in acquiring files using FTP is knowing exactly what is needed and where it is stored, because all that comes up on the screen is a directory of files that give little or no indication of what each file contains. Fortunately most institutions and libraries are now available on the World Wide Web, which is much more user-friendly and easier to access.[9]

Commercial information services

With so much information available electronically it is no wonder that over the past few years a host of companies have grown up to sell that information to people who need it. Generally these commercial information services are expensive to use, and in most newsrooms their use is restricted to librarians who can navigate quickly to the area they need. A lot of the time the information sold by these companies is already available freely, but might take some expertise or a lot of time for an individual to compile. For example, it might take all day for a journalist to trawl through the electronic archives of daily papers to get background information on breaches of standards in nursery schools, whereas a commercial service like Nexus would be able to produce the information within the hour – but at a cost. Similarly, the financial background of a particular company is freely available through Company House who have archives on CD-ROM and a limited amount of information on the Internet, but the information provided by a commercial organisation like Dun and Bradstreet is more likely to be in a form that is easily understood.

There is no doubt that the commercial information services offered online are extremely useful, but in the main they are also extremely expensive and outside the reach of most freelance journalists. Their main use is in established newsrooms on stories that need information to be checked quickly.

Spreadsheets and databases

It is generally accepted that facts and figures can be presented in such a way that certain aspects of the story are obscured, and this is especially so if those aspects could show the information supplier in a less than good light. This is where spreadsheets and databases can help investigative journalists to check information and analyse it independently without spending endless hours with a calculator.

Spreadsheets are used for analysing numerical information such as national or local government budgets, company finances, trends in the salaries of public officials, crime rates, or looking at changes in census information. Database management systems are like electronic filing cabinets that keep your information organised. They are used to find patterns in information. For example, if a reporter is investigating the decline of a neighbourhood they might first of all use a spreadsheet to look at crime rates over the past few years, compared with those in another neighbourhood. Using the spreadsheet to analyse these figures would help a journalist to determine whether or not rising crime was a factor in the decline of the area, and if it were, provide them with information to grill the police about what they are doing to improve the situation.

Taking the same information and using it in a database management system would give a journalist a different perspective. By entering the location of the crime, the type of crime, the time it was committed, the gender, age, race and home location of victims, they would be able to tell whether the neighbourhood's crime problem was primarily because of violent assaults, car crimes, burglaries, racist attacks or domestic violence. Obviously an area where there are a lot of violent assaults against ethnic minorities, but few against the majority group has a different problem to one where there are very few assaults of any kind, but a large number of burglaries. The database manager could also allow you to build up a detailed picture of the particular streets where it is most dangerous to leave unattended cars, which have the highest burglary rate, and where it is most dangerous to walk around. Again, all this information would give a reporter valuable ammunition in questioning those responsible for running the neighbourhood. As Neil Reisner of the *Miami Herald* says:

> The analytical tools desktop computers make available allow journalists around the world to gather information more efficiently, to analyse the information they gather, to ask better more probing questions of their sources, and to write or broadcast deeper, more insightful stories.

They give journalists access to the same tools that officials have been using for years. They level the playing field.

(Reisner 1997)

The use of spreadsheets and databases by journalists in America is already standard mainly because obtaining information on disk is common. In Britain it is extremely difficult because of the Data Protection Act, which is often used by local authorities and the like to stop information they have from being passed on to reporters electronically.[10] In America reporters routinely receive information on disk, ranging from city council budgets to pet licensing, political campaign financing to government contracts, birth, death, marriage and divorce statistics to voter records. This gives reporters there enormous scope to use spreadsheets and databases to their best ability, and has produced stories that previously would have taken months of research. One of the most famous cases was in St. Louis, where a reporter linked the database for the city's death records with that of the city's voting records and found that a substantial number of 'dead' people had voted in the last city election.[11]

Nonetheless, there is evidence that the situation in Britain is changing with some local authorities posting committee minutes on their web sites, Court of Appeal verdicts posted on the Web, and the prospect of court transcripts being available on the Internet.[12] On top of that there is already a wealth of statistics available from government web sites, and country specific data is available from organisations like the United Nations, the World Health Organisation and European Community. Even when the information is not available electronically it is often available in paper format, and, although more time consuming, journalists can make their own databases by typing in the information given to them on paper, and still gain by using the computer to analyse the information far more quickly and accurately than with paper and a calculator.

The future

While the tools described above are available for use by journalists, it should be remembered that in this, as in accessing all information, journalists in Western democracies have no privileges over other citizens. The problem is that the amount and varied quality of information makes accessing it akin to what Trevor Haywood, Professor of Human Information Systems at the University of Central England, described as 'those old cartoons where the farmer shoots off a wide-barrelled blunderbuss full of nails and rusty bits in the hope of hitting something and a host of unexpected animals drop from the sky'.[13]

This effectively means that 'more than ever, the task of journalism (in print and every other medium) will lie in filtering relevant issues from an increasing supply of information in a crowded domain and its fragmented segments. Journalism evolves from the provision of facts to the provision of meaning'

(Bardoel 1996: 297). According to Philip Meyer, to overcome this 'information overload' journalists have to apply social and behavioural science research methods, to become 'precision journalists' and abandon the twin traditions of journalistic passivity – whereby they accept stories given to them by official sources – and journalistic innocence – whereby they accept the official version of those stories as being correct. This does not mean that journalists need to abandon the ethos of objectivity in their work as happened with the 'new journalism' of the 1960s,[14] but it does mean that they have to become more active in tracking down the right information, not just the information that is most readily available, which is usually from interested parties who are pro-active in getting their version of a story across through press releases.

As Meyer (1991) points out:

> The underlying theme in most modern criticism of journalism is that the media are too easily dominated by powerful politicians and their skilful 'spin-doctors' whose desires too easily determine what is defined as news and what is not. To defend against being manipulated, the media need more self confidence, and the best route to self-confidence is through knowledge.

That knowledge is readily available through technology. As Brian McNair says: 'the arrival of the Internet effectively destroys the traditional controls enjoyed by elites over information and its dissemination' (McNair 1998: 141).

Tom Koch goes even further. He argues that new technology empowers reporters by allowing them to access information that is equal to, or even greater than, that of those they are interviewing. This means journalists will no longer have to rely on the information given out by public officials, like spokespeople from the police, fire and hospital services, private officials like press officers, or people immediately involved in a story. Instead they can quickly access independent expert opinion which will allow them to dictate the context of the story. As Koch writes:

> At the very least, this potential informs writers or editors in a significant way, empowering them, through this electronically-gathered, background information, with a perspective that allows them to question critically an official posture, no matter how politically powerful its official source may be.
>
> (Koch 1991: 118)

This was evident in the Clinton–Lewinsky scandal already mentioned, and in Britain when William Straw, the son of Cabinet Minister Jack Straw, was named on the Internet as the 'government official's son' who was the subject of a cannabis bust in 1997, despite the government trying to keep his identity a secret.

On one level then, technology can be seen as liberating information, but it has to be remembered that this is not a universal liberation, and that just because the information is accessed electronically does not mean that it is unbiased. As Trevor Haywood points out:

> we note that alliances are being forged, almost on a daily basis, between media content providers and those who provide the drivers and connections to the new networks; and we also guess that these alliances have more to do with profit than with high ideals or unsullied altruism.
>
> (Haywood 1997: 8)

An early example of this is Microsoft's *CityScope*, an online magazine launched in 1995. Since then almost every major publication in both Britain and America is also available electronically, despite the fact that few, if any of the electronic publications make a profit. The purpose of publishers extending their interests onto the Internet is to stake a claim in the medium, and make sure their influence can be felt.

Haywood also points out that the Internet in the main is limited to First World countries, with only two in a thousand Africans having online access, and most of those are in South Africa. Moreover, even in Western countries, access to the Internet is restricted to those who can afford it. He writes, 'There will be great riches and great opportunities from Internetworking but there are no certainties and we have little evidence, so far, to suggest that all economic groups will secure similar benefits' (ibid.: 26). That said, in both Britain and America the use of computers and the Internet is becoming standard in newsrooms. A survey of online newsgathering trends in American newspapers published in 1997 by Bruce Garrison of the University of Miami concluded:

> The Internet is not just a new distribution vehicle for journalists. It has become a highly valuable resource for news gathering and, in time, the World Wide Web, electronic mail, and other Internet tools most often used will take their place at all newspapers alongside other time-tested resources of news rooms, such as reference books and the telephone.
>
> (Garrison 1997)

The importance of journalists knowing their way around the Internet is apparent in an edict of the Reuters news operation in America, which instructed its reporters to spend half an hour a day in company time surfing the Internet to keep up to date with new sites. Even in Britain, where a survey published by the Department of Journalism of City University, London in 1997 found that widespread use of the Internet by British journalists was less than that of their American colleagues it was found that:

> there is some evidence that journalists are attempting stories that would not otherwise have been written because the Internet is providing them with additional sources. It is also possible that stories generally may be beginning to have more breadth. Terrorist Web sites have been accessed to get a background to articles not possible before, and electronic versions of newspapers are experimenting with links to full text documents.[15]

The City University survey found that the journalists in Britain who most used the Internet and its facilities were freelances and those working for smaller publications in the provinces. What both these groups have in common is lack of access to large cuttings libraries like those of national publications, and economic constraints. National newspaper journalists can call on their libraries to do a background search (either of traditional cuttings or electronically) and even use commercial information providers – a luxury few freelances and small publications can afford. This means that the Internet is levelling the playing field for journalists by giving everyone equal access to information no matter where they work and what their budget.

In Britain one of the first large organisations to embrace the Internet for journalists was News International. Gertrud Erbach, the Information Services Manager for News International comments:

> Most journalists at News International now have access to the Internet. It is a useful tool despite the vast amount of useless information on there. Staff in the Information Services department use the Internet on a daily basis to answer enquiries and its use is increasing regularly.[16]

As well as the Internet, News International also have an Editorial Services Intranet[17] with Internet links, which are added to regularly, divided into subject areas and links to sites relevant to big stories. For example, during the investigation into the Stephen Lawrence murder there were links to the McPherson report, and during the war in Yugoslavia there were links to Kosovo sites. Smaller organisations also benefit. Nigel Pickover, an editor with Eastern Counties Newspapers who have a string of weekly and evening newspapers in South East England, says the Internet has transformed the way his journalists work and the kind of stories they are able to cover. He cites the example of a local man doing a charity walk across the Negev Desert in Israel who was able to send reports of his progress back to Ipswich by e-mail, and another of a reporter being sent to Boston in America on the trail of a master criminal who researched the project on the Internet and made contact with journalists on the *Boston Globe* to help him when he arrived. While Pickover acknowledges that these stories could have been done without the Internet, he believes using it produced better stories. 'Only fools – and people who shouldn't be journalists in the first place – would resist this mighty extra tool,' he says. 'There have been two massive developments in my twenty-five years on daily papers – full page electronic make-up and the Internet.'[18]

Investigative journalist Danny Rosenbaum acknowledges that in Britain the use of the Internet for researching stories is still behind that of America, but believes that will change. 'I think it (the Internet) will prove more valuable than it is now,' he says. 'At the moment its main use is finding stories and providing ideas.'[19] In his work, which includes documentaries for Channel 4 in Britain, he says he finds journalism 'lists' very useful for contacts, and has used the government's search database on several stories including deaths in prisons, deaths in car crashes involving the police, the use and misuse of methadone, and fraudulent and badly-run charities.

Conclusion

In the past two decades there has been a general lament in Europe and North America about the commercialisation of the media, the commodification of information and the demise of 'serious' journalism. Media commentators like Anthony Sampson blame this on 'the narrowness of [their] competition, the pressures of advertising, the centralisation of [their] power' (1996: 49). In particular Sampson laments the way political analysis, foreign news and investigations have been lost to 'human interest' stories and sound-bite news broadcasts, and he looks to new technology to redress the situation. 'If mass communication has become too distorted and corrupted, it may be thought that the Internet and e-mail will provide the new technologies to rescue [us] from the old ones, to build up more reliable systems of information across the world,' he says (1996: 51).

While this may be a tall order, I hope I have shown that at the very least the Internet and computer technology can aid journalists and provide them with a degree of autonomy from the economic, political and professional constraints of late twentieth century journalism. For investigative journalists the Internet has the potential to allow them to access a wide range of sources from all over the world so that a more objective viewpoint can be gained. By doing background research on the Internet, journalists are now able to get enough information easily to make their questioning more pertinent and probing. Accessing the right people to interview, be they officials, experts or 'victims' contacted through newsgroups, is also easier. Even more importantly, getting a more objective viewpoint is also possible. Traditionally journalists have always tried to check information they receive from one source against that of another – known as double sourcing – but the constraints of time and space often made this difficult. The Internet and e-mail reduce both time and space and make it easier for journalists to track down and access people.

Most important, the Internet is a new forum for journalists to disseminate information that traditional outlets deem too sensitive, or to bypass restrictions in areas where there is political upheaval and censorship. This was shown to good effect in Serbia in December 1996 when Yugoslav President Slobodan Milosevic tried to stop the broadcasting of reports by the independent Serbian radio station Radio B-92 about anti-government demonstrations over the annulment of municipal elections. After the station's transmitter was switched off, the station posted print versions of its news on its web site, and also began using RealAudio to broadcast their voice online. Further attempts by the Serbian government to put filters on independent media web sites to prevent Internet users in Serbia from accessing those sites, also failed as Radio B-92, among others, used 'mirror sites', which are alternative web sites that contain the same information as the original site. Moreover, the station was able to disseminate information to 30,000 people subscribing to its e-mail mailing list.[20]

The negative side of the technology is that while journalists can use it to track others down, it can be used to keep track of journalists. Every time anyone goes online they may give away information about themselves, where they are and what they are accessing. In repressive regimes therefore, the technology could be used to stifle rather than liberate information. There is also a danger that by not checking the source of information on the Internet, disinformation will be spread.

Nonetheless, the *potential* of the technology is to create a more equal and free arena that goes some way to meeting the criteria of the ideal of the 'public sphere' as defined by Jürgen Habermas. The key characteristic of Habermas's concept of the public sphere is guaranteed access; within that public sphere there is no social hierarchy and any subject of importance or interest can be discussed. The public sphere he envisions is also autonomous in that it is free from either political or economic control, and it embodies a democratic ideal through the provision and exchange of knowledge and information.[21] Critics have pointed out that the arena of seventeenth-century coffee houses on which Habermas based his theory did not in fact have these characteristics, in that it was restricted to those who could afford to use the coffee houses who were mainly the bourgeoisie and nobility and were exclusively male. Nonetheless it serves as an ideal concept for democratic societies to work towards.

Similarly, the Internet is not freely accessible, being restricted to those with the economic ability to purchase the necessary hardware, generally those in affluent Western societies. But at the moment it does provide a forum within which there is equality and freedom, and unlike Habermas's coffee houses it is not limited to a particular size, or a particular geographic space. On accessing the Internet there are no restrictions on what can be discussed, or who can take part in those discussions, and to a large extent it operates without being controlled by either politics or the market. This 'freedom' does of course raise other issues of taste, decency and cultural imperialism that will have to be addressed at some stage in the future. But as a forum for the free exchange of information and knowledge the Internet appears to satisfy the basic criteria of a public sphere open to all citizens. Whether commercial interests and governments will allow it to remain so is an issue we will all have to consider in the future. As Brian McNair comments:

> The coming years will demonstrate if this is misplaced utopianism or a realistic assessment of the liberating potential of a technology which is uniquely difficult to police and regulate, thus uniquely free from the commercialisation and elite control which have eventually subdued all other media forms in human history.
>
> (1998: 142)

In any event the future of investigative journalism looks brighter because of technological advances. The Investigative Reporters and Editors Incorporation in America have a down to earth definition of the job of an investigative journalist:

> On average it's nine-tenths drudgery, endless hours sifting through mostly meaningless documents, protracted negotiations with defensive bureaucrats, frequent meetings with dry sources and mentally disturbed crusaders, long nights, cold coffee, busted trails, bottomless pits and, occasionally, heady success.
>
> (cit. in Northmore 1996: 10)

With the technology now available this definition could well become redundant.

NOTES

1 For example Rupert Murdoch's refusal to publish Chris Patten's critical evaluation of the Hong Kong hand-over to China in 1997, because at the time he was negotiating broadcasting rights in China and did not want to upset the Chinese.
2 See, for example, Tindall and Shi 1989; 118 and 124.
3 Quoted in *Journalism and the Internet*, www.soi.city.ac.uk/~pw/j1_results.html
4 NetMedia 97, City University, London 3–4 July 1997.
5 Figures from *Journalism and the Internet*, www.soi.city.ac.uk/~pw/j1_results.html There is enormous debate over determining the size of the Internet, with various methods used. However, while the actual figures are open to debate, the fact that the Internet is continuing to grow is not.
6 *Journalism and the Internet.*
7 Ibid.
8 Ibid.
9 For more information on FTP see Reddick and King 1995.

10 Although it is a moot point that local authorities and other official bodies refuse to pass on information electronically, in practice they do, and as yet no official ruling has been made.

11 The story called 'Dead or Alive: City's Ineligible Voters Number in the Thousands', by Tim Novak and George Landau, was published in the St. Louis Post-Dispatch on 9 September 1990.

12 Lord Justice Saville made British judicial history in June 1998 in a landmark Court of Appeal verdict by directing that it be posted immediately on the World Wide Web. 'Wig, Gown and Laptop' by Duncan Campbell, *The Guardian Online*, August 1998. (www.guardian.co.uk)

13 Paper delivered at the first Ameritech Information Society Lecture, Edinburgh 1997.

14 For example the journalism of Tom Wolfe, where journalists reported through their direct experience. See Wolfe and Johnson 1975.

15 *Journalism and the Internet*, www.soi.city.ac.uk/~pw/j1_results.html

16 Interview with the author, May 1999.

17 An intranet is a corporate internal web site that can only be accessed by those within the organisation.

18 Interview with the author, October 1998.

19 Interview with the author, May 1999.

20 Information from 'Big Brother Watches the Internet in Belgrade' by Julie Moffett, *www.rferl.org/* January 1999.

21 This is a very simplified version of Habermas's theory. For more details see Habermas 1989.

BIBLIOGRAPHY

Bardoel, J. (1996) Beyond journalism: a profession between information society and civil society. *European Journal of Communication*, 11 (3): 283–302.

Boyd-Barrett, O. and Newbold, C. (eds) (1997) *Approaches to Media*. London: Edward Arnold.

Curran, J. and Seaton, J. (1995) *Power without Responsibility: The Press and Broadcasting in Britain*. Routledge: London.

Garnham, N. (1979) Contribution to a political economy of mass communication. *Media, Culture and Society*, 1 (2): 130–4.

Garrison, B. (1997) Online news gathering trends in American newspapers. On the Internet at http://gehon.ir.miami.edu/com/car/stpete.htm

Golding, P. and Murdock, G. (1996) Culture, communications and political economy. In J. Curran and M. Gurevitch, (eds.) *Mass Media and Society*, 2nd edn. London: Edward Arnold.

Habermas, J. (1989) *The Structural Transformation of the Public Sphere: An Inquiry into a Category of Bourgeois Society* (trans. T. Burger and F. Lawrence). Cambridge: Polity Press.

Hall, S. (1982) The rediscovery of 'ideology': the return of the repressed in media studies. In M. Gurevitch, T. Bennett, J. Curran and J. Woolacott (eds) *Culture, Society and the Media*, London: Methuen.

Haywood, T. (1997) *Praise the Net and Pass the Modem*. Edinburgh: Merchiston Publishing.

Koch, T. (1991) *Journalism in the Twenty-First Century*. London: Adamantine Press.

McCombs, M. E. and Shaw, D. L. (1972) The agenda-setting function of mass media. *The Public Opinion Quarterly*, 36 (2). Reprinted in O. Boyd-Barrett and C. Newbold (eds) (1997) *Approaches to Media*. London: Edward Arnold: 154.

McNair, B (1998) *The Sociology of Journalism*. London: Edward Arnold.

Meyer, P. (1991) *The New Precision Journalism*. Bloomington: University of Indiana Press.

Moffett, J. (1999) Big Brother watches the Internet in Belgrade. On the Internet at www.rfelr.org January 1999.

Nicholas, D. (1998) *Journalism and the Internet*. On the Internet at www.soi.ac.uk

Northmore, D. (1996) *Lifting the Lid: A Guide to Investigative Research*. London: Cassell.

Reddick, R. and King, E. (1995) *The Online Journalist*. Fort Worth and London: Harcourt Brace.

Reisner, N. (1997) Introduction to computer-assisted reporting. Paper delivered at NetMedia 97, City University, London, 3–4 July.

Sampson, A. (1996) The crisis at the heart of our media. *British Journalism Review*, 7 (3): 42–51.

Smythe, D. (1981) *Dependency Road: Communications, Capitalism, Consciousness and Canada*. Norwood, New Jersey: Ablex.

Tindall, G. B. and Shi, D. E. (1989) *America*, 2nd edn. London: W. W. Norton: 118 and 124.

Wolfe, T. and Johnson, E. W. (1975) *The New Journalism*. London: Picador.

FURTHER READING

Reddick, R. (1995) *The Online Journalist*. London: Harcourt Brace.

Part 2

PRACTICE

10

INVESTIGATING CORPORATE CORRUPTION

An example from BBC's *File on Four*

Hugo de Burgh

The medium of radio in the UK

The BBC was founded in 1922 as a national, publicly regulated corporation. It was founded in this manner because the unregulated US radio sphere was seen as chaotic (Franklin 1997: 117) and a negative model. One of the most important influences upon the development of BBC radio, which itself influenced the institutions created for television after the Second World War, was the personality of the first Director General, Lord Reith, who exemplified many of the values admired by his generation.

Lord Reith believed that the medium should 'inform, educate and entertain'. By this he meant that its principal responsibilities included the provision of impartial information upon which citizens could base their decisions; the expression of a national consensus in matters of morality and taste, a consensus guided by his own Presbyterian instincts; that quality of output should always take precedence over profit. The institutions were created through a number of measures, of which the most important were the Acts based on the Crawford reports, which made Reith's vision possible to implement.

Independence from the politicians was assured by the creation of an independent board of directors whose main function was to defend the BBC from political pressures; public funding was provided in ten year tranches so that the BBC was not required to raise money in the market.

As a result of these arrangements Lord Reith was able, in 1926, successfully to resist calls by politicians to take the side of the government of the day over the General Strike; this was a propitious moment in the development of the BBC, since it defined its position. This event, together with its metamorphosis into a 'national institution' to which everybody listened during the crisis years of the 1930s and the Second World War, enabled it to emerge from that war as a national institution of authority and influence, respected at home as abroad for its high standards of reporting and production.

Competition from television and technological developments menaced the

Corporation in the 1960s, as did social and cultural evolution. It was the period of the establishment of commercially produced popular music, of the expansion of advertising and of that expansion's impact upon the media and of the start of modern consumerism. In 1967 the Pilkington Committee recommended the introduction of local radio, and in the same year the BBC set up Radio 1 in acknowledgement that the existing services catered only inadequately to varieties of taste.

In 1972 the Sound Broadcasting Act established Independent Local Radio, which expanded hugely under the free enterprise impetus of the Thatcher government from 1979. These commercial stations were intended to be profit-making; their owners were not necessarily imbued with the public service ideal. Their views on the media were expressed in the 1990 Broadcasting Act which changed British radio broadcasting dramatically by not requiring the new radio stations to educate or inform, by limiting the involvement of the government in the monitoring of quality and by selling the right to broadcast to the highest cash bidder.

In 1992 the first British whole-nation commercial channels went on air; there are now three (1992 Classic FM, 1993 Virgin, 1995 Talk Radio). A BBC response to this was to launch BBC Radio 5. The 1996 Broadcasting Act stabilised this situation and also permitted more cross-ownership; however it did confirm the BBC's special status for the moment.

Faced with competition from commercial channels, the BBC is criticised for becoming much more populist in order to compete with commercial channels. The reforms undertaken in the 1990s in order to try to make the BBC more competitive are widely believed to be to the detriment of radio, cutting investment in radio, forcing newsrooms to go bimedia. The paring down of established schedules and diminishing of highbrow content do not appear to have solved the perceived problem of the BBC which, according to figures in late 1998, has lost audiences at an even faster rate (Hellen 1998).

File on Four

There are two principal vehicles for investigation on BBC radio, *File on Four* and *Face the Facts*. The *Face the Facts* team, which in 1998 had its number of slots reduced, also inputs into news. Other BBC programmes with a tradition of investigative work are *You and Yours, The Food Programme, Farming Today, The Today Programme, World at One* and *World this Weekend*. As yet there are few if any outlets for investigation on commercial radio in the UK, which is a pity since radio has many advantages over television in this field; people are more likely to talk into a marantz (tape recorder) than a camera and issues of identification are much easier to deal with.

The two BBC series are complementary. *Face the Facts* is a popular, 'getting wrongs put right' programme whereas *File on Four* attempts the stories with wider ramifications and issues of policy behind them. *File on Four* was first transmitted in October 1977. It is transmitted for 40 minutes weekly and has an audience of one million per week for its two broadcasts, an audience which is more male than female, whose members are in their 30s and 40s and who are dedicated Radio 4 listeners. It is produced in 4 weeks, butted up to transmission. The production team consists of the series editor and aide, the producer, responsible for structure and the reporter who does the writing and interviewing. The Reporter takes responsibility and must have the authority to convince the listener of the significance of his case and individual arguments, as well as the communication skill to make significant or interesting 'sometimes quite dreary bits of fact' (Heggie 1997).

Facts that have been investigated in recent years include the lack of controls on locum doctors, the poor conditions and lack of legal protection for child labourers, the regulatory framework for small airlines, corruption in Palestine under Yasser Arafat, the morale of the Russian army, hormone disruption chemicals, phoenix directors (those who reappear with new companies after the destruction of the old) and the exploitation of the citizens of poor countries for medical research. The editor 'never employs specialists' but takes pride when his programmes are admired by experts in the field with which they have made themselves familiar. For example *File on Four* has been awarded both Gold and Silver awards of the Medical Journalism Association (Ross 1999).

According to David Heggie, one of the producers of *File on Four*, the programme is investigative in every sense. It finds its own stories – there is 'nothing that comes off diary'; it has an utterly different agenda from news; it is long-form programming with the implications this has for the nature of the subject and the kinds of treatment. The subjects have major policy implications and matter to large numbers of people; therefore once embarked upon, a subject has to be treated thoroughly so that no listener can imagine that the programme is dressing up a 'cheap scandal' as something more significant. The editor, David Ross, is very clinical early on as to what the core of the subject is and starts by writing the billing. 'We are ostentatious about dotting Is and crossing Ts and only make claims that we can substantiate; moreover we believe that the plural of fact is not data and that facts in themselves are not truth'. *File on Four's* team believes that its reputation depends upon its evidence: 'there is no rhetoric except that coming from other people' and it does not campaign, 'campaigning is for others. We produce the facts' (Heggie 1997).

This characterisation is endorsed by editor David Ross, who talks of *File on Four* as being not investigative journalism but 'evidential reportage': the 'reportage' is in the getting away from the daily debate and trying to look at the effects of policy and decisions on how people actually live, the 'evidential' is looking for evidence first hand. It is the level and quality of detail that marks out *File on Four*. What is the difference between evidential and analytical? 'Not wheeling in the experts but getting out and seeing what's going on' (Ross 1999).

It is programmes dealing with aspects of business that he mentions when asked to illustrate his method, and in particular business interfacing with the public sector. In 1996 his team looked at the background of US companies coming into the UK power market (*FoF* 30 January 1996). 'We found that you need very strong regulation if you are to deal effectively with these power companies. We questioned the effectiveness of the regulatory mechanisms' (Ross 1999). Similar lessons were learned from an investigation of the outsourcing of public service computer contracts by the Department of Social Security and Immigration Service; here were 'massive contracts and things not going right' (*FoF* 2 March 1999).

The same theme has run through several investigations into fraud in the European Commission since January 1998, well before the European Parliament publicised such fraud in early 1999. Through his contacts in Brussels reporter Richard Watson opened up the scale of the fraud by revealing that over 200 agriculture projects were under investigation. One of those he exposed was a project where the recipient company in Ireland received hundreds of thousands of pounds for work done in Sicily costing minimal amounts (*FoF* 6 January 1998).

Business issues and investigative journalists

Government is a clear target, businesses less so. There are thousands of businesses carrying on unimaginably varied activities. Whereas we are all affected by public administration, for an investigation into business to be appealing to an audience, and therefore worth doing, a journalist must feel confident either that its name is sufficiently known, or its activities sufficiently heinous, for impact to be possible. The kind of activities that investigative journalists in the UK have found their public to be interested in include the production of goods which harm substantial numbers of people; apparent price-fixing, so that consumers are short-changed; faulty manufacturing and safety procedures which result in death; dishonest use of investment funds; tax evasion by the rich; anti-competitive practices by well-known companies and, at least in the case of one well-known company with a following of popular shareholders, the cheating of its owners; the failures of professional regulation.

Opportunities are provided for the investigative journalist by the fact that regulatory bodies and professional codes exist, in some cases as a result of revelations by earlier journalists. They provide the touchstone against which business may be judged, rather than against mere abstract moral laws of behaviour. There are the consumer protection watchdogs and the industry watchdogs such as the Gas Users' Council. In the UK the Financial Services Acts spawned several regulatory bodies for the investment industries and there is the Monopolies Commission. The Companies Acts provide the basic rules of operation. These are the structures which police business – apart from the general laws – and even a cursory knowledge of them opens the eyes of the investigative journalist to opportunities.

One common fact emerges from the examination of some of the best-known cases of business malpractice which have been investigated. It is that companies often create their own moralities, forgetting their responsibilities to the larger society; this is potentially dangerous when their actions can affect so many people, and particularly so when they are insulated from the consequences of what they do either because the regulations are inadequate, perhaps because nobody in the public domain really understands what they do, or because, being transnational, they can be made subject to no national laws, or because law itself allows them to create structures which ensure that blame can be isolated or deflected from the principals. Eddy makes this point very well, in his summing up of the DC10 investigation (Eddy 1976), when he quotes Cavour saying, 'if what we did were not done for Italy, what criminals we would be'.

In an attempt to undermine the socially negative aspects of these cultures, a UK pressure group, Public Concern at Work, has promoted the Public Interest Disclosure Bill (1998) which came into force in 1999. In effect, it supports whistle-blowers, giving them protection for revealing their employers' malfeasance. Its effect on investigative journalists is dealt with by Gill Moore in Chapter 7.

Doubtless there are many scandals awaiting exposition; Walter Ingo's *Secret Money* (1985) hints at the opportunities for the investigative journalists in tracking tax avoidance by multinationals; Anthony Sampson's series of books on multinational arms dealers, computer companies, oil moguls and bankers tells us of their awesome power to circumvent regulation; Davis' *The Corporate Alchemists* (1984) suggests ways in which the unchecked power of the chemical industries needs to be exposed. In the following brief sketch of the extent of the investigation of business, I exclude those stories where the emphasis has been on the relationship of business to public administration (political party funding, for example) or to political policy (breaking of embargoes, selling of military or police equipment or services).

There are two outstanding stories that have investigated how it was possible for products which have either killed or maimed large numbers of people to be manufactured and distributed. First, the thalidomide story is well described in several books, succinctly by Evans (1983) and in more detail by Rosen (1979), and the *Sunday Times* Insight (1973 and 1979); it is briefly summarised in Chapter 3.

The other major manufacturing story also comes from the 1970s:

> The worst air crash the world had then seen occurred just outside Paris on a fine Sunday. Ten minutes after taking off for London from Orly Airport, at 12.30 pm on 3 March 1974, a DC-10 airliner operated by Turkish Airlines plunged 11,500 feet into the Forest of Ermenonville at 497 miles per hour. There were 346 victims. They died violently because the DC-10 had a lie in it.

It took 2 years to trace that lie, and with it the disaster that should never have happened. It brought us into conflict in a California court with McDonnell Douglas which built the doomed DC-10, their Ship 29, and it raised the question, as did the thalidomide tragedy, of how far the press should go on behalf of the citizen in challenging corporate power. It was piquant that in this contest with McDonnell Douglas they quoted the thalidomide campaign as an example of our irresponsibility.

(Evans 1983: 26)

In essence, the *Sunday Times* discovered that a known fault had not been corrected; its implications had been clear for two years, yet no action had been taken and that therefore many travellers' lives were at risk. The investigation, which required that the journalists become experts in the subject in hand to a remarkable degree (Eddy 1976: 302ff), and without which the important facts of the case might never have come to light, indicted the civil aviation industry for its procedures, the failure of the agency responsible for the public control of safety standards and the commercial and political pressures upon the manufacturers to which it accorded much of the blame.

Price-fixing is a perennial issue, presumably because editors know that it riles their audiences. In 1998 there was a series of exposures in several media of the fact that British consumers pay more for their supermarket food than those on the continent of Europe; in 1991 the *Sunday Times* had already shown that mark-ups by British supermarkets, at 60 per cent, were much higher than in the US or Germany (Neil 1996: 335). Bank charges are a similar staple. At the time of going to press the British government claims to be taking serious action to deal with these issues identified by journalists.

One impressive group of investigations into price-fixing, covered by television and several newspapers, concerned the by now well-known fact that UK consumers pay vastly more for cars than their continental counterparts. At least one television programme (BBC *Panorama* 1998) exposed the unethical practices that achieve this, and the way in which a coalition of manufacturers and dealers had ensured that it was virtually impossible for British consumers to buy right-hand drive cars on the Continent; it also demonstrated how the second-hand car market was being rigged to support the excess profits being made in the new. As an example of how millions of people's incomes and necessities are affected by business malpractice, this could hardly be bettered.

There have been many after the fact investigations of investment malpractice. The 1960s saw the introduction of a number of invest and save schemes including that of IOS, Investors Overseas Services, run by a Bernard Caulfield; his operations were the subject of extensive journalistic investigation by Insight, described in Raw (1971), who went on to cover the Slater Walker financial scam, written up in Raw (1977). In June 1988 the Barlow Clowes scandal broke, 'an immense deception carried out with almost farcical ease by one man against major financial institutions, government departments and over sixteen thousand private investors' (Lever 1992). It illustrated well the failure of auditors to identify problems, the limitations of legal regulation and, probably, the lack of competent journalists in this important field.

The earliest example of the investigation of tax evasion of which I am aware is the series of articles by Philip Knightley on 'The Gilded Tax Dodgers' in the *Sunday Times* during 1980. Knightley later went on to write up the story of the family that had made tax avoidance a core principle of its business since the First World War in his *The Vesteys*, providing a beginners' guide to methods which, it may be speculated, have since become widely applied. In 1988 the *Sunday Times* reported that the Kuwait Investment Office, despite having a £15 billion portfolio of British shares, 'did not pay a penny of tax' (Neil 1996: 329); in 1990 Insight also exposed how the 1981 British Finance Act had made possible large scale tax avoidance through offshore trusts (ibid.: 330). More recently there have been stabs at understanding how Rupert Murdoch's business empire has succeeded in paying very little tax.

Anti-competitive practices are probably only of general interest when the companies involved are well-known and the story has a touch of the thriller about it. The latter was so when National Car Parks, Europe's biggest, was exposed as having 'conducted an industrial spying campaign against (its rival) Europarks' (the *Sunday Times*, 5 August 1990). Better known is the 'dirty tricks campaign' mounted by British Airways against its rival, Virgin, also exposed in the *Sunday Times*. The investigation became really popular when agents of British Airways were caught trying to steal the household refuse of the *Sunday Times*'s business editor.

The most notorious examples of management abuse of shareholder funds are those of Guinness – which resulted in the imprisonment of the Chief Executive of that world-class company – Polly Peck and BCCI. Insight found that Polly Peck's managers were buying their own shares in order to lift their price, and using the company's own money in order to do so. This investigation was made more intriguing by the fact that Polly Peck's founder, Asil Nadir, fled bail and took refuge beyond British law by his associations with politicians and donations to the Conservative Party and by the extraordinary saga of contacts between the exiled entrepreneur and the British government.

The Bank of Credit and Commerce International (BCCI) was being investigated by journalists in 1990, well before its collapse a year later. Essentially, the BCCI story is that of a bank set up to cheat the gullible; millions of devout Muslims or others with a Muslim connection put their money into BCCI because they believed it would be run on Islamic lines by their co-religionists. In reality the bosses siphoned off much of the money either for themselves and their families, or for their pet political or charitable projects, as in the case of *South* magazine. Much information about what was going on had been available for a long time beforehand, had anyone read the accounts of BCCI and its subsidiaries. One of the journalists who worked on the story, Nick Fielding, makes a number of points relevant to investigations in this area. He believes that the regulators (the Serious Fraud Office) in the UK need to be much more proactive in gathering intelligence on potential fraud; that liquidators are a source of important information that is rarely exploited by journalists because not published; that qualifications on company accounts need to be highlighted publicly for them to be accessed by journalists in the UK (Fielding 1993).

Finally, employee exploitation is also a staple of UK media investigations. One that aroused considerable interest was 'Pesticides in Kenya' (1996), which had more audience response than any *File on Four* for the previous few years, suggesting that its listeners are not parochial if the topic is made relevant and addresses existing concerns. 'Pesticides in Kenya' aroused much wrath among listeners; for different reasons it did so too in Kenya, with Kenya Radio denouncing the *File on Four* team as spies (Heggie 1997).

The original intention of the team was to make a programme about pesticides in the UK but *File on Four* failed to find any adequate evidence of malpractice. By that time *File on Four* was in contact with the Pesticides Action Network which suggested Equador. While examining Equador they came across two researchers, one of whom was a Kenyan with convincing evidence of medical problems caused to agricultural workers through pesticide handling and the other a postgraduate student who had studied pesticide labelling in Kenya. *File on Four* was able to build upon both of these.

The kernel of the story then became the impact upon poorer countries of Western market demands. Its achievements included the fact that the journalists managed to provide incontrovertible evidence of what had first aroused their investigative urges; that they were able to bring together information with which to confront the authorities; that they showed that the large transnational corporation Del Monte imported banned chemicals.

Example: insolvency practitioners

'Insolvency Practitioners' is a *File on Four* that deals with the failure of professional regulation – regarded in legal and social theory as an important bulwark of society. There are 2,000 insolvency practitioners in the UK, working mainly for the banks who lend out money to businesses, and regulated by their own professional body working closely with other professional bodies such as the accountancy regulator. When lenders or creditors are concerned about the future of their investments in a company, they call in insolvency practitioners to examine the best method of protecting their investment. The law gives insolvency practitioners great discretion, yet the rules that bind them are, according to the programme 'few, vague and not always enforced'.

In other words, it is widely believed that insolvency practitioners act more in their own interests than in the interests of their clients, let alone those whom they are investigating. Since they stand to gain, it is argued, from declaring a company insolvent and disposing of its assets, they will always prefer this option to any other. This is hard on the companies which, sometimes through no fault of their directors, have difficulties that may often be remediable; furthermore it is damaging to society and to the economy if businesses are closed unjustly and unnecessarily.

The treatment

The programme starts with an image that – this being radio – has to be described to us. It is of a Mr Barrie Chapman standing before the house he used to own as we are told that it was taken from him when his 100-year-old business was closed down unnecessarily. It then goes on to state the case of the programme very succinctly, first in the words of the reporter, Jolyon Jenkins, who says, 'most people involved in insolvency are losers, but one player always wins – the insolvency practitioner'. Whereupon another voice is heard (that of Prem Sikka, who will be introduced later) giving the rationale for the programme:

> you will find that these insolvency practitioners do not owe a duty of care either to unsecured creditors or shareholders or employees. What we need is more public scrutiny because what is at stake is not only the particular fortunes of a company, but the fortunes of our economy.

All of this has happened within 30 seconds and precedes the signature tune that leads us into the programme proper. In the traditional way the programme will tell stories that illustrate the points and provide evidence in the form of verifiable facts and testimony. Thus, having heard the case stated at the outset, we will then listen to it being built up and be able to decide whether the investigation has proved it.

In this particular story, we could divine that illustrations from victims of the insolvency practitioners' procedures would follow, providing evidence of specific cases. These cases would be generalised with reference to data on the number of cases taken on by insolvency practitioners and the 'destruction rate'; it is possible that further statistical colour might be found by trawling government agencies' publications. Insolvency practitioners themselves, here set up as the villains, would be asked to comment, individually in the matter of the particular illustrative cases used, and as a body through their professional association on the general charges. Such might be anticipated. How does the programme actually deal with the story?

Illustration A

Farm noises tell us that we are in the countryside and Jolyon explains where we are and that we are with a farmer, Thriepland, whose farm used to be a 'multi-million pound business until Mr Thriepland got embroiled in the curious world of the insolvency practitioner'. Thriepland shows us around the buildings in which he used to produce cheese and the reporter explains that when the price of cheese fell he went to his bank for advice. The bank appointed an investigating accountant, KPMG Peat Marwick, to assess Thriepland's business.

Thriepland gives his comment on what then occurred. A very young man was sent by KPMG to assess the value of Thriepland's stock, whose value he decided – seemingly arbitrarily and without any experience or knowledge of the industry he was assessing – to halve. The one day report by the youth cost £3,000 and was charged to Thriepland. As a result of that report the bank thought the business was failing and appointed an insolvency practitioner to take control of the business and sell off any assets.

Mr Thriepland refused to cooperate and obtained another valuation backing his contention that the business could survive. A wrangle took place over many months of meetings. Thriepland was lucky in that he had excellent contacts, including a banker and a senior lawyer who represented him without charge; the bank was represented by KPMG who then charged him. Thriepland won in the sense that he forced the bank to back down over declaring him insolvent but the case was costly and he was obliged to sell off his cheese-making operation. Furious at his treatment, he tried to sue KPMG upon the assumption that they had failed in their 'duty of care' to him but found that, legally, they owed him no duty of care, so he had no grounds for complaint.

Illustration B

This time we hear the sounds of the demolition of buildings formerly belonging to the Bass Group, another long-established company, this time in packaging and timber. Again the Bank had commissioned a report when the company wanted extended terms; again the report was done speedily by a firm of accountants, Ernst and Young. This firm recommended that the Group be handed to administrators to manage, which it was. The 'even more lucrative task of carrying out their own recommendations', says reporter Jolyon Jenkins, was awarded to Ernst and Young.

There then follows an interview with a senior executive of Bass who believes that the interpretation of the accounts by Ernst and Young was quite simply wrong and that the company was making a profit. The reporter goes on to describe the efforts by the board of the company to obtain a third opinion from a business academic; the academic found it extraordinary that the company he investigated and saw as basically successful and with good potential in its new products should be 'presented as a dead duck'. The academic also pointed out that assets of the Bass Group were undervalued by Ernst and Young. A building valued by Bass at £300,000 was revalued by Ernst and Young at a mere £170,000 and its sale obliged; yet a few months later it was going for £360,000.

After five months of administration by Ernst and Young, the Bass Group ceased trading and administrators gave way to liquidators. The liquidators were Ernst and Young. They sold off the assets and raised enough money for 'nearly all' the debts owed to the creditors to be paid back. 'Not bad' as the reporter says 'for an allegedly insolvent company', especially as about £1million was paid out in fees, a good deal of it to Ernst and Young.

This very strong case against the system is now given a further twist. Former directors of Bass Group want to complain formally, yet the evidence they require to back their case lies in the Group's books which are held by Ernst and Young and to which they, being no longer directors, have no access.

This predicament is put by the reporter to the Head of Professional Ethics at the Institute of Chartered Accountants, the professional body that regulates Ernst and Young, but he receives no support for his suggestion that the directors should be provided with the information necessary.

The moral that the reporter takes from this story is that investigating accountants should not be allowed to recommend receivership and then become the receiver. He finds that specialists in this area have been arguing for the dual role to be banned. Prem Sikka, a university Reader in Accounting and Finance, believes that businesses are less likely to be recommended for liquidation if investigating accountants have nothing to gain from doing so.

At this point the reporter, as we predicted, produces such statistical evidence as he has. He claims that in general there is 'striking statistical evidence that banning insolvency practitioners from acting as receivers for companies they've investigated would mean more companies surviving' and cites the Royal Bank of Scotland as having decided not to commission insolvency practitioners to do both jobs. However, the accountants themselves are very keen that the Royal Bank's example not be followed, and this is stated by the professional body's spokesman who believes that his members are scrupulous about all the various threats to their objectivity.

Having failed to get any agreement on his point from the 'villains', the reporter then proceeds to undermine the case that accountants do bind themselves by rules of impartiality. One such professional rule is that there should be no close connection between the accountant selling off the assets of a bankrupt company and those to whom the assets are sold. Jenkins gives the example of a Nottingham printing company. According to him, not only did the receivers, accountancy firm Grant Thornton, refuse a higher offer for the business than they subsequently accepted, but Grant Thornton's manager for the receivership was the main person to buy it, and was apparently improving it before he actually became its main owner. This is definitely unethical and against the profession's rules. The reporter returns to the professional body. Such action as described is unethical, he establishes, and would be subject to complaint and disciplinary action. Yet nothing has been done.

Having verified his point that the regulatory bodies cannot be relied upon to 'police the system with small companies', the programme moves on to a bigger field, showing that similar, or worse, behaviour can take place at capital or national level. Corporate Communications, a major public relations company, went into receivership, in other words was bankrupt and had its management taken over by accountants supposedly acting in the interests of the creditors. This happened, it was alleged, at least partly due to the greed of the executive directors who took far too much out of the company; yet when the accountants were called in they promptly sold the assets back to those directors, but conveniently excluding some major shareholders. The old company, the shareholders not in on the plot and its creditors were thus put out of the way. Cork Gully, the insolvency arm of accountancy firm Coopers and Lybrand, managed the whole affair so fast that the shareholders and creditors had no time to challenge the process yet, according to the programme, were left with no money because the asset sale had not raised enough.

Here we come to some sleuthing by the programme that reveals that the trick was premeditated. The researchers discovered that:

1   the receivers had been consulted before they had even been appointed, and the whole process had been planned in advance;
2   the claims that speed was essential if the business was to be saved and that there was no other buyer for one particularly sensitive part of the business cannot be substantiated and were probably false;
3   a rule of the Society of Practitioners of Insolvency was broken in that Coopers & Lybrand was both a consultant to the company well before liquidation and then its receiver.

The programme has documentary and testimonial evidence to support these allegations. It then goes to the Society and asks in general terms whether the kind of things described above would be against the rules and are informed that they are. However, its expert witness, Prem Sikka, warns that self-regulation does not work, pointing out that regulatory bodies made up of committees, many of whose members represent firms making hundreds of millions of pounds from these practices, are not very disposed to control them.

Jenkins has the last word:

Last year, 5,000 companies went into receivership. The insolvency practitioners who took them over had virtually unlimited and unchallengeable powers to dispose of them as they saw fit. But our cases show that what they do is not always in the best interests of the company. The accountants have not yet been called to account.

Discussion

The world of insolvency is full of arcane terms and business jargon and the programme very effectively deals with this by first giving a helicopter view of what the theme is and going on to very simple and concrete examples. It is everywhere clear, at least in part because the stories are well told, with disciplined testimonials. Expertise is only used to clarify or to offer comment where comment by the reporter would be out of order.

To undertake this programme for television would have been extremely expensive; for it to have been written as a newspaper feature would have demanded such space as to tax the concentration of all but the most dedicated readers. Yet it is entertaining as well as informative as radio, suggesting that radio is an excellent medium for investigative journalism, something that has not been fully exploited.

As to the content, the remarkable implications, in particular of the Corporate Communications case, were not fully spelt out: if it is illegal to privilege some creditors of a liquidating company over others and if directors' liabilities and responsibilities of good governance mean anything, how was it that Corporate Communications' original directors and their advisers were not prosecuted? The way in which this aspect was dealt with was not as decisive as the earlier parts of the programme.

Nevertheless this programme is a classic example of dealing with a business story in investigative journalism because it satisfies the conditions of a good investigation and a good human interest story. It identifies cases that represent issues with far-reaching implications; challenges villain with victim; clarifies complex issues by going to the root of the matter; uses whatever techniques are required to gain that access or information that provide the appropriate evidence. These are necessary conditions of investigative journalism.

BIBLIOGRAPHY

BBC (1996) *File on Four.* 'Pesticides in Kenya'. Manchester: BBC.
BBC (1997) *File on Four.* 'Insolvency Practitioners'. Manchester: BBC.
BBC (1998) *Panorama.* 'The Car Cartel'. London: BBC.
Crook, T. (1998) *International Radio Journalism.* London: Routledge.
Davis, L. (1984) *The Corporate Alchemists.* London: Temple Smith.
Eddy, P. (1976) *Destination Disaster.* London: Granada.
Evans, H. (1983) *Good Times, Bad Times.* London: Phoenix.
Fielding, N. (1993) Investigating BCCI: a journalist's experience. *Crime, Law and Social Change*, 20 (4): 311.
Franklin, B. (1997) *Newszak and News Media.* London: Edward Arnold.

Heggie, D. (1997) 'File on Four' Talk given to students on the MA Investigative Journalism course at Nottingham Trent University, 23 November 1997.

Hellen, N. (1998) Boyle to go in Radio 4 disaster. *Sunday Times*, 1 November 1998: 9.

Ingo, W. (1985) *Secret Money*. London: George Allen.

Jordan, G. (1990) *The Commercial Lobbyists: Politics for Profit in Britain*. Aberdeen: Aberdeen University Press: 13–46.

Knightley, P. (1980) The gilded tax dodgers. *Sunday Times*, Oct–Nov 1980.

Knightley, P. (1993) *The Rise and Fall of the House of Vestey. The True Story of How Britain's Richest Family Beat the Taxman – and Came to Grief*. London: Warner.

Lever, L. (1992) *The Barlow Clowes Affair*. London: Macmillan/Channel 4.

Neil, A. (1996) *Full Disclosure*. London: Macmillan.

Raw, C. (1971) *Do You Sincerely Want to be Rich ?* London: André Deutsch.

Raw, C. (1977) *Slater Walker*. London: André Deutsch.

Rosen, M. (1979) *The Sunday Times Thalidomide Case: Contempt of Court and the Freedom of the Press*. London: Writers and Scholars Educational Trust. For the British Institute of Human Rights.

Ross, D. (1999) Interview with Hugo de Burgh, BBC Manchester, 24 March 1999.

Sampson, A. (1973) *Sovereign State: The Secret History of ITT*. London: Hodder and Stoughton.

Sampson, A. (1978) *The Arms Bazaar*. Sevenoaks: Coronet.

Sampson, A. (1981) *The Money Lenders*. London: Hodder and Stoughton.

Sampson, A. (1993) *The Seven Sisters: The Great Oil Companies and the World They Made*, 3rd edn. London: Coronet.

Stephens, M. (1997) *A History of News*. Fort Worth: Harcourt Brace.

Sunday Times (Insight Team) (1973) *The thalidomide children and the law*. London: André Deutsch.

Sunday Times (Insight Team) (1979) *Suffer the children: the story of thalidomide*. London: André Deutsch.

FURTHER READING

Crook, T. (1998) *International Radio Journalism*. London: Routledge.

Franklin, B. (1997) *Newszak and News Media*. London: Edward Arnold.

11

LOCAL POWER AND PUBLIC ACCOUNTABILITY

An example from the East Midlands

Mark D'Arcy

Introduction

At the turn of the century Lincoln Steffens exposed the corruption of US local politics in his *Shame of the Cities* (cit. in Ekirch 1974: 92); in the 1970s British investigator Ray Fitzwalter, in what became known as the 'Poulson Saga', revealed to an incredulous public how politicians of both major political parties could be bought. Today in Britain the scope of public administration, and therefore of maladministration, is greater than ever before, yet many fear that journalists are not up to the standards of Steffens and Fitzwalter. This chapter argues that monitoring the activities of the local state (which now extends well beyond elected local government) should be a principal task for investigative journalists, particularly in the local and regional media. It shows that the job is becoming more difficult because of the changing nature of the local state, and that the emphasis of reporting is now changing towards what editors see as a more reader-friendly agenda. Although based upon the British experience, the lessons are equally relevant to other countries.

English local administration

About a quarter of total government expenditure is delivered through elected local councils to provide us with services ranging from community care to highways and schools. Much of this activity is of direct and daily importance to viewers, listeners and readers of the local media. It is their children who suffer if the schools are sub-standard; it is their cars that are damaged by pot holes in the roads; it is they or their relatives who are at risk if community care services are inadequate; it is their council tax bills that rise if local politicians are corrupt or incompetent.

Local authorities are just one component of an increasingly complex and unreported local state. With opting out for schools, colleges and hospitals, power in key services is more diffuse and at the same time the potential for wrong-doing and unaccountable decision-making is greater. In my experience, the activities of Training and Enterprise Councils (TECs) are virtually unreported, except when they decide to press release something themselves. Yet these bodies will take an increasing role in employment training under the Labour government's New Deal programme, so their performance will directly affect the lives of thousands of unemployed people, who might lose their benefit if they do not participate in their training programmes. Police and health authorities have been reformed in the cause of 'leaner, fitter' decision-making; but this has entailed a far more closed style of decision-making, and their activities often escape systematic scrutiny. And what of the appointment and training of their members, and come to that, of local magistrates? The latter, after all, can send people to prison.

A good principle to observe is that the use of state power and public money should be accompanied by proper checks and balances. Where an organisation can operate in the knowledge that no-one is watching, all kinds of problems can quickly develop. In the late 1990s, the local state is full of faraway bodies of which we, the public, know nothing.

Reporting the wrong subjects?

The local state, in all its manifestations, presents an obvious and legitimate target for scrutiny and investigative reporting. But if anything, the local media are reducing their coverage of local public life. Fewer and fewer papers now devote the acres of space which would once have been allocated to reporting a council meeting with quasi-parliamentary coverage of speeches and questions. Fewer and fewer local radio stations cover council committees or even full council meetings. This is perceived to be a retrograde step, a blow to local democracy. But perhaps the real story is more complex. I doubt there was ever a halcyon era in which a breathless public crowded the streets, agog to read the latest reports of their local council's Policy and Resources Committee. If there was, that era is now over; market research by focus groups has identified, apparently, that this kind of coverage of local affairs is not what the viewers, listeners and readers want.

One reason may well be that, as far as the readers were concerned, such coverage simply did not deal with their real concerns. First, it was seldom sufficiently analytical; insults traded in the council chamber would be faithfully reported, with little or no explanation of the significance of whatever was being debated. It sometimes seemed that the journalists in the council chamber had lapsed into trial reporting mode, and were quite consciously avoiding any comment or judgement upon their story. But without some background and analysis readers would often be left with little idea of what the argument was actually about. A second issue is that much local government reporting dwells on subjects that simply don't interest the readership. In two and a half years as political correspondent with the *Leicester Mercury*, I spent much of my time covering power struggles in the Town Hall. This was investigative journalism in the sense that it involved revealing information that those in power would have preferred to keep private. There would be whispered tip-offs, careful checking with other sources, even the occasional leaked document. In retrospect, I was probably devoting too much time to reporting the micro-politics of local government, which were of limited interest to most readers. Perhaps the verdict of the focus groups was not so surprising after all. But perhaps the wrong conclusions are now being drawn from it. Many editors and policy-makers have made an unjustified leap from arguing that traditional local political reporting is too fixated on process and micro-politics, to the belief that all stories about local politics (in its broadest sense) are boring.

For instance, what I and my colleagues in other local media outlets in Leicester failed to notice, was the appalling standard of education provided by many of the city's schools. This only came to light when the county council lost responsibility for them and the new city education authority took its place close to the bottom of the government's education league tables. Here was a story with real public appeal and far more lasting importance. The local media should be ready to pounce on the failure of essential services; in practice, it seems to me that they seldom attempt to audit the performance of bread and butter services, even where doing so would produce some startling results. One starting point for this kind of reporting is The Audit Commission's Annual Performance Indicators for local services, which cover everything from exam results to the efficiency of council tax collection. These will give a clear indication when a local authority is falling behind in the standard of service it provides, and should prompt local reporters and editors to start asking why.

Such reporting still requires a specialist who can find his or her way around a town hall, who has some credibility with politicians and officials and who has a sufficient understanding of the workings of local government to spot a potential story. The trouble is that, on the principle that 'all council stories are boring', fewer and fewer local media outlets employ such a specialist – even on a part-time basis. All too often the reporter attending council meetings is some puzzled junior with little idea what is going on and who is speaking – and in many authorities there is no one there at all.

Bob Satchwell, President of the Guild of Newspaper Editors, and editor of the *Cambridge Evening News*, believes that many newspapers are consciously shifting their reporting agenda to meet the needs and tastes of their readers, as identified through focus groups and market research (Satchwell interview 1998). He con-tends that the recent revival in readership figures, led by local weekly papers and now being observed in regional dailies, is evidence that this process is indeed delivering what the readers want. But he also conceded that in some cases it has led editors to concentrate on a narrow news agenda and pay less attention to monitoring the performance of public services. This can lead to important stories that would appeal to readers being missed.

'I don't decry focus groups, but the downside of using them is that you can become over-focused,' Satchwell says. 'You do have to keep some perspective, and be prepared to have people trawling through council minutes and going to meetings that don't immediately seem newsworthy, in search of the stories that may be there.' An essential part of the process, he believes, is maintaining specialists who have the background knowledge to interpret information, and can develop contacts and gain the trust of potential whistle-blowers. But he insists that most local newspapers are doing 'a very, very good job' of monitoring the local state, and he rejects the idea that there was some lost golden age of serious local political reporting.

Ed Glinert, who compiles *Private Eye's* 'Rotten Boroughs' feature, a regular round-up of sleaze, abuse of power and municipal pomposity from town halls across the land, is less sanguine about the performance of the local media. He says most of his stories come from 'disaffected journalists, who find they can't get some stories printed, or are forced to tone them down, because they are about local councils which advertise in their paper.' Indeed *Private Eye* lacks the resources to obtain such stories itself, and his role is mainly to check the details. Often the stories he dealt with were reasonable accounts of events, which had been rejected because editors were afraid of causing offence. 'I think a lot of local newspapers are doing a really bad job, because they're so in hock to their local establishment that they never run anything that is detrimental to it,' Glinert said. He identifies a number of reasons why local papers may shy away from exposing wrong-doing in local public life:

> If a story focuses on wrong-doing by a particular individual, editors will often be reluctant to risk accusations that they are conducting a witch-hunt. For some reason this seems a particularly potent response to criticism of an individual, however powerful. This may result in stories being sanitised so that names are not named.
>
> (Glinert 1998)

This can be risky. A story which related, for example, tales of unnamed drunken councillors misbehaving, may provoke a writ from innocent and uninvolved local politicians, who feel they have been implicated. In the case of heavy-weight political scandals, there may be a cynical assumption that the readers will not understand or wish to read about some complex tale of wrong-doing. Glinert cites the example of the collapse of the Bank of Credit and Commerce International (BCCI), which had painful financial results for those councils which had invested in it. Some local papers thought the details of how their local politicians and officials had ignored the warning signs about the BCCI, and thus opened up their councils to substantial losses, were too complex for their readers.

Another barrier to investigative reporting can be a misguided local patriotism, which may induce some editors to give uncritical support to a prestige local initiative, rather than question whether it was money well spent. Glinert suggests that the English city of Manchester's bid to host the Olympics should have received more scrutiny and less uncritical coverage from the local media. Too often, he believes, the flaws in many flagship local projects only become apparent after a spectacular and expensive failure. Other examples may include grandiose regeneration projects, perhaps City Challenge schemes, or developments funded by Millennium Commission money. Typically such initiatives are hyped up as a great leap forward for a particular area; often the reality can be rather more mundane.

Financial and political corruption

Few stories confirm prejudices more satisfyingly than those about council corruption. The image of the councillor with his fingers jammed firmly in the till may be unfair (sitting in committees for hours to decide planning applications for garage extensions or whether to take a particular child into care is neither a financially nor emotionally rewarding activity). In Britain, council corruption is mostly a small-scale, often quite pathetic affair, involving expenses fiddles, favours and patronage, rather than grand pay-offs for massive council contracts. The latter are not entirely unknown, but are not particularly widespread.

The Audit Commission's 1997 bulletin on council fraud put the cost of the 208,000 cases of fraud detected in 1995–96 at £76 million within the context of total expenditure by local government of close to £40 billion (Audit Commission 1997). The main component was housing benefit fraud rather than corruption by councillors or council staff. In the last six years the number of corruption cases recorded by the Commission involving councillors or paid officials has varied between twenty and sixty a year. The cases included a storekeeper in a vehicle maintenance workshop who accepted gifts and holidays for placing orders with a particular supplier, and a market inspector who took pay-offs in return for allowing unlicensed stalls to trade in his market. All this hardly suggests that corruption is pervasive in Britain's town halls. But as the Audit Commission points out, corruption is difficult to detect and prosecute. These figures represent the tip of an iceberg, and the damage such cases can do to public confidence may be out of all proportion to the actual sums involved.

What is often missed is the political dimension in many corruption cases. It is not uncommon for junketing, expense-fiddling and other forms of freeloading to be used as instruments of political control by political leaders. They can be rewards for loyalty – and, if exposed, can be used to punish the disloyal. At least one political boss, on a council where many of the elected members were unemployed, was reputed to punish his critics by giving the DSS details of the attendance allowances and other payments they had received, which in several cases resulted in criminal prosecutions. Glasgow

City Council has been shaken by allegations that councillors were offered places on attractive 'fact-finding' trips abroad in return for their votes on contentious issues. Here we see corruption as a political tool. Greed is harnessed for a political purpose rather than being indulged for its own sake. This kind of abuse tends to take place in one-party states – councils where the opposition is minimal or non-existent. The collapse of the Conservatives in local government in the 1990s has led to a substantial increase in the number of councils where the checks and balances provided by democratic scrutiny have ceased to function. There are signs that the Labour leadership nationally is increasingly worried by the political culture in moribund party fiefdoms. There are fears that the record of many Labour councils could be used to discredit the party and that such councils could present a soft electoral underbelly to opponents like the Liberal Democrats and the Scottish National Party. British Prime Minister Tony Blair has spoken scathingly about council-lors finding themselves 'trapped in the secret world of the caucus and the party group'.

The huge range of services provided by councils offer a vast array of opportunities for corruption. In the author's experience, typical abuses may include:

Housing: big city councils typically rent out tens of thousands of flats and houses. Many thousands of people will be on the waiting list for homes that are usually allocated through a complicated points system, designed to give priority to the most deserving cases. Potential abuses include manipulating the system to provide homes for friends or families of councillors or staff – or even conniving at illegal sub-letting of properties.

Employment: councils are big employers with huge potential for nepotism. For example in 1995 Professor Robert Black QC's independent inquiry into Labour-run Monklands Council found evidence of widespread nepotism and favouritism. He found thirty-three council staff who were either prominent members of the local Labour Party or relatives of prominent members; among them were a window cleaner who refused to climb ladders and a gardener who did not know how to use a hoe.

Contracting out: the drive to encourage competitive tendering for council services – everything from cleaning contracts to building work – has been accompanied by strict rules to ensure fairness and honesty – but it has actually increased the potential for a range of 'sweetheart deals' with favoured compa-nies or businessmen.

Planning: councils' powers to grant planning permission or allocate land for certain types of development are one of the most tempting areas for corrup-tion. A stroke of a pen can transform an anonymous field from a modestly priced piece of agricultural land near a motorway junction into a valuable development site for an out of town superstore. The decision-making process by which such transformations can occur often goes entirely unnoticed. And the rules under which it operates are so complex that any suspicion of corruption may be impossible to prove.

Internal democracy: most councillors win office as the candidates of a political party – and control of who is nominated is one of the key props of local political power. This can lead to all kinds of abuses. Addresses may be falsified so that people can qualify to vote in a particular ward selection (which may include making illegal false declarations in order to get onto a particular electoral register). There may be mass signing-up of members who are used as a kind of block vote, or opponents may be removed from the list of those entitled to vote or stand for selection as candidates.

Perks: one of the classic signs of a public body going sour is the extravagant pampering of those in power. When leading councillors are chauffeured too and fro in plush limousines, booked into expensive hotels, enjoy elaborate meals and free drinks on a regular basis at the expense of their council, public duty has been subverted to private pleasure. Council work has always carried a few minor perks – few would object to free sandwiches at council meetings, or tea and biscuits during a committee – but constant junketing and freeloading is another matter. Often, the problem is one of definition – is it excessive to fly first class? What standard of hotel is appropriate when councillors travel at public expense. The District Auditor's report (September 1997) on the 'Donnygate' scandal gave an illuminating picture of a culture of perks: bar bills of thousands of pounds paid by council credit card; trips to Paris, Genoa and Singapore, with hundreds of pounds spent on phone calls, videos and drinks; a chauffeur waiting for a councillor for 9 hours, outside a bar. A further issue is accepting gifts or entertainment. At what point does watching the local football team from the directors' box become the corrupt acceptance of a gift? In Doncaster, councillors and officials went to Euro 96 football matches and accepted gifts of travel vouchers worth hundreds of pounds from a developer working on a flagship project with the council. The District Auditor has criticised the council's Chief Executive and Treasurer for allowing the abuse to continue. Two councillors have been jailed for expenses fiddles.

Such cases are legitimate targets for investigative journalists – but they should also be on the lookout for activities which, while they may not be overtly criminal, also represent misuse of public money or the distribution of favours for political purposes. For example, many urban councils now support extensive networks of local organisations, perhaps championing a particular community, locality or cause. These groups may be influential within a particular political party – some may even deliver a 'block vote' at local party meetings, perhaps ferrying its members to the party meeting with a minibus loaned by the council. At best, this is unhealthy. At worst it can lead to the creation of an extremely undesirable form of machine politics, in which local bosses with influence at the town hall are able to dispense favours – jobs, leisure facilities, planning permission – to what amounts to a client community. In return they deliver their supporters' votes, both at elections and in internal party contests. In an extreme form this can harden and institutionalise 'ethnic' divisions, for, in effect, the needs and concerns of a section of the electorate are filtered through a network of local bosses who may, or may not, make the effort to address them. For example in Monklands, it has been alleged for at least fifty years that the Protestant community of Airdrie has been discriminated against, in favour of Catholic Coatbridge. An even more extreme example is Mayor Daley's Chicago in the 1950s and 1960s – where the city connived at a virtual system of apartheid[1] and political careers depended on maintaining it.

In 1994 the *Sunday Times* accused Birmingham City Council of using money supposedly set aside to improve 'environmental conditions in areas of deprivation' to win middle-class votes with cosmetic schemes in marginal wards. Conservative Westminster City Council has been accused by the District Auditor of using public money to 'gerrymander' marginal wards for the 1990 Borough elections. The strategy of attempting to 'gentrify' eight key wards, selling off council homes and hostels for the homeless to move out potential Labour voters and attract in more Conservative voters, was in conflict with the council's statutory duty to homeless people, according to the District Auditor, John Magill.[2]

Masons and others

Much attention in Britain has been devoted to the activities of Freemasons and similar groups. (For example, the Monklands scandal in Scotland highlighted allegations about the conduct of councillors who were members of the Catholic Knights of Saint Columba.) In Leicestershire in 1990, a rather out of date masonic handbook for the county was discovered in a suitcase bought by a Labour Party member at a jumble sale. The book confirmed that a large number of senior Conservative county councillors and senior council officials, including the then Chief Executive and the then Treasurer were masons. It didn't prove anything else – and no allegations of corruption were ever made, let alone proved. Even so, the incident generated a certain amount of unease about possible links between some of the county's most influential figures – out of sight of voters and colleagues. In another example in 1995 a leading Conservative member of Medina Borough Council on the Isle of Wight resigned, complaining of masonic influence – he claimed twelve of the eighteen members of the council's ruling Conservative group were Freemasons. Tensions between masons and non-masons remain an important factor in the politics of many of the cities of North East England.

Another area where masonic influence is often perceived to be pervasive is the criminal justice system. In February 1998, the chairman of Parliament's Commons Home Affairs Select Committee, Chris Mullin MP, clashed with the United Grand Lodge of England over his attempts to establish whether the police officers involved in the Birmingham bombing investigation were masons – culminating in a threat to bring proceedings for contempt of Parliament if they did not cooperate. In another case, two men were charged with assaulting drinkers in an upstairs bar in a hotel in the Home Secretary Jack Straw's constituency, Blackburn. It later emerged they had walked into a private function for police officers from a local masonic lodge – they were set upon when they objected to being asked to leave. The two were acquitted and later received £170,000 ($272,000) in damages from the Lancashire police – but the case underlines the problems that can arise when police, solicitors and even the hotel manager were all members of a particular lodge.

Masons, not unreasonably, resent the implication that membership is *prima facie* evidence of corruption and influence peddling. Commander Michael Higham, Grand Secretary of the United Grand Lodge of England, pointed out in his testimony to the Home Affairs Select Committee that wrong-doers are expelled and that masons are 'strictly enjoined' against acts that subvert the peace and good order of society. Nevertheless it is clear that such networks *can* become channels for improper influence. Knowing about such links is an important task for an investigative journalist. Increasingly public bodies require their staff and elected members to declare membership of the masons and similar bodies – judges[3] and police officers are among the groups who are now required by the government to declare their membership.

The changing system

Planned reforms will make the problem of lack of scrutiny of the local state more serious. The current British government is in the process of reforming local government. A new tier of regional institutions is being created – including development agencies and quite possibly emergency services. It is entirely possible that these will be virtually ignored by the local media, despite their considerable powers. Councils may opt to be run by executive mayors rather than be organised in the traditional 'mini-parliamentary' way, and their decision-making will probably become less accessible as a result. The increased use of private contractors further blurs lines of accountability, while the tendering process by which council agencies compete against the private sector for public contracts provides a rich source for investigation and revelation.

Two white papers, *A Mayor and Assembly for London* (HMG 1998) and *Modern Local Government: In Touch with the People* (HMG 1998a), have set out the government's vision of a more streamlined local state. The proposal for a Mayor of the Greater London area (not to be confused with the more ceremonial figure, the Lord Mayor of London) will create the most powerful directly elected official in the land, commanding a budget of £3.3 billion ($5.3 billion) at 1996 prices. The mayor will have formidable powers of patronage. He or she will personally appoint the heads of powerful executive agencies like the new transport and economic development agencies and a range of other public sector appointments and members of the proposed new Metropolitan Police Authority. And the mayor will be responsible for devising strategies on economic development and transport which will touch the lives of millions of people. Leaving aside the issue of whether these arrangements will make for better government, it is likely that much of the decision-making will remain private for far longer than would have been possible under the existing model of local government. Eventually key decisions would come before the London Assembly and be debated in public, but the initial work would be done by the Mayor's private advisors and the crucial early discussions would happen in his 'cabinet' of key officials, again in private. In short it will be a lot harder to find out what they're up to – and investigative journalists with a keen ear for gossip and sources of information inside the bureaucracy and political establishments will have a greater role in keeping the public informed.

Similar arrangements may also operate outside London, where the government is now proposing several methods of organisation that councils could adopt. As with London, a move to a directly elected Mayor would need to be endorsed by a referendum – but it is quite likely that a number of cities will soon have such mayors, with a cabinet of councillors running local services. Again, it is likely that these cabinets would sit in private, and that their decisions would emerge rather later in the policy-making process than under present arrangements. Councillors left outside the cabinet would have the role of scrutinising its decisions and spending more time looking after their wards. They would still have the power to reject or amend the council budget every year, but they would not have a direct voice – or vote – in decision-making. For a journalist this of course means fewer sources of information about what a council is really thinking, but it would be easy to overstate the influence wielded by backbench councillors. In practice the new structures formalise what actually happens in many councils already.

Whatever the merits of the new arrangements in terms of improving the quality of local decision-making, the danger exists that they could concentrate even more power into the hands of the kind of local oligarchies described above. For many local bosses, they could mean a better salary and far less tiresome interference from critics or dissidents. They could go further, faster, in greater secrecy. Like any set of democratic arrangements, they require a powerful opposition, or at any rate a large number of independent minded critics, in order to work properly. Unfortunately, oppositions and independent minded critics are currently something of an endangered species in many local authorities.

One possible side-effect of the creation of high-profile, powerful elected officials to oversee local services, however, is greater public interest in their activities. Indeed, raising the profile of local government is one of the major arguments for change. Prominent council leaders of the 1980s such as Ken Livingstone in the Greater London Council, Ted Knight in the London Borough of Lambeth, Derek Hatton in Liverpool and David Bookbinder in Derbyshire certainly attracted attention to their local authorities, although the coverage they received seldom amounted to a sober assessment of the issues confronting their local authority. It would be hard to argue that the traditional model of local authority decision-making has been a resounding success; however, it is by no means clear whether the proposed changes will give the much needed 'new life' to local government.

Reforms over the last decade have already made scrutiny of the local state much more difficult. The system has become much more complex and devolved, to the point where few local newspapers or radio stations have the resources to monitor it. More unaccountable centres of power have emerged, as a result.

The health service

A classic example of this kind of change is the National Health Service (NHS), which like local government, spends well over £100 billion of public money every year. Until the late 1980s the NHS was administered through a structure of district and regional health authorities, reporting to the Department of Health. Now there are more than 400 NHS trusts, with substantial independence from the district and regional authorities. Decision-making has become much more diffuse. Matt Youdale, the BBC's regional health correspondent in the East Midlands recalls that when he took up his post in 1994, he could go to a district health authority meeting and pick up most of the significant NHS stories in that district. Any important controversies or clinical problems in the district would normally be discussed. No longer. Now he has to try and maintain contacts in a much wider range of bodies – trusts running individual hospitals or units like the ambulance service – to get anything approaching the same coverage. In addition, there are fewer meetings open to the press – all most health trusts are required to do is stage an Annual General Meeting. Since so many investigative stories depend on an initial tip-off from a trusted source, this decentralised structure constitutes a serious barrier to investigative journalism across large tracts of the National Health Service (Youdale 1998).

Above the districts were the Regional Health Authorities (now abolished) which usually had dedicated press officers and a relatively open attitude towards the media. Where these large authorities tended to be relatively open and accessible, many of the smaller units that have replaced them are far more suspicious of the press and far less likely to disgorge even the most innocuous information.

Example: Corby

In 1994–5 the Labour Party purged almost all its sitting councillors in Corby, a small former steel-making town in Northamptonshire, England, which curiously was inhabited by the grandchildren of Scots transferred from Monklands. Corby had been controlled by a clique of local councillors for fifteen to twenty years. When the local steelworks closed in 1980, with the loss of a third of the town's jobs, these politicians proved highly effective in attracting in new employers and reviving the local economy. But ten years later the same local elite was still in place and had become the target of a wide range of allegations. These included incompetence and neglect of basic services like council house repairs, and extended to claims of nepotism and favouritism and to innuendoes of outright corruption. Labour had targeted the Parliamentary seat in three elections, but the local Conservative Member of Parliament held on by running, in effect, against the council.

At the count for a local election, a Radio Northampton reporter overheard a conversation between a regional party official and a local activist which made it clear that the national central office of the party was planning a clear-out in Corby. Similar rumours reached the author, after a conversation at a new year's party. Conversations with a Labour official and a series of off the record meetings with local activists – who were at first reluctant to talk for fear that the local establishment would learn that they had blabbed, produced more evidence. After some reassurance they were mostly willing, indeed eager, to dish the dirt, and the result was a cornucopia of corrupt practice stories. The credibility of some of the claims was increased by cross-checking with Labour Party members in other parts of the region who had some connection with Corby. For example, one contact had been sent there to preside over an appeal hearing for a councillor who had had the whip withdrawn for complaining about the number of free trips taken by senior councillors.

My contacts also allowed me to keep abreast of Labour's timetable for action. I put some of the allegations to the Corby leadership, and their response did not seem credible. Critics were dismissed as acting out of jealousy, or stories were not denied but met with counter allegations of similar behaviour – 'if you got that from him, he's a fine one to talk … .' In the absence of solid evidence for most of the stories, my editors were not keen to broadcast specific allegations – not least because the level of local feuding was so intense it was difficult to distinguish the malicious allegations from the true ones. So our strategy was to report the battle to remove the local leadership, who were known to be litigious, (and indeed later issued writs against the national and regional Labour Party) without going into detail about the allegations against them. This was safe, but unsatisfying. Listeners were being told about the deselections, but not the reasons for them. The local watchdog was not entirely silenced, but the bark was certainly muffled. A danger with this approach is to try and fill the yawning gap it leaves where the explanation should be. But with a generalised reference to 'council sleaze', which can be interpreted as a blanket allegation against every councillor in a particular authority, you can end up libelling far more people.

For television, the story had an additional difficulty. Aside from a few pictures of buildings involved in various controversies, there was little to film. A cameraman was dispatched to the annual Corby Highland Games in the hope of filming inebriated councillors in the official council hospitality tent; the results were not particularly incriminating, although the pictures of marching pipe bands were useful in illustrating Corby's Caledonian heritage. Permission was also secured to film a council meeting in progress.

One area where it was possible to go into specifics was the extraordinarily high level of travel and subsistence allowances paid to councillors on official duties. This was because the council's annual Management Letter (an annual assessment of their financial performance which all councils receive from the District Auditor) pointed out that if Corby brought its spending into line with that of all the other Northamptonshire district councils, this budget could be cut by 85 per cent. This was a rare instance where it was possible to use solid information from an unimpeachable source.

Another issue with the Corby case was that we did not wish to become a pawn of the Labour Party officials who were leaking much of the information – so we made a point of saying the party was engaged in a purge. This made our stories an issue in the legal action that followed the deselection of the local leadership – they complained their fate was decided in advance of formal party hearings, which indeed it was, and which we reported before the hearings were held. The deselected councillors eventually ran against official Labour candidates in the 1996 borough elections, under an independent 'Corby Labour' ticket. None was elected. Investigations into the conduct of Corby Council are still going on at the time of writing.

Example: Frank Beck

The failure of dozens of local authorities to protect children in their care from sexual, physical and emotional abuse is one of the worst stains on the record of British local government. The roll call of scandals ranges from the oppressive disciplinary regime in Staffordshire, called 'pin-down', to sexual exploitation of children in care in Clwyd in North Wales, to the brutal quack-psychological therapies and sexual abuse revealed in the Frank Beck case in Leicestershire. New allegations emerge almost monthly, and it is now clear that abuse of all kinds has carried on unchecked, in some cases for decades, across much of the child care system.

Such scandals are dangerous territory for the media; there can be few more damaging allegations than to accuse someone of child abuse, so legal worries will never be far from an editor's mind. Such dangerous cases are far more safely reported from the courtroom, with the protection of qualified privilege. Moreover, complaints from former residents at children's homes – the most likely people to bring their stories to the media – might seem to lack credibility. They might have criminal records or drug problems or have been emotionally shattered by the abuse they had suffered. As a result, they might not be taken seriously, or might be thought dangerous witnesses on whom to rely if a story resulted in a libel action. Indeed, this has typically been one of the major reasons for failures by the police and other agencies to investigate complaints of abuse. The moral here is to avoid making the kind of assumptions about individuals which mean that important stories are dismissed out of hand.

In 1989 Frank Beck, the former head of a Leicestershire County Council children's home, was arrested on charges of abusing children in his care. At the time, the author was Political Correspondent for the *Leicester Mercury*. The case was to reverberate over the next seven years, with a sensational trial that revealed more than a decade of appalling crimes against children, an inquiry and official report revealing an amazing catalogue of management failure, and a hard fought and frequently harrowing compensation action brought by Beck's victims. Every stage of this process provided opportunities for investigative journalists to deal with.

Beck's arrest was completely unexpected and, because proceedings against him were active, only the barest details could be reported – but several reporters began to sniff around the case. It quickly became apparent that officials at County Hall were deeply worried by the ramifications of the case. An outside official (in this case a retired Assistant Director of Social Services from neighbouring Nottinghamshire) had been called in to prepare a report on Beck's activities. His conclusions were shocking; that Leicestershire County Council had repeatedly ignored alarming evidence from credible sources about the physical and sexual abuse of children – mostly boys – in homes run by Beck. Not only had a major child abuse scandal emerged in Leicestershire, but the County Council should have detected the problem and dealt with it long before the case actually came to light. Even when Beck was sacked over complaints that he was sexually abusing junior social workers, he was allowed to walk away despite allegations that he had also abused children. Later, he had been given a reference that allowed him to work with children.

Spotting that they might get unwelcome media criticism, the County Council began to prepare the ground. A leading local journalist – by then semi-retired – was consulted on the formation of a PR strategy. His advice to the council was that it should build up a cushion of good news about social services and that it should try to avoid the precedent set by the Cleveland case, in which a local authority was linked directly to a high profile social services failure. They did not want the case to be referred to as 'The Leicestershire Scandal'. This advice was acted on. Council press officers invariably referred to 'The Beck Case' in conversations with local journalists, and, subliminally, their terminology was absorbed and used by journalists. Meanwhile, favourable stories about the activities of social services began to appear. A team of top officials and the leaders of the three political parties (Leicestershire is a hung council) met regularly to consider the County Council's response. In the era of the spin doctor, investigative journalists are now far more likely to encounter such tactics.

The internal report and its damning conclusions were supposed to be highly confidential, but the County Council's political divisions meant that it was soon leaked to local and national reporters. They were unable to publish while the case was *sub judice* (the *Mail on Sunday* was prepared to risk the wrath of the court by publishing during the case) but the process of contacting and interviewing key witnesses began in earnest. Many of those involved had good reason to talk: some of Beck's victims wanted their ordeal made public; some officials wanted to defend their careers, others were horrified at the failures of their management; some politicians could see votes in the affair – Beck was a Liberal Democrat councillor at the time of his arrest and the Conservatives in particular were arguing that Labour and Liberal Democrat policies had made it easier for him to abuse children, because they had made his particular home more important within the Leicestershire child care system. Reporters were not, therefore, short of sources, but the material they delivered had to be weighed carefully in the light of their various agendas. Often, individuals were more concerned with promoting their version of a relatively minor part of the affair, for example their role in a particular instance where evidence against Beck had not been investigated. This was often at such a level of detail that it was unlikely to be reported – while journalists were much more interested in the source's information on the major events of the case.

By the time Beck's trial began, local newspapers, radio and television had all accumulated a substantial body of material about the case, and the trial provided the chance to interview further witnesses, for broadcast after the verdict. One of the pitfalls of having such a devastating report, together with appalling accounts of abuse and mismanagement, but being unable to publish them for months was that reporters became almost bored with its conclusions, even though they would undoubtedly astonish the public when they were revealed. It was important not to allow this familiarity to distort editorial judgements.

There were further legal complications. Initially, the trial judge banned all reporting of the case because it was anticipated that Beck might face a further trial or trials on additional child abuse charges after this case was completed. This ruling was overturned by the High Court after an appeal by several newspapers. And because the verdicts on the dozens of charges faced by Beck dribbled out over a period of two days, background interviews and analysis could not be published or broadcast until well after the first guilty verdict had been announced.

After Beck's conviction, the then Health Secretary, William Waldegrave, announced an inquiry into the case, to be conducted by Andrew Kirkwood QC, a leading barrister and expert in child protection law. Kirkwood decided to take most of the evidence in private, a decision he refused to revoke, despite questions in Parliament and intense pressure from the media, which included attempts to persuade some witnesses to demand that their evidence should be heard in public. But for the most part, the media were restricted to taking pictures of witnesses arriving at the inquiry. Even so, there were substantial and detailed leaks of the evidence, including some damaging accounts of Leicestershire County Council's inept and complacent management of Beck. The greatest interest, however, was in Kirkwood's conclusions. He did manage to keep these confidential until the publication of his report, but since he was not willing to take questions about them at a press conference, and would do no more than read out a prepared statement, it was hard for the media or the public of Leicestershire to make a judgement about the soundness of his conclusions – particularly when the evidence upon which they were based had been heard in private. The media were left to take the report or leave it; and of course they were in no position to leave it – but Kirkwood's restrictions had created a position where no reporter could credibly comment on his conclusions. It would be impossible to comment that a particular criticism was a bit harsh, or that a particular individual had got off lightly.

The next event in the Beck case was the struggle by some of his victims to extract compensation from Leicestershire County Council. This eventually came to court in 1996, but the negotiations and clashes between the plaintiffs and the defendants regularly featured in the local and national news. The case itself provided a sad postscript to the whole Beck affair, with witnesses recounting the abuse they had suffered and council officials being summoned to testify as to whether the County Council had fulfilled its duty of care towards the children in its homes. Amazingly, the defendants at one stage denied that they had a duty of care towards children in their care – a legal argument that deeply embarrassed officials and councillors at Leicestershire County Hall. Much of the reporting of these events amounted to a rehash of earlier coverage, but an important theme was the long drawn out and painful process by which victims of crime had to seek compensation. More than one remarked that it felt like further abuse.

Cases like that of Frank Beck provide a long drawn out test for the media. It is often easy to focus on the horrific details of child abuse cases, while failing to give detailed attention to the rather drier details of the policy failures or management mistakes which made them possible. But these failures ruin lives. Cases like these should be as much the territory of those who investigate the local state as of crime reporters. What the proliferation of child abuse scandals demonstrates is that there are plenty of catastrophic failures in public policy and management out there for reporters to expose.[4]

Process

Leaks and tip-offs are the stock in trade of the investigative reporters covering the local state. But when dealing with political organisations they will need to be more than usually careful about the motives of their sources and the spin attached to the information they receive. It is an iron law of politics that there's always an opposition; if there are no opposition parties, internal divisions inevitably surface. Factional tensions and personal hatreds are among the main reasons for significant leaks and any information received should be weighed in that knowledge and should be cross-checked in some way. Relying on a single source may mean that the reporter ends up parroting the party line of some individual or faction. This discredits the reporter and fails the reader.

As well as bias, there is also the danger of manipulation. A leaked Labour Party document[5] advised local organisations to 'use a backbencher or loud mouthed staffer' to let the press know 'what you really think.' In other words, that candid unofficial source may simply be feeding out another subtle version of the party line, with the full knowledge of the people at the top. The same document also urged the use of smear tactics against opponents: 'check their declarations of interest and their records. Find one flaw and smear them all. Go negative until swamped by complaints. Then do it again … '. So beware of the spoon-fed exclusive about a political opponent; the Westminster cult of the spin doctor is spreading and local journalists will not escape its touch. Fortunately, some politicians are not only immoral but also infantile, as this document reveals. No really sophisticated would-be Machiavelli would ever be foolish enough to write such things down – but for many the urge to boast about how tough and unethical they are can be irresistible. So when they start boasting in the bar, believe them.

Earlier in the chapter I referred to the need for reporters to understand the structure and workings of local councils, if they were to investigate their conduct effectively. The same applies to political parties. Labour, for example, has an elaborate structure of district and regional parties that comes into play when corruption or misconduct is alleged. These little known bodies may be the forum in which the most serious and far-reaching allegations are discussed and action decided. They may also be a useful 'one stop shop' at which a reporter can seek information about a wide variety of stories or potential stories, across a wide geographical area.

It is noticeable how few of the recent tide of council corruption stories have been brought to light by local reporters (there are of course honourable exceptions, Doncaster for one). One of the dangers of traditional council reporting is that the journalist becomes a prisoner of his or her contacts, and becomes unwilling to antagonise them. But a more substantial reason is the reluctance of editors to commit the time and take the legal risks inherent in investigative journalism. And even where investigations do reveal something, there may be little enthusiasm for the resulting story – 'too parochial, readers in other council areas won't be interested … ', 'Who cares, everyone assumes they're on the take anyway', 'It's too complicated … people won't understand it'. There are other outlets – *Private Eye*'s 'Rotten Boroughs' feature, for example. And some national newspapers and television or radio programmes are willing to pick up local stories that the local media fear to print. This however, hardly amounts to the classic role of a local watchdog – often it seems safer for the watchdog to bark by proxy.

NOTES

1 For an account of the politics of Chicago in this era see Royko, M. (1971) *Boss: Richard J. Daley of Chicago*. Dutton and Co.
2 Report on Westminster City Council, John Magill, District Auditor, Deloitte and Touche, 9 May 1996.
3 Out of 5,400 Judges, 200 declared themselves to be freemasons and 50 refused to answer the question. Written reply to a parliamentary question by Geoff Hoon MP, then Minister of State, Lord Chancellor's Department, 22 March 1999.
4 For a fuller account of the Beck case see D'Arcy and Gosling 1998.
5 'Beating the Liberals', internal Labour Party document quoted in *Red Pepper*, October 1998.

BIBLIOGRAPHY

Audit Commission (1997) *Protecting the Public Purse*. London: HMSO.
D'Arcy, M. and Gosling, P. (1998) *Abuse of Trust: Frank Beck and the Leicestershire Children's Homes Scandal*. London: Bowerdean Publishing Company.
Ekirch, A. (1974) *Progressivism in America*. New York: Viewpoints.
Fitzwalter, R. et al. (1981) *Web of Corruption: The Story of John Poulson and T. Dan Smith*. St Albans: Granada.
Glinert, E. (1998) Interview with Mark D'Arcy, 19 November 1998.
H. M. Government (1998) *A Mayor and Assembly for London*. CM 3897. 25 March 1998. London: HMSO.
H. M. Government (1998a) *Modern Local Government: In Touch with the People*. CM 4014. 30 July 1998. London: HMSO.
Satchwell, R. (1998) Interview with Mark D'Arcy, 16 November 1998.
Youdale, M. (1998) Interview with Mark D'Arcy, 17 October 1998.

FURTHER READING

Burke, R. (1979) *The Murky Cloak: Local Authority Press Relations*. Croydon: Charles Knight.
Clarke, M. (ed.) (1983) *Corruption*. London: Frances Pinter.
Doig, J. (1983) You publish at your peril – the restraints on investigatory journalism. In M. Clarke (ed.) *Corruption*. London: Frances Pinter.
Franklin, B. and Murphy D. (1991) *What News? The Market, Politics and the Local Press*. London: Routledge.
Franklin, B. and Murphy, D. (1997) The local rag in tatters? The decline of Britain's local newspapers. In M. Bromley *A Journalism Reader*. London: Routledge.
Murphy, D. (1976) *The Silent Watchdog: The Press in Local Politics*. London: Constable.
Murphy, D. (1983) Journalistic investigations of corruption. In M. Clarke (ed.) *Corruption*. London: Francis Pinter.

12

SCRUTINISING SOCIAL POLICY

An example from Channel 4's *Dispatches*

Hugo de Burgh

Channel 4 *Dispatches* in the public sphere

In 1982 a fourth national television channel was inaugurated in Britain, among the responsibilities of which were the reflection of perspectives and issues ignored by the other channels and the commissioning of programmes from independent producers rather than in-house production. In 1986, much derided by the then current affairs establishment, David Lloyd took this to 'the extreme' by deciding to commission his creation, *Dispatches*, from a different supplier every week.[1] Nearly 400 *Dispatches* have been transmitted since November 1987 and the variety of stories and treatments is possibly greater than for any other series or strand in the same period. There can be few aspects of British public affairs that have not been touched upon by *Dispatches* and, in consequence, it has upset many and found itself regularly fielding legal challenges.

A famous *Dispatches* episode is 'The Committee', which was the subject of a court case under the Prevention of Terrorism Act; 'Mother Russia's Children' won awards as a revelation of life for street children in St Petersburg; in 'Who Pays the Gas Bill?' *Dispatches* joined the race to expose the British Parliament's 'Cash for Questions' scandal; *Dispatches* claims to have been first with revelations about the effect of CJD on humans in January 1994; its 'Obscene Telephone Calls' programme resulted in British Telecom being forced to introduce systems to deal with a problem they had denied; another inquest was held after *Dispatches* investigated the Marchioness Ferry disaster (Stott 1998).

Since the classic studies of British producers (*inter alia* Elliott 1972, Silverstone 1985) there have been many changes in the ways in which producers operate, not least the turn to commissioning independents; yet the sense of élitism among the, now increasingly independent, producers is scarcely reduced. They are, though, subject to all the pressures of an astoundingly competitive freelance market. One indication of just how competitive that is is the statement by the Commissioning Editor for *Dispatches* that he has at times received twenty times as many proposals as he has slots (Lloyd 1998a). Producers are very keen to make a *Dispatches*; the series is usually considered to be the 'flagship' strand of C4 TV, whose remit is to take risks, to champion the under-represented and to ask the questions that have not been asked (McNulty 1996: 19). To produce for *Dispatches* is a badge of honour, as is producing for *World in Action* or *Panorama*, its ITV and BBC equivalents. The C4 viewer is positioned as being educated, wealthy and liberal so that, possibly more than any other channel, it talks to an élite.

Dispatches and social policy

When *Dispatches* was launched, investigative journalism was largely assumed to do with what David Lloyd calls 'the gloaming' – the hidden areas of life where sordid deals between cocaine criminals and arms barons take place and where investigative journalists can practise the skills of the commando and the spy. However, while *Dispatches* continues to screen programmes with the modern equivalent of that profile, such as 'Saddam's Secret Timebomb' (1998) in which Gwyn Roberts courageously investigated the current consequences of Iraq's germ warfare programme against the Kurdish minority, its proportion of programmes dealing with topics of more immediate concern to British citizens at home has risen. This is less in response to market forces, suggests Lloyd, and more the result of a deliberate policy of using the techniques of investigation upon important issues and stories at home, such as the 1999 films on foreign prostitutes in Britain, which required elaborate stings and secret filming ('Sex Slave Trade', 29 April 1999), and a year long undercover investigation of the Animal Liberation Front ('Animal Liberation Front', 10 December 1998) both commissioned by Lloyd's successor as Commissioning Editor, Dorothy Byrne.

These are examples of investigative journalism in the traditional sense, but both Lloyd and Byrne consider that *Dispatches* is in the business of widening the conception of what investigative journalism might be. Programmes that are original in the way they counter orthodoxy are also investigative, he claims; they 'inquire anew on some area of social policy that people think they know about – but actually, when you quarry just a few layers down you find that what you are being told is at serious variance with the evidence' (Lloyd 1998b).

Perhaps the best known product of this approach is the series *Dispatches* made about Aids in the 1980s. Joan Shenton and her team identified an unreported analysis of the Aids illness made by scientists who denied the link between HIV and Aids and claimed that all contemporary research was wrong – and determinedly so since its direction suited the big pharmaceutical companies, among other interests (Shenton 1990). Lloyd does not offer this example of his work when asked about the impact of *Dispatches*, though once the subject is raised he defends the programmes – which attracted more

232

hostility than perhaps any other *Dispatches* – on the grounds that 'although the extreme thesis that there is no connection between HIV and Aids is now discredited', nevertheless there is still no certitude as to the catalytic factors. His defence of the polemical style of those programmes gives insight into his view of investigative journalism; he argues that the medical establishment at the time simply would not admit that the scientists whom he screened could or should have any kind of voice in the debate; they were excluded, as were all counter-orthodox views of Aids. Now, he says, such a programme would not be necessary as the medical establishment is chastened by its failure to solve the problem and is more open to discussion and challenge.

Dispatches has transmitted many programmes on health issues; it claims to have been the first medium to demonstrate CJD transmission to humans, to reveal the major British scandal of deaths in the surgery wards at Bristol Hospital, to reveal problems of cervical screening and to show, via the story of the Yorkshire Hospital Trust, how health service reforms were not working as intended. It has also tackled the problems of British education.

A belief that the quality of school education provided to the majority of British children was inadequate and deteriorating spread out beyond the specialists in the 1980s to the extent that by the 1990s it was a major political issue, the subject of radical government policies and a central plank in the Labour Party's victorious 1997 election campaign. *Dispatches* played a part in the dissemination of this view, principally through one programme in 1991, 'Every Child in Britain', followed by 'All Our Futures'.

'Every Child in Britain' argued a view that was widely held by specialists but barely understood in the wider agora, that by virtually any measurement most British state schooling was inferior to its rivals and crippled its products through low expectations and poor teaching methods. 'All Our Futures' proposed that one of the solutions to the problem – quality vocational education for those for whom academic courses were inappropriate – had gone wrong and was as hopelessly inadequate as that which preceded it. In 1998 *Dispatches* went on to examine another of the solutions, the Office of Standards in Education (Ofsted), whose Chief Inspector wholeheartedly endorsed the analysis advanced in 'Every Child in Britain'. Chief Inspector Chris Woodhead, although appointed by the Conservatives who encouraged his radical inspection policy, was confirmed in office by the new Labour government, despite opposition within the Labour Party, and by 1998 was widely treated by the political classes and much of the media as being the fount of all wisdom in education. There was widespread agreement in society that school inspections were good and raised standards; rather than attend to the issue of principle therefore *Dispatches* interrogated the data and sought to see if Woodhead had feet of clay by questioning his methodology.

'Inspecting the Inspectors' demonstrated that:

1   critical school inspections have a powerful effect upon schools, in one case virtually destroying the school overnight, as the parents of all bar one pupil removed their children;

2   school inspections are demanding on teachers;

3   there may be contradictions in a system in which schools may have good Inspection Reports but atrocious SATs (examination) results;

4   a review of inspectors' judgements by the Professor of Education at Durham University showed them to lack system;

5   inspectors' attention to detail and understanding of what they are inspecting may be limited, as evidenced in the CCTV footage available to one head teacher, himself a trained inspector;

6   Ofsted appeared to accept criticism only grudgingly;

7   there were comparative studies made by Ofsted inspectors that were not published, perhaps because their findings were inconvenient;

8   the use of data in the Chief Inspector's annual report to Parliament could be questioned;

9   and that Ofsted was accountable only in a limited sense.

The case made against the Chief Inspector, whose interview with reporter Spiller was used extensively, was rather weakened by considerable use of his arch-opponent, Professor Tim Brighouse, which appeared to bring polemic and personal animosity into what was otherwise detached.

In what senses were these three programmes investigative? First, there is the originality, the overturning of generally held assumptions; second, there is the attack on interest groups, there were undoubtedly people who did not want those questions asked; third, there is method – the careful analyses of data upon which policies and programmes are based, the investigation for alternative or supplementary sources of data and the unexpected comparisons. All these modes led to the building of cases opposed to those which people were being asked by authority to believe.

In particular there were several aspects to 'Inspecting the Inspectors' that made it investigative rather than analytical; they were points 3, 4 and 5 (see above), and to a lesser extent 7 and 8. The fact that it is possible for schools to have good Inspection Reports but atrocious SATs results is a fascinating revelation for many parents now very aware of the differences between schools that are being revealed by the high profile inspection system; detailed information from two very different sources, academic research data plus the evidence of CCTV footage, fortunately presented to us by a head teacher who is himself an inspector, provides very strong evidence that attention needs to be paid to inspection methodology. Points 7 and 8 appeared weaker, and were more easily brushed aside by the Chief Inspector.

An analysis of the inspection system as might have been undertaken say in the *Times Educational Supplement* or a less consistently investigative series such as *Panorama*, might have examined the issue in detail without either challenging the methodology or demonstrating that flaws in that methodology had already been detected by critical observers. The level of detail into which the programme went in order to cast doubts upon the statistics used is also indicative of a investigative approach.

Example: 'Holding the Baby'

Treatment

In 1989 the producer who was to make his first *Dispatches*, 'Holding the Baby', a year later was, among other things, producing and presenting an ITV chat show series, *Night Flyte*, on controversial issues. The scouting for this threw up an article by a *Daily Mail* reporter on the business plans of a US company, Kindercare, which intended expanding into the UK. Kindercare, said the article, offered round the clock baby parking and could solve all the problems of the mother who wanted to get a job outside the home. The writer implied that this was production line, McDonalds style, baby care and, in tune with the *Daily Mail's* editorial line, that it was reprehensible (Gerrie 1987).

Thus 'nursery care' came to be the subject of one of the *Night Flytes*. The transmission demonstrated strong passions both on the programme itself and at audience feedback and informed the production team that there had been 'problems' with institutional childcare in the US, including maltreatment of children by care providers and claims by academic researchers that institutional childcare stunts growth. The producer, who had already worked up programmes on corruption in the Scottish law courts and bad practices in financial services for the *Dispatches* Commissioning Editor, therefore wrote up a first proposal on about a page (HTB 1998) and sent it to the same patron.

Commissioning editors view vast numbers of proposals and are moved by many considerations. One of the most important is survival – to survive they must show that they are having impact. With the BBC or ITV this is usually, though not always, proved by ratings figures. With C4, as with broadsheet newspapers, impact may equally well be interpreted as response among the target audience of opinion-formers and decision-makers. So when the *Dispatches* Commissioning Editor decided to look further at this topic, he was moved by the following:

- he had received numerous proposals in this general area and knew that producers were interested
- he believed that it would add to his series profile.

His impact upon the proposal was significant; it went in stages through a series of meetings over a period of six months when he asked for:

- evidence that childcare was a business in the UK ripe for development;
- evidence that the US entrepreneurs wanted to expand into the European market;
- evidence that there were scandals in the USA;

and, later,

- proof of research evidence demonstrating that children might be harmed by childcare and
- proof that people in a position to know were ignoring such research evidence.[2]

By this time the producer was fielding a team at these meetings which included the reporter (writer of the *Daily Mail* article) and director (the first producer–director of *Hard News*).[3] The team was nervous initially that – after investing time and effort – the angle was becoming too skewed towards research, as it did not look as if there were much conclusive evidence revealing whether or not childcare was good or not for children. Although he was disappointed that there was little or no UK research, the editor decided that they should see this lacuna as a strength. He said that '*Dispatches* will argue that it is disgraceful that HMG should encourage more mothers of young children to work when the effects have not been considered' (HTB 1998). The programme he eventually commissioned was very different from that initially envisaged by the proponents and, during the process, they had been obliged to substantiate every statement that he had hypothesised.

The final documentary treatment conformed to the classic current affairs approach in which there is a victim, villain and various subplots that eventually integrate to make the case. The case was made through the media of several stories, or component elements of the long-form documentary, in order to personalise and pictorialise. They included the story of:

- a particular little girl
- a childminder
- various young mothers
- a particular nursery and its proprietor
- how the research of an academic psychologist, Belsky, had been undertaken, replicated in other countries and received in the academy.

It also featured, by way of additional testimonial,

- a US nursery that it constructed as providing impersonal mass production
- clips from secret filming of US nurseries showing neglect and malpractice by staff.

During the course of filming in a high profile nursery, an example of bad practice occurred and was shot. The piece of film was then shown to a psychologist and she was herself filmed at the viewing showing her professional disapproval, even horror, and reinforcing the message that commercial organisations could not be trusted to deliver reliable childcare.

Since she was now the object of attack, the proprietor of the nursery 'investigated' was shown the material that reflected upon her institution and was invited to respond on camera, as is usual practice on *Dispatches* – an invitation that she took up, further condemning herself by the unsympathetic interview she gave.

Not only were companies in the business of child care implied to be flawed but the child care establishment – officials and academics – could be construed as appearing shifty and perhaps malevolent. This was partly on account of their own behaviour in refusing to answer questions directly, and partly because of the way their interviews were cut.

In summary, the documentary's main arguments were:

- child care is one of the biggest issues society faces;
- for their own interests it suits business – both those that profit from child care and those that profit from creating a market in low wage second earners – that mothers enter the job market;
- these interests have used the rhetoric of feminism and choice as a cover for their interests;
- they have won the support of institutions such as the CBI and of government to promote what interests them, not what is in the interests of children;
- the research there is says that this is bad for small children;
- yet the establishment of government advisers and managers, wanting to exert power over ordinary people and afraid to admit that their ideas are motivated more by political correctness than by the interests of those affected, won't listen.

Discussion

'Holding the Baby' had a very high audience rating for *Dispatches* and attracted much comment, mainly hostile. It has continued to be talked about in the television profession and used as a model, not least because of Caroline Gilbey's very effective direction. The production team at the time thought that it was being very advanced, challenging and creative, while its critics read the programme as reactionary. Within the context of the emerging discourse of child care and the subsequent development of programming on this subject, it now seems more realistic to say that the team was responding to the 'corporate expectations' (Cottle 1995: 162) of C4 for a certain type of programme – as was the Commissioning Editor, albeit with his more strategic antennae. C4 demands the kind of programme idea that is slightly in advance of cultural change, but only just (or no one will watch it). If it is not in advance, no one will be angry about it, which would be unfortunate for C4 and for its executives' careers. This and the subsequent development of the discourses of child care may explain the cultural locus of 'Holding the Baby'.

The expert debate was over the interpretation of the social science research and in particular over two questions: was the (US) research of Belsky generalisable and did the combination of his research with a UK, a French and a Swiss study amount to a general conclusion of recent research that institutional day-care at too early an age could be damaging intellectually and emotionally? Underlying it was a further debate on the selective use of research.

Today it is unlikely that a *Dispatches* on this topic would focus so heavily upon research and, in particular, in a manner that denied the value of earlier research in comparison with current research. The focus would be on 'a dereliction of standards that are true whatever you believe about day-care' (Lloyd 1998b). This is in part because the latest ITC protocols have made the provision of 'due impartiality' more important, as discussed in Chapter 3; 'the other side has all sorts of purchase on the piece you do' and these are formalised in statute. The advantages of this, according to Lloyd, is that it forces you to make a clear distinction between opinion journalism and investigative journalism, no matter that both are evidenced and witnessed. Without this, much can be called investigative that is not; 'in the past you could deliver a parallel argument and make it feel investigative, but this is now less easy' (Lloyd 1998b).

The investigative journalist and the evidence

Mark D'Arcy argues in Chapter 10 that, if only by virtue of its scale and its influence on our daily lives, local administration is a fitting target for investigative journalism. The same can be said for national social policies. More public money is spent on social policy implementation than in any other area of government; demographic changes have made topics such as age[4] and child development of central importance to the UK's economic future; education is keenly argued over for the same reasons; problems from unemployment to delinquency, nutrition and health have huge consequences and constituencies and thus experts of every political persuasion.

The proposals of those experts, politicians and pressure groups need to be analysed, but, more than analysed, their premises require examination, especially since they, and justifications for current policies, are usually based upon statistical data and social science research. The journalist applies the 'social scientific' method to the scientists. Indeed, as Tankard (1976: 45) has pointed out, there are similarities between social scientists and journalists. Journalists rely upon verification by observation or testimony; they aspire to making only those statements that can be corroborated or verified and thus achieve impartiality; they attribute or cite opinions or findings and they aim at internal and external validity.

While Tankard's observations are flattering to journalists, he also points out that they regularly commit errors such as generalising from unrepresentative samples, misunderstanding the methodologies employed in research and making invalid causal associations. In theory, at least, journalists argue their conclusions deductively from the evidence, although they are often attacked for the opposite, making the evidence fit as in the case of a much reviled *Panorama*, 'Missing Mum', on a similar subject to the example above (e.g. BBC 1997).

Research methods

A knowledge of the procedures of the social sciences is essential to the investigative journalist. Social science research has driven much of the debates over the family, the underclass, welfare and schooling that have become central in UK politics – as in other rich countries. Take the UK education debate. Many research studies have been undertaken and have been used to prove this or that theory in education. A 1998 survey of education research was sceptical of the value of much of it, complaining that it was often highly biased in its premises and incompetent methodologically as a consequence (Gold 1998).

In 1996 the National Foundation for Educational Research (NFER) was commissioned by two media organisations associated with opposite political leanings[5] to undertake a study of reading skills in the UK, a study that had already been undertaken in thirty-two other countries and the format of which was considered uncontroversial by the customers. It had been accepted internationally, as in the UK, as telling something worthwhile about the differences between countries in the acquisition of reading skills. At the data analysis stage, however, the methods required to replicate in England and Wales the study that had been undertaken in the other countries were confusing to the NFER, and NFER's application of them was confusing to those who had designed the methods. The NFER changed its mind twice about the results and their implications, and different officials offered different interpretations of them.[6]

Not surprisingly the C4 News journalists covering the story[7] found this confusing, and a verdict had to be sought from specialists at the London School of Economics and Paris University as to whether the NFER was implementing the study properly; the verdicts were only just supportive. Worse, once the NFER had finally agreed its official interpretation, it was found that luminaries of the education establishment were so opposed to the very idea of such a study that they were unavailable to comment dispassionately on the results;[8] the one finally persuaded to do so said that the results told nothing; 'The wrong things are being measured' (C4 1996).

In effect, the educationalists approached did not accept the validity of the research. In that case, and the journalists at the time felt that this was far more coloured by their prejudices than by any soundly based critique of the research, the reliability or generalisability didn't matter. Shipman (1981) discusses several controversies within social science in *The Limitations of Social Research*, including an example, as quantitative as the NFER study, which, when replicated, gave utterly different results. Some of his cases are controversial because of the methods of the researchers, others because of their biases. He cites the famous qualitative study of Samoa by Margaret Mead which deserves to be part of journalistic folklore, as it is of academic. *Coming of Age in Samoa* (1943) was fun because it dealt with sex; it was influential because journalists interpreted it as demonstrating that in our emotional and sexual practices we are constrained less by biology than by culture. Mead's findings showed that the Samoans were uninhibited in their relationships and suggested that this was more natural than Americans' (then) repressed or discriminating behaviour. However, later research (Freeman 1984) made clear that her method of investigation was flawed; that she did not know the language sufficiently well to understand that she was being teased and that she fundamentally misconstrued Samoan society which, in reality, had many of the same rules as Western society. Methodology aside, the study was not generalisable (what can knowing about teen sex in Samoa tell us about teen sex in Wyoming?) anyway, but at the time nobody thought about that, perhaps because her views were so welcome.

Until 1997 and the publication of a new book on Alfred Kinsey,[9] Kinsey's 1947 study *Sexuality and the Human Male* was widely accepted as valid but neither generalisable nor reliable. It now seems quite clear that it was and is a farrago of little or no scientific value. In fact, the truth about Kinsey's methods had been exposed in a study that failed to seize the attention of journalists when published in 1989. By 1997–8 the media were ready, and a television documentary complemented two high profile books on the subject. These famous examples serve to illustrate the dangers of journalists' failure to understand key conditions for reliable social research.

Statistical data

In covering topics as varied as financial affairs and defence estimates journalists are faced with data provided them by the Government Statistical Service, policy units, pressure groups, company and government agency finance officers and the university research community. We assume that all journalists gatekeep the material, but the active journalist is surely one who is able to check out the material before use.

In 1989 *Dispatches* produced a useful illustration of how politicians bamboozle with statistics in its programme 'Cooking the Books'. It showed, *inter alia*, how the then British government had recently announced that it was building '380 large hospital schemes'. The definition of a hospital scheme was not clear, nor was the fact that every building project of over 1 million pounds was classified as a separate scheme even if it was really part of a larger, say 30 million pound, scheme. Thus the '380 large hospital schemes' included several car parks. Similarly, an increase in the number of hospital beds was claimed, whereas there was no net increase if the beds abolished elsewhere were taken into account (C4 1989). It is now well established that early ideas about the dangers of Aids were based on quite fallacious statistical projections and that these projections were used to justify expensive and often irrelevant publicity campaigns as well as the diverting of health service resources from problems of much greater concern to the majority of the population. For the student examining the use of statistics in investigative journalism a number of books listed at the end of this chapter may be useful.[10]

In sum, the investigative journalist deals with the evidence of documents, fieldwork, the findings of scientific and social science studies, testimony and statistics. The problems for the investigative journalist include its provenance, methodology and checking procedures. In the face of these problems, the investigative journalist in effect applies methods developed in academic research and called 'scientific method'. He or she tries to make only those statements that can be corroborated or verified and thus be impartial; attributes or cites opinions or findings and aims at internal and external validity (Tankard 1976); and argues conclusions deductively from the evidence.

More specifically, in dealing with social research, the investigative journalist must first review the literature to understand the context of the research under discussion; a simple review of the literature on a subject will often astonish by its paucity or by its limitations. It is also useful for journalists to remember that the peer group review system is not everywhere of the same rigour and that there is a much-loved repository called the *Journal of Inconvenient Research*!

Having had a sceptical look at the environment of the topic in question the investigative journalist will want to consider reliability (is the method clearly understandable and could the same results be achieved by other researchers using the same method?), validity (does the research really reflect what was going on?) and generalisability (does this research tell us about any situation apart from the one researched?). This can be taken further. Katzer (1978) proposes what he calls 'Standardised Integrity Tests'. My own version, here, borrows from Katzer, Simon (1978) and de Burgh (1987):

Checklist for integrity testing

- The problem statement: what exactly is being defined?
- Compare the problem statement with the findings: has the researcher answered their own question?
- What are/were the research design options? Why this one?

- Are his or her operational definitions credible? i.e. is not crying by infants a sign of happiness and therefore an indication that children in day nurseries do not miss their parents? (see Katzer 1978: section 4)
- Methodology: what exactly is being measured?
- What are the potential sources of bias? (due to research plan, researcher, behaviour of subjects)
- What did the researcher do to compensate for or eliminate bias?
- What assumptions are being made about the population?
- What are the sampling procedures?
- What has been done about noise (e.g. the Hawthorne Study[11])?
- Distortion by noise/unsystematic error (e.g. the way in which teachers react to league tables test measurement is not uniform – there is random variability)
- Validity
- Reliability
- Interpretation – is it fair and correct? Does the summary do it justice?
- Causal relationships – are they wrongly assumed?
- Generalisability? Could this be a fluke? Does this research really apply anywhere else? Do the findings matter?
- Replicatability? (can the research be repeated and get the same result?)
- Has the study been triangulated? (i.e. the problem looked at from two other angles or using two other methods)
- What do rivals say?

In conclusion, in evaluating evidence the investigative journalist is confronted with at least four problems: the errors of testimony, the identification of expertise and the authenticity of documentation and filmed material are just the beginning. The limitations of social research – and, surely, 'hard' scientific research, too, – need to be clearly understood; if the meaning of statistics is too large a topic for any one investigative journalist to feel on top of, at least he or she has access to some excellent books that will support his or her scepticism with revelations of the ways in which figures can be manipulated.

NOTES

1   Bored by the fear of conflict, repression of minority opinion and consensus-seeking that he regarded as typical of the UK media, the first head of Channel 4, Jeremy Isaacs, commissioned a deliberately opinionated weekly current affairs programme, *Diverse Reports*, from the company set up to produce the series by a former BBC associate. When, however, in 1986 David Lloyd was appointed from the BBC to head Current Affairs at C4 he went one step further; he decided that each week's programme should be produced by a different supplier. At the time his decision was derided on the grounds that current affairs required a resource base that no small company or individual could provide; Lloyd claimed that though he might lose because of the weaknesses of his suppliers' resources he would gain in diversity, innovation and courage. Events have borne him out.

2   In a recent talk (Lloyd 1998a) he compared other programmes on the same subject with 'Holding the Baby' and asserted that it was superior because of its use of that evidence.

3   Namely Anthea Gerrie, Caroline Gilbey and Hugo de Burgh. The media with which they had been associated just before this project were both 'right' (*Daily Mail*) and 'left' (C4 *Hard News*) but there were never any differences of approach among the team; the 'story' took precedence.

4   By 'age' I mean not only the issue of how smaller workforces in Europe will fund larger numbers of pensioners but matters of retirement policy, age prejudice or ageism.

5   Channel 4 Television and the *Daily Mail*.

6   The files on this programme are contained in the journalism library at Nottingham Trent University. See ISPSR 1998.

7   Hugo de Burgh and Peter Morgan. The feature was transmitted on 25 July 1996.

8   Eight senior figures in the field were approached in turn to give an overview of the significance of the research, conventionally an essential element of such a feature. Finally, and with many caveats, one did agree.

9   See Jones (1997). Tim Tate (see Chapter 16) made C4 *Secret History* 'Kinsey's Paedophiles' in 1998 on the same subject; the trail had been blazed by Janet Riesman in 1986 when she published her book but orthodox opinion was probably not ready to accept what, thanks to her, was known in the academy well before 1997.

10 The Department of Journalism at City University, London offers a module for its journalism students called Quantitative Methods for Journalists, which addresses some of the issues.

11 The Hawthorne Study illustrated how research can be affected by the research process itself.

BIBLIOGRAPHY

BBC (1997) *Biteback* [TV audience response programme], 2 March 1997. London: BBC.

Channel 4 TV (1989) *Dispatches*: 'Cooking the Books' (Producer: Christopher Hird). London: C4 TV.

Channel 4 TV (1991) *Dispatches*: 'Holding the Baby' (Producer: Hugo de Burgh). London: C4 TV.

Channel 4 TV (1996) *Channel Four News*: 'International Comparisons of Primary Reading' (Hugo de Burgh and Peter Morgan). London: C4 TV.

Channel 4 TV (1998) *Dispatches*: 'Inspecting the Inspectors' (Producer: Sarah Spiller.) London: C4 TV.

Cottle, S. (1995) Producer-driven television? In *Media Culture and Society*, 17 (4): 159–66.

de Burgh, H. (1998) Audience, journalist and text in television news. Paper delivered at the Annual Conference of the International Association for Media and Communications Research, 27 July 1998.

de Burgh, H. and Steward, T. (1986) *The Persuasive Screen: Video Applications in Business*. London: Century Hutchinson.

Elliott, P. (1972) *The Making of a Television Series*, London: Constable.

Fishman, M. (1980) The perspectival nature of events: fact by triangulation. In M. Fishman *Manufacturing the News*. Austin: University of Texas Press: 116–29.

Freeman, D. (1984) *Margaret Mead and Samoa*. London: Penguin.

Gerrie, A. (1987) Are mothers really necessary? *Daily Mail* 12 November: 13–14.

Gold, K. (1998) Tooley, madly, deeply. *THES*, 31 July 1998: 13.

Hird, C. (1983) *Challenging the Figures*. London: Pluto.

Hooke, R. (1983) *How to tell the Liars from the Statisticians*. New York: Marcel.

House of Lords (1991) *Weekly Hansard*, No. 1498: 11/3–14/3.

HTB (1998) The 'Holding the Baby' Documents Box, containing draft scripts, research notes, meetings minutes, interview tapes etc. of the production and subsequent research, held in the Library of the Centre for Broadcasting and Journalism, Nottingham Trent University

Huff, D. (1954) *How to Lie with Statistics*. London: Penguin.

Irvine, J. (1981) *Demystifying Social Statistics*. London: Pluto.

ISPSR (1998) *International Comparisons of Primary School Reading*, programme production file, Library of the Centre for Broadcasting and Journalism, Nottingham Trent University.

Jones, J. H. (1997) *Alfred C. Kinsey: A Public/Private Life*. London: W. W. Norton and Co.

Karpf, A. (1988) Outside the box: medical expertise and the power to define. In A. Karpf *Doctoring the Media: The Reporting of Health and Medicine*. London: Routledge: 110–34.

Katzer, J. (1978) A step by step guide for evaluation. In J. Katzer *Evaluating Information*. Reading: Addison Wesley.

Lloyd, D. (1998a) Talk to the students of the MA Investigative Journalism course at Nottingham Trent University, 19 February 1998.

Lloyd, D. (1998b) Interview with Hugo de Burgh, London, 9 October 1998.

Lloyd, D. (1998c) Quoted by Jancis Giles in a letter and notes to Hugo de Burgh, 25 October 1998.

McCombs, M. (1976) *Handbook of Reporting Methods*. Boston: Houghton Mifflin.

McNulty, M. (1996) Dispatches rider. In *Broadcast* 18 October 1996.

Mead, M. (1943) *Coming of Age in Samoa: A Study of Adolescence and Sex in Primitive Societies*. London: Penguin.

Meyer, P. (1991) Journalism and the scientific tradition. In P. Meyer *The New Precision Journalism*. Bloomington: Indiana University Press.

Nissel, M. (1995) Vital statistics. *New Statesman and Society*, 27 January 1997.

Shenton, J. (1998) *Positively False*. London: I.B. Tauris.

Shipman, M. (1981) *The Limitations of Social Research*. London: Longman.

Silverstone, R. (1985) *Framing Science: The Making of a BBC Documentary*. London: British Film Institute.

Simon, J. (1978) *Basic Research Methods in Social Science: The Art of Empirical Investigation*. New York: Random House.

Stott, R. (1998) [press officer for C4 *Dispatches*] Conversations with Hugo de Burgh.

Tankard, J. W. (1976) Reporting and the scientific method. In M. McCombs *Handbook of Reporting Methods*. Boston: Houghton Mifflin.

FURTHER READING

Katzer, J. (1978) *Evaluating Information*. Reading: Addison Wesley.

Shipman, M. (1994) *The Limitations of Social Research*. London: Longman.

13

EXPOSING MISCARRIAGES OF JUSTICE

An example from BBC's *Rough Justice*

Hugo de Burgh

The problem

In 1974 an IRA bombing in Birmingham killed twenty-one people; the men convicted in the subsequent trial were later found to have been convicted wrongly on the strength of flawed evidence and forced confessions. The same year, 1974, bombings in Guildford and Woolwich resulted in the conviction of four men who were to be released in 1989, having been found innocent.

From very soon after the Birmingham trial, there were doubts about the convictions. On various occasions over 13 years, two Home Secretaries reviewed the case, as did two Directors of Public Prosecutions, eleven judges and four police inquiries. Over many years a journalist (and from 1987 Member of Parliament), Chris Mullin, kept presenting and re-presenting his evidence that the men were innocent and claiming not only that he knew the names of the real perpetrators, but that the police also knew. As a result of his work, the verdict of the forensic scientist in the original trial was re-examined by the Home Office and found unsafe.

Mullin, who wrote a book on the Birmingham investigation (Mullin 1986) made no great claims for his skills. When asked how he uncovered those whom he believed had really carried out the Birmingham bombings, he replied 'by simple detective work of the sort one would commend to the West Midlands police' (Lennon 1991). 'Most people travelling on the buses noticed that there was something wrong in these cases, Guildford and the Birmingham Six' said Mullin, wondering why the judicial system got them so wrong.

> Stupidity would be one possible explanation for the behaviour of a succession of judges, but I am inclined to the view that it is a pre-occupation with protecting the credibility of the legal system which takes precedence over a commitment to justice.
>
> (cit. in Lennon 1991)

In the 1970s miscarriages of justice appear to have proliferated. Another famous instance was the case of Carl Bridgwater in which four men were imprisoned for the killing of a newspaper boy in 1978; after twenty years of research and campaigning by investigative journalist Paul Foot, the men were finally released in 1996. The apparently large number of miscarriages, and of course we can only speculate as to how many there really are for only a tiny number are taken up by journalists in relation to all committals, may simply be a function of the huge increase in recorded crime over the past fifty years. While there is no agreement regarding how much of this increase reflects more crime and how much better identification of crime, it is generally accepted that crime itself has burgeoned.

Whatever the wider context in which rising crime and its control can be seen; whatever the factors in the notorious cases of miscarriage of justice named above, it has long been the contention of interested journalists that there are serious flaws in the judicial system which make it essential that there be investigative journalists prepared to subject cases to scrutiny. One of these is the fact that, contrary to popular opinion, it is not easy for the convicted to get leave to appeal, in fact virtually the only grounds for appeal is error in legal procedure. The other principal accusation is that the lack of a system of independent investigation as available in France or Italy results in courtrooms being presented with evidence that has been inadequately researched, or is partial, or is presented in a confused manner because insufficient examination has been made of it before trial.

Ludovic Kennedy, involved in exposing many miscarriages of justice over many years, sees police manipulation of evidence, the 'childish' adversary system in the courts which obscures rather than reveals truth and 'cavalier' assessment of evidence by the Court of Appeal as the main problems. Among the reforms he and others have advocated is the replacement of trial by conflict with trial by discovery. He says:

> In the short term the remedy is quite simple. It is that in all cases of serious crime, murder, manslaughter, rape, armed robbery, offences for which the penalty's likely to be many years of imprisonment, the questioning of suspects be taken out of the hands of the police and given instead to an examining magistrate ... who will direct the police in their inquiries.
>
> (Kennedy 1991: 312)

In a short summary Tom Sargant describes the typical miscarriages of justice and how they come about, miscarriages which 'take many forms and are far more numerous than anyone in authority is prepared to admit, or is in a position to estimate' (Sargant 1985). He also points to the accusatorial system above all because it 'is more of a battle than an inquiry into the truth and is operated under wholly inadequate safeguards and controls' (ibid.: 218). The legal system, in other words, provided the opportunity, even the necessity, for investigative journalists to investigate. We are not talking simply about some corrupt or inadequate policemen but of a system that promotes such inadequacy to influence the trials.

Some argue (Haywood 1999a) that it is now easier to get to appeal and that the system is much more responsive to the concept of miscarriages; the Criminal Cases Review Commission was established in 1997 and this they credit especially to *Rough Justice* which has made everybody involved in the criminal justice system more sensitive to the possibility of miscarriages and more aware of how they can come about. There is such scepticism now that, as Steve Haywood, former editor of *Rough Justice* and now responsible for C4's equivalent, *Trial and Error*, talks of

> a whole coterie of solicitors and barristers who will work on behalf of people claiming to be victims of miscarriages plus a political bandwagon which will provide any claimant with a support group to go politicking and junketing, trying to get others interested.
>
> (Haywood 1999a)

He points out that programmes like those on which he has worked are important because which cases go to appeal courts are not based on judicial considerations, 'politics has a lot do with it ... if you can build up a level of public concern to the extent that the case *must* be dealt with then you stand a much better chance' (Haywood 1999a).

Examining the cases selected by *Rough Justice* and investigative journalists working in other media, it's easy to be struck first by the extraordinarily great gulf that separated the lives of the journalists from those of the people they were investigating – whose lives were often detached from community or family or prospects for an orderly life, which made it much easier for them to be exploited by unscrupulous or incompetent police – and second by the dedication with which reporters, and a few other individuals, fight on behalf of these, very different, citizens. Peter Hill, founder of *Rough Justice*, explains his motivation as 'outrage' that people with power can do shoddy things to people without power.

Time line of some recent, publicised, miscarriages of justice in Britain

1957   Founding of the organisation Justice
1982   First transmissions of *Rough Justice*
1982   UK government re-opens cases investigated by *Rough Justice*
1985   Granada TV decides to resource Mullin's search
1989   Release of the Guildford Four
1990   March Granada TV drama documentary 'Who Bombed Birmingham?'
1991   Release of the Birmingham Six

1996   26 November *Rough Justice* transmits programme on Ryan James
1996   26 July *Rough Justice* on Bridgwater Case
1998   Bentley hanging conviction quashed

BBC's *Rough Justice*[1]

Rough Justice first transmitted in 1982, examining three cases all of which were subsequently re-opened by the Home Office. The authors were influenced by the efforts that had been made over many years by the rights campaigner and founder of Justice, Tom Sargant, and by the merits of the three cases in question. In each case the convictions seemed implausible and the evidence questionable, to say the least. According to Young and Hill (1983) *Rough Justice* was typically drawn to cases where:

- defence solicitors became involved too late;
- the police could not find things that journalists could;
- institutions attempted to thwart the journalists.

The *Rough Justice* investigators have usually been treated with suspicion and suffered from attempts to thwart them. For example, according to Young and Hill (1983), in a modest investigation without any wider or political ramifications, they were denied access or simple help by the Ministry of Defence, British Rail, the Broadmoor Hospital authorities, the Department of Health and Social Security (as it was then), the medical authorities and the police. Sargant found great difficulties in obtaining copies of statements taken by the police, the names of psychiatrists who had examined prisoners or court transcripts (Sargant 1985: 237). Little has changed today.

Rough Justice started after BBC reporter Peter Hill was driving in North London and found himself accused by a policeman of jumping a red light; the fury he felt at wrongful accusation started him thinking about the nature of miscarriages and he contacted Tom Sargant of Justice. The programme he and Michael Young persuaded their BBC managers to let him launch, *Rough Justice*, started with a very clear idea of what it behoved it to do. This is how Young and Hill (1983) put it:

> we chose to observe a number of constraints. The first was that the programme should deal in facts, not opinions. We would corroborate these facts as far as possible. We would authenticate any documents that we quoted or used.
>
> The second constraint was that we should not yield to the temptation to become judge and jury, to draw inferences from the conduct of the original investigation and trial.
>
> We decided, too, that the prosecution case must be fairly and fully represented in each case. This was a third constraint. We guessed that

people were going to ask, 'But just how did he get convicted?' We wanted to be able to say that all the salient facts that the prosecution had presented against the defendant had been reported in our films.

We asked our lawyers to check the script on each occasion against the transcript of the judge's summing up to ensure that we had been fair to the presentation of the prosecution case.

Allegedly the programme experienced a difficult phase in the late 1980s because of the failure of the BBC to support its reporters when they were under attack. The two most distinguished journalists of the team were given the opportunity to work on programmes other than *Rough Justice* after it was alleged in court and in the media that they had dealt unfairly with the subject of an investigation. [2]

The investigation in question was of a woman called Anne Fitzpatrick. She had picked out in an identity parade one Anthony Mycock, known to the police in Manchester, as having forced her into her flat, assaulted and tied her up before stealing from her. The *Rough Justice* team investigated the case in 1985 and became certain that no burglary had taken place; they learned that Fitzpatrick had trashed her own flat in a fit of pique with her partner and that her pretence that there had been a burglary was an attempt to explain this event to that partner. They suspected that the identification of the suspect was fraudulent and a further cover-up in that the police had not been too scrupulous in checking, since Mycock was a 'usual suspect'.

Hill and Young traced Fitzpatrick to Los Angeles and interviewed her, securing her admission. This was reported in the BBC staff newspaper *Aerial* as a great coup. The programme went out in 1985 and the case was reinvestigated by Manchester Police, although a history of antagonism between the programme and Manchester Police meant that there was little or no cooperation, indeed Steve Haywood (then producer) believes that he was intimidated by the police at that stage (Haywood 1999a). Furthermore, he believes that the police told Fitzpatrick she was guilty of perjury and liable to a severe sentence which in reality was most unlikely, though it served to frighten her.

After the programme 'The Case of the Perfect Proof' went out on 3 October 1985, Mycock was at last given leave to appeal and at the hearing it was quickly found that the case against Mycock could not be sustained. However, in the course of the hearing it was alleged that the reporters had pressurised Fitzpatrick to the point of threatening her in order to get retraction and, although this was by then tangential to the hearing, Lord Chief Justice Lane spent a great deal of time examining the two reporters and impugning their methods.

As a result of Lane's examination of the reporters, BBC managers removed them from *Rough Justice*. They also made every effort to hush up the matter, presumably because they lost their nerve after criticism in the press (e.g. the *Daily Mail*); they also feared legal actions starting in the USA which were expected to follow because the BBC failed to refute the accusations made against their reporters.

Why did Lane bother, and why did the BBC fail to defend its reporters? Other journalists on *Rough Justice* at the time believe that after the early successes of the programme in reporting failures of the police and courts, those believing themselves under attack felt antagonism, fuelled by the belief that the scepticism inflamed by the programmes was harming the justice system as a whole. In an interview at the time, one of the UK's most important judges, Lord Denning, said 'it was better that a guilty man remain in prison than that the integrity of the system be questioned'. The hostility was such that the team began to believe that if *Rough Justice* was involved the subjects' chances of release were being hindered. That was the worst period *Rough Justice* went through.

Today

This genre of programming has a problem very particular to it: 'You only have one person to talk to you – if you cannot get to that person, you are finished' (Haywood 1999a). This conditions the choice of topic, or at least demands particular skills. The story is told of how in the first series Peter Hill needed to speak to a woman – call her Jean – whom he was doubtful of being able to persuade to see him. He undertook to visit several people over several months on the housing estate in which Jean lived and to interview them instead; on each occasion he mentioned that he would be meeting Jean 'because she is such an honourable woman'. After a couple of months of this everyone on the estate knew that he would eventually be seeing Jean 'because she is such an honourable woman' and, not surprisingly, he did.

The ability to plan strategically in this manner and to doorstep effectively are two of the skills that researchers on *Rough Justice* require. Equally important, though, is an analytic brain. 'By sitting and reading through a case again and again you can often crack it just sitting there.' The lawyers did not manage it because of the pressure of events, because they had no time, because they're 'not as good as us' (Haywood 1999a). Good contacts are not so significant – 'they find you' – although, since the best contacts are in the police it is useful to know how to relate to them. More important is a grasp of how the medium works, since filling 50 minutes so that people keep on watching demands many different skills. The kind of topic a producer looks for has three essential sequences. Although the format has been changing the traditional one is made up of:

- part one – **conviction**, i.e. all the prosecution evidence
- part two – **human story**
- part three – **the handful of hair**, i.e. production of the evidence which destroys the prosecution case.[3]

In sum, this is documentary-making in current affairs with the added spices of requiring a specific narrative form, much carefully sifted detail, the risks of exposure to legal action and problems of identifying and communicating with sources that would rarely be found elsewhere in journalism. Not surprisingly, therefore, it is generally held by those in the business that *Rough Justice* is quintessentially the kind of programme that requires a public service umbrella, since there must be the freedom to select topics on moral criteria, to abort programmes, and to research them to the utmost degree. There is a risk otherwise that topics will be selected only because they are already guaranteed to attract attention or where there is certainty that they can be concluded; that producers will rely upon the information provided by solicitors rather than upon their own original research. Commercial pressures, in other words, endanger quality.

When *Trial and Error*, C4's equivalent of *Rough Justice* introduced in 1993, was commissioned conditions that were quite unique at the time were written into the contract in order to protect its integrity, to take account of the fact that a great deal of research might be done only to have the programme for which it was intended pulled. The essential provision was that the 2-year contract did not stipulate the number of programmes required to be made – an unimaginable condition in any other sector of the industry.

For two reasons a different type of case is now being taken up by these programmes. Audiences for this genre of television are declining and the introduction of the Criminal Cases Review Commission (CCRC) has changed the environment. The CCRC investigates miscarriage allegations which in the past would only have been undertaken by television; there are however some cases that they do not take up and it is among these that *Trial and Error* finds its subject matter (Lloyd 1999).

Contractor Steve Haywood (whose company also made the C4 series *Clear My Name* in 1998) says that in today's climate it is difficult to do cases other than 'high profile' ones. He believes that today it would not be possible for him to take on a case such as that of Jacqueline Fletcher in the 1991 'Murder or Mystery'. The victim of this miscarriage was a woman, accused of murdering her child, whom he characterises as poor, unhealthy, uneducated, exploited and ignorant; 'and yet she was innocent'. Because he was sure of this, and of the injustice of the accusation, Haywood 'had a go' and eventually, with the unstinting help of the pathologist whose original error he exposed, proved that the child had probably died of natural causes. 'Lord Justice Lane was obliged to let her out.' Haywood believes that Fletcher would still be in prison if that *Rough Justice* had not been made. His defence of the programme as it was then is eloquent: 'Miscarriages of justice don't happen to people like you or me, people with large incomes or powerful friends; they happen to poor people' (Haywood 1999a).

Example: Death in the Playground

On an afternoon in May 1992 a 3-year-old child, Karl, disappeared in a play area of some cultivated and some rough and overgrown land near a housing estate. The police were called and among those who helped them search was the teenager Paul Esslemont, the last person known to have seen the child; he had been practising golf strokes on the grass at the time. When, partly thanks to Esslemont's help, the child was found in the bushes, he had been battered to death.

Subsequent police investigations included interviews with Esslemont who gave three statements over 8 days, statements that contained inconsistencies. Moreover forensic tests revealed, according to the police case, blood on all his clothes and on his golf club. He was tried in May 1993 and the inconsistencies in his statements were declared to be not lapses of memory but lies; he was found guilty and his appeal was rejected. Incidentally, his parents' home was firebombed.

Rough Justice decided to examine the story on the basis that the idea of Paul Esslemont murdering anybody was incredible. The team talked to people who knew Esslemont, including those for whom he had been a baby-sitter, and became convinced that there was neither motive nor psychological explanation. Furthermore, at least one jury member was not convinced of his guilt.

Early in the programme, *Rough Justice* states that it clarified quickly that there was no motive and that Esslemont does not fit the psychological profiles of a killer, profiles that are well recognised. They noted that the police interviews had pushed Esslemont into admitting irritability with the small boy and they thought that the forensic evidence might be uncertain since Esslemont had been searching through the undergrowth with the police looking for the child, which might explain the bloodstains on him.

In fact no forensic scientist had visited the scene until *Rough Justice* commissioned one to do so (BBC 1994). The scientist pointed out that in such cases a map of bloodstains should be made, yet none had been. The undergrowth had been mown in order to find the weapon, possibly destroying evidence. The forensic scientist commissioned by *Rough Justice* constructed a model to see how far blood could travel in the case of the child's battering. This made it plausible that Esslemont might innocently have flecks of blood on him. He went on to find that there was little or no evidence that the murder weapon was a golf club, as claimed by the police; indeed he went further and said that the weapon could not have been a golf club. He proceeded to give an innocent explanation for the appearance of blood on the tongue of the accused's trainer; demonstrated that the blood on Esslemont's jeans was not that of the victim but the accused; and showed that, while the accused's T-shirt had no blood on it, the killer's upper garment had to have blood on it, such were the dynamics of the assault.

This study pointed, too, to the fact that the police had failed to follow up the lead on another possible killer who was in the vicinity at the time; they had plumped for Esslemont, perhaps because he was handy and easy to manipulate, allowing themselves to be convinced by inadequate forensic evidence. In July 1997 Esslemont was released. He had spent 3 years in jail.

Discussion

People involved with this genre of journalism appear uneasy about some of the cases. The distinction is commonly drawn between a case of corruption of justice and a case of miscarriage. Thus it is asserted that in at least one of the well-known bombing cases there may have been corruption but no miscarriage. It was also suggested that further examination of other recent cases might lead one to question whether there was a miscarriage of justice, or whether inadequate evidence was the problem.

The following example of the distinction was given to me. In the Sheila Bowler case, dealt with in three programmes transmitted over 1994–5,[4] in which a spinster was accused of effecting her (supposedly unable to walk) aunt's death by taking her to a river. The *Trial and Error* team argued that the proposition that the aunt might have walked the distance was never properly examined by the court, which thus made erroneous assumptions. It was on the basis of that that there was a re-trial. The programme did not prove at any time that the aunt did walk, but only that in order to have a fair trial this matter should have been explored. By comparison, in the case of Brian Parsons, accused of murder during a burglary, there was a good deal of proof that Parsons could not have done it and some evidence that someone else had. This was a true miscarriage of justice (BBC 1996).

In either type of case, investigative journalists can be more successful in their research than the professionals of the legal system because some witnesses will speak to journalists but not to police or lawyers. Since they investigate after the event more truth may be available than at the time, and, moreover, they are usually building upon some initial police work, however flawed. Investigative journalists should be able to bring to the case a cast of mind that is quite different from that of the professionals. They have no *interest* in the case; their *professional integrity* is not impugned if the case has to be re-thought, or if no villain is found, although today such a failure may have *commercial* implications.

Journalists are not bound by the rules of evidence used in court cases, by professional conventions, by considerations of career within the system they are scrutinising or (it is hoped) by the fear of spoiling relationships within that system. It is also possible that journalists may be more intelligent in the sense that they can bring to bear a different set of intellectual skills and lateral thinking from those professionally involved. They may be educated in a different manner and be more contextually aware investigators than the police or solicitors.

The work of journalists brings them in touch with the widest possible range of people, in relationships of equality equally with those who have prestige and power, or none. This often makes them sceptical of the hierarchies and procedures that less free individuals use to protect themselves from examination. Moreover, through working in a variety of other environments, they develop specific skills and knowledge that they can employ in scrutinising the justice system. For these reasons, in examining miscarriages of justice in Britain, investigative journalists act as expert check on the activities of police or solicitors, running repeat investigations, gathering new witnesses and constructing models.

NOTES

1   While I was writing these chapters the editor of *Rough Justice* was Elizabeth Clough and I made great efforts to meet her, to talk to her on the telephone or to have her designate a spokesperson to tell me about the programme today. Unfortunately, because of her personal commitments and difficulties at the time I was unable to draw upon her knowledge.

2   My account of this situation derives from discussions with Peter Hill (1999), the chapter of a book he has in preparation, an interview with Steve Haywood (1999a) and the original BBC transcripts of interviews conducted by Hill and Young for the programme in question.

3   The expression 'Handful of Hair' emanates from the first series of *Rough Justice* in which there was the case of the murder of a student of Goldsmith's College, London; the conviction was overturned on the production of evidence by *Rough Justice* that the hair grasped by the murdered woman in the moment of death was not that of the convicted. 'Handful of Hair' represents the irrefutable, what the producers are looking for.

4   The first two were in the series *Trial and Error* (reporter David Jessel, producer Steve Phelps) transmitted 20 September 1994 and 9 November 1995; the third was a fly-on-the-wall of preparations for the re-trial called *The Music Teacher*, produced by Steve Rankin. (Information supplied by Steve Haywood 8 June 1999.)

BIBLIOGRAPHY

BBC (1994) *Rough Justice*: 'Death in the Playground'. London: BBC TV.

BBC (1996) *Rough Justice*: 'The Vet's Wife'. London: BBC TV.

BBC (1997) *Rough Justice*: 'The Bordon Baseball Bat Murder'. London: BBC TV.

Haywood, S. (1999) Being an investigative journalist today. Talk given to the students of the MA Investigative Journalism course at Nottingham Trent University, 22 April 1999.

Haywood, S. (1999a) Interview with Hugo de Burgh in Blackheath, London, 6 May 1999.

Hill, P. (1999) Interview with Hugo de Burgh, 18 May 1999.

Hill, P., Young, M. and Sargant, T. (1985) *More Rough Justice*. London: Penguin.

Kennedy, L. (1985) In P. Hill, M. Young and T. Sargant *More Rough Justice*. London: Penguin.

Kennedy, L. (1991) *Truth to Tell: Collected Writings of Ludovic Kennedy*. London: Bantam Books.

Lennon, P. (1991) Meddler after truth. *Guardian*, 2 January 1992.

Lloyd, D. (1999) Information provided to Hugo de Burgh, 10 June 1999.

Mullin, C. (1986) *Error of Judgment: The Truth about the Birmingham Bombings*. London: Chatto and Windus.

Sargant, T. (1985) In P. Hill, M. Young and T. Sargant *More Rough Justice*. London: Penguin.

Young, M. and Hill, P. (1983) *Rough Justice*. London: BBC.

FURTHER READING

Hill, P., Young, M. and Sargant, T. (1985) *More Rough Justice*. London: Penguin.

Kennedy, L. (1991) *Truth to Tell: Collected Writings of Ludovic Kennedy*. London: Bantam Books.

14

GRAVEDIGGING

The case of 'the Cossacks'

Hugo de Burgh

Background

From 1989 to 1993 a historical investigation became news in tabloid and broadsheet media alike as argument raged over the merits of the combatants in a struggle over who might have done what over a few days in 1945. The case of 'the Cossacks' has been perhaps the single most prominent example of historical investigation to be turned into journalism, not only in the acres of newsprint devoted to the story and based upon the several books on the subject but also in a programme in the BBC historical series, *Timewatch*. We will come to the part played by *Timewatch*[1] shortly; first, the background.

A month after the Second World War ended in May 1945, British troops in occupied Austria appear to have contravened orders and deported large numbers of defenceless people to their enemies for certain suffering and likely death. The case has been much discussed in the British, and latterly the Russian and North American press, ever since a book by Nicholas Bethell was published in 1974, *The Last Secret*. The case achieved international prominence when a libel action was brought in 1989 by a British retired officer who had been accused of ordering the deportation. Exactly why it was done and who was responsible has not been finally established. However, many influential and well-known people in Britain have been involved in the controversy, and there have been charges of conspiracy to suppress the evidence as well as charges against the integrity of both sides.

The case is interesting to journalists for the following reasons. It is generally agreed that an injustice was done to many thousands of people in May 1945 (the story is told below) and thus there is, to any journalist, a case worth investigating. When it is argued that the injustice was committed against the expressed orders of the highest authority, the case becomes intriguing. The difficulties of establishing the truth because of the passage of time, the apparent evasiveness of some of those in a position to help, the death of witnesses, the complexity of the written records and the strong emotions conjured up by the story are all stimulating to the hunter.

The investigation of the incident was initially carried out primarily by two writers, Nicholas Bethell and Nikolai Tolstoy, and provides an ideal illustration of the problems of complex data trawling in several countries' archives and using several languages. Problems of obtaining evidence from public bodies appear to have been exacerbated through intentional obstruction and, it is claimed, illustrate how well-connected parties can obfuscate the work of the researcher and how official files can be weeded before being put in the records (Faulkner 1998).

At the time of initial research Russian and some German archives were not accessible; they now are and are claimed to throw new light upon the case (Tolstoy 1997); this may demonstrate how research interpretations can be stymied because of partial sourcing. The arguments over the libel case have already shown how important access to documents at the right time can be in determining judgement (Mitchell 1997: Appendix A).

Both writers have come up against opposition merely for tackling the study, and have been vilified. Tolstoy's involvement in the case drew him into a series of court actions, the first of which bankrupted him, and the subsequent ones have been draining without achieving any satisfactory result (to him). The case is widely thought to have illustrated flaws in the British legal system, in particular Britain's notorious libel laws. Aspects of it have also made legal history.

The story

In May 1945, after the total German surrender, British troops occupied much of what is now Austria. There was no more fighting, but there were considerable problems involved in keeping the peace and ensuring communications and supply of necessities to the population.

Western Europe was awash with refugees, known then as Displaced Persons, who were put into Displaced Persons Camps for screening, that is checking for war criminals or potential sources of information. Refugees included the millions of slave labourers brought to Germany by the fallen government; members of minorities persecuted in Poland and other countries of Eastern Europe; escaped prisoners of every variety; German colonists in flight from revenge; participants in the ill-fated armies of liberation that had sought to free the East from the Soviets but found themselves exploited by the Germans; families and camp-followers who joined the fleeing German armies in their stampede West.

At a meeting at Yalta between Stalin, Roosevelt and Churchill in 1945 it had been agreed that former Soviet citizens among these should be repatriated. However, down in the camps it was not always easy to ascertain who was a former Soviet citizen; moreover it was generally recognised by the Allies that anyone so deported might be liquidated.

In these circumstances, Harold Alexander, Allied Commander in Chief in Italy, in concert with Prime Minister Winston Churchill, decided that the refugees should not be deported. This was particularly pertinent in Austria, where British troops looked after large numbers of refugees not very far from the border with the Soviet zone. They tend, and tended, to be referred to as 'the Cossacks', although actually how many were Cossacks, recruited by the Germans in an anti-Soviet crusade, as opposed to other kinds of refugees is unclear. Over half of them were women and small children and a large number were easily identifiable as never having been Soviet citizens. Many were expecting to be able to emigrate to Canada or Argentina while others waited clearance to return to their homes in France or Germany. In these circumstances, and because of deteriorating relations with the Soviets, Alexander and Eisenhower, the Supreme Commander, agreed that the refugees should be moved further from the Soviet border. This was a concrete decision such that an allocation of resources was made and 800 trucks were supplied.

These facts were well known to the officers of the British army of occupation, although in the 1980s and 1990s it was to be suggested that this was not so. In May 1945, very shortly after Alexander's order had been issued and those vehicles been released to enable the refugees to be transported to safety, an operation began to hand over the refugees to the Soviet side. The vehicles were sent back. The question that has exercised researchers since is why, and on whose initiative was this action carried out.

It could be circumvented. For example, the Sixth Armoured Division under General Murray held a large number of Cossack refugees in the Drau Valley. Once Murray's officers knew that force was about to be used on the refugees some of them warned them to flee (de Burgh 1995). Murray himself remonstrated with the command, on the grounds that many of the refugees were not Soviet citizens, but he was overruled. There was, therefore, an impetus behind the initiative that would not be gainsaid. Many refugees were savagely beaten by British troops before they could be forced over the border to the Soviet side where whips and bullets were ready for them.

What has intrigued researchers is that the person or persons responsible not only contradicted the instructions of the Commander in Chief but also quashed requests by senior officers that the task be reconsidered, ignored the well-known fact that many of these people were not appropriate for repatriation, and turned a blind eye to the known fate that would befall them. Malice of this kind seems implausible, so that commentators have proposed a 'banality of evil' explanation – that it suited the career aspirations of an officer and an official so well that they were prepared to contradict the Commander in Chief.

While Bethell's book apportioned no blame, elsewhere it was suggested that Brigadier Toby Low (Lord Aldington from 1962) had been involved; subsequent publications with which Tolstoy was concerned went further and suggested that Low, who would shortly leave the army to fight a parliamentary seat, was keener to please his political patron than his Commander in Chief.

His party patron was Harold Macmillan, then Political Adviser at Allied HQ for the area, and an important politician whose influence would presumably be useful to Low, just starting out in politics. Macmillan would later be British Prime Minister.

If this is to be believed, then some motivation has to be ascribed to Macmillan; thus far Tolstoy has not convinced many that he has successfully explained this motivation. Unfortunately those who object to Tolstoy's view (Horne 1998, Johnson 1990) have not themselves come up with a satisfactory attribution of responsibility or explanation of motive.

Time line of story and legal case

1945   In May 1945 an officer or officers in the British army of occupation in Austria, apparently contradicting written orders from superiors, initiates an operation, itself grossly inhumane, that results in the savage treatment and/or murder by Russians and Yugoslavs of many refugees under British protection.

1957   Polish historian Josef Mackiewicz publishes *Kontra*, an account of a brutal handover of Cossacks by British troops.
       Nikolai Krasnov, great-nephew of Don Ataman Krasnov, is released from prison in the Soviet Union and publishes *Hezabyvaemoe* [The Unforgettable].

1962   Ataman of the Kuban Cossacks Vyacheslav Naumenko publishes Volume 1 of *Velikoye Predatelstvo* [The Great Betrayal]; the second volume is issued in 1970.
       Toby Low is created Lord Aldington.

1973   US writer Julius Epstein publishes *Operation Keelhaul* based on US documents of the case.
       The British Public Record Office receives the files for 1945 from the Foreign Office and War Office, and makes them available.

1974   Lord Bethell publishes *The Last Secret*.

1977   Count Tolstoy publishes *Victims of Yalta*.

1978   Tolstoy discovers that relevant UK Foreign Office files have been destroyed; obtains duplicates from Washington.

1981   Aldington claims he left Austria on 25 May 1945.

1985   Tolstoy publishes *The Minister and the Massacres*.
       Nigel Watts, for reasons not connected with the case, publishes a pamphlet critical of Lord Aldington. *Inter alia*, it refers to Aldington as the officer responsible for the infamous initiatives of May 1945. He had consulted Tolstoy on the detail of the case.
       Lord Aldington brings an action for libel against Watts. Tolstoy, sure of his case, asks to be included in the indictment.

1987–8 Aldington prepares his action; his costs, it emerges, are to be underwritten by the Sun Alliance Insurance Company; he gets access to files denied Tolstoy.

1989   Main trial from 2 October to 30 November; Tolstoy found culpable and Aldington awarded damages and costs totalling £1.5 million, the largest ever libel award.

1990   Tolstoy appeals; Aldington proposes the appeal be subject to Tolstoy proving he has funds to pay costs; Registrars of the Court of Appeal reject this; Aldington appeals against this decison and wins; Tolstoy is required to deposit £124,900 which he cannot do; appeal dismissed. Tolstoy declared bankrupt.

In Strasbourg Tolstoy appeals to the European Court of Human Rights that the award to Aldington violated his rights to freedom of expression under Article 10 of the Convention.

1991   The BBC makes a film in the *Timewatch* series, 'A British Betrayal'. Before it can be released, Lord Aldington writes to the BBC 'reserving the right to sue on the grounds that it is libellous'. BBC goes ahead and shows the programme (once).

An injunction is taken out prohibiting Tolstoy from speaking publicly or writing about the case.

1993   Tolstoy applies to the Court of Appeal for leave to adduce new evidence. Application rejected.

1994   Tolstoy issues a writ against Aldington in the High Court, applying for an order to set aside the 1989 judgement on the grounds of fraud.

Mr Justice Collins strikes out the writ as abuse of process. He then, in a decision which made legal history, orders Tolstoy's *pro bono* lawyers to pay 60 per cent of Aldington's costs, thus effectively ensuring that Tolstoy will be unable ever to find lawyers to help him again.

In Strasbourg the European Court of Human Rights declares that the award to Aldington violated Tolstoy's rights to freedom of expression under Article 10 of the Convention.

1996   In February Tolstoy appeals the High Court judgement. Refused leave to appeal.

The data sources used by researchers

From 1957 to 1970 several memoirs of the events were published in Russian, and one in Polish. German survivors of the war were also writing their memoirs, and these included those who had served with the so-called Army of Liberation. For those interested in the case and with facility in those languages (which both Bethell and Tolstoy have) there was a good deal of raw material already available on the case in general.

However, as interest began to focus more and more on the responsibility and the motivation for the initiative, and once Bethell and Tolstoy had realised how orders had been ignored that the initiative might be taken, then the data sources which mattered were those of the Allied forces. Details of these sources may be found in the references in Tolstoy's books, and a discussion of them, and of those which mysteriously disappeared when needed in evidence during the 1989 trial, are described in the appendices to Mitchell (1997).

The extraordinary story of how an ostensibly impartial inquiry was undertaken into the issues raised by Tolstoy (the Cowgill Report); of how Lord Aldington obtained special help over the documents from party political contacts, help that was denied Tolstoy; of how the Foreign and Commonwealth Office lost files when they were most needed and then found them when it was too late is described elsewhere, particularly in Mitchell (1997).

If Aldington was indeed the officer responsible then Tolstoy must prove that he retained the command on the days when certain orders were given. Two key orders were given pertaining to the operation on the afternoon of 22 May and on 23 May, and they were given on the authority of the Brigadier General Staff for V Corps. Although on earlier occasions Aldington had said he had left Austria on 25 May, by the time of the trial he was saying that he had left before the fatal order of 22 May, so that he could not have been responsible for it (the military title would have applied to his successor), and that he had left before a meeting at which it was decided to shoot at those resisting deportation. Because of the absence of documentation and the vagueness with which those involved have answered questions about dates, it has not been possible to finalise this issue. Tolstoy has not proved his case.

The work of investigation

Why did these two men undertake this investigation? For many years after the Second World War the full extent of what the Germans did to their subject peoples, and in particular to minorities, was not generally or fully understood. Even once it was understood, it was not universally agreed that all those involved in the vast project of cruelty should be held to account or that it was necessary to put resources into finding them. The competitive spirit of the Cold War encouraged the Allies not to do anything that would besmirch the Allied side. Thus, war criminals from Germany or those countries now part of 'the West' who had worked with the Germans were often left in peace. The goodness attributed to the Allied cause in the Second World War was now transferred to the 'West' in the Cold War. To suggest otherwise could at times be dangerous, as the McCarthy period in the USA shows.

These factors may account for the failure to question how the Allies found it expedient to cooperate with criminals from among their former enemies, or indeed to question the Allies' own conduct during the Second World War. Times change. The Case of the Cossacks was always known to enough people, and enough people who felt ashamed, that it was never forgotten. They believed that this was 'Britain's war crime' and, while it might appear insignificant beside the horrors inflicted by the Germans, it should not be allowed to be forgotten.[2] If there be a guilty party then he must be revealed so that justice may be seen to be done, even over fifty years after the crime. There were survivors who longed for their loved ones' sufferings to be recognised and for some explanation of the deed.

Bethell was one of those who had always been aware of the case and who directed his attention to the documents dealing with the place and the period as soon as they were made available in the Public Record Office. Tolstoy, an established historian before becoming a public figure as a result of this case, was more emotionally involved with the story. Having been brought up in part in the White Russian émigré community in England, he was familiar with the tale from an early age. Furthermore, one of his childhood heroes, Ataman Krasnov,[3] was killed as a result of the deportations. Tolstoy wanted to find an explanation for this, and his sense of chivalry revolted against the manner of his hero's treatment (Norman 1990).

In making what Aldington has argued is an unjust and unsubstantiated allegation that has besmirched his reputation, Tolstoy has inflicted tribulations upon himself too. After losing the 1989 libel case his supporters set up a Forced Repatriation Defence Fund (Norton-Taylor 1990) to enable him to appeal. However, the trial judge, Mr Justice Michael Davies froze that fund. This meant that in future he would not be able to pay lawyers and he at first decided to conduct his own case; when, in 1994, in a further action, lawyers agreed to conduct his case *pro bono*, Mr Justice Collins ruled that those lawyers should pay 60 per cent of the costs of the other party's lawyers, in effect fining them heavily for helping Tolstoy. It is not perhaps surprising that Tolstoy believes that every opportunity is being taken by highly prejudiced judges to make it impossible for him to make his case.

The *Timewatch* documentary

Timewatch is the BBC's historical strand, with a remit 'to cover, in a succession of one-off, predominantly 50 minute films on BBC2, historical issues, ideas and stories from twentieth and pre-twentieth century history'. Its objectives are to 'excite the viewer about pre-twentieth century history and show the resonance of the distant past to today' as well as to ignite debate, as in its programmes about Second World War bombing or the history of immigration (BBC 1999). Its rival is Channel 4's *Secret History* strand.

'A British Betrayal' is a good example of British documentary art. Not only does *Timewatch* here tell the story clearly and systematically, but it does so with well-selected footage used without redundancy. It contains archive material which either shows the story as it unfolds or illustrates excellently the tenor of the times.

It starts – and this assertion is repeated towards the end – by stating that the libel trial completely vindicated Lord Aldington, but that this does not mean that interest in the case itself is reduced. Late in the programme it notes that Tolstoy's defeat was based upon his having made a mistake in the date of

Aldington's departure from Austria, and therefore wrongly attributing blame. It nowhere mentions the controversy surrounding that date, or the fact that Aldington is alleged to have changed his mind about it. In this sense the programme can be said to accept the verdict of the libel trial, namely, that Aldington was not to blame. It nowhere suggests that the trial was anything but fair.

Aldington's position is put by his allies and associates, Brigadiers Tryon-Wilson and Cowgill. Cowgill's claims of operational necessity are given due space and respect. Sir Charles Villiers, a partisan specialist in the Second World War and later a very distinguished industrialist and writer, can also be said to be on the Aldington 'side' in the sense that he explains the initiative in terms of the prevailing political and military climate. He does not however subscribe to the view that the refugees were deported out of fear of imminent war with Tito's Yugoslavia, one of the arguments in defence of the initiative.

While being scrupulously polite to the Aldington case therefore, the producers do not in any way disguise the belief that the initiative was shameful and not worthy of an army that had claimed to be on the side of truth and justice. An array of testimonials attest to the dishonesty practised on the refugees in arranging their deportation and the brutality with which it was executed. British officers of different ranks and backgrounds and regiments admit their part, supporting the evidence of survivors. One, a (then) young girl who, getting away from Auschwitz concentration camp during the German collapse, joined herself to some Cossacks and their families only to find herself being beaten and shot at by British troops, is particularly arresting. A very moving witness, she was one of the few who escaped in the chaos as the troops coerced the refugees into accepting deportation.

Everything is done by the programme makers to avoid legal action, and to be impartial in the manner required by the *BBC Producers' Guidelines* (BBC 1996). For example, in defence of the initiative it has often been said that there was chaos in Austria at that time, or that the British authorities were under extreme physical, political and administrative pressure. Although these claims are not always borne out by the recollections of British survivors, the programme nevertheless repeats them, presumably in an attempt to be fair to those responsible for the initiative. Moreover the British troops are put in as favourable a light as possible; the stress some of them felt at having to comply with orders requiring them to be dishonest and brutal is emphasised. One officer tells how he wrote a critical report of the proceedings, mentioning the distaste his soldiers had for them, which he was ordered to repudiate in a later report (Nicholson, speaking in BBC 1991), reminding the viewer that not all documents are factual, even if they are old and official.

The question of responsibility is examined carefully. No explanation is presented as to how it was that clear policies by superiors Churchill and Alexander should have been ignored at the executive level. British officers on the ground 'knew there was something wrong ... many of them had no connection with Russia' in the case of the identifiable Cossack units (Davies, in BBC 1991); about a thousand separately encamped Germans were handed to the Russians (about 80 per cent allegedly died in slave labour) following an order of 24 May which included Germans and camp followers (i.e. women, children, the elderly) although it was known to all the British that they were not Soviets; the Yugoslavs deported against precise orders from Prime Minister Churchill appear to have been butchered as they anticipated and as their British guards expected. The man who negoti-ated with the British and then organised the mass slaughter is interviewed arrestingly, as is one of the British officers who, with repugnance, lied to them so that they could be tricked into deportation (Nicholson, speaking in BBC 1991). The mass graves are found and filmed. Official documents, loca-tion shots and primary testimony are woven together well to create a convincing case.

No one is named a war criminal, nor is anything negative attributed to any named person, with the exception of the Yugoslav officer who condemns himself. The producers have been extremely careful to obey the BBC's guide-lines which stipulate, 'We must not use language inadvertently so as to suggest value judgements, commitment or lack of objectivity' (BBC 1996: 7).

Lord Aldington is himself treated with kid gloves. He is introduced as 'a bright young officer who, at thirty years of age, was the second youngest Brigadier in the army' (BBC 1991). When, later in the programme, there is a description of the deception practised upon the women and children to ensure that they also be handed over, the narrator gives Aldington's own justi-fication:

> despite the fact that those civilians were not told where they were going, Brigadier Low (now Lord Aldington) said at the libel trial that he felt that he had probably let them accompany the men out of compassion.
>
> (Commentary, BBC 1991)

The treatment is not at all sensationalist, yet is sensational in the sense that its witnesses are moving – those who suffered as well as those who are ashamed of carrying out the orders which caused them to suffer. What is telling is the failure of the more senior officers, the decision-makers of the time or their defendants, to acknowledge any kind of responsibility or even admit the enormity of what was done, although this may be a producer's device.

The impartial viewer would, I believe, come away with the strong belief that a wrong was done and that someone somewhere is not coming clean. The fact that the accusations have not stood up to scrutiny does not mean that there is no villain, or villains. Although describing Tolstoy as discredited, in allowing him to explain why the case matters the producers demonstrate that this is an important story: 'I'm not saying that what I say is the truth, but if somebody doesn't fight for the truth to be investigated and recognised, and that's what I want, terrible events like this will be repeated' (Tolstoy in BBC 1991).

Ruthless men, in other words, must know that they will be held accountable for their actions even fifty years later; the rules of decency apply just as much to the victors as to the vanquished; the same type of criminal person can appear in every society if he be but given the opportunity or if he thinks he will not be found out; the representation of unbesmirched British honour must not be defended with lies and evasions; in this case ideals such as justice and compassion were betrayed and it is necessary to know why.

Discussion

For British society, the most immediate lessons of this case have been legal ones. In various legal actions to which he was party, Tolstoy was allegedly treated without the respect accorded to Aldington, a disrespect amounting to partiality. There were failures to take account of evidence, failure to acknowledge the damage caused to Tolstoy's side by the 'disappearance' of evidence and the failure to keep (or supply) transcripts. The size of the award against Tolstoy was extreme; at the time it was the largest ever such award. It was unfair in that it was clearly calculated to destroy Tolstoy; Lord Aldington's case was being underwritten by the Sun Alliance Insurance Company (an interesting issue in itself, but one mainly for the shareholders of that company).

At a conference of lawyers and senior journalists in September 1990 the Tolstoy–Aldington case was cited as demonstrating that 'the present legal arrangements [in libel cases] were unreliable in the extreme and should be reformed' (Norton-Taylor 1990). Charles Gray QC, Aldington's barrister when he won £1.5 million damages from Tolstoy, stated that he believed juries should not be used at all in libel trials. Another leading lawyer, Michael Beloff, 'called for a curtailment of judges' powers to ban reports of court proceedings, powers which were unknown in America or continental Europe' (Norton-Taylor 1990).

There were alleged obstructions to Tolstoy's attempts to appeal which have been detailed above. The ban on discussion of the case has also excited interest. As a consequence of a decision of the Court of Appeal in 1987, it is held that an injunction 'against one is for all' (Welsh and Greenwood 1999). The injunction put upon Tolstoy in 1989 not to disseminate his views was, after 1991, regarded by the BBC as extending to 'A British Betrayal', screening of which would apparently be in contempt of court; when the Series Editor (and Producer of 'A British Betrayal') was invited to speak about the case to students he regretted that he could not, because of the injunction. Moreover it is technically contempt of court for Tolstoy to carry out research and supply information to the media.

There are more general lessons from the case. A few years ago, before the

Birmingham Six, Guildford Four, Scott Inquiry and so on, it was hardly credible to British people first that connivance in covering up could be possible, and second that judges could be so biased, ignorant and wrong. The Tolstoy libel case has probably further undermined faith in the system. It has also focused attention on the cavalier way in which elected politicians can deal with public records in Britain, and on the need for rules and systems to prevent this.

Many people regretted that the issue came to light because of how it reflected upon British chivalry, and some allowed their regret to cloud their sense of justice; others gloried in the undermining of what they saw as a nonsensical myth. Neither attitude is very laudable. However, they do point up the emotions aroused and the issues raised by the investigation of history.

Historians are forever reinterpreting history, knowing that each period's history is influenced by the passions, prejudices, policies and limitations of its time. They can bring to bear new evidence, new techniques and new attitudes. They are not necessarily aiming at a permanent solution, but may be trying to challenge the prevailing interpretation because that is a worthwhile contribution to debate in itself. Not all historical reinterpretation will be of immediate influence upon us; Joseph Needham's empirical researches for Science and Civilisation in China have both changed our understanding of science and trade history and challenged our Eurocentrism, but it may take generations for these to permeate daily life. Emmanuel Todd's theories of development and political process may be in the same category. Of more immediate relevance, in 1999 an amateur Irish historian produced a startling piece of research, the evidence of which was meticulously transparent and respectfully applauded in reviews; he demonstrated from the historical evidence that the image of Oliver Cromwell as the butcher of Drogheda, an image so powerful in Irish history as to have been almost a justification in itself for the existence of nationalist terrorism, is a myth. Moreover, it was a myth invented intentionally by an identifiable individual in the nineteenth century, whose ghost (we must suppose) has since had the satisfaction of seeing the nonsense he created being repeated by eminent historians and political propagandists alike.[4] That is the rethinking of history with immediate relevance.

Investigative journalists are interested in the here and now of the past. The investment of time and resources is such that they will usually select topics which they believe will have, or can be made to have, wide general interest, perhaps a mass audience. They can appeal to the thrill of dark secrets; to the revelation which comes from overturning assumptions. They can make use of availability of documents earlier kept classified or the accessibility of people who, either because circumstances have changed or because they themselves have changed, are willing to talk. They can build on memories kept alive by resentments and anguish.

The story of the Cossacks did all this. Part of its fascination is that guilt has not been finally ascribed.

NOTES

1 Laurence Rees, editor of *Timewatch*, was not able to make himself available to discuss his team's work, hence the limited information on *Timewatch* itself. Nevertheless it seemed to me that the story has been so very prominent, and has so many aspects of interest to investigators, as to be the obvious example.

2 I believe that this is a reasonable summary of the position of some of Tolstoy's partisans, including Sir Bernard Braine, Viscount Cranbourne, Nigel Nicholson, Chapman Pincher, Alexander Solzhenitsyn, and Roger Scruton.

3 Krasnov was a Russian soldier who held out against the Bolsheviks during the Civil War of 1917–1920; after the White defeat he fled to France. Following the German invasion of the Soviet Union he helped inspire an Army of Liberation that was intended to free Russia initially from the Communists, and then from the Nazis. Krasnov was one of those in the Displaced Persons camps who would be handed over and killed.

4 Doubtless this subject will be revisited, but in the meantime Tom Reilly (1999) seems to have the best of it. See also R. Dudley-Edwards (1999).

BIBLIOGRAPHY

BBC (1991) *Timewatch*: 'A British Betrayal'. London: BBC. (Producer: Laurence Rees)

BBC (1996) *Producers' Guidelines*. London: BBC.

BBC (1999) 'Timewatch Remit'. Notes supplied by *Timewatch* office.

Bethell, N. (1974) *The Last Secret*. London: André Deutsch.

Booker, C. (1997) *A Looking Glass War*. London: Duckworth.

de Burgh, J. (1995) interview with Hugo de Burgh at Naas, 12 May 1995.

Dudley-Edwards, R. (1999) The Good Soldier. *Sunday Times*, 23 May 1999.

Faulkner, R. (1998) Tolstoy Pamphlet. On the internet at www.tolstoy.co.uk

Horne, A. (1988) *Macmillan, Volume 1: 1894–1956*. London: Macmillan.

Horne, A. (1998) Letter to *Times*, 30 October 1998.

Johnson, D. (1990) A vindication that came too late. *Times*, 19 October 1990.

Mitchell, I. (1997) *The Cost of a Reputation*. Lagavulin: Topical.

Needham, J. with Wang Ling (1954) *Science and Civilisation in China*. Cambridge: Cambridge University Press.

Norman, M. (1990) 'I loved the romance of the Tolstoys': Count Nikolai Tolstoy: a childhood. *Times*, 11 August 1990.

Norton-Taylor, R. (1990) Tolstoy conducts his own libel appeal. *Guardian*, 11 January 1990.

Rayment, T. (1996) The massacre and the ministers. *Sunday Times*, 7 April 1996: 2.

Reilly, T. (1999) *Cromwell: An Honourable Enemy*. Dublin: Brandon.

Todd, E. (1987) *The Causes of Progress*. Oxford: Blackwell.

Tolstoy, N. (1977) *Victims of Yalta*. London: Hodder and Stoughton.

Tolstoy, N. (1986) *The Minister and the Massacres*. London: Century.

Tolstoy, N. (1997) Investigating the forced repatriation of the Cossacks. Talk given to the students of the MA Investigative Journalism course at Nottingham Trent University, 13 November 1997.

Tolstoy@enterprise.net OR http://www.uvsc.edu.tolstoy

Welsh, T. and Greenwood, W. (1999) *McNae's Essential Law for Journalists*. London: Butterworths.

FURTHER READING

Mitchell, I. (1997) *The Cost of a Reputation*. Lagavulin: Topical.

15

PILLAGING THE ENVIRONMENTALISTS

An example from *The Cook Report*

Hugo de Burgh

In this section we look at two phenomena, widespread concern about the environment with reference to the problems and opportunities this poses investigative journalists; and how *The Cook Report* has made investigative journalism into popular theatre. Taken together they focus our attention on how complicated scientific issues can be dealt with by the media, and the risks of trivialisation, of tendentious sourcing and of misinformation.

The media and the environment

Environment issues became mainstream news in the 1970s; in the UK the industrial correspondents started to disappear and were replaced by environment correspondents. Their popularity may now be on the wane as readers and viewers become inured to doom-mongering or at least more sceptical as to whether environment reports have immediate relevance to them.

Research has shown that citizens of rich countries, especially women, have until now evinced much concern about the environment; the spectacular burgeoning of pressure groups which, in some cases, have developed from being eccentric fringe protesters into large, wealthy and sophisticated policy pushers, is one indication of the trend. However, there is little agreement on the role that the media have played in this (Anderson 1997: 171). One model of communication effects is perhaps pertinent here. Anderson (following McQuail and Windahl 1981) suggests that:

> individual opinions are highly dependent upon what is perceived to be the 'majority' view on any given issue ... individuals gain clues as to the relative prominence of particular points of view. If an individual's own position does not seem to accord with the dominant view then they are seen as being much less likely to express their opinions than if they are perceived to have wide support.
>
> (Anderson 1997: 78)

Thus opinion polls, reported in the media, influence people's behaviour; high profile campaigns such as that for lead free petrol (see Chapter 16) have a dual function; they may achieve the stated objective, say a change in government policy, but they do this in part because the very prominence of the issue created by the campaign has convinced many people that the campaigners' assessment of the situation is the dominant view and that they should come on board. Brosius' and Kepplinger's (1990) ideology diffusion model shows how pressure groups have their influence extended through specialist magazines, which then have their articles picked up by general magazines whose concerns are picked up by the popular media from which they diffuse into the general public. Other studies cited by Anderson (1997: 179) suggest that the influence of the media on the general population in respect of environmental issues is small; the impact that they have is upon policy-makers. This ties in with theories of media influence described by Wayne Parsons (1995). Other research (Bell 1991) tells us that only if people already have awareness of the issue in question do they learn anything more from the media.

Climatic change resulting from ozone depletion and global warming became an international political issue in the 1970s. Bell (1994) has studied its treatment by the media in New Zealand, the economy of which is particularly sensitive to climate, as well as the effect of this reporting upon the populace. Bell's findings on treatment of the issue are salutary for journalists. He shows how scientists' views have been distorted by journalists and he shows the processes through which the information they provide to journalists goes, and why it ends up so distorted. Five techniques are applied:

1 'illocutionary force' is used to *assert* what scientists prefer to *speculate* upon;
2 overstatement;
3 proposition of imminence, presenting phenomena as certain or imminent;
4 imaginability, picturing the topic graphically so that a strong and memorable impression is created;
5 confusion, the blending of information such as that on ozone depletion or the greenhouse effect are, for example, merged into one great awfulness.

As a result of the application of these techniques readers may see a multi-faceted catastrophe all around them; they may be taught to believe that a given phenomenon, upon which scientists are merely speculating might touch us in hundreds of years, is certain and imminent, if not already here (ibid. 1994). Another reaction is that they may cease to believe anything on the subject at all.

Sources and the problems of sourcing

That sourcing may pose problems for journalists is very well illustrated by Matt Ridley's salutary essay collections, *Down to Earth* I and II (1995 and 1996). In them he looks afresh at the environmental issues of the moment: acid rain, fisheries policy, fuel resources, culling of pests, population, famine warnings, rising sea levels, dangers from sunlight and so forth, and either questions the science upon which the scares are based or questions the proposed solutions, intentionally taking a sceptical or 'contrarian' (as he calls it) view.

He shows on many occasions that the fashionable view is not necessarily that of the scientists closest to the issue in question, for example on acid rain and the melanomas supposedly resulting from greater exposure to sunlight. He provides a convincing reminder that it is easy for journalists to get sucked into fashions if they do not carefully examine their bases. An illustration of this not cited by Ridley is the way journalists have, over some 35 years, failed to interrogate the overpopulation scare. This has been the most famous and long-running series of apocalyptic predictions for which journalists have fallen; the result of failure to question the evidence adequately or to consider alternative views in the scientific community have been policies that have affected the lives of millions (Simon 1992, Kasun 1988).

Ridley accounts for gullibility on environmental issues by blaming the pressure groups who use hyperbole, he says (Ridley 1996: 79, 87, 101) in the competition for funds.[1] In dealing with the environment, journalists are faced with some wealthy and powerful interest groups, public relations officials and campaigners, and he recommends knowing the sources of your information and the background of your informants.

Shoemaker has argued that it is not the justice of a source's case that affects journalists' selection of sources but the source's extroversion, assertiveness, credibility (assigned to them by the journalists!), accessibility and quotability (Shoemaker 1996: 182). In the UK the most active environmentalist operations are Greenpeace and Friends of the Earth. There are several hundred other bodies from the Nature Conservancy Council to the Royal Society for the Protection of Birds and the National Trust. Some of these organisations are believed to be both rich and influential, with policies and monetary interests to defend. Greenpeace is suspected by some of launching some of its campaigns to boost membership rather than to call attention to a real problem (Ridley 1996); it has been argued that the National Trust, Britain's best established conservation body, has argued to serve sectional interests while presenting itself as altruistic (C4 1994). Their weapons are those of all pressure groups and include briefings by plausible experts, press releases in print, video or audio form, pseudo events and contacts in the worlds of the decision-makers and the opinion-formers. Journalists on the whole like sources that seem established and mainstream; in a study of the coverage of environmental disasters by newspapers, it was found that journalists were more likely to rely upon government sources than upon scientists (Hornig 1991).

The Cook Report

Central Broadcasting is one of the fifteen regional Independent Television (ITV) companies in the UK (London has two) and is part of Carlton Communications, which has two ITV licenses: (weekday) London and the Midlands (Upshon 1997). In its portfolio Carlton also has substantial percentages of Meridian TV, the London News Network, GMTV and Select TV. Central Broadcasting's franchise covers a quarter of England with a population of nearly 9 million. The conditions of the franchise require that Central supply certain types of programmes, in particular regional programmes and news, although the core schedule, as with other ITV regions, is provided by the Network Centre to which Central is a substantial contributor of programmes.

Its network output is large and famous; perhaps the most famous are *Family Fortunes*, *Inspector Morse* and *The Cook Report*. *The Cook Report* was started in 1985 by Roger Cook, the New Zealander who had been the creator of the BBC's investigative programme *Checkpoint*[2]. Among other things, the series has exposed child pornography, protection rackets in Northern Ireland, baby trading in Brazil, loan sharks, the ivory trade, war criminals in Bosnia and the Russian black market in plutonium. 'A number ... have been followed by successful police prosecutions of the villains or major changes in the law' (Central Television 1997). Cook is proud of 'our after-sales service' by which he means giving evidence in court that will convict the villains and cites among the programme's achievements legislation on child pornography, an extradition treaty between the UK and Spain and the closure of a Hong Kong refugee camp.

> What we are trying to do is to reveal what we think is damaging to the public, whether it be child pornography or gangsters. And taking people off the streets who shouldn't be there like the members of the UDA [Ulster Defence Association] who were making money through extortion of building companies. It was our evidence got them convicted. The object is to take the case of the victims as far as you possibly can; I see investigative journalism as public service broadcasting at its best.
>
> (Cook 1999)

The Cook Report is expensive to produce, over £180,000 a programme, and needs a star presenter of courage and initiative. In 1996 the Network Centre (which takes *The Cook Report* from the ITV company making it for the national ITV network) considered abolishing the programme as part of a revamp of current affairs, notwithstanding that it achieved remarkably high viewing ratings for current affairs.[3] However, it thought better and *The Cook Report* remains in the form of hour-long specials approximately every two months.

The hallmarks of *The Cook Report* are that a popular topic is selected, in the example below canned lion hunting with its implications of cowardly killers parodying the noble hunter of yore, set within a theme that triggers off some satisfying emotions such as, in this case, those associated with the battle to defend the environment, and endangered species. The story form is employed and as layer upon layer is revealed you can almost hear the master storyteller whispering 'and then?' as each twist in the tale is made to increase your involvement. The viewer expects, and gets, the elements appropriate to the genre: a righteous champion (Mr Cook), a villain, assumed identities, a sting, a chase, victim or victims who will be vindicated, even rewarded. In other words, the drama narrative style is typical, rather than the upturned pyramid of straight reportage.

That characteristic of *The Cook Report* has been copied by other programmes since, but when first used was very remarkable, as were the atmospheric effects including the hand-held camera and eerie music (Beckett 1995). Viewers at home anticipate a dramatic confrontation; according to audience research they 'like to be made to sit on the edge of their seats' (Cook 1999). Criticisms have focused on whether these narrative methods diminish the seriousness of the issues under consideration, or make it impossible to tackle some issues. Tim Tate, formerly one of *The Cook Report*'s producers, jokes that editorial meetings revolved around the question of 'who's going to hit Roger this time?' (Tate 1997). Cook denies this vehemently. For all his modesty, however, *The Cook Report is* the man; he is a hero to many, known to have received death threats, and seen on screen being assaulted by indignant villains as he braves their wrath.

To draw attention to the artefact is not to diminish the work of investigation nor the public service motivation of teams who seek to right wrong and overcome evil. In the Cook investigation into the pop music business (Central 1997b), the fact that Cook managed to hold our attention for two programmes on the subject was surely due both to the narrative skill and to the research, research that revealed suspected but hitherto unproven naughtiness in the manner in which 'successes' in the pop records charts could be effected by the spreading of a little money here and there. Cook found an attractive but otherwise ordinary girl, created a pop group for her, produced her song and promoted it in order to demonstrate the entire process of manufacturing pop celebrity. The programmes were entertaining and, like some other Cook Reports but unlike some other investigative journalism whose shelf-life is limited to the duration of the topic in question, would likely hold interest as repeats.

The programme has been fiercely criticised from time to time, never more so than over its two programmes on cot deaths (1994) and one that investigated monies donated to help the strike of the National Union of Mineworkers

(1990). In March 1990 *The Cook Report* combined with the *Daily Mirror* in what the *Mirror*'s proprietor, the late Robert Maxwell, described as 'classic investigative journalism'. The investigative journalists exposed not only that the National Union of Miners (NUM), which had been battling with the then government for 10 years over restructuring of the energy industry, had been in receipt of foreign funds during its strikes, but that some of the money donated by Soviet miners and Colonel Ghaddafi of Libya had been used to make life more comfortable for senior officials of the NUM.

In his book on the issue, Seamas Milne argues not only that the details were wrong but that the journalists involved were the dupes of the miners' leaders' political enemies and of the notorious secret services who planted ideas and clues and provided surveillance reports and convenient interpretations of them to the reporters (Milne 1995). These accusations are rejected entirely by the journalists involved. Suggestions that the programme was 'manipulated by the Secret Services' are risible, says Cook. Allegations made in the programme were all at least dual sourced and all facts thoroughly checked (Cook 1999).

The Cook Report was attacked in another television programme, this time C4 *Dispatches*, which also used the trademark Cook doorstepping technique on Cook himself. It was successfully shrugged off by Cook, whereas by common consent its use on NUM leader Arthur Scargill had been damaging to Scargill, who was seen at a disadvantage, uttering what seemed to be legalistic phrases about requiring notice to questions. The *Daily Express* described it as 'trial by television' (Milne 1995: 49).

The cot deaths programmes put forward a theory from a leading consultant scientist that the fire retardants recommended by the government for use in the manufacture of baby mattresses could, in some circumstances, produce poisonous gases. According to one commentator, there followed a panic among parents of young children who bought up new mattresses in large quantities and expressed their fears in tens of thousands of letters and telephone calls to the media and to advice sources (Beckett 1995). The BBC's science programme, QED, examined the claims by *The Cook Report* and attacked them. Cook defends his programme on the grounds that it gave a platform to the views of the most respected scientific authority, views that have never been disproven as one of the causes of cot deaths, that its attackers used research that was itself flawed and that, regardless of the mechanisms which connected mattresses and deaths, the withdrawal of the mattresses resulted in a further decrease in cot deaths (Cook 1999).

These two serious criticisms must be seen within context. If you accept that investigative journalism must happen, then you accept that there will be opponents of it and that, from time to time, the research will be characterised as selective, the authorities as eccentric, the researchers over-enthusiastic, the managers as failing to make the right checks and for failing to spot the hidden hand of outside interests. In the long career of *The Cook Report* it is hardly surprising to find some carping.

Example: 'Making a Killing'

The public interest basis for this programme is that, while there is an international agreement to protect species that are facing extinction – rhinos, turtles, elephants, tigers and so forth – thanks to mankind's taking over more and more of the earth's surface, this agreement, CITES or the Convention on International Trade in Endangered Species of Wild Flora and Fauna is known to be widely flouted. Evidence of this has been obtained by, for example, the Environmental Information Agency (despite its official sounding name, a pressure group of activists with skills in video production and investigation) (Grundy 1996) and in this case by journalists. 'Making a Killing' tells the story of a chase: how Roger Cook got evidence of the trade in species supposedly protected by CITES, how he recorded the illegal and cruel killings of such species and then took his evidence to the South African High Commission (Embassy) to demand action on behalf of us all.

The transcript of this programme is self-explanatory and relatively short. I have therefore decided to incorporate it, slightly edited, and am grateful for permission of Central Television to do so. Readers should, in reading this script, note

- the tease at the start that suggests you will see a kill;
- the gradual accumulation of evidence, some obtained with covert filming;
- the appeal to our sympathies and to our anger at the dastardly customers;
- the sting on the dealers;
- the build-up to confrontation;
- the confrontation;
- the declaration to the world.

'Making a Killing'

Generic montage of dramatic shots of guns, chases … exciting music … Cook driving a 4-wheel in Africa …

ROGER COOK Tonight, hunting down the hunters – we expose the men who make big money from the killing of protected and endangered animals.

South African 'gamekeeper' beside stuffed lion.

SANDY MCDONALD Two-thirds down, one-third up, right on the shoulder blade. Smoke it in there and he'll bounce around and make a lot of noise and run off and die probably …

Montage ends with the generic 'Cook confrontation' picture, cut to overheads of Kruger National Park.

ROGER COOK This is the Kruger National Park, perhaps the world's best known reserve for wild animals running free in an area the size of Wales. Here, millions of tourists, the majority of them British, have enjoyed seeing the well protected big game that gives South Africa its reputation as a safe haven for the continent's endangered species.

Our investigation has uncovered the shocking truth these tourists have not been told – no animal here is safe, even the King of the Jungle.

We've discovered that even lions are being stolen from under the noses of game wardens to die at point-blank range and end up on some rich man's wall.

Change of scene, general views Costa del Sol.

Spain's Costa del Sol, playground of the wealthy is where *The Cook Report* has come to uncover the unacceptable face of big game hunting – the wealth is conspicuous, less obvious are the unscrupulous middle men who cater to the basest of instincts – middle men like José Iglesias and Luis Gomez, on the face of it legitimate sportsmen, but for the right money, they'll arrange for you to shoot anything you like, any way you like, anywhere in the world – however endangered.

Change of scene – meeting.

ROGER COOK Within minutes of meeting Mr Gomez, *The Cook Report* undercover team was offered the illegal shooting of gorillas, tiger and jaguar.

As his credentials, he offered this video of a jaguar hunt in Bolivia complete with posturing client and prohibited kill.

Change of scene – company office.

Back in Marbella, we set up a bogus company, we pretended to be agents for rich people who wanted hunting trophies, no matter how illegally obtained.

Cook to camera:

This is a story of cruelty and greed. From an office in this country renowned for its devotion to hunting in all its forms world wide, we set up a cover company which offered rich rewards to game hunters who could arrange for our clients to shoot anything at all. The response was astonishing.

The Spanish hunters recommended South Africa for the sort of hunting we were interested in.

Change of scene – back to Africa.

ROGER COOK Our team found this ranch run by professional hunter Chris Sussens on the edge of the famous Kruger National Park.

The distressing pictures you're about to see, taken on a legal Sussens hunt, were to massage his French client's ego.

Hunter shown killing a lion in the bush.

It was a short trek but a slow death for this lion.

It took several minutes and six more shots than we're going to show you for the lion to die. They didn't want to spoil the trophy by shooting him in the head.

Covert filming.

Sussens can also arrange the illegal shooting of big cats in small enclosures in what's called a canned hunt.

Covert filming.

CHRIS SUSSENS The only time I can actually guarantee an animal, it's going to be like a canned animal which I don't like doing and that's normally not done in this area, we have to go up towards the Free State, we'll give the odd operator there that's got lions in big camps and you can go into a big camp and you can shoot a lion there. Basically, this camp where this chap's got the lions is about a 20 hectare camp.

Change of scene – young man in view.

ROGER COOK Bruce Hamilton was once a farm manager on what he thought was a lion breeding project. When he discovered the speciality was actually canned hunting, he left in disgust having taken this video.

Actuality of lioness beside wire, cubs other side, unhappy.

The lioness has been separated from her bewildered cubs who still follow their mother's steps on the other side of a wire enclosure. As they look on, a German hunter is preparing for the kill.

BRUCE HAMILTON It's totally disgusting what happens here in South Africa. A lot of wealthy game ranch owners make a lot of money out of shooting lions which have been bred in cages and purely for that purpose. They take them out either by darting or by baiting them out of these cages and an overseas client will come in sitting on the back of a Land Rover or on foot and just shoot it for his own pleasure.

ROGER COOK Roy Plath is the wealthy man who owned that lioness. We contacted him to see if he'd sell us another of his tame lions for a canned hunt. Keen to take our client's money, he lets us film examples of the prey without showing the wire enclosures to preserve the illusion of a fair free-range hunt. We asked him to record a personal invitation to our bogus client. He was happy to oblige.

Pitch to camera by:

ROY PLATH Mr James Rogers, nice to meet you, look forward to meeting you in South Africa. I'd like to say, as you can see, it looks like we've got just the lion here for you and we look forward to you being able to come out and shoot this lion and have a trophy for your office or home as it pleases you.

We see the lion.

ROGER COOK Mr Plath had also wanted to kill this young lioness, Shamwari, because she had rickets. Conservationists stepped in, and one of South Africa's few lion sanctuaries is now her home. Safe from what the owner regards as a barbaric practice.

SIMON TRICKEY Canned lion hunting is like shooting fish in a barrel, it's unethical, it's bloody easy, and it's earning a lot of people a lot of money.

Airport scenes.

ROGER COOK For the moment, away from lion hunting to a different quarry in London as Luis Gomez, the Spanish middle man, arrives to explain how his plans for the illegal gorilla hunt are progressing. We meet him at Heathrow and take him to the man we've told him is the brother of a hugely wealthy client.

Covert filming of a meeting between Cook and dealers.

Gomez, on the left, has already offered us gorilla but is guarded in front of our interpreter but he confirms we'll get exactly what we want and wants another 12,000 dollars to smuggle the gorilla's head out of the country.

ROGER COOK And in the meantime, what I'm going to do, just to keep you going, I'm going to give you 2,000 dollars in advance ...

Gomez refuses to give a receipt but will supply the coordinates of the hunting ground in Cameroon so we can fly out undetected.

Scenes of gorillas.

ROGER COOK The hunt in prospect horrifies gorilla experts like Ian Redmond who says there are only 12,000 of these imposing animals left.

IAN REDMOND *(Interviewed)* They are almost human and to go and shoot one, it's I guess, it's a ... it's a sickening insight to the kind of species that we belong to.

Back to the covertly filmed meeting.

ROGER COOK Gomez says we can also hunt endangered tigers in Malaysia using his corrupt contacts.

Tigers in wire enclosures ... splendid tigers.

But why risk being caught hunting endangered tigers in Malaysia when you can shoot captive ones in a private canned hunt in South Africa for 100,000 dollars apiece?

This is another wealthy businessman, Farnie Roberts, his farm has Bengal tigers, black leopard and jaguar. Like Roy Plath, he's eager to hide the wire enclosures from our wealthy clients and even cuts a hole in the wire for our camera.

No hunting permit would ever be given to shoot these cats and certainly not in the canned conditions Mr Roberts has on offer.

Covert filming.

FARNIE ROBERTS I have got enclosures which are like 100 metres by 100 metres. Something like that. Where you and your clients and the tiger can't come out.

Undercover researcher in discussion with Roberts.

FARNIE ROBERTS And this one is available to shoot …

Picture of a jaguar.

ROGER COOK This beautiful jaguar is surplus to Mr Roberts requirements so for 100,000 dollars, our client can shoot him too.

We showed our evidence to actress Virginia McKenna who's been devoted to the wellbeing of the big cats of Africa ever since she starred in *Born Free* with Elsa the lioness in the 1960s.

McKenna testimonial at her home.

VIRGINIA MCKENNA I don't think anyone except someone with a sick or warped mind could call this kind of hunting sport and from the evidence that I have seen on your programme, it should be banned from this moment onwards.

Lions in shot.

ROGER COOK South Africa again and more doomed lions. This time it's hunter Mossie Mostert who runs another outfit operating on the edge of the Kruger Park. He wants to sell our client one of his eighty-six caged animals for hunting including his rare white lions in 5 years' time when they've bred enough to spare.

White lions.

But it's in Kruger National Park, the world's best known conservation area that the King of the Beasts is quietly and secretly disappearing.

Cook looking at elephants.

In 3 days in Kruger, we've seen lots of wildlife but neither hide nor hair of a lion, the very symbol of this national park. One good reason perhaps why lions are less often seen than they used to be is that they're being lured across the border and into the sights of the canned hunters.

Taxidermists' operations.

ROGER COOK It's easy to see why the pressure is on to provide big game hunters with a steady supply of prey – the Americans alone spend 110 million dollars a year in South Africa obtaining trophies like these and it's a market which is growing rapidly as the taxidermists of South Africa work round the clock to send their wealthy customers their bloody souvenirs.

Covert filming in McDonald's office as she counts her money.

TRACEY MCDONALD So many are allowed to be exported because they feel that they're endangered, which is also a load of nonsense.

ROGER COOK This is Tracey McDonald, who runs what she claims is one of the biggest hunting outfits in Southern Africa with her husband Sandy. Last year, she boasts her company arranged the shooting of more than a thousand animals but we've discovered many of the most profitable ones are actually stolen.

Once again, we pay a hefty deposit and, captured by our secret camera, she explains how the tourist and the South African government are being cheated as Kruger Park lions are stolen for canned hunting through the boundary fences.

TRACEY MCDONALD You just dig a little bit under the fence and you leave her a little piece of rotten meat on that side and then you drag it with the blood running through and that lion picks that scent up so easy and it just comes through.

Back in the bush.

ROGER COOK Stealing lions from Kruger these days is literally a push-button job. One, to turn off the electric fence and the other, to start the lion call tape on your ghetto blaster. It doesn't take long for the lions to answer the call and come right under the fence.

And this is the fate a Kruger lion will face – death in the closely controlled-conditions of a canned hunt. Bruce Hamilton explains how the lioness met her end.

Lioness and cubs again.

BRUCE HAMILTON The lioness had three cubs. We took her out of the camp that morning into a hundred hectare enclosure, which is not legal, and she was still running up and down the fence, she wouldn't leave the cubs even though a bait was used to try and lure her away from the fences so that ... the hunter wouldn't see the fences and be caught up in the illusion.

Over shots of violent death of lioness:

ROGER COOK Some illusion.

Gunshot.

BRUCE HAMILTON Even though she wouldn't leave the fences, he still shot her. You could see the cubs on the other side of the fence but that didn't bother them. Even when the lioness was skinned and the milk was pouring out of her teats, it didn't bother the hunter nor the professional hunter that she was still producing milk for those cubs and now they didn't have a mother.

VIRGINIA MCKENNA Just unbelievable isn't it really? To separate a lioness from her cubs, to wound the animal so that she dies in agony; how anyone could actually find pleasure in that kind of hunting so-called must be really sick, that's all I can say.

Change of scene – hotels etc.

At lunch table with friends/targets.

ROGER COOK In Barcelona we're about to meet José Iglesias and Luis Gomez who think they're collecting 40,000 dollars from us for the illegal gorilla hunt in Cameroon. All the animals they've offered us in perfect English are protected by international law under what's called the CITES convention.

I think you should know something – I am a television reporter and you have been offering us three animals, protected to shoot. We can shoot gorillas pictured in this book which you've just shown me, the gorillas that we could shoot, you're offering us jaguar, that's CITES too, that's illegal. You've offered us tiger, you are offering us the opportunity to kill CITES 1 animals, this is illegal. Illegal animals to kill.

Gomez/Iglesias, rather surprised, forget how to speak English, mumble, rise to go; Cook shows he's miked up.

ROGER COOK And what's more, you speak perfectly good English. ... What's more, Mr Iglesias, I've been recording you speaking perfectly good English on that microphone ...

Iglesias and Gomez beat a retreat but they'll be hearing from the Spanish authorities now we've passed on a dossier of their illegal hunting activities.

Change of scene – South Africa and a hunt – Cook in hunting gear.

ROGER COOK The South African hunters think they are taking businessman James Rogers, alias Roger Cook, for a ride. He's not meant to know this is a canned hunt. In fact, we're conning the hunters by recording the event for what we say is a vanity video.

Wheezing and puffed up to play the part of an incompetent and unfit hunter, in need of all the help he can get, and easy prey for Mossie Mostert who owns the land and Sandy McDonald who runs the hunt.

SANDY MCDONALD It's not too bad once you're here, it's on the road you know, it's pretty bad out there.

Let's step inside, having something to drink and go through a bit of a procedure here and what ...

A park house, McDonald the 'gamekeeper' beside a stuffed lion.

Voice-over scenes in 'Gamekeeper' training room

ROGER COOK They split the 18,000 dollars being paid for this one-hour expedition. No television programme has ever before got this far inside the secret and sordid world of canned hunting but first, a quick lesson in lion killing.

SANDY MCDONALD Being a park lion, he's not too wary about humans, cars and that sort of stuff which means he's pretty relaxed, but once he's stood up we've got his attention, it's very important, the shot placement is very important, our first shot is the most important shot. After that we'll sort any problems if there are any. And what you've got to remember Mr Rogers is that we want to try and break a limb, that's the most important thing on any cat. Now he's got ... just follow his leg up, two-thirds down, one-third up ... is the vital spot and to break a leg. We really want to get him that, if it so happens that he'd be wounded, he's got one leg less which makes it a hell of a lot easier for us. It's easier on the dogs, it's easier on everything else. Now he'll have a bigger mane than this, maybe a bit longer this way than this one. So, it's important that mentally, you don't take the mane for his chest, remember that ...

SANDY MCDONALD ... remember that his chest inside there, it's behind. All you need to do is when he's either looking straight at you, which is probably what he'll do, if you shoot him just under the chin here. Just shoot him in there ... because he'll be looking down at us, because the grass is thick. It's hot, he's in a cool place. Side on, two-thirds down, one-third up, right on the shoulder blade. Smoke him in there and he'll bounce around and make a lot of noise and run off and die probably and they're not difficult animals to kill, they're soft skinned, they have a very highly-developed nervous system which means that all the shock effect from the bullet is taken into their body and absorbed and it hurts them.

ROGER COOK McDonald admits he's offering us a Kruger Park lion but he's not telling Mr Rogers what he told our undercover team earlier on.

Covert shots filmed earlier.

SANDY MCDONALD It's a canned lion, make no mistake, but it's a very nice size but it's at a bait and it's going to be fairly easy for him to have a first shot at it.

Back to the main story and the hunting expedition.

ROGER COOK Every part of the crooked business is recorded on tape as Mr Rogers' cameraman filmed their so-called client's expedition.

SANDY MCDONALD What we'll do is we'll go to the camp and let your have a few shots at a target.

Cook does target practice – and he's good at it. They look at the target he's hit.

ROGER COOK What you mean two went through there?

SANDY MCDONALD Two went through there which is really good because you can …

Target practice over, the pretence of tracking a roaming wild animal resumes. Music. The vehicles drive over the park, stopping every so often to find the spoor of the lion (!)

Covert shots filmed earlier.

SANDY MCDONALD From our side it's all fixed, you guys … and I'll keep him happy, I know what to say at the right time and all the rest of it.

SANDY MCDONALD Right, basically what's been happening is that, er, this area is adjacent to the Kruger National Park and what we have is a move-ment of usually old male lions that come out. Once they come in here, we keep them in by virtue of the fact that we have a pretty good bait out there and being an animal that is lazy by nature, he's going to stick around by the bait and this is a really good time to get him then because he's lying at the bait.

ROGER COOK The conspiracy continues as we move closer to the lion now dazed by drugs and unable to escape.

Covert shots filmed earlier.

SANDY MCDONALD I've tranquillised it, it's a hell of a nice lion … . nobody will suspect a thing.

UNDERCOVER RESEARCHER Right.

SANDY MCDONALD We do a lot of them.

In the vehicles.

ROGER COOK Out in the bush the hunters go through charade of tracking down the prey, although they know precisely where it is. All this is just for show.

They 'find' the lion. Cook's voice-over:

And here he is, after 20 minutes of circling the same small area of bush, we find our Kruger lion. Lured from the reserve with meat, then drugged, to give the hunter the chance to kill it close range without the slightest risk to himself.

SANDY MCDONALD (*instructs his client*) I want you to look at him through the scope. I want you to find his eyes. I want you to follow his neck down, then shoot him where the mane ends, on his shoulder. Shoot him and, take your time, do a good shot. Remember it's a lion. It's hot, he doesn't want to move away, but if we get out of sight, the wound is bad. You have to shoot him from here.

ROGER COOK (*changing tone and confronting McDonald who for several minutes fails to understand what is going on ...*) Well, let me tell you why I'm not going to shoot this lion, he doesn't stand a chance and you know he doesn't and I'm not a businessman, I'm a television reporter making a programme about canned hunts, and that's what this is, isn't it?

SANDY MCDONALD There is your lion.

ROGER COOK This is a canned hunt isn't it? I'm not shooting that lion, it doesn't stand a chance. It's been drugged, you told us earlier, you know it has.

My colleagues are all from the same television company, let this sink in. This is a canned hunt, I am not shooting that lion, and neither are you. It doesn't stand a chance. It's been tranquillised. It's a lion that's come across or been baited across ...

SANDY MCDONALD (*his predicament has still not sunk in*) It has been baited.

ROGER COOK ... it's been baited across, from the National Park ...

SANDY MCDONALD Yes. Yes.

ROGER COOK ... So he actually belongs to somebody else.

SANDY MCDONALD No, he belongs to here.

ROGER COOK ... and he's been baited and that's not ethical is it?

SANDY MCDONALD No, that's ethical.

ROGER COOK He's been darted, that's not ethical. He's been shot from a vehicle, that's not ethical.

SANDY MCDONALD He's from the park.

Let us end here. ...

ROGER COOK No, we're not going by foot, we're turning round and going back, I'm paying for this. We're not shooting that lion.

Caught red-handed McDonald pressured us to hand over our tapes, then, when we tried to leave the Mostert Farm with them, the mood turned ugly.

ROGER COOK We found a road-block of heavily armed men, stopping us reaching the safety of the public highway.

Covert filming of armed thugs menacing Cook's party.

Even when the police arrived, they wouldn't let us go.

Eventually the gate was opened, but the hunters made it very clear they still wanted our tapes of the canned hunt.

During an hour of negotiation, we smuggled out the tapes, and got a stern warning from the police not to return.

Change of scene – Trafalgar Square, London

ROGER COOK Back in Britain, we took our dossier on canned hunting to the South African High Commission.

Our findings shocked the New Republic's Deputy High Commissioner.

DEPUTY HIGH COMMISSIONER – HAPPY MAHLANGU Look, I'm really appalled, I'm really appalled that something like this is still going on in my country. I promise you, I'm saying to you after this I'm going to be talking to some people from the environment, in the ministry and make them aware of what you guys found out and ask them if they could look into this because, it must be stopped and it must be stopped immediately.

ROGER COOK Sadly that will be too late to help our drugged canned lion. Before we left, the hunters told us he would only survive until the next wealthy foreigner came to take his life – for money.

Discussion

Critics say that *The Cook Report* overdramatises mundane matters, goes for small-time, accessible crooks and doesn't understand the wider implications of its stories. These critics miss the point. Successful communication reflects the cultural values of those with whom you wish to communicate. Successful communication, transforms 'what you already know' by providing a new cast within a trusted format or genre just as the epic poem in the ancient world could be peopled with different warriors or lovers but deliver the same satisfactions because of its use of familiar techniques and its grounding in shared outlook. In other words, as a vehicle for popular investigative journalism, *The Cook Report* knows its audience. Yes, the topic is one that he can be sure the viewers will be in sympathy with, it is in no way counter-orthodox. A less conventional theme would be, as Ridley might say, how the CITES convention itself endangers the survival of the species, but a story based on that would be very complicated and although it might expand viewers' horizons, it might also come up against the communications difficulties identified above. The goal of this particular *Cook Report* is a lesser one, but it is well achieved: it demonstrates how regulations, international, national and local, are flouted by people prepared to plunder everybody's heritage for the sake of personal enrichment, and it does so very effectively. Villains have been nailed, their villainy evidenced and reported.

The programme performs another unusual task. In investigative journalism the gulf between what is aimed at the broadsheet market – serious investigations with public interest dimension – and what is aimed at the tabloid market – exposure journalism, is large. *The Cook Report* bridges the two by doing subjects of public interest in a popular format.

NOTES

1 Ridley himself is not, as he admits (1996: 41), without a point of view; he argues that it is property rights that defend, rather than ruin, the environment, a view contrary to that held by many international and national agencies.
2 For his own gripping account of his life and adventures, see Cook (1999) *Dangerous Ground*. London: HarperCollins.
3 Various conversations over 1998 with David Mannion, former editor of *The Cook Report*.

BIBLIOGRAPHY

Anderson, A. (1997) *Media Culture and the Environment*. London: UCL.

Beckett, A. (1995) Looking for Mr Big. *Independent on Sunday*, 21 May 1995.

Bell, A. (1991) *The Language of News Media*. Oxford: Blackwell.

Bell, A. (1994) Climate of opinion: public and media discourse on the global environment. *Discourse and Society*, 5 (1): 33–63.

Brosius, H. and Kepplinger, H. (1990) The agenda setting function of television news. *Communication Research*. 17 (2): 183–211.

Central Television (1997) 'Roger Cook'. Briefing sheet supplied by Central Television Department of Current Affairs, June 1997.

Central Television (1997a) *The Cook Report*: 'Making a Killing'. Nottingham: Carlton Central Television.

Central Television (1997b) *Putting the Record Straight*. Nottingham: Carlton Central Television.

Channel 4 (1994) *Without Walls*: 'J'accuse the National Trust' (reporter: Stephen Bayley). London: Fulmar for C4 TV.

Cook, R. (1997) *The Cook Report*. Talk to students on the MA Investigative Journalism course at Nottingham Trent University, 30 October 1997.

Cook, R. (1999) Interview with Hugo de Burgh, 14 June 1999.

Grundy, R. (1996) *How Do They Do That?* London: Environmental Investigation Agency.

Hornig, S. (1992) Framing risk: audience and reader factors. *Journalism Quarterly*, 69 (3).

Kasun, J. (1988) *The War against Population*. San Francisco: Ignatius.

Lowe, P. et al. (1984) Bad news and good news: environmental politics and mass media. *Sociological Review*, 32: 75–90.

McQuail, D. and Windahl, S. (1981) *Communication Models*. London: Longman.

Milne, S. (1995) *The Enemy Within: The Secret War Against the Miners*. London: Pan.

Parsons, W. (1995) *Public Policy: An Introduction to the Theory and Practice of Policy Analysis*. Aldershot: Edward Elgar.

Ridley, M. (1995) *Down to Earth I: Combating Environmental Myths*. London: Institute of Economic Affairs.

Ridley, M. (1996) *Down to Earth II: Combating Environmental Myths*. London: Institute of Economic Affairs.

Shoemaker, P. (1996) *Mediating the Message*. White Plains: Longman.

Simon, J. (1992) *Population and Development in Poor Countries*. Princeton: University of Princeton Press.

Tate, T. (1997) The making of *Laogai*/ Talk to students of the MA Investigative Journalism course at Nottingham Trent University, 6 November 1997.

Upshon, L. (1997) Interview with Hugo de Burgh, 10 June 1997.

FURTHER READING

Anderson, A. (1997) *Media Culture and the Environment*. London: UCL.

16

HIGH POLITICS AND
LOW BEHAVIOUR

The *Sunday Times* Insight

Hugo de Burgh

Insight and British public life

Insight is a news-gathering and analysis operation of the *Sunday Times* parallel to and separate from the departments of Home News and Foreign News and, like them, answering to the Managing Editor of News. Insight has no dedicated space and no requirement to produce a story each week; its manpower has usually been around five experienced journalists, many of whom have written books based upon their investigative work (some are listed at the end of the chapter).

Insight is the by-line most associated with investigative journalism in the UK press, although there have been other teams and units in other newspapers which have competed with it, particularly, in recent years, the *Guardian*. Insight first appeared on 17 February 1963. At the time advertisers were growing in number and in their demands; more space for advertisements was resulting in expanded space for editorial copy, and there was space to allow journalists to write at length. The first major story covered as a result of these developments was a 6,000 word piece on UK government minister John Profumo, accused of lying to the House of Commons over his association with a potential spy published on 9 September 1963. What was unusual about the piece at the time were first its narrative presentation, and second the 'close attention to detail which was to become an identifying feature of Insight' (NICAD 1997). Then

> came the Rachman exposure, an account of the rise of a Polish immigrant whose name has now entered the language to mean a grasping, unscrupulous, slum landlord. In October [1963] Insight published a story headed 'Backstage at Blackpool: hour by hour in the fight for power'. The story told the problems within the Conservative Party after the Prime Minister, [Harold] Macmillan fell ill just before the party conference.
>
> (NICAD 1997)

The 1970s are widely regarded as the great days of UK investigative journalism, and where this is so it is because of Insight. 'Insight was the role model of the period, with huge investigations, plenty of time, large budgets and a strongly supportive editorial approach' (Doig 1992: 46).

There was always a strong sense of purpose and idealism, infused above all by the *Sunday Times* editor Harold Evans. Under him Insight's main achievements of many, were the thalidomide and the DC-10 air disaster stories, both described elsewhere in this book, as well as the Philby Spy Scandal (see Knightley 1997 and 1998). Careful groundwork was expected:

> The idea was that you became as expert on the subject, whatever it was, as those involved in it, so that when the time came to confront Mr Big, or to explain why his technicians had inserted a faulty bolt in the flange bracket, you not only knew as much about the business as he did, but you could probably sell his phoney insurance policy or build his bridge as well, if not better, than he had done.
>
> (Linklater 1993: 19)

By the late 1980s, the combination of new proprietor Rupert Murdoch's change of style at the *Sunday Times* and the willingness of television executives to spend money on investigations meant that the best investigative journalism was appearing on television. Knightley (1999) believes that newspapers' loss of enthusiasm for investigative journalism came about because, first, before new technology, the salaries element of the total costs of production of newspapers was very small – he says 11 per cent; however, once new technology came in, salaries came to a much larger percentage of total production costs and were seen as ripe for cutting. Second, he says that new technology made it possible to see instantly the productivity, in terms of words per pound spent on salary and overheads, of any particular journalist. Since investigative journalists had typically produced much less copy, they were vulnerable. 'Efficiency was judged by quantity published in the newspaper. Investigative journalists who don't get their story into the paper for a year don't look very cost effective' (Knightley 1999).

Television salaries and benefits were famously very good in the late 1970s and early 1980s, and this may have contributed to the strength of investigative journalism, as well as the glamour of an industry still in its discovery stage and attracting top talent. However, Linklater believes that economics was less significant in the change of tone at the *Sunday Times* than ideology, since, after all, the company owning the *Sunday Times* is enormously wealthy (Linklater 1993).

Former Insight people believe that by the late 1980s there was little sympathy for the craftsmanship of the 1970s, and Linklater mentions in evidence for this lack of sympathy the 3-year investigation of a tycoon's financial affairs by the distinguished financial journalist Charles Raw, which he describes as 'one of the most brilliant pieces of financial investigation I have ever seen', that was spiked by Murdoch (Linklater 1993: 20).

Although claimed by Andrew Neil (Neil 1996: chap. 12) as one of Insight's 1980s successes, there are question marks over the story of 'Arthur Scargill's Libyan Connection', which declared that the senior employee of the National Union of Mineworkers was seeking financial help for the then strike from the most reviled regime in the world. Although the trip certainly took place and was a spectacular own goal for the miners' union, the man who undertook it was later found to be in the camp of the Union's enemies; the story ideally suited the UK government at the time and it has been suggested that the British intelligence services had a hand in ensuring that Insight got the details of the story (Milne 1995: 148–56).

When in 1986 a rail crash took place in Clapham, South London, Insight reporters claim that they were the first to find the culprit, a technician who had failed to insulate wires; however the editor would not publish the identification of the culprit as he believed this would constitute an 'unfair, vindictive attack on an individual' (Leppard 1997). Another 1986 success for Insight was the revelation, made on 5 October 1986, that Israel had secretly developed a military nuclear capability and that it was of an unimaginable extent and advancement. The story fell into the lap of Insight because other newspapers failed to see its significance, or failed to find the informant, Mordechai Vanunu, credible. Vanunu was only too genuine and had photographs taken within the nuclear installations that were even more so, as Insight reporter Peter Hounam realised and as was confirmed to him by the experts he employed. Two matters diminished the glory; first, the *Daily Mirror*, whose proprietor and Foreign Editor were both involved in different ways with the Israeli security services, according to Hersh (1991: 307–15), published a spoiler shortly before in which they rubbished Vanunu and diminished his revelations; second, the *Sunday Times* failed to hold onto their informant, Vanunu, whom they allowed to become so lonely as to fall for a secret service honey trap that led to his being kidnapped and taken home for trial. Finally, in the 1980s, Insight ran a series of articles called 'The Water Rats' exposing 'the top industrialists poisoning Britain's rivers' for a lengthy period in 1989.

Stories in the 1990s included Asil Nadir and the Polly Peck Scandal (share manipulation by a colourful businessman), offshore trust tax loopholes and how National Car Parks waged a commando style industrial espionage war against its rival. A fraudulent story, claiming that the then leader of the Labour Party Michael Foot had been the agent of a foreign government, led to the aggrieved party winning damages from the *Sunday Times*.

Insight is after 'the big story, not dodgy insurance salesmen or councillors or medical reps bribing doctors' (Leppard 1997) and the target must be above a 'certain threshold', people near the centre of power, whether civil servants or politicians, who are wrong-doers. Insight will eschew the story of a minister's dishonestly conducted affair, but might investigate how others set the minister up, as they did in the case of a disgraced Conservative minister, David Mellor, when his mistress sold recordings of his intimate conversations to the *People* in 1992; in 1993 when other newspapers revealed the existence of the 'Squidgy-gate' tapes, providing evidence of Princess Diana's extramarital affections, Insight's story dealt with the manner in which the tapes had been obtained because of what this revealed about public agencies.

In 1995 Insight set up an elaborate sting in order to trap corrupt members of parliament. A company was set up which purported to be looking for MPs prepared to ask questions about pharmaceuticals, and the newspaper was later to be accused of entrapment for so doing. At the same time the *Guardian* was carrying out its own investigations in this area, which became the 'Cash for Questions' scandal (see Chapters 1 and 3).

In recent interviews the Insight editor has claimed that Insight has found 'the stakes raised by the (British) government's establishment of a Rapid Rebuttal Unit, and by its PROs' vitriolic abuse and intimidation whenever reporters appear to be near a story' (Leppard 1997). Specifically Insight claims to have been warned off examining the business connections of the husband of a minister; these connections became pertinent to central issues of corruption and undue influence when the *Financial Times* and *Sunday Telegraph* revealed how the Prime Minister had allowed himself to be addressed on policy matters by their wealthy associates (Leppard 1997).

Despite these warnings, Insight has continued its close interest in the government's appointments, examining the responsibilities of millionaire minister Lord Sainsbury of Turville; the Sainsbury family are major benefactors of the Labour Party and, as shareholders of a massive supermarket and banking operation, stand to be affected by planning decisions to be taken by the Deputy Prime Minister in his executive capacity. In the late 1990s concern about genetically modified foods surfaced in Britain, and it became a matter of controversy that the same Lord Sainsbury had had connections with the genetically modified food lobby in the recent past. In such a climate, everyone who visits the Prime Minister or who is appointed by him is of potential interest, as of course are those companies that donate to the governing party. Leppard (1997) believes that he will in time establish that some of these are foreign defence companies, acting via lobbyists; were this proved so it would be ironic, given the capital made by Labour when in opposition out of the connections of the Conservatives with arms companies, and out of the 'Arms to Iraq' affair, to which we turn later in the chapter. Before we do so, however, it is appropriate to consider the context within which this kind of investigative journalism is deemed important.

Public opinion, public policies and journalists

Journalists have ambivalent relationships with high politics. Former *Sunday Times* editor Andrew Neil describes in his memoirs how he would chat to

Prime Minister Major on the telephone (Neil 1996); the place settings at one of John Major's dinner parties gives an indication of the intimacy that is possible (Tunstall 1996); national journalists go to the homes of ambitious politicians as well as meeting them regularly at Westminster or the many other meeting points for the political elite. Yet the journalists are always on the look out for the weak point, the revelation, the scandal; the greatest fame attaches to those who can bring down a national politician.[1]

For many journalists, as doubtless for many observers, Watergate (see Chapter 3) is the quintessential investigative journalism. This is partly on account of its methods, partly on account of its execution, which 'encapsulated and exemplified all of the difficulties and challenges' (Leppard 1997), involving source development, triangulation, tensions with editors and tremendous political risks, and partly on account of its influence on journalism everywhere. Most of all, however, it is quintessential because of its target. For Insight in particular, investigative journalism today is about national policy and national policy-makers. Its reporters want to know that policy is being made for the right reasons and that policy-makers are behaving in accordance with the principles they profess.

Hence the classic status of Watergate, which demonstrated misdemeanours and derelictions out of keeping with society's expectations of the executive. Hence also the significance to journalists of British equivalents. In the 1970s the UK had the Profumo affair and Poulson, because it implicated a prime minister in waiting; in the 1980s, while the USA was attending to the Iran-Contra story, which undermined the Reagan administration – a premonition of the forthcoming British arms scandal – Rinkagate was the big UK story, in which a senior politician was investigated for incitement to murder. In the 1990s, the two biggest British investigations of the conduct of people in high places, 'Cash for Questions' and 'Arms to Iraq', were significant for similar reasons.

The importance ascribed to such investigations is based on a number of premises. One is the theory of journalism's social responsibility, upon which we have already touched. Another is the assumption that public persons are accountable to public opinion for aspects of their lives once deemed private; another, the theory that public policy should defer to public opinion.

That it is not possible to make public policy without carrying public opinion is now probably well established in the folklore of high politics, at least since the Poll Tax fiasco when Prime Minister Thatcher was forced by hostile public opinion to withdraw an important element of her tax reforms; thus governments increasingly try to persuade people of their policies. The effort and money government now puts into the manipulation of public opinion is enormous (Franklin 1994). The connection between the public and those seeking to make or to influence public policy via public opinion is made by the media. The media can set the agenda of debate by highlighting some matters more than others (Iyengar et al. 1984); they can 'gatekeep' or exclude some matters; they can prioritise or hype (Cohen 1972, Edelman

1988); they can popularise the concerns of elite groups (Mayer 1991). Public policy is sometimes made in immediate response to public opinion as mediated by the media; for example, recent British legislation on handguns, dangerous dogs and terrorism is widely regarded as a manifestation less of legislative fore-thought than of public opinion as represented by the media. By contrast, public opinion is insufficient when the political elite, presumably in cahoots with the mediators, sets its face against a policy; the obvious examples in the UK are capital punishment and privacy. The 'establishment model' of policy-making (Parsons 1995: 110–22) suggests that a major institution needs to take up an issue for it to become sufficiently important to change public policy.

Outsiders have two main choices in trying to influence public policy; the backdoor, lobbying mode, which is increasingly systematised and used by many professional and trade organisations, plus individual companies and countries (Jordan 1990), and the public mode. When campaigners for lead-free petrol came to the conclusion in 1981 that their lobbying had failed against more powerful resistance from counter-lobbies, they decided to go for a public campaign (Wilson 1984), bearing in mind the successes of such high-profile campaigns as those on housing (Shelter), family benefits (Child Poverty Action Group) and recycling (Friends of the Earth). They called it CLEAR (Campaign for Lead Free Air).

The CLEAR campaign forced the government of the day to change public policy by mobilising public opinion. Factors included the quality of CLEAR's argument and of its presentation, together with the acceptability of its scien-tific testimonials; it was also executed in a carefully planned and efficient manner. Arguably the most important factor, however, was the targeting of journalists who were leaders and opinion-formers, not only by virtue of their jobs but because of the respect they commanded in their profession.

CLEAR's approach accorded with theories of the processes by which the media influences public opinion. The *pluralist* conception (the media is a marketplace of ideas making free debate possible) is largely discredited, as is the *hypodermic* model (the media injects, and we believe); it is widely agreed that the media set agendas, gatekeep, in that they can include or exclude issues from debate, and, in Mayer's 'reflection and reinforcement model' (Mayer 1981), that they reflect concerns of knowledgeable minorities and then blow them up into public issues. The role of media owners and of advertisers in this process may be considerable, but is more difficult to pin down.

What is the evidence that the media have a significant influence in the formation of public opinion? Studies exist which demonstrate how, in the USA, the media influenced public opinion of the Vietnam War, particularly in deromanticising it, and therefore influenced public policy towards that war, although many disbelieve the studies. Important attitude changes, for example the increasing acceptance of homosexuality in the UK after the liberal legisla-tion of the 1960s may be attributable to media treatment, but the dynamics of this have yet to be explored. There have been periods in UK public life when the media have been thought to have set the public agenda, notably in the 1960s with the issue of police corruption. Iyengar et al.'s study demonstrated the influence of media coverage on US Presidential policy in the 1980s. In the UK there are claims as to the influence of the media upon the presentation of legislation to Parliament, and in the 1990s the National Commission on Standards in Public Life and the Scott Report came about as a consequence of the media's direct influence upon public affairs.

That journalists themselves might have strong opinions that should be listened to was an idea that, grudgingly, the political classes came to accept in the middle of the nineteenth century. Journalism was the Fourth Estate – after the monarchy (or the spiritual peers), the Lords and the Commons – because it represented the views of large numbers of people in a manner other than by election or by interests, and could influence those people. That journalists might have better information than political decision makers and business people (Desmond 1978: 320ff) was another idea that began to catch on as foreign correspondence developed. But that journalists had a social obligation to criticise, expose and exhort was a development to which those in authority did not take kindly – it suggested that journalists had a kind of moral authority perhaps superior to that of anyone else. From observers and informants they became brokers of information, and then the determinants of what constitutes significance, and the creators of the agenda.

Their power came from their signalising role and also from their access to readers, an access which politicians needed; they were sometimes trusted by their readers because of their supposed impartiality, or at least clear-mindedness; they could deny such access to those in authority or those with whom they disagreed. These were the foundations which made it possible for journalists to use their various tools, sometimes in combination: investigation and exposure would be one way; moral censure another; analysis, argument and criticism a third.

In these ways it may be said that the journalist is important in creating the relationship between public opinion and policy-maker. The manner in which s/he reacts to pressure from interest groups, government or politicians probably determines which policy ideas conquer public opinion and which do not. Furthermore, the vigilance with which journalists scrutinise the doings of politicians determines how effective they can be at promoting or executing their policies; the last Conservative government can be argued to have been disabled by the revelations of journalists in the 'Cash for Questions' and 'Arms to Iraq' stories, examples of journalists taking the initiative rather than responding to events or simply mediating facts.

The 'Arms To Iraq' affair

This matter spread throughout UK public life, and to a much lesser extent also touched upon the EU and USA for at least 17 years. Because of its alleged influence upon the decline and, in 1997, the defeat of the Conservative government of John Major, its detail may have become confounded in lay minds with the 'Cash for Questions' affair; some Conservative supporters may simply think of it as one of those weapons with which hostile journalists sought to beat the government and bring nearer the possibility of a victory for Mr Blair.

Although there were doubtless many who wanted to exploit the affair to discredit the government, it is much more than that. Not only did the affair reveal moral muddle and incompetence within the public administration; it also found ministers attempting to prevent the revelation of truth. It dealt with an area of life – arms sales – of concern to many people, either because their livelihoods depend upon them or because they find the trade repugnant.

'The Arms to Iraq' affair: glossary

DTI	Department of Trade and Industry
MI5	Military Intelligence 5 (the UK secret service)
HMG	Her Majesty's Government
Export Licences	permits
HMCE	Her Majesty's Customs and Excise (the organisation that polices imports and exports)

'The Arms to Iraq' affair: time line

1980	Iran–Iraq War starts
1984	HMG decides not to take sides in the war and bans sales of arms
1985 October	Geoffrey Howe, Foreign Secretary, announces Guidelines
1987 November	MI5 records the fact that UK machinery is being used to make weapons
1988 January	DTI tells Matrix Churchill (an arms making company) that its Export Licences have been frozen
1988 February	Matrix Churchill receives Export Licences for machine tools used to make shells
1988 August	Ceasefire between Iran and Iraq
1988 December	Guidelines on exports to Iraq relaxed
1989 February	DTI Approval for further Matrix Churchill exports
1989 November	DTI Approval for further Matrix Churchill exports
1990 April	Parts for an Iraqi 'supergun' seized by HMCE
1990 June	HMCE raids Matrix Churchill
1990 July	DTI Approval for further Matrix Churchill exports
1990 August	Iraqi invasion of Kuwait
1990 October	Arrest of directors of Matrix Churchill
1991 January	Gulf War

1992 February	Directors of Ordtech Ltd convicted of illegal exporting of arms-related equipment to Iraq
1992 June–September	Signing of Public Interest Immunity Certificates by ministers which would prevent the disclosure of information that would have assisted the Matrix Churchill defence
1992 November	Matrix Churchill trial starts, and collapses (because of admission by minister Clark)
	Prime Minister John Major appoints Judge Sir Richard Scott to conduct an Inquiry on ministers' role
1993 May	Scott Inquiry begins
1996 February	Scott Report published, concluding that Parliament was misled

(with acknowledgments to the *Sunday Times*, 18 February 1996)

In essence the story is as follows. In 1980 war broke out between Iran and Iraq. Neither regime was very attractive to the West, Iran's leaders having declared their extreme hostility to the West and equated that hostility with the very raison d'être of their theocracy; Iraq was ruled by a racist, totalitarian and utterly brutal Arab government. Western governments perceived Iraq as less of a threat, and were therefore less hostile to her and her supreme leader, Saddam Hussein.

The Western media were able to publish extensive detail on the war; two items in particular stuck in the popular imagination. One was that the Iranians were sending hordes of boys as young as 8, virtually untrained and armed with little more than faith, to attack and be slaughtered; the other was that the Iraqis were using chemical weapons upon these children, and upon minority Kurdish inhabitants of Iraq with horrible consequences. People were killed, maimed, disfigured and died in great agony. Iraq was doing, it was remarked at the time, what even Adolf Hitler feared to do on the battlefield (Sweeney 1993).

The UK government decided, in the light of this, to ban sales of arms to either side. However, some manufacturers, including a company called Matrix Churchill, whose ultimate owner was the Iraqi government, continued to export. Export licenses were issued to Matrix Churchill by the DTI; yet, in June 1990 Matrix Churchill was raided by HMCE under suspicion of exporting illegally. On the face of it this was an example of lack of coordination by the administration: the DTI was permitting what HMCE was forbidding. If it was indeed government policy that there be no arms sales, then the DTI was wrong. If, on the other hand, the policy had been relaxed, then HMCE was wrong.

However, the situation was not so clear cut. The Gulf crisis blew up with Iraq's invasion of Kuwait in August 1990, and it was evident that the UK might soon be involved in a war with Iraq, which indeed did break out on 16 January 1991. Furthermore, the information that had enabled HMCE to raid Matrix Churchill had come from within Matrix Churchill, whose directors not only believed that they had been encouraged by the DTI to continue their sales, but who also contained among them at least two agents of MI5. When the directors of Matrix Churchill were arrested and charged with breaking the export ban in October 1990, it is not surprising that they were peeved.

Thus the affair became not merely one of how companies flouted government policy or even of how government agencies encouraged them to do so, but of how UK agents were being sacrificed to hide the hypocrisy of the government. The story took a further twist when, in 1992, ministers attempted to prevent a proper self-defence by the Matrix Churchill directors through their action in signing Public Immunity Certificates, which are orders preventing the disclosure of apposite documents on the grounds of national security.

The 'Arms To Iraq' affair and journalists

The story developed in nine stages:

1 reporting, often critical, of the arms trade
2 suspicions that Western firms were involved in the arming of Iran and Iraq
3 evidence that British companies had breached the guidelines
4 evidence that parts of government knew this was happening
5 evidence that ministers had encouraged this
6 evidence that ministers had tried to prevent the truth coming out
7 media revelations resulting in a public inquiry
8 the public inquiry analysed for its lessons
9 the influence of the affair upon public opinion.

Various newspaper journalists had been involved in different aspects of the story up to December 1990 when the *Sunday Times* brought the story up to stage 5 with its Insight article 'Minister helped British firms to arm Saddam's soldiers'.

> Straddling the metalled highway that runs south out of Baghdad towards the Kuwaiti border lies the Taji industrial plant, a sprawling complex that is the centre of the Iraqi arms industry. Behind two huge ornamental gates, past the fortified guardhouse, thousands of production workers are feeding President Saddam Hussein's burgeoning war machine.

Inside shed C, one of the largest of the work areas, stand row upon row of computer controlled lathes programmed to making the casings, fins and nose cones of mortar shells. The lathes were supplied by two leading British companies. In shed D, more British equipment stands ready for plating shells and missile parts.

Only a few miles to the west, at Al-Iskandariya, is the Hutteen factory complex where British made machines are mass producing shells and ammunition. It is the same at the Badr and Qaqa establishments to the west of Baghdad, on the road to Ramadi, where Farzad Bazoft, the British journalist, tried to take soil samples and photographs before he was arrested, then hanged as a spy last March ...

The *Sunday Times* Insight team has investigated how this British equipment came to be in Iraq and discovered that a government minister allowed firms to break the spirit of the government's arms embargo forbidding the export of military goods to Iraq.

(*Sunday Times*, 2 December 1990)

How had the *Sunday Times* arrived at this? According to Leppard, once the Gulf War had begun in late 1990 'with fears of a nuclear war between Israel and Iraq, the whole news agenda shifted to the Middle East'(Leppard 1997). UK-based journalists, unable to compete in the coverage from the Middle East, sought a domestic angle and decided to look at the trade which had allowed Saddam to build up such a mighty military force. Was government involved in allowing that trade to take place? Insight trawled the trade press for companies selling machine tools to Iraq and made a short list, always aware that sanctions-busting by a few companies would not be a significant story, whereas government complicity would be. Leppard had a list of six companies to telephone and by chance called the Matrix Churchill Managing Director Paul Henderson '45 minutes after he had been sacked' and was in the mood to talk. He offered Leppard the memo of a meeting with minister Alan Clark advising him to keep on with his business in defiance of sanctions.

What followed Leppard's good fortune is best described in the words of the Scott Report:

2 December 1990:The Sunday Times 'Insight' article entitled 'Minister helped British firms to arm Saddam' was published.The main thrust of the article was that Mr Alan Clark, while Minister for Trade, had encouraged machine tool manufacturers, when applying for licences to export to Iraq machine tools intended for the manufacture of munitions, to cloud the truth and stress the civil manufacturing potential of the machines in order to facilitate the grant of export licences. One effect of the article was to highlight the political implications of the Matrix Churchill investigation and a future prosecution.

(Scott 1996: 1098, see also p. 1156)

Another effect was that

> on the morning of 3 December 1990 a meeting at the Cabinet
> Office was attended by a number of very senior officials ... The
> purpose of the meeting was to discuss the *Sunday Times* article and
> the answer that might be given by the Prime Minister (to a letter on
> this subject).
>
> (Scott 1996: 1161)

Later that day 'Mr Clark met the Prime Minister, Mr John Major, to discuss
the *Sunday Times* article' (Scott 1996: 1098). A later effect was that at the
Sunday Times Christmas party minister Alan Clark threatened editor Andrew
Neil that he'd 'have his balls' and sue the *Sunday Times* (Leppard 1997).

The story then took off, especially when Insight established the extraordinary contradiction that HMCE was bringing Matrix Churchill to court but
that MI5, another arm of government, was using the company for intelli-
gence-gathering.

'Arms to Iraq' has been denigrated as a journalistic investigation by other
journalists, first on the grounds that it 'was just an ordinary news story, not an
investigation in the true sense' (Knightley 1999) and secondly on the grounds
that

> The role of journalists and their respective media institutions in that
> case, as in the case of the numerous fraud trials of the time, was to
> observe merely the proceedings from the sidelines and provide a
> detailed 'analysis by post mortem'.
>
> (Northmore 1994: 319)

If all investigations are to be measured for their length and complexity by
the standards of the thalidomide and DC-10 stories, then 'Arms to Iraq'
cannot compare. Yet, despite Northmore there was investigation, even if it did
not require the kind of investment made, unnecessarily if we are to agree with
Bruce Page (Page 1998), by the *Sunday Times* in the thalidomide story. In his
essay Northmore offers a useful list of suggestions as to what sources investigative journalists might have used to get to the Matrix Churchill story
earlier (Northmore 1994: 330–1); in fact some of these sources were used, but
the story was not an editorial high priority until, first, war with Iraq seemed
likely, and second, the *Sunday Times* managed to establish the role of minister
Alan Clark.

Insight continued to publish on the story after that exposure, but it can be
argued that little more original investigation came from its reporters, who
relied upon the court cases and the Scott Inquiry to disclose new facts.
Equally it should be said that Insight had done its bit, ensuring that the
government could not hide its role.

From a humanitarian and moral viewpoint the story always mattered, but it was not significant in terms of public policy and political leadership until the December 1990 article. Once that article had made the vital link, all the other factors joined to make 'Arms to Iraq' an important investigation because of:

1   the consequences of Western companies' success in supplying Iraq, i.e. the wars against Iran, Kuwait and finally the Allied Coalition;
2   the awfulness of the direct results of that supply upon defenceless populations, including minorities within Iraq;
3   the fact that ministers had broken their own rules and connived at the continuance of a trade which they condemned in public.

What made the story an achievement of investigative journalists was that, in large measure as a result of their efforts, government was not able to hide the chaos and corruption, but was obliged to set up an inquiry which then consolidated their case. Contradictions in public policy were revealed, and the resulting revelations probably contributed to the further discrediting and ultimate electoral defeat of the then government.

NOTE

1   Peter Oborne (1999) interprets the change in relationship between journalists and politicians since the 1970s as the rise of a new 'media class', and describes the features in Chapter 7.

BIBLIOGRAPHY

Booker, C. (1994) *The Mad Officials*. London: Constable.
Cohen, S. (1972) *Folk Devils and Moral Panics*. London: Paladin.
Desmond, R. (1978) *The Information Process: World News Reporting to the Twentieth Century*. University of Iowa Press.
Doig (1992) Retreat of the investigators. *British Journalism Review*, 3 (4).
Eddy, P. (1976) *Destination Disaster*. London: Granada.
Edelman, M. (1988) *Constructing the Political Spectacle*. Chicago: CUP.
Franklin, B. (1994) *Packaging Politics*. London: Edward Arnold.
Gibbons, T. (1998) *Regulating the Media*. London: Sweet and Maxwell.
Henderson, P. (1993) *The Unlikely Spy*. London: Bloomsbury.
Hersh, S. (1991) *The Samson Option: Israel, America and the Bomb*. London: Faber and Faber.
Home Office (1998) *MI5: The Security Service*. London: HMSO.
Iyengar, S., Kinder, D. R., Peters, M. D. and Krosnick, J. A. (1984) The evening news and the Presidential evaluations. *Journal of Personality and Social Psychology*, 46: 778–87.
Jordan, G. (1990) *The Commercial Lobbyists: Politics for Profit in Britain*. Aberdeen: Aberdeen University Press.
Knightley, P. (1997) *A Hack's Progress*. London: Jonathan Cape.
Knightley, P. (1998) The inside story of Philby's exposure. *British Journalism Review*, 9 (2).
Knightley, P. (1999) Interview with Hugo de Burgh, 22 May 1999.

Leigh, D. (1980) *The Frontiers of Secrecy: Closed Government in Britain.* London: Junction.

Leppard, D. (1997) The Watergate model in UK journalism. Talk to students on the MA Investigative Journalism course at Nottingham Trent University, 27 November 1997.

Linklater, M. (1993) An insight into Insight. *British Journalism Review,* 4 (2).

Mayer, R. (1981) Gone yesterday, here today: consumer issues in the agenda setting process. *Journal of Social Issues,* 47: 21–39.

Milne, S. (1995) *The Enemy Within.* London: Pan

Neil, A. (1996) *Full Disclosure.* London: Weidenfeld and Nicolson.

NICAD (1997) Briefing from News International Corporate Affairs Department, 10 September 1997.

Northmore, D. (1994) Probe shock: investigative journalism. In R. Keeble *The Newspapers Handbook.* London: Routledge.

Norton-Taylor, R. (1985) *The Ponting Affair.* London: Cecil Woolf.

Oborne, P. (1999) *Alastair Campbell: New Labour and the Rise of the Media Class.* London: Aurum.

Page, B. (1998) A defence of 'low' journalism. *British Journalism Review,* 9 (1).

Parsons, W. (1995) *Public Policy.* Aldershot: Edward Elgar.

Scott, Sir R. (1996) *Report of the Inquiry into the Export of Defence Equipment and Dual-Use of Goods to Iraq and Related Prosecutions* (The Scott Report). London: HMSO.

Sweeney, J. (1993) *Trading with the Enemy: Britain's Arming of Iraq.* London: Pan.

Tunstall, J. (1996) *Newspaper Power: The National Press in Britain.* Oxford: Oxford University Press.

Wilson, D. (1993) *Campaigning: The A–Z of Public Advocacy.* London: Hawksmere.

FURTHER READING

Parsons, W. (1995) *Public Policy.* Aldershot: Elgar.

Sweeney, J. (1993) *Trading with the Enemy: Britain's Arming of Iraq.* London: Pan.

17

INTERFERING WITH
FOREIGNERS

An example from *First Tuesday*

Hugo de Burgh

The idea of the universal journalist

Anglophone journalists tend to believe that there are only two types of journalism, good and bad. Thus, David Randall:

> There is no such thing as Western journalism ... there is only good and bad journalism. Each culture may have its own traditions, each language a different voice. But among good journalists the world over, what joins them is more significant than what separates them ... Good journalists, universally, agree on their role.
>
> (Randall 1996: 2)

Journalists from cultures that lack some of the underpinnings of Anglophone journalism – journalists from African or Asian countries, for example, where the legal, cultural and political premises can be different – often agree that they are underdeveloped, and make efforts to conform to Anglophone norms (Golding 1977). Journalists in countries as diverse from each other and from the Anglophone world as Italy, Turkey and Germany have waged heroic struggles to have this vision of journalism accepted. The key tenets (after Allan 1997) of this vision are as follows:

- objective reality exists out there to be apprehended and reflected by journalists and
- it is the relationship of the journalist to this objective reality – in which relationship he or she applies certain principles – that is the touchstone of being a *real* journalist rather than stooge, PR person or partisan.
- Journalists who do not behave as journalists should are not yet up to the mark, or are perverted by ideology, usually forced upon unwilling journalists by politicians.

- What Anglophone journalists adhere to is not, they believe, an ideology, but a group of tenets that reflect the essence of journalism.

The question here begged, however, is whether there exist 'facts', or 'objective reality'. Is there such a thing, or does reality depend upon the observer? In journalism, as in academia today, not everyone agrees. What is agreed in journalism studies is that the media prioritise different aspects of reality, depending upon

- who owns them (the *Sun*, a British tabloid with the largest circulation in Europe and a very distinct set of priorities, is a product of Rupert Murdoch's particular genius);
- the political system surrounding them (compare China with the US);
- the audience for which journalists mediate, the expectations of which may be different, and their own education and social background;
- the resources currently available from camera teams to information sources;
- the news context, i.e. what stories are thought necessary to provide a good mix that particular day, how often similar stories have appeared, etc.

If all these are influences upon what bits of reality become news, then the ideal of the universal journalist as impartial and disinterested truth-finder can seem compromised.

The organisation of the global media

It has often been observed that the world's principal suppliers of news, the news agencies, and the main buyers of news are Anglophone corporations and that this gives an Anglophone bias to the selection and depiction of events.[1] Not only do the stringers and agents on the ground, the ultimate sources for news, strain to sell to their masters what their masters will perceive to be news but the editors and schedulers gatekeep the information received; the significance of this system in political and cultural life is debated and the evidence is contradictory (Tracey 1985: 30–1).

The news agencies are the wholesalers of the world media; suppliers such as CNNI, BSkyB, Fox, StarTV and BBC World Service Television (WSTV) are the retailers. Boyd–Barrett (1997) argues that, for all of them, Anglophone definitions of what constitute news are paramount; that the news provided originates in the Anglophone capitals and responds first to their own rich domestic markets. News aside, that the world market in entertainment provision is also predominantly Anglophone has been much observed (Tomlinson 1997: 134ff and 143ff), as is the fact that the Anglophone countries are virtually impervious to non-Anglophone cultural products (Tracey 1985: 30).

Going further, Chambers and Tinckell (1998: 15) suggest that the so-called global media are agents of Anglophone values which privilege norms of 'competitive individualism, *laisser faire* capitalism, parliamentary democracy, consumerism'. They see the presentation of the English language as international as a further feature of Anglophone dominance. People are, they suggest, defined according to their relationship to Anglophoneness. Those who are not quite 'wasp', but nearly, are 'subalterns', that is the English speaking Irish or Indians or Jews, compared to the real Anglophones who are Australians, Americans and English.[2] Their assertions are complemented by a number studies (Smith 1980).

Concern about this cultural imperialism transmitted by the media has been expressed regularly over the past thirty or more years. In the 1970s it was identified in the promotion by UNESCO of the idea of a 'New World Information Order' that would provide more impartial (or more positive?) information on non-Western countries; more recently it has seen expression in the arguments over GATT, in which some countries (e.g. France, China) have sought to defend their cultural integrity by banning imports of foreign media products. These matters are discussed thoroughly in Tomlinson 1991.

How foreign countries are seen

Edward Said has argued for many years that the west has created images of 'the Orient' that have then been used as bases for political, economic and foreign policy decisions, to say nothing of informing culture generally (Said 1995). He has written mainly of the Arab world, but the West's image of, and therefore attitudes to, China, as expressed in contemporary culture, have changed markedly over the centuries in accordance with its own self-perceptions (Christiansen and Rai 1993).

The magic Tartary of a splendour and technical superiority that Europe could not match (fourteenth and fifteenth centuries) gave way to Voltaire's China, in which philosophers eschewed superstition, ruled according to reason and had meritocratic institutions. This was useful at a time when Europeans of the Enlightenment were confused at the decline of the old certainties. Then came the China of silk and ceramics and superiority in arts and crafts so popular in the early stages of Britain's industrial revolution. This image of China ceded place to the grotesque and contemptible tyranny that could not withstand either modern might or manifest destiny during the imperial period of say the 1870s to 1930s; she became pitiable, weak and easy to exploit by adventurers, open to spiritual reconstruction by missionaries, tricked by politicians. During the Second World War, China was admired as a plucky ally against Japan; during the Cold War that followed, excoriated as the 'Empire of the Blue Ants'. In the 1960s the European left hailed the communes as a 'new civilisation' while the right discussed the Yellow Peril; by the 1980s China was once again loved for its quaintness and for the business opportunities it offered ('the last great market'); after Tiananmen China was condemned as the world's moloch – rival, giant and thug.

The dynamics of how other societies are depicted today have been looked at in particular by Galtung and Ruge (1965) who found that foreign news is reported in various categories and in partial ways conditioned by our own cultural prejudices. Evans (1997) has given an example in his description of how Soviet President Gorbachev's test ban announcement was treated by the US media in 1985. Although the test ban was unilateral and real, it was consistently represented by all the media as propaganda, demonstrating not only gullibility to political spin but unwillingness to check facts when the facts might not suit the belief. During the Gulf War the *Guardian* examined the language being used by the press in one week, and reported:

> We have Army, Navy and Airforce; they have a war machine ... We dig in; they cower in their foxholes ... We launch [missiles] pre-emptively; they launch without provocation ... Our missiles cause collateral damage; theirs cause civilian casualties ... Our men are lads; their men are hordes ... Our boys are professional; theirs are brainwashed ... Ours resolute; theirs ruthless ... Our boys fly into the jaws of hell; theirs cower in concrete bunkers ... We have reporting guidelines; they have censorship ... We have press briefings; they have propaganda.
>
> (cit. in Leapman 1992: 266)

Keeble, in a book that dissects our assumptions about the Gulf War which, he suggests, are made up of a whole collection of myths and half truths, also draws our attention to research on the way in which the *Sun* and *Star* newspapers used war news selectively to make convenient points (Keeble 1997: Chap 16) and Hume suggests that the 1999 war in Yugoslavia should be seen as self-projection (various articles, Hume 1999).

A study of the 1997 handover of Hong Kong to China in the UK and Chinese media shows that 'the reporting of both countries has sharply different perspectives and therefore each presents equally different perspectives to their respective readers' (Cao 1998: 15). According to Cao British accounts are infused with a 'history-oriented nostalgia for the empire and present-oriented myth of democracy' whereas Chinese accounts are infused with the myth of victimhood and reinforce the myth of the Communist Party (CP) as saviour of the Chinese.[3] An interesting aspect of Cao's study is that whereas the homogenous view of the Chinese media might well be anticipated from the fact that it is centrally-owned and directed, the UK media are not, and yet on this story at least are similarly homogenous in their approach. This point (ibid.: 16) appears to bear out the argument that the influences of culture are very powerful.

Thus, empirical research of media content complements the research on news agencies.

Ethical imperialism or human rights?

On page 301 I listed a number of the conditions within which journalism is practised and by which it is moulded. Beyond these, it is widely acknowledged (Shoemaker 1996) that the conventions of journalists and their work practices determine the limits of news, selecting certain types of events rather than others for processing, privileging certain themes and then shaping events into pre-specified formats such as the TV news package, so that they become elements which make up a conventional news programme.

The exact relationship between these various influences, which are the more powerful or more explicit, is probably impossible to determine. Nevertheless culture, meaning 'the social practices and beliefs of a given group of people who share them' (Jandt 1995) is surely fundamental. A central message of cultural scholarship over the past few decades has been that 'what you see depends both upon what you look at and what your previous experience has taught you to see' (Jandt 1995: 157). Stuart Hall and others have shown how our culture affects the ways in which we represent others – other individuals, societies, institutions and so on – according to where we ourselves are situated. Where we are situated may mean our degree of prosperity, our gender, our cultural identity and so on.

So, when can a foreign story tell us about the society reported and how much is it a reflection of our own culture? It may appear to others not as truth but as 'their reality', or even *ethical imperialism*.

I first heard the term used nearly ten years ago by the then Turkish ambassador lambasting the BBC for reporting British Liberal politician Lord Avebury's concern over the Kurds. He sneered that Avebury was behaving like a typical British colonial governor and used this term *ethical imperialism* as abuse. He touched a nerve, for there is unease, if not among journalists, then among media academics, as to whether we have the right to investigate other countries, declare some aspect of their society wanting according to our lights and demand that they conform. Child labour, political imprisonment, industrial diseases ... these are among the ills that offend the Anglophone sense of human rights and, *prima facie*, require investigation and condemnation. Some people in the investigated, and therefore perhaps labelled and demonised, societies may disagree. The matter of their disagreement may, of course, be opportunism; some have attacked the Anglophone media on the grounds of offending their values when in fact they resent interference in their own nefarious activities. However, let us assume for the sake of argument that resistance to Western journalism is disinterested.

The notion of human rights transcending those of institutions is fundamental to Anglophone attitudes today, yet when critics of the Anglophone media, or of politicians' raising human rights issues make their criticisms, they commonly refer to the colonialist antecedents of these notions, presenting them as arrogance, a kind of imperialism of the heart.[4] Prime Minister Blair's crusading zeal in the bombing of Serbia and Kosovo in 1999 has doubtless reinforced such reaction and may be seen by non-Anglophones as contradicting simultaneous claims of promoting human rights.

Over the last thirty years in Anglophone societies it has been widely declared that different cultures must be respected, that the Anglican way of life is no more valid than that of the Sikh, the Rastafarian or the Sufi. Those who do not respect other cultures but seek homogenisation through language, media, commerce or political domination are cultural imperialists. Despite this, to non-Anglophones, what we see as the defence of human rights is simply a manifestation of that very imperialism. Moreover, journalists who have a missionary conception of their calling and seek to reveal wrongs are simply the servants of Anglophone interests, dressed up as morality.

Outside of the Anglophone world the idea of the journalist as missionary, defender of the defenceless, sceptic and critic of the way things are is probably held by few. Even where, as in China today, an investigative role is acknowledged for the journalist, it rarely extends to interrogation of the leadership or virtual political opposition. Critics of the Anglophone conception share the widely-held belief that journalists are partial; that the selection of events as newsworthy and the processing of those events into stories (conflict seeking, counter-factual, identifying victims and villains) are culturally biased and reflect the needs of the observers' culture rather than the 'objective reality' of the observed. More sophisticated critics reject the very concept of objectivity as anything more than a professional device to evade responsibility.

Some observers from poorer countries believe that the news needs of their communities and those of the rich and developed ones are different and that the Western 'construction of reality' is positively harmful. Anthony Smith quotes an Indian journalist:

> In our environment there is, and there will be for a long time to come, much that is ugly and distasteful. If we follow the Western norm we will be playing up only those dark spots and thus helping unwittingly to erode the faith and confidence without which growth and development are impossible.
>
> (Smith 1980: 94)

Smith adds 'A journalist would have to share the commitment to the ideology of development before he would see the objective story in a developing society'.

Going further along this path the English political thinker John Gray has suggested, as a fact upon which to base mutual respect between incompatible systems, that some rights that we value little are better defended in other cultures. He is thinking of the right to community, to economic security and to freedom from chaos (Gray 1995: 140).

Coverage of China: the ultimate other

This however comes perilously close to saying that the Chinese, for example, are so different that we cannot apply any of our values. At the extreme this ends up in claiming that, for example, the Tiananmen massacre was an invention of the Western media because what was going on was something too Chinese for our scandal hungry media to understand. This view has been criticised by Zhang Longxi (1992) but as he acknowledges in two interesting essays, although it might seem absurd it has a distinguished pedigree.

For, as we have already mentioned, China has indeed often been reported by Westerners in terms that revealed their own longings, prejudices and political assumptions. For generations, writers up to, in our own time, Foucault and Borges have helped to perpetuate the China that is 'the image of the ultimate other' in the manner in which, as Edward Said has so well demonstrated of the Middle East, the West created 'the Orient' (Zhang Longxi 1988). More prosaically, a group of Chinese academics and journalists, all claiming to have gone to study in the USA filled with admiration for their host country, have published a bitter book full of impressive evidence of the misrepresentation of China, which they call 'Demonising China'.[5] So we should always look at a text on China and say: what do we understand about ourselves from this?

Example: *Laogai*: inside China's gulag

Harry Wu is a Chinese man who spent 19 years in prison camps in his homeland and who has made it his life's purpose to expose the extensive penal system of the People's Republic of China.[6] He is the author of several books on Chinese prisons and the head of a foundation researching them (Wu 1997). His ability to provide first-hand information, his contacts, courage and eloquence have all ensured that he has been taken up by the Anglophone media and that his story has become famous, particularly since 1995 when he was released from prison, apparently so that the wife of the US President might be .prevented from cancelling a visit to China at the instigation of human rights activists. [7]

The style of his writing is rather sensational:

> The American passport was tucked into the pouch on my belt. Occasionally I would reach for it the way a cowboy in a Western movie might feel for his six-shooter, just to know it's there. Everybody wants an equaliser. It was June of 1995, and I was riding in a taxi through a remote corner of Kazakhstan, trying to slip into China. I felt a shiver, half-love, half-terror. My US passport would not protect me if they caught me inside my homeland. China has a most-wanted list, and I was on it.

> (Wu 1997: 3)

Description of the programme

The film *Laogai*, transmitted by Yorkshire Television on the national ITV (commercial) network in August 1993 for the *First Tuesday* strand,[8] argues that pressure should be put on China to reform its penal system, and that this should be done by shaming it in international fora such as the UN and by the trade authorities of Western countries refusing to accept imports that have originated in forced labour camps.

Wu and his wife disguised themselves as business visitors or tourists, depending on the occasion, and used US passports. They filmed with hidden cameras in the vicinity of several camps; on one occasion Wu donned police uniform to get nearer and on another represented the family members of a prisoner to get access. There are testimonial interviews on the extent and general harshness of the camps with Robin Munro of the human rights pressure group Asia Watch and on individual cases of brutality with several former prisoners of different generations.

The treatment is dramatic. *Laogai* starts with sequence showing illegal immigrants 'on their journey to freedom' being picked up by (then British) Hong Kong police and, probably incorrectly, allows the impression that these immigrants are largely political refugees. At various points in *Laogai* we see the careful preparations made for undercover filming. There are many shots of the grim landscapes in which the camps are situated and there is one risky encounter with guards, from which Mrs Wu flees.

As to the quality of the information contained in the programme, the main corroboration comes from Munro of Asia Watch. We are told that there have been approximately 25 million political prisoners since 1949; that the population of the camps may now be as much as 10 million; that 10,000 activists were arrested after the 1989 massacre in Beijing, of whom 'many are still behind bars'; 'inside these walls are prisoners whose only crime is to think' we are told at one point, and it is suggested that they may comprise Tibetan independence activists, students and priests. We learn that many prisoners are working in 'cruel and degrading conditions', exposed to toxic chemicals; there is torture; the ethos is that of the Nazi camps.

The second part goes into detail on the economic significance of the camps whose products are exported to thirty countries, we are told, although China has been obliged to sign a pledge to the effect that gulag exports have ended. Harry Wu is seen setting up a sting in Hong Kong to see if he can buy from Chinese government brokers goods that originated in the camps. He signs the contract and it is then confirmed by US Customs that the subjects of the contract are indeed the products of prison labour.

Wu goes to Congress to present his findings to sympathetic politicians who will use them as ammunition in their battle with China over human rights and trade. He then turns his attention to the UK and the case is made that much of the tea consumed in the UK may come from prison farms, notwithstanding the fact that as long ago as 1897 the UK banned all prison-made products.

At the end, as earlier, Wu makes an impassioned case for action by the West, explaining his motivations as the urge to make up for the youth that the camps took from him, the hope to see an end to the system that devoured his friends and the longing for an end to communist power in his country.

Critique of the programme

The programme can be faulted on three grounds. One is that it exaggerates the importance of the issue selected, i.e. lacks real truth by being selective and that it does so on the basis of incomplete (if understandably incomplete) data; second is that it takes no account of the changes for the better that have taken place since the 1970s, in other words it lacks context; third is that it panders to Western prejudices and interests.

There is no reason to doubt the veracity of the cases described or of the descriptions of the camps visited. It is possible that the overall figures quoted for the size of the prison system are correct, although in the absence of authoritative statistics, judgement must be suspended. 'Around 10 million' is a prison population of 1 per cent; the proportion of political prisoners appears to be entirely speculative.

As to treatment, it is very likely that brutality exists in these camps since there are no institutions that can inspect or expose them. It is quite compre-hensible that former prisoners will have passionate views, but it is equally possible that they are not representative. It is also arguable that the number of people being maltreated is not as important a fact as that some are being maltreated. Nevertheless, if the overall impression given is one that contributes to prejudice rather than to enlightenment, then the journalist is open to criticism.

Such criticism is answered by Tim Tate, producer and main author of the programme after Wu himself, with the point that if a wrong is wrong, then demanding detailed statistics is asking the wrong question; what matters is that the main thrust is right (Tate 1997).

Grant McKee, Executive Producer of *Laogai* when at Yorkshire Television, says that such a programme would be most unlikely to be made now. A few years ago ITV did many foreign stories. Why *Laogai*?

> We'd been going for easy targets such as multinationals based in the West, and a totalitarian regime such as China and Russia presented a challenge. After all, it's easy to go after malfeasance in democracies, every so often we ought to do something a bit more difficult! Also it was very relevant at the time because China was being considered for most favoured nation status and the question of what kind of rela-tions we should have with a country which had such a poor human rights record was being discussed everywhere.
>
> (McKee 1999)

He was scathing of the suggestion that his programme was part of systematic demonisation of China.

> The reaction of the Chinese is an indication of great insecurity. I am proud of being English but I would not have the slightest hesitation in exposing or seeing exposed the murky corners of my country. Are they suggesting that what Harry Wu saw should be kept hidden in the cause of some greater balance? Well, I do not wear that. Human rights are universal. Should we not show that people are stoned and tortured to death in Africa or Arabia? Of course I understand that if you are African or Arab and do not have a long-standing tradition of press freedom and human rights behind you then it is rather galling that it is always foreigners exposing things; but we are not trying to be imperialistic. We are just saying 'look this is going on, don't you want to know about it?'
>
> (McKee 1999)

The context in which this programme is made and filmed is one of trade war between major powers, disagreement between China and the USA on international issues and a fear of eventual rivalry between the USA, currently the sole superpower, and China. China sees the USA as a threatening military force moved by ruthless business interests and irresponsible politicians; indeed, there are interests in the USA that want to see China tamed for commerce and weakened politically. Thus the characterisation of China as an abuser of human rights, its demonisation, serves political purposes as well as being a contribution to enlightenment. In such circumstances investigative journalists would probably do well to consider whose interests they serve; they will still expose, but they might expose with more circumspection.

Channel 4 has transmitted some unrelentingly critical programmes about China's most sensitive aspects: the population programme, the treatment of non-Chinese citizens, the nuclear project and its effects upon ordinary people. Head of News and Current Affairs David Lloyd, questioned about his attitude to China, considers that 'you have to judge a country by its worst aspects' (Lloyd 1998). He makes an analogy:

> If 5 per cent of the Royal Ulster Constabulary are bigoted persecutors of Catholics, they must be followed up, even if 95 per cent are not, because the damage is being done by the 5 per cent. ... Investigative journalism very properly looks for the worst case; investigative journalism stands for human rights, transparency, ability of people to have some control over their futures ... it is, if you like, the people's tribune.
>
> (ibid.)

China is a 'big story' both because it is becoming a big economy and because of the discrepancy, to Western eyes, between its economic ambition and its political system. There are two ways of factually representing China to people; witnessing the unfolding of real life, for example through an observational documentary series such as the lyrical *Beyond the Clouds* or the much admired portrait of a big city, *Shanghai Vice*; and investigation. Lloyd denies being Anglocentric: 'We are not Martians, we have to relate China to British perspectives, we have to mediate for British people'. Taken to task for spreading, through C4's investigations in China, a partial view of China that has great impact for its sensational revelations, he says that he 'speak[s] as someone who must hold the torch of investigative journalism' and that C4 has also covered many aspects of China in ways that are not investigative (C4 has also transmitted Chinese opera, modern films, features on Chinese economic successes). Coverage of China is, however, like that of other countries 'intermittent and not coherent', partly because of the attitude of the Chinese government and partly because of the scepticism among British broadcasters as to whether international subjects can win audiences.

Discussion

There is an established British tradition of investigating and reporting on other countries; in addition to the general current affairs series already mentioned there are programmes exclusively dealing with foreign countries, such as BBC *Assignment*, C4 *Correspondent* and BBC *Foreign Correspondent*. These media, and the broadsheets, usually home in on some aspect of foreign countries that excites reproof or even condemnation; individual reporters, in particular John Pilger and Martin Gregory, have concentrated upon the responsibility of their own society for the issue in question.

How do we account for Anglophone journalism's interest in other societies? We can point to the idea of social responsibility and see travelling abroad as an extension of that. Our present interest in suffering in other countries then appears to be the heir to a noble tradition of concern, from anti-slavery to women's rights. There is the one-world view which sees no man as an island; we are all our brothers' keepers. These are arguments that could be used to defend the missionary moralism of Spanish priests in sixteenth-century Latin America or Protestant pastors in nineteenth-century China. Then there is the camp of ethical relativism, using this kind of argument: 'Anglophones and Africans have different cultures and therefore different standards; we mustn't be judgmental'. This is also the defence of those who want to preserve the *status quo* in, for example, Africa.

More pragmatically it can be argued that we are not justified in investigating foreign countries and revealing what we consider to be abuses simply because we understand so little about them. It is often observed how few correspondents know the languages, let alone have a deep knowledge of the cultures of the countries they report; indeed this is often regarded as a disadvantage for a correspondent. In such conditions the journalist can encounter many problems in trying to understand another society, and probably often gives up, whether allowing others to mediate for him or her or simply accepting that his or her perspective is the limited one of seeing that society only insofar as it touches upon the political or economic interests of his or her own.

At its worst, foreign reporting is merely the use of exotic locations to show up squalor, with the underlying message that the reporter's society is superior; furthermore, in a culture with different traditions, in which not only is the reporter ignorant of the culture but also the host society is unaccustomed to the reporter's style of journalism, the case for the defence may never be put. The report is then subject to less stringent standards of fairness than would be possible at home. To some extent, these problems could be resolved by education of journalists, sensitising them to other societies; however such sensitising might be seen to go against the ideology of social responsibility and the professional values of anglophone journalism, exemplified in the quotation from Randall, above. John Pilger (1999) responds to the critics thus:

> To a great extent they are right. The reach, monopoly and power of the Western media is a new form of imperialism which interprets countries to themselves in the light of Western interests as well as seeing them only in the light of those interests.
>
> More aware critics will recognise though that nationalism should be separated from the right of people to know, no matter from where that knowledge comes, and that both Chinese and Western journalists 'speak culturally'. [As far as the Western journalist's investigations are concerned] if you do not do it in your own country then you have no right to do it in foreign countries. As to the demonisation argument, the reporting of Russia today is typical; we see the horrible things but we never understand why. For if you do not place your investigation within the political context, explain it, then you are at risk of demonising.

Laogai therefore raises a number of issues in the Anglophone reporting of other societies.

NOTES

1   The largest news agency in the world is quite possibly Xinhua (New China), but its influence on the media outside China is probably negligible.
2   Interestingly, they see two attempts to escape from this as confirmation of the trend: the efforts to create International Cultural Studies they see as a further example of Anglophone cultural imperialism, imposing Anglophone categories, and the introduction of the norms of multiculturalism and hybridity in the UK,

Canada, USA and Australia they see as further reinforcing the dominant position of the Anglophone majority.

3 Both the Chinese myths are debatable; it is quite possible to see China as a victim of itself rather than of Western imperialism as the Communist Party (CP) has sought to portray it; many Chinese by no means subscribe to the myth of the CP as saviour. No less suspect are the British myths. Whereas the British media criticise China for its society today, the Chinese media are defensive, perhaps acknowledging in so being that in a world whose ethical leadership is Anglophone there is no mileage in attacking its assumptions.

4 In the early imperial period there was a hierarchy in which many non-white people were seen as having different or conditional rights. Conrad's novel of the exploitation of the Congo, *Heart of Darkness*, puts this point, although it may also be the case that the notion of universal human rights was strongly felt at least among British colonial officials in the twentieth century. This may account for the many attempts to ameliorate the lot of subject peoples, particularly where such amelioration was against the interests of the colonial rulers, for example in the attempts to eradicate paederastic sodomy and clitoral circumcision in West Africa.

5 Li Xiguang and Liu Kang (1997) *Yamohua Zhongguo de Beihou* (Behind the Demonisation of China). Peking: Zhongguo Shehui Kexue CBS.

6 Accounts of Wu's life appear to originate exclusively from him and, as far as I am aware, are not corroborated by disinterested sources. To say this is not to denigrate him, but to utter a caveat.

7 Wu was by this time a US citizen and had returned to China specifically to make a film there which was sure to stimulate the wrath of the authorities.

8 *First Tuesday* was ITV's flagship documentary series from 1983–93, screening monthly a highly acclaimed range of programmes of many different kinds and winning many international awards. The highest ratings ever obtained were 12.5 million for *Katie and Eilish; Siamese Twins* (August 1992); the most controversial arguably was *Windscale: the Nuclear Laundry* (November 1983). In its ten-year period it had two Series Editors, John Willis and Grant McKee. Information supplied by Chris Briar, Group Controller of Factual Programmes, to Hugo de Burgh by telephone on 4 November 1999.

BIBLIOGRAPHY

Allan, S. (1997) News and the public sphere: towards a history of news objectivity. In M. Bromley and T. O'Malley (1997) *A Journalism Reader*. London: Routledge.

Boyd-Barrett, O. (1997) Global news wholesalers as agents of globalisation. In A. Sreberny-Mohammedi (ed.) *Media in Global Context*. London: Edward Arnold.

Cao, Q. (1998) Discourse, ideology and power: a comparative study of the reporting of the handover of Hong Kong in the British and Chinese printed media. Paper delivered at the 21st Conference of IAMCR, Glasgow.

Carlton TV (1994) *Death of a Nation* (Reporter: John Pilger). London: Carlton TV.

Chambers, D. and Tinckell, E. (1998) Anglocentric versions of the international: the privileging of Anglo-ethnicity in cultural studies and the global media. Paper delivered at the 21st Conference of IAMCR, Glasgow.

Christiansen, F. and Rai, S. (1993) *Theories and Concepts: shifting views of China*. Coventry: University of Warwick PAIS Working Paper 117.

Evans, H. (1997) Prometheus unbound. Iain Walker Memorial Lecture, Green College Oxford, May.

Galtung, J. and Ruge, M. (1965) The structure of foreign news. In J. Tunstall (1970) *Media Sociology*. London: Constable.

Golding, P. (1977) Media professionalism in the third world: the transfer of an ideology. In J. Curran, M. Gurevitch and J. Woollacott (eds) *Mass Communication and Society*. London: Edward Arnold.

Gray, J. (1995) *Enlightenment's Wake*. London: Routledge: 140.

Hall, S. (1997) The spectacle of the 'Other'. In S. Hall (ed.) *Representation: Cultural Representations and Signifying Practices*. London: Sage.

Harrison, P. (1996) *News Out of Africa*. London: Shipman.

Hume, M. (1999) The war against the Serbs is about projecting a self-image of the ethical new Britain bestriding the world. It is a crusade. *Times*, 15 April 1999.

Jandt, F. E. (1995) Culture's influence on knowledge. In *Intercultural Communication*. Thousand Oaks: Sage: chap. 9.

Keeble, R. (1997) *Secret State, Silent Press*. Luton: John Libbey.

Leapman, M. (1992) *Treacherous Estate*. London: Hodder.

Lloyd, D. (1998) Interview with Hugo de Burgh at Nottingham Trent University, 19 February 1998.

McKee, G. (1999) Interview with Hugo de Burgh, 17 May 1999.

Pilger, J. (1999) Interview with Hugo de Burgh, 29 June 1999.

Randall, D. (1996) *The Universal Journalist*. London: Pluto.

Said, E. (1995) *Orientalism: Western Conceptions of the Orient*. London: Penguin.

Sandford, J. (ed.) (1990) *Gunther Wallraff: Der Aufmacher*. Manchester: Manchester University Press.

Shoemaker, P. (1996) Influences on content from outside media organisations. In P. Shoemaker *Mediating the Message*. White Plains: Longman.

Smith, A. (1980) *The Geopolitics of Information: How Western Culture Dominates the World*. London: Faber and Faber.

Tate, T. (1997) The making of *Laogai*. Talk to students on the MA Investigative Journalism course at Nottingham Trent University, 6 November 1997.

Tomlinson, J. (1991) *Cultural Imperialism*. London: Pinter.

Tomlinson, J. (1997) Internationalism, globalization and cultural imperialism. In K. Thompson (ed.) *Media and Cultural Regulation*. London: Sage/Open University Press: 117–62 (chap. 3).

Tracey, M. (1985) The poisoned chalice? International television and the idea of dominance. *Daedalus*, 114 (4): 17–56.

Wu, H. (1997) *Troublemaker*. London: Village.

Yorkshire TV (1993) *Laogai: The Chinese Gulag* (Director: Tim Tate. Reporter: Harry Wu). Leeds: Yorkshire TV.

Zhang Longxi (1988) The myth of the Other: China in the eyes of the West. *Critical Inquiry*, 15 (Autumn).

Zhang Longxi (1992) Western theory and Chinese reality. *Critical Inquiry*, 19 (Autumn).

FURTHER READING

Gray, J. (1995) *Enlightenment's Wake*. London: Routledge: 140.

Hall, S. (1997) The spectacle of the 'Other'. In S. Hall (ed.) *Representation: Cultural Representations and Signifying Practices*. London: Sage.

Tomlinson, J. (1991) *Cultural Imperialism*. London: Pinter.

ENDWORD

There are thousands of examples of beneficial disclosure of fraud and waste, dangerous consumer products and environmental practices – the revelation of radiation experiments on citizens; the chaos in blood donor centres threatening to introduce Aids-tainted blood into the system; the many unreported mishaps at 141 nuclear power plants; lethal defects in tyres; the spying on domestic dissidents.

(Evans 1997)

Harold Evans' words above refer to the USA. Many UK journalists look enviously at the USA, believing that in Britain there are huge swathes of local and central authority without effective surveillance, powerful businesses that collude to keep prices high, politicians who have been shown to be as putty in the hands of business and central government which can even wage war, with all the implications this has for our foreign relations and our domestic economy, to say nothing of those we kill, without the permission of Parliament. John Pilger, one of those who worked on the Vietnam War, is scathing about the way the British media has covered the foreign stories of the 1990s:

Investigative journalists are people who should lift rocks, look behind screens, never accept the official point of view or (as Claud Cockburn said) never believe anything until it is officially denied. The 'Pentagon Papers' and the 'My Lai massacre' stories told you how the US war system was working; they revealed how people manipulated that system to cause such havoc. If the Kosovo bombing had happened in the 1960s journalists would have investigated how it came about and whose interests it serves; today the British press is degraded by its ludicrous drum beating and rhetorical jingoism.

(Pilger 1999)

If Pilger is correct, then there are many reasons for such degradation, some of which have been referred to in this book. One, surely, is the weak sense of professional pride and identity shared by British journalists. There are various possible ways of dealing with this, such as increasing professionalisation or improving education and training; one is by the clarification of their rights. If they are to be expected to delve and reveal, it is said, investigative journalists need their rights established and their access assured. Freedom of speech means little without the freedom to find out. This is why many of them want a strong freedom of information law to limit what authority can hide and to give the investigator rights. If these rights are only to be used for salacious purposes – as is often feared, given the predilection of much of the UK media for voyeurism and the humiliation of its targets with no observable public benefit – the citizenry, which appears to have little sympathy for journalists' aspirations for more rights, may demand a privacy law, too. Harold Evans, however, is probably in the company of most British journalists when he argues that the benefits of freedom of information far outweigh the problems it brings.

At the start of this volume we proposed that investigative journalism might be considered as the first draft of legislation. By this was meant that investigative journalists show up the deficiencies in our systems of regulation in the light of the principles we profess. The examples provided in the subsequent chapters have indicated how they can be seen to have done so in recent years in Britain. Seen in this way, investigative journalists are not the enemy of order, as some politicians and officials have seen them, but its champion; not disloyal to their country and institutions, but at least as loyal as the temporary custodians.

The scope for investigation has grown wider and wider as the state has penetrated more areas of our lives and as big companies clash by night to control our environment, our spending, our feeding and our thoughts. So never has the investigator, motivated by his or her belief in finding the truth, been more needed. Nor has the difficulty ever been greater, as institutions employ battalions to tell the story their way. The state probably needs to be the prime target for suspicion; after all, although commercial companies provided the gas that exterminated the innocents in German camps under Hitler and the bombs that slaughtered the wretched Cambodian peasants in 1969–70, the power to command such immense evil is so far only in the hands of states.

Although states seem so strong, in some ways they are much weaker. The citizenry no longer believes in the icons – Majesty of the Law, Mother of Parliaments, Blue Lamp, City Gentleman – but wants them to come clean and admit their faults, the better to function properly as the servants of the polity and the colleague of the citizen. Our institutions have all suffered the fate of the House of Windsor: the light has been let in upon them and there is no mystery. In this situation the investigative journalist is the tribune of the commoner, exerting on her or his behalf the right to know, to examine and to criticise.

So although there is gloom among those who work in or with investigative journalism, who see the power of its enemies growing and the outlets for its efforts diminishing, if we compare the situation with that of investigative journalism a hundred years ago the pessimism can seem exaggerated; the idea of investigative journalism is generally accepted, new types of outlet are developing and information is more readily available and testable. Who knows, it may be that the career of investigative journalism has only just begun.

BIBLIOGRAPHY

Evans, H. (1997) Prometheus unbound. Iain Walker Memorial Lecture, Green College Oxford, May.
Pilger, J. (1999) Interview with Hugo de Burgh, 29 June 1999.

INDEX

317